Gaining Ground in College Writing
Tales of Development and Interpretation

SMU STUDIES IN COMPOSITION AND RHETORIC
General Editor: Gary Tate, Texas Christian University

Gaining Ground in College Writing
Tales of Development and Interpretation

RICHARD H. HASWELL

Southern Methodist University Press

DALLAS

First edition, 1991

Requests for permission to reproduce material from this work
should be sent to:
    Permissions
    Southern Methodist University Press
    Box 415
    Dallas, Texas 75275

Library of Congress Cataloging-in-Publication Data

Haswell, Richard H.
    Gaining ground in college writing : tales of development and
interpretation / Richard H. Haswell. — 1st ed.
        p.   cm. — (SMU studies in composition and rhetoric)
    Includes bibliographical references (p.   ) and index.
    ISBN 0-87074-322-8 (cloth) — ISBN 0-87074-323-6 (paper)
    1. English language—Rhetoric—Study and teaching.   I. Title.
II. Series.
PE1404.H39   1991
808'.042'07—dc20   90-53580

Previous versions of parts of chapters 3, 5, 7, 10, and 11 were first published in
professional journals:
"Toward Competent Writing in the Workplace," by Richard H. Haswell, *Journal of
Technical Writing and Communication* 18 (1988): 161–73. Reprinted by permission
of *Journal of Technical Writing and Communication.*
"Error and Change in College Student Writing," by Richard H. Haswell, *Written
Communication* 5 (1988): 479–99. Reprinted by permission of Sage Publications, Inc.
"The Organization of Impromptu Essays," by Richard H. Haswell, *College Composition
and Communication* 37 (1986): 402–15. Copyright 1986 by the National Council of
Teachers of English. Reprinted with permission.
"Dark Shadows: The Fate of Writers at the Bottom," by Richard H. Haswell, *College
Composition and Communication* 39 (1988): 303–15. Copyright 1988 by the National
Council of Teachers of English. Reprinted with permission.

This bit of ground is dedicated to
Alice Sherwood Haswell and Richard Ellis Haswell
"a lot of lives"

Contents

Contents

Acknowledgments

Pieces and versions of chapters 3, 5, 7, 10, and 11 were first published in professional journals. I thank them for permission to reprint: "Toward Competent Writing in the Workplace," *Journal of Technical Writing and Communication* 18 (1988): 161–73; "Error and Change in College Student Writing," *Written Communication* 5 (1988): 479–99; "The Organization of Impromptu Essays," *College Composition and Communication* 37 (1986): 402–15; and "Dark Shadows: The Fate of Writers at the Bottom," *College Composition and Communication* 39 (1988): 303–15.

As these dates show, this book was long in the making. The first version was completed in 1985; the second—the majority of it new—was begun the fall of 1987 and finished the following summer. (Had the work taken only a bit longer, it would have incorporated the insights of Louise Wetherbee Phelps in *Composition as a Human Science: Contributions to the Self-Understanding of a Discipline,* but as it is I can only acknowledge my gratitude for the chance affinities involving hermeneutics, Gadamer, Ricoeur, development, the teaching of writing, even the Necker cube.)

So my work was twice raised, and both times many community hands helped. Initial backing in time, funding, and facilities came from the Basil and Ella Gerard Endowment Fund, the Washington State University Humanities Research Center, the Washington State University College of Sciences and Arts, the Comisión Fulbright of Quito, and the Instituto de Lenguas y Lingüística of the Universidad Católica de Ecuador. As for co-workers, I had the collaboration of three year-generations of teacher-students—too many to be named here; the co-labor of five research assistants: Laura Bloxham, Irene D. Hayes, Bill Kreiger, Linda Stairet, and Susan Wyche-Smith; and the collegiality of Evelyn Ashton-Jones, George Kennedy, Richard Law, Roy Major, Susan McLeod, Tracy Montgomery, Barbara Sitko, Jan Tedesco, Dene Thomas, and Gorden Thomas.

Above all I must thank Kenneth Eble, Anne Gere, Ken Kantor, Eleanor McKenna, and Charles Suhor, who somehow saw light in the first version and offered much needed encouragement; Janice Hays, whose presence shines throughout this final version; and of course Gary Tate, without whose insight, support, and patience this final version would not be.

Gaining Ground in College Writing
Tales of Development and Interpretation

Alienation:
Loss of the Student and
Tales of Development

> You made me into an object of contemplation. Just like the
> landscape. I have made it unreal by endlessly looking at it
> instead of entering it.
>
> —Iris Murdoch, *The Unicorn*

IT IS ONE OF THE PARADOXES OF THE PRO-
fession that the longer we teachers stay in it, the farther we
stray from its subject. By *subject,* I do not mean writing. We are
not teachers of writing. We are teachers of this eighteen-year-
old, writing. And year after year this writer, eighteen years old,
walks into our classroom or into our office, while year by year
we grow more removed from the time we were eighteen, writing an essay for freshman composition. From our perspective,
of course, it is the subject who becomes a more and more distant
figure. There comes a day—if it hasn't happened in your career, it will—when the student's essay on the desk lies empty, a
container of words without an author, a landscape seen for so
many years out an office window that the scape remains but the
land is gone.

The paradox reflects one way the teaching of students to
write is entangled with the happenstances of human development. There are other ways. The career development of

teachers intertwines with the development of the domain of writing. This decade, the field has executed its unique turns—outside the university with desktop publishing, steno pools, style shifts toward the informal; inside the university with computer labs, writing-across-the-curriculum reform, burgeoning of technical writing and ESL courses. The focus of this book, however, will be on a third ingredient in this developmental mix, the individual student. This eighteen-year-old continues to mature as a writer and as a person during the four undergraduate years, although there are many of us who prefer to not believe it.

To all kinds of development, in fact, teachers often shut their eyes. This is not a perversity but a matter of being human and of being members of a Western culture that historically would rather envision life as stable than changeful (see Jerome Kagan 1980). But professionally shut eyes are a matter worth looking at. When the profession tends to deal with this decade's increase in upper-division composition enrollment by continuing to assign to the beginning course young teachers who do not also teach the advanced and to assign to the advanced course older teachers who no longer teach the beginning (and sometimes never did), when the profession continues to treat the curriculum of the two courses as essentially identical, when it continues to imagine the students in the two courses as essentially identical, then it is time to take a determined look at writing development in college and to see what that development recommends by way of changes in our teaching. Such a look itself will be developmental. The fact rests on a basic law of mature change in humans: gain in development always begins with reflection on development.

Gain in development also always begins with a sense of alienation and loss. This is a fact of such consequence that it must be made clear from the start. Imagine how the jaded eye of the ten-year teacher might see the all-too-familiar student essay, stripped of its author, atop the stack of papers:

are, however, certain basics which are common to all. Children as well as adults seem more attracted to people who are well-groomed, well-dressed, and confident of manner. Children seem more apt to base all of their judgements on these three criterion, while adults are more likely to recognize physical beauty, or potential, under a shy or poorly dressed person. On the other hand, children are quick to ostracize an extremely homely or handicapped individual in spite of that person's efforts at being well-groomed and outgoing. I find that as I grow older I am more likely to incorporate someone's personality into my conception of their looks. When I was a child, though, I didn't wait to get to know a person. I formed a

Most writing teachers will instantly protest that they cannot imagine this passage (or *paysage*) without seeing the rest of the essay. But in fact this window of vision suffices for most of us in the act of marking papers. Would we look any further to query the generalization that children are more likely than adults to be attracted to <u>well-groomed</u> people, or to mark the misspelling of <u>judgements</u>? More to the point, do we want to look any further? Our view may be a tunneled vision, but a tunnel can afford both security and convenience. To enlarge the frame to include the rest of the essay will entail a certain loss of security and convenience. The final paragraph may retract the generalization. And if the frame is extended farther to enclose information outside the text, as the developmental perspective requires, more of that security and convenience are lost. With <u>judgements</u>, the student may turn out to be British and brassy and ask classmates why the teacher doesn't know how the Queen's English is spelled.

The point is that any effort to regain the student through an enlargement of perspective will destroy parts of any former perspective. The developmental approach shares this problem with other recent approaches that widen the context by which student writing is understood, whether that context be ethnographic milieu, political power entitlements, academic service, gender boundaries, or technical employment. The difficulty in imagining pedagogical change faithful to new context has always been in convincing teachers that a shift to new ground will not necessarily incur an alienation of old ground.

That is a difficulty this book cannot avoid but wishes to face openly. Its aim is to expand the teacher's knowledge of college-age development and to reflect on the ways that such knowledge will alter the understanding, evaluation, and teaching of student writing. The last book on writing development during college was published in 1963 (Kitzhaber). The current book will draw on much new information about development, new theory about human change, new investigations of normal change after adolescence (sometimes called "life-span" or "life-course" studies), and new research into change in the writing of students during college, including my own study of the writing of freshmen, sophomores, and juniors. There is much new ground to be gained and with it, I think, a way to regain a part of the student that perhaps many of us never noticed we had lost.

What we do or do not notice depends on our particular assumptions about human change. How teachers use their assumptions to attend, read, and react to student writing I call interpretive tales of development. It is a concept central to this book and in need of a few comments about four of my own assumptions. They involve the concept of development, the act of interpretation, the intellectual mode of narrative, and the way the three together will be deployed in this book.

Development. Readers expecting the time-honored treatment of composition and development will be disappointed, or perhaps relieved. This book will not present developmental research findings such as in Kellogg W. Hunt's or Walter Loban's books, nor apply to the classroom any particular developmental theory such as Jean Piaget's or William Perry's. It looks instead to synthesize research and theory by extracting the underlying concepts. It is the interpretive modes of development, by which people make sense of human change, that

4

have undergone radical change. Freud, Gesell, and Piaget's old biological perspective of development as thoroughly inner, lock-step, stage- or age-bound, and finished by adolescence—a perspective writing teachers in the past have found unproductive or even inimical to college instruction—has been replaced by new theory suddenly very friendly to college instruction.

I will mean *development,* in its broadest sense, as any human change that both lasts and leads to further change of a similar cast. Development, then, includes some but not all instances across the entire range of changes: physical accidents, experiential growth, physiological maturation, cultural maturing, skills expertise, book learning. A severed finger may be developmental depending on whether or not it leads to adjustments in behavior or view that lead to further development. Puberty or balding, usually developmental events, may produce fixation in life perspectives of prepuberty (neurotic attachment to a parent) or of prebalding (neurotic attachment to a hairpiece), and then they are not developmental. The definition has more impact than may appear. Writing skill learned to pass a course but unused thereafter is learning that is not developmental.

This image of development is hard to grasp. Specialists in psychology and sociology have recently converted the image to a full-blown model of development, but their names for the model may not much help teachers of writing: "contextualist-dialectic" (Lerner and Busch-Rossnagel), "interpenetrative" (Meacham). Nor does my image of development fall readily into either of two camps now familiar to composition teachers: expressivism and social construction. For instance, Joseph M. Williams identifies two popular models of growth in writing: a competence that grows like strength or weight, "mappable onto the doorjamb that we use to measure our children's increasing height," and a competence that grows like knowledge or skill, mappable as the path of an outsider entering into the bounded circle of a discourse community (1989: 254). My model includes and therefore transforms both of these maps. It sees writing development as three-dimensional, perhaps best pictured as an ascending spiral. It is not just an inner, maturational growth nor just an outer, social acculturation, nor even the interaction between the two, but an educational life-process or lifework composed of three main forces or vectors, all on the move. Where the developments of student, field of writing, and teacher meet and are furthered by the meeting, there genuine educational development takes place (see figure 1). Teaching becomes developmental when the work of the course achieves the individual development of the eighteen-year-old student, the three-thousand-year-old field, and even the ten-year, jaded teacher.

Interpretation. If development is a "natural three-dimensional matrix," as Stephen Toulmin says, with student, craft, and mentor "all incorporated fully into the script" (265), then precisely that element of *script* or interpretation must emerge. Whether a vision of one's own life, a salary step system, a standardized curriculum, or a theory of development, notions about human change are fabricated partly to fit "the facts" and partly to fit the needs of the human. Throughout, this book will explore the premise of Jerome Bruner, Bernard Kaplan, Mark Freeman, Richard J. Bernstein, Bertram J. Cohler, and other recent developmentalists that to some extent all notions of development are partly

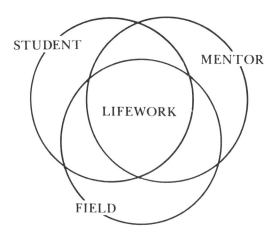

Figure 1.

invented or fictive. To introduce a distinction from Jürgen Habermas—a philosopher of social change whom I will turn to often—developmental frames are not "explanatory laws" but are "general interpretations" that have a persuasive and not a coercive force in instructing students.

For teachers, a developmental theory serves exactly as does any other knowledge framework. They will use it, or not, to interpret or make sense out of the puzzles of life. To adopt the distinction of Hans-Georg Gadamer—a hermeneutic philosopher whom I will rely on as frequently as on Habermas—instruments can *measure* matter, and science can *explain* matter, but "life *interprets* itself." With the teaching of composition, I take the approach of Frederic Jameson in literature, Hayden White in history, Clifford Geertz in anthropology, and many others, that in fields involving human subjects there is no genuine insight free or innocent of interpretation. Students of the discipline or mentors in it stand perhaps innocent but not free if they do not reflect on that fact. We have to try "somehow to understand how it is we understand understandings not our own" (Geertz: 5). Theories of development are no more free of interpretation than any other theory. For these theories to be used wisely by a teacher, their underlying mechanisms must be bared and judged. As Bruner puts it, "Theories of development require a meta-theory of values concerning the cultivation of the good man and the good society" (1986b: 27).

Narrative. The developmental frame differs, nonetheless, from many other knowledge frames in that it is a narrative one. Its way of understanding the understandings of an eighteen-year-old sets the present situation within a connected time-scheme of prior history and subsequent possibility. This book does not argue that such storytelling is the "central function or instance of the human mind" (Jameson: 13), although there is now ample precedence for such a stand (e.g., Walter R. Fischer in public rhetoric, Erving Goffman in communication, George Klein in psychoanalysis, R. C. Schank and R. P. Abelson in social action, Victor Turner in anthropology, A. C. Danto in epistemology). I remain with Kenneth Burke's rich and fundamental insight that the two ways of making sense of life—narrative and nonnarrative—are "convertible," or in his terminology, that essence may be temporized and temporality may be essentialized (1945: 430–40). There is nothing pedantic or arcane about this. We make the conversion all the time. We think of a plane accident as "tragic" and then, compulsively, imagine the last minutes of a passenger in it. Though convertible, however, the two ways of knowing may be more or less appropriate to the teaching situation and may have quite different effects. Certain teachers define, essentialize, certain students as "lazy." Certain researchers observe the situation and define, temporalize, the same students as those making the most demands on teacher time and school resources (Gubrium and Buckholdt: 121). Imagine the different pedagogical advice for the author of the piece windowed on page 3. One teacher essentializes the essay's tendency to indulge in black-white dichotomies and in personal experience, categorizing it "simplistic." Another temporalizes it by setting it in a common developmental history in which twenty-year-old college students, such as the author of the piece, often feel disillusioned with dichotomous thinking and intuitively use autobiographical knowledge to help them struggle free of it. (As it turns out, applying developmental knowledge to this particular piece discovers it to be quite eccentric. We will return to the essay at the end of the book, in chapter 14, when we can appreciate the pedagogical consequences of that fact.)

Just *imagining* such consequences, of course, is an exercise in temporalizing. I agree with Linda Brodkey that narrative knowing is unjustly devalued in the academy, and this book will push such knowing rather relentlessly. My major claim is that writing teachers have essentialized certain elements of the professions that were better temporalized: evaluation, models, diagnosis, curriculum. To conceive of these pedagogical tasks as narrative—as "historicized," in Gadamer's word, or as "dramaticized" in Habermas's—is to reach the central vision of this

book and what it calls interpretive tales. I see the way teachers
interpret student writing as narrative in the sense that they always begin with a mental frame, then accommodate the text to
that frame, then apply the accommodation by using it to evaluate
or diagnose the writing and the writer. Clearly there are so
many different interpretive tales to tell about teachers and their
encounters with text because we start with such a hardware-
store assortment of interpretive frames, some more temporal,
some less. Much of this text is devoted to describing the clashes
between developmental and nondevelopmental tales of interpretation. The dean of cognitive scientists, John H. Flavell, calls
them "mechanisms-of-development stories" (1984: 191), and I
will have no apologies for giving them story-like titles or for
illustrating them with works of creative fiction. They are works
of creative fiction.

Method. I assume that the interpretive tales of the profession can be bettered. But how does one go about rewriting
them? Not from the beginning. If a tale is truly interpretive, it
will be circular, without any beginning. Mental frames make
sense of life and therefore lead to action and involvement, out
of which are generated mental frames. Research hypotheses
(essence) create experiments (temporality), which confirm hypotheses. Theory invites the teaching practice that inspires the
theory; biological structure explains the function that defines
the structure; change in maturing requires the learning that
qualifies one as mature. At the root of all these logical dilemmas
lies the famed "hermeneutical circle," which describes how any
whole cannot be understood as a whole without recognition of
the parts that constitute it and how the parts cannot be defined
as parts without recognition of the whole.

Following the advice of Thomas S. Kuhn (336) and
Richard J. Bernstein (1983: 131–9), my approach to the interpretive dilemma is pragmatic, namely to present as much of the
circle as I can and to trust to what logic might deny but what
experience teaches: that with enough circling between part and
whole, things change. Action changes social frames, research

findings alter hypotheses, teaching practice modifies theory, and so on. The aporia or logical circle pragmatically turns out to be a developmental spiral or what Paul Ricoeur calls a "living circle." Only when one point in the circle is dwelt on, or dwelled in, do the other points stagnate. Focus long enough on the text, and the student disappears.

The logic (if that is the word) of presenting the whole interpretive circle or tale explains the unorthodox organization of this book and the dizzying way it will keep switching from lofty theory to gritty textual analysis. Generally each chapter starts with theory, usually a conflict in theories, then turns to research findings and then to application, analyzing student texts and proposing classroom practice, thereby returning to test the theory. As a whole, the book deals with underlying universal mechanisms of writing development in parts 1 through 3, qualifies them with a more individual approach to the teaching of several aspects of composition in part 4, and then recommends specific application in part 5. I let my full understanding of development evolve. Chapters 1 and 2 arrive at a rather simple tale of growth, chapters 3 and 4 revise it to a more elaborate tale of maturing, and chapter 5—long and abstract—elaborates it to my best candidate for an interpretive tale of development useful for teachers of composition (the "transformative"). Various practical concerns of writing teachers are taken up where this evolving concept seems most to enlighten them: standards and evaluation in part 1, writing models in parts 2 and 3, stylistic features in part 4, and curriculum and diagnosis in part 5. General theory of development is synthesized in chapter 5 and concrete findings of the theory ("life-span studies") in chapter 12.

This book's method of interpretive circling also embraces a rather extensive piece of personal research on writing changes during the undergraduate years. I refer to it as the Sample, not from conceit but for convenience. The study analyzed first-week diagnostic essays written by eighteen-year-old freshmen, nineteen-year-old sophomores, and twenty-year-old juniors and end-of-course essays written by eighteen-year-old freshmen—all compared with similar essays from college graduates employed in business, government, and industry. That comparison responds to the need for "as rich and detailed a description as possible of the qualitative differences between experts and novices in any task domain" (Brown: 109). The method of the Sample is empirical in order to test subjective interpretations, and it is analytic (over a hundred measures were applied) because such breakdown of writing skill has proven to be the only way to detect development in writing—a point of major implication, as it turns out. Findings related to the undergraduate writing are presented in chapter 1, to the employee writing in chapter 3, and to the end-of-course writing of the freshmen in chapter 13, but material and data from the study are interpreted and reinterpreted throughout.[1] This research study began my own effort as a teacher to regain the student by regaining lost developmental ground, common ground to both of us, as I finally discovered.

Of course, all research begins with a sense of alienation or loss, as the *search* in the word *research* reminds us. The tales we tell and listen to—whether they be on the screen or in the page or behind our understandings of the world—begin with a suspenseful inkling of something unfulfilled. The call of a piece of student writing to be interpreted rather than just evaluated

---

[1] For a full account of design and methodological issues, see Haswell 1986a and Haswell 1991. Haswell 1989 and 1990b speculate on findings only slightly covered in this book. The present book does not intend to offer a systematic account of this research nor of any other on college-age writing development. However, I have documented thoroughly theory and research in the area—Richard Beach, Patricia Bizzell, Aviva Freedman, Janice Hays, Barry Kroll, Joanne Kurfiss, Susan Miller, Ian Pringle, among others—as well as in developmental studies generally. As a result, the Works Cited stands as a fairly complete bibliography for writing teachers interested in development. Theoretically, my approach to writing development combines the "socio-cognitive perspective" of Hays et al., which views human development as including "cognitive, social, moral, affective, and other components," with constructivist assumptions that developmental studies must be narrative, dialectical, and hermeneutical (cf. Mark Freeman).

begins somehow with the thwarting of our expectations. Development itself, biological or cultural or psychological or cognitive, happens only in a state of incompletion, or who would ever want to change? It may seem strange to recommend teachers to take on such perspectives of loss. And certainly many teachers do not think their teaching needs research findings, can't imagine that their livelihood could or does advance by means of anything fictive, find it puzzling to imagine student writing needing to be interpreted, and look on the notion of development as an irrelevancy in the classroom. This book was written for them, among others.

Here at the start, I pose two cryptic questions. If the teacher feels no loss, what has been lost? Will students gain ground if the teacher does not?

PART I

The Status of Growth

Grown don't mean nothing to a mother.
A child is a child. They get bigger, older,
but grown? What's that supposed to
mean? In my heart it don't mean a thing.
— Toni Morrison, *Beloved*

CHAPTER 1

Growing

IN WESTERN CULTURE, THE OLDEST TALE OF growth—at least the oldest to survive Western culture intact—begins in the middle with the hero in trouble and on alien ground. One of our newest educational tales starts in a similar manner. It begins in the sophomore or junior year and finds the hero, the student—in strange plight and in strange territory indeed—writing midway through college with skills that have not grown since the freshman year. It is a surprise beginning. Students are writing no better after two or three years of college. Although surfacing only at times with teachers and scholars of composition, the story runs deep.

The implications for teaching also run deep, and have not been fully sounded. Is this just a saga that educators tell one another to purge their worst fears and to gird their loins for the daily fray, or is it a true history of the present curriculum, in which students are not learning to write? The way teachers answer this question will affect the way they interpret student writing and every other way they teach their course, whether it be advanced or beginning composition.

Let's begin at the real beginning, with learning itself. It would seem that two terms are essential for any definition of learner: *status* and *standard*. To qualify as learners, students must have a status of novice, nescient and receptive; to succeed as learners, they must achieve some set standard, say, writing three pages of prose that nowhere befuddles a reader. Learners are beginners who meet standards. It follows that if sophomores or juniors cannot better freshman standards, then either they are still novices who have failed the freshman course and therefore must begin it or some form of it again or else the freshman course has failed them and ought to be revamped.

But what if this notion of learner is wrong to begin with? Or more insidiously, what if it is incomplete and therefore not a safe notion with which to begin? In fact, I believe that the notion omits a third term whose presence defines everything in learning anew: *change*. Change may appear a self-evident factor in learning, but as we will see, teachers can conceive of certain acts of education without it. In Burke's terms, adding the factor of change converts an essential notion of learning to a temporal one, with radical effect. For one instance, it doubts the epic vignette of writing students sulking in their tents (with a status of malingerer refusing to fight for standards) and begins the construction of a different tale with different implications for the teacher. It will produce, as in this chapter, a more adequate view of the status of people learning to write in college. All it takes to see this is to resist the lure of beginnings (as I have noted, interpretive tales have none) and instead to take the earliest, perdurable way—to plunge in, in medias res.

Course Learning and Developmental Learning

Consider the strange things that happen when the bearers of standard, the teachers, meet a new student midcourse—not at the start when they install values that they suppose will define an act of learning, nor at the end when they suppose the values will judge the act, but somewhere midstream. Say the student is newly from Greece, twenty-two years old, delayed in transit, entering the freshman writing course at the fourth week. What is her status? No teacher would assume it to be beginner, since she may have been long versed in the writing of sturdy, British-style essays. Nor would it be finished, since as a latecomer to the English language and to the course, she must have many things to learn about idiom and audience and conventional form that the other students already know. And what should the standards be for her? Should she be required to begin with paragraph exercises too? It would be the beginning teacher who would refuse to modify certain procedures—in assignment, in attendance, even in critical judgment (in this student's essay, for instance, the teacher would read differently that word spelled *judgement*).

Teachers may think there are ways to appease or outmaneuver these problems in the determination of status and standard. A "diagnostic" essay, not truly diagnostic but still a declaration of status, might recommend that this exceptional student forget about the exercises and classroom discussion and just hand in a certain number of essays sometime before the end of the semester. Some standards, such as attendance, might have to go by the board, but others, such as stable grading systems and preset course objectives, can still handle the exceptional case. But this solution entails a shift in interpretation, from diagnosis to placement. The teacher may not notice the shift, but it is a violent one (see chapter 14). The teacher has maneuvered the two concerns of status and standard out of one area, learning, and into another, academic credit. If this foreign student in a new land is to continue in the role of learner, new standards will have to be set for her, and to some extent they will not be the same as those set for the other students.

The point is not that there are two standards, one an exception for aliens or latecomers. It is that if learning continues, standards and status change. The Greek latecomer may be an unusual case, but she is not an exception. All students enter all courses in medias res, all are on alien ground. Like her, they are not beginners, empty urns waiting to be filled, but already experienced, and their experience grows with each step of the course. Consequently their performance changes in value as the course advances. Paragraphing an essay may seem to have a fixed value in a teacher's whatnot of standards, but a failure to paragraph first happening in the third essay means something different from such a failure in the first and second. Only from the perspective of academic credit is an "A" essay that is turned in the first week also an "A" essay when turned in the last week. From the perspective of learning, it is failure. The status of students also shifts as the course advances. It shifts, again if we are talking about genuine learning and not grade earning, from adept to more adept. Learning so entails change that were the students in a course, even passing students, not to relinquish old ways and move to new ones permanently, their status would still change, from novice to dropout. What always qualifies any determination of status or standard in an act of learning is the sense of growth.

I introduce these primitive concepts here—standard, status, change—because they underpin even the most primitive concept of writing development. The terms give us an axiomatic, though minimal, grasp of that eelish notion. Development in writing involves a change in status not from beginner to finisher but from experienced to more experienced, and with that change comes a shift in evaluative or interpretive or pedagogical standard.

But I also start with these terms because they reformulate the question of growth in a student's writing during college. From the standard perspective of grade earning or course mastery, the "advanced" writing student should begin where the freshman finished. By this standard, most teachers would expect to find sophomores and juniors not having changed in their writing in the year or more since leaving freshman composition. But as I have said, other teachers tell different stories. One will find that students have forgotten a good deal of whatever knack of writing they had picked up in the beginning course. A second, alarmingly, will find that their skills have actually regressed since they entered college.

From the perspective of developmental learning, all three of these positions are alarming. I will look more closely at them as interpretive tales in the next chapter, but here the crucial point can now be made. When teachers imagine that student writing waits or grows rusty or decays over time, they explicitly or implicitly also imagine that learning has not continued, that is, that it never really took place. They believe that for a year or more students stop growing or forget to grow or even, perversely, ungrow. In contrast, development assumes as a norm that, compared with the freshmen they once were, the sophomores and juniors will be more experienced writers, although to define that experience (more adroit with words? wilier with forms?), it recognizes that standards will be changed along with the status of students as "advanced" or "upper-division." The last thing development assumes is that students will delay and reject their own natural growth. "After all, our pupils are alive," Alfred North Whitehead reminds us, each a "living organism which grows by its own impulse towards self-development" (38–39). Whitehead reminds us, in fact, how odd yet how easy it is for teachers to do three things: to imagine that the same standards can be applied to different contexts, to think of students as ciphers before and after they enter the classroom, and to forget that human growth and learning are synonymous.

My triad of terms, primitive as they may be, formulates some questions badly in need of asking. At midstream in college, have undergraduates changed in their writing? By which standards—for the freshman or for the postfreshman? By whose standards—the teacher's or the student's? Earning what status for the student—learner, advanced, recalcitrant, malingerer, laggard, recidivist? Answers to these questions will not be found readily. The rest of this chapter centers on the third question. It looks for evidence of undergraduate growth in writing and change in status, first from the perspective of the students' motives, then from a perspective momentarily relieved of motive (the eighty-four empirical measures of the Sample), and then, perhaps most convincingly, from the angle of the students' self-descriptions. The next chapter will look at the way growth and status are perceived in different ways by teachers.

Evidence of growth one way or the other is requisite for any effort to envision a working undergraduate writing program. If the answer is negative, supporting the tale of the tent-bound student, it will strike not only near the life of the basic course, whose breath is finally measured not by how the students change during it but by how long they keep changing afterward, but right at the life of any curricular sequence that hopes to send students into the world outside of college with the skills and motivations to keep on learning to write all their life.

Change in Status: Freshman to Junior

Homer knew that plunging into the midst of the action forces his audience to raise these same three crucial questions: What is the status of Achilles? How is he to be judged? Will he change? In the same preemptive way, the Sample intruded into the middle of the educational careers of three classes of students—freshmen, sophomores, and juniors. Let's turn to that context and judge, as best we can, the status of the students who provided the sample of writing that will force so many similar questions in the following pages. We will set aside the end-of-the-course freshman essays and focus on the first-week "diagnostics." Were there differences in motive that would lead one to expect, and help one to interpret, changes in the writing of the more experienced students?

The freshmen are spending an August hour of the second day of their college career writing the first essay for their freshman composition teacher. They have been told it will be used to assess their writing skills for a course that all must take but few know much about. The topic gives them little trouble. It asks for a well-written essay offering to hypothetical researchers any opinion about one of two familiar subjects, American codes of conduct or American ideals of physical appearance. The thirty-two writers ending up in the Sample—half of them female and half male—represent quite faithfully the range and distribution of verbal ability of all entering freshmen, less the 3 percent who chose Honors classes, and they will finish their course in "regular" composition with an equivalent range and distribution of grades. None of the group write English as a second language, and all are eighteen years old (our student from Greece is too confounding).

During the same hours of the same day, a group of nineteen-year-old sophomores and twenty-year-old juniors are writing a "diagnostic essay" for an advanced-composition teacher—same topics, same purpose. When freshmen a year or two years earlier, the students in these two groups had brought a range and distribution of precollege verbal skills and high-school grades equivalent to the freshman group's. Just like the freshmen, the older students are in a writing course largely because it is required for graduation—required, in their case, by the majors they have declared (which are about the same as the ones the freshman group predicted for themselves).

But if the sophomores and juniors seem more or less the same kind of students as the freshmen, and in the same writing pickle, they do not approach that task out of the same status. In one word, they are no longer "fresh." All have written this kind of diagnostic essay before, all know how one college writing teacher made use of it, and all know what is intended by the word *essay,* since they have written eight or so for freshman composition and have survived. They have also survived, by making "regular academic progress in," at least twenty-seven (if sophomores) or fifty-seven (if juniors) semester hours of other courses. None of their courses were in composition but about a third (the national average) required them to write extended pieces such as library research papers, summaries and reviews, lab reports, case studies, and discursive examination answers. Their language sense has been hardened in the long fire-and-water treatment of academic prose. They have read literally thousands of pages of texts whose academic style can set meteorological records on the Fog Index and have packed a quantity of spiral notebooks with raw gobbets of this style. Compared with the status of second-day freshmen, theirs certainly warrants the expression "more experienced," and to ask them to sit in the stead of such students would be much like asking them to wedge into primary-school desks. Obviously, such status gives the older students the right to ask that a teacher expect some significant growth in their essays.

Or obviously not—and by the same tokens. Part of the self-image of any student who has made regular progress through a year or two of college is of image bearer, of one who prepares a face to meet the face that one meets behind the podium with test in hand. In a skills course, the experienced students may decide it is good strategy to write a bad essay, since the skills they can be most sure of acquiring are those they already possess. If it turns out that they truly occupy a level of skill lower than that projected by the teacher, the nearer they are to finals when they reach it, the better. In short, the experienced students may write a first essay more as a diagnosis of the teacher than of the student, more as a topic assigned to the teacher. They will read the grade on their essay as the teacher's essay that will determine their own course objectives. They may suppose that if the whole class writes at the standard of entering freshmen, then the teacher will give them a course they can enjoy because they have already had it.

Students are sensible people, and some such perverse image-making is not unlikely. Academic experience teaches the value of such ploys. Experienced students may have learned that the writing they do in the third or so of their courses outside of English counts for much less than that percent in final grade, or learned that the writing teacher's focus on writing is usually overpowered by the subject teacher's focus on content, or learned that freshman composition is one of those courses, like ethics, that it actually pays to forget. But note: this is learning. It marks a change of status from naive to savvy. Long ago in a piece of research with questionable methods but answerable results, Phil C. Lange showed that the same students during the same semester wrote much worse for other classes than for their writing class. Half of the students submitting "remedial" papers for a sociology course were submitting, in the same weeks of the semester, acceptable papers in English. When the students got their sociology papers back, they were able to correct a third of their errors on their own. They said, "Why didn't you warn us?"[1]

Change in Performance: Evidence from the Sample

So change in status leads us to expect an ambiguous growth in performance, either an advance or a manipulation to feign stasis or even recidivism. This may explain why afterwards, in conference, advanced-writing students sometimes greet their first essay with a gesture of embarrassment or deprecation. Still, I would not expect these students to be surprised to hear that when these same first-week efforts of freshmen, sophomores, and juniors are compared by means of objective measures, free of status or motive, the evidence is unambiguous. The underlying intent may or may not change, but the performance certainly does. On the eighty-four preset measures, twenty-one, or a fourth, register a statistically significant difference between either the sophomore or junior essays and the freshman essays.

That difference is of clear importance to this study, with each of the twenty-one measures deserving a sustained look. For the moment, here is the gist of the shift. *Organization:* On the whole, the essays for the advanced-writing course are shaped by schemes that are more complex logically. The top

---

[1] Lange's piece was published in 1948. The same year English teachers at Franklin and Marshall College initiated a program to catch writing recidivists, under the slogan "Eternal vigilance is the price of English undefiled." In the spirit of today's random drug-testing, they "lifted" quiz and examination papers of unwarned students and scrutinized them for surface errors. Deficient writers had to write an impromptu essay, and those who failed it had to enroll in a junior remedial writing course. In eight years 1,176 students were tested, 237 screened, and 46 (or 4 percent of the original) had to take the course (Adams). In the next chapter, we will see dashed more of these hopes to find large-scale postfreshman deterioration in writing skill.

level of organization embraces more embedded levels, and it more often embraces the entire piece, resulting in fewer "double-thesis" essays. *Specificity:* Focus broadens, with subjects of sentences increasing in generality or topical reach. But the number of sentences with the generic *you* as grammatical subject drops, while the number with *I* rises steeply. *Coherence:* Titles are more apt to point ahead to a thesis, introductions to direct the reader to the purpose and scope of the whole essay, and conclusions to summarize the essay in full or to further its implications. In contrast, explicit logical connectors decrease. *Diction:* Vocabulary expands—the words tend to be longer, and they tend to be less common (judging by frequency counts of words in print). *Syntax:* Style becomes less verbal and more nominal: a larger share of the words in the essays are put to use modifying nouns, and the modification grows more complex. Sentences lengthen. To be blunt, they sprawl. Fewer nouns are compounded, more modification is placed after the nominal head, more free modification and adverbial expressions are placed after the main clause, more appositives and less syntactic parallelism are used everywhere.

Without doubt it is a gaunt and quirky list, tethered by the original choice of quantifiable measures. This may be hard evidence for a shift of some sort and may be evidence consisting of differences in group means, which, as statistically significant, carry with them the credentials of group tendencies. But how substantial is this difference? Does this sparse outgrowth of traits reflect a change in writing skill profound enough to satisfy the older students' intuition of a gain in experience and central enough to earn the writing teacher's interest? I believe so. Later chapters will argue that these traits bond more closely and at greater depth with the rhetorical competence critical to growth in undergraduate writing than a first glance might suggest. Here we can use these disembodied traits to interpret some of the writing from which they were abstracted. We will find between the beginning and advanced writing differences that may please both students and teachers.

Two of the diagnostics are transcribed on pages 26 and 27. Their comparison has a certain justification. Essay F was written by the freshman who fell at the median in the distribution of precollege verbal scores for the freshman group. Essay J (without title) was written by the junior who fell at the same median for the junior group. Since both groups expressed the distribution of precollege verbal scores for the entire matriculating class, the two writers presumably brought to their task a similar middling writing ability. Later chapters will explore the rich and fascinating border regions of exceptional performance, but these two pieces speak from Missouri, the stable midlands of the youngest and oldest groups, as befits our present concern with general growth. The two writers are my best candidates for population center of the crowd of first-language students in our colleges. By luck, both are the same sex and both wrote essays of almost the same length, ridding the comparison of two vexing constraints. I encourage giving these two pieces a careful reading, since they will serve also in following chapters.

Essays F and J do not display all twenty-one of the group changes. They would be ontogenetic museum pieces if they recapitulated such phylogeny so perfectly. Of the two, it is the freshman essay that exhibits an appositional phrase, for instance, and the junior essay more parallel structures. But these departures from the norm do not much weaken the instructive way the two essay writers render the shared style of their classmates. Fifteen of the group changes are present, enough to generate a sense of a shift in technique. Consider five familiar rhetorical competencies: organization, coherence, specificity, diction, and syntax.

Organization. The argument of the freshman Essay F may seem more graphic. It develops by means of four examples arranged as a simple contrast between present leaders in the first three paragraphs and past leaders in the fourth. The argument of junior Essay J, beginning with the third sentence and running to the end, is too complex to be expressed so readily. Logically, it is arranged as a dialectic, progressing through an antithesis

Essay F
The affect of phisical appearances in politics

When our current president, President Carter, was running for president, his big, warm smile attracted many voters. Many people thought he was a different kind of man than past presidents. He fit our needs perfectly. He, we though, would be a down-home president who really cared.

Now, three years later, the situation has changed. Cartoons make fun of his smile now that he isn't as popular. In politics the same physical appearance can change from good to bad depending on how we feel about a person. It can also change because of what we want to see of them. His smile went from friendly to ludicrous or sinister.

This election year we have another prime example. Govener Reagon has nothing special to offer, but we musn't forget that he is very good-looking for an older man. For example: Women have been heard saying this sort of thing, I don't know how good of a president he would make, but he sure is good-looking". This quote shows that just because he is good-looking for an older man he can attract votes. What people should realize is that good-looks cannot run a country.

Another example of the affect of physical apperances is to take a quick look at past presidents. Many presidents got elected by simply portraying themselves as an active individual. Dwight D. Eshinhower and Ullyses S. Grant were both army heros, but the didn't know the first thing about running a country.

If all the facts are put together a theory like this comes into grasp: If a person has a certain style, grace or good physical appearance they can win votes if the only have an I.Q. of 50.

Essay J

Codes of conduct play a considerable role in our lives. The role in wich these codes play in many ways is harmful and many ways is beneficial. Benefically these roles help as a guide to what should or shouldn't be done, said or considered. These codes give us an understanding of what is expected of us as individuals interacting in society. How we act on a date, How we conduct ourselves in day to day interactions among our peers, What we do in day to day situations are all governed to a great extent by the codes we are taught by our parents, schools, and friends. These codes are used and maintained to help society to keep some sort of order. Without these codes much of our social structure would break down as a result of the disorder between individuals.

The harmful effect such codes play in society can be seen as a result of the restraint that they put on us. Codes of conduct restrict the individual to where in many cases one feels he/orshe can not function in the way they wish. This type of restraining is not always the case and is usually found where codes of behavior have been strictly enforced, to the point of near intrapment. Deviance within society falls in many cases as a result of this, one is attempting to achieve a freedom that has not before been there. These ethical codes seem to manytimes surpress a free and creative spirit within us.

The best of all posible worlds is found in moderation of codes of conduct. Let the codes be set down and maintain but at the sametime let the creative spirit act around these codes as guide lines. Without such codes there would be disorder, but with codes that surpress disorder would result as well. The happy medium between harmful and beneficial effects keeps society running smooth.

(the beneficial and harmful effects of conduct codes), to a synthesis (the resolution in a policy of moderation).

Coherence. On the surface, F looks more cohesive. It provides a title and furnishes explicit logical connectors—such as For example, Another, and but—at three times the rate of J. But F's title serves as its only introduction, and its one-sentence summary turns out to be incomplete and even misleading. Though lacking a title, Essay J coheres more pervasively, with a functional introduction and a conclusion logically evolving out of the body.

Specificity. F creates a strong sense of concreteness by narrowing the distance between topic and sentence lens. Semantically, most of the subjects of F's main clauses have a reference at least as restricted as the subject of its second sentence (many American voters). None of the subjects of J are that specific. Compare our current president, Cartoons, Govener Reagon, Women . . . heard saying this sort of thing in Essay F with Codes of conduct, our social structure, Deviance within society, The best of all possible worlds in Essay J. Instead, J moves toward a greater interest in logical relationships, syntactically rendered by a downward zooming as sentences proceed. For instance, J devotes about half of its words to restriction of nouns, F about a third. Compare passages (with head nouns in uppercase and modifiers in italics):

> In politics *the same physical* APPEARANCE can change from good to bad depending on HOW WE FEEL *about a person.* It can also change because of WHAT WE WANT TO SEE *of them. His* SMILE went from friendly to ludicrous or sinister. (Essay F)

> Without *these* CODES MUCH *of our social structure* would break down as a RESULT *of the disorder between individuals.* The *harmful* EFFECT *such codes play in society* can be seen as a RESULT *of the restraint that they put on us.* (Essay J)

Diction. Despite the deft stroke of sinister in Essay F, the junior essay shows a wider command of word choice. If we mark words that occur in print ten times or less in every one million words (according to Edward L. Thorndyke and Irving Lorge's standard count), J ends up with three times the rate of F. Actually, these "unusual" words are unusual only in comparison with the mass of repeated basic words. In F, the "unusual" words are down-home, ludicrous, and sinister; in J, beneficially, interacting, interactions, governed, disorder, restraint, strictly, entrapment, deviance, suppress, and medium.

Syntax. Something of the same easy flair for words shows up in J's sentences. The sentences in F seem both more controlled and less sure of themselves. They average nearly four words shorter than J's and stack up over a third of their nominal modification before the noun head. J is more inclined to put ideas in postpositioned structures. J places twice as many words in adverbial expressions at the end of main clauses and twice attaches free modification to the end of a main clause, whereas F does so not once. Compare When our current president, President Carter, was running for president, his big, warm smile attracted many voters (F) with This type of restraining is not always the case and is usually found where codes of behavior have been strictly enforced, to the point of near intrapment (J).

Though even more gaunt, this catalogue of differences begins to paint a round enough portrait of two writers with quite distinct styles. The freshman is reluctant to move far from the facts, secure in lists and a few practical generalizations, direct and colloquial in sentence and vocabulary, cautious and rather uncivil in a focus on one part at a time, reliant on the direct verb more than on the complex noun. The junior is enamored of abstract ideas, eager for analysis and debate and idealistic resolution, more learned and elegant in phrase and word, more easily cohesive from essay logic down to sentence structure, reliant more on the elaborated nominal than on the verb. In sum, F has a kind of upstate blunt pragmatism, J a dressier, more formal urbanity.

The temptation, of course, is to explain the familiarity of these two approaches by assigning them personal styles and to explain away the difference between the two essays as the luck of the draw. On the other hand, the point the statistical analysis of the twenty-one quantified measures makes—an unfamiliar point—is that the two styles or approaches gravitate toward different university classes. By circling from the statistics back to the essays, I have deliberately set these two individual writers and their particular essays against the developmental frame, with its inbred hypothesis of growth norms, erected by the group comparisons. This is bound to raise muddy but fertile questions. How much of the styles of Essays J and F reflects personality and how much age and experience? Evidently, if personality and growth are to be separated, it will be by a willingness to ask how surface traits such as logical organization and free modification respond to deeper motivations, such as cognitive style and cognitive development, and by a willingness to admit that personal and developmental styles interact. The separation will not be easy or definitive ever. But it has to be attempted if the developmental factor enters into teaching in any large and honest way. I make my trial in chapters 6 through 11.

Here it is enough to see that the evidence argues for substantial writing changes between the freshman and junior years in students representing a wide range of writing competence, a growth that teachers might encourage the older ones to be proud of. Apparently the students are alive, on the stir, living and learning. It remains to be seen whether the direction of this mobilization requires a tactical shift in teaching standards to counter or to join the shift in student writing. But one general change seems to follow right away. That is our appreciation of the self-perceived status of the older students.

The Student's Tale of Growth: Freshman to Junior

According to the Sanskrit *Hitopadesa,* a work nearly as venerable as the *Iliad,* "Learning is a companion on a journey to a strange country; learning is strength inexhaustible." What is wrong with assuming that students, on their trek toward upper-division status, will keep only those companions who will serve them most faithfully? Aren't there good reasons for them to arrive at the advanced writing course with many old skills dropped by the wayside or grown rusty since freshman composition? As I have admitted, many students find writing devalued in other courses and associated almost totally with grades and graduation requirements. Surely they often also find it of unproven intrinsic worth or of suspect cultural standing, inducing anxiety and undermining self-esteem and poorly defined in terms of quality and appropriateness. Given the terrain, how will many students, no matter how well intentioned, enter an advanced writing course other than somehow as laggards or recidivists?

Against such an arsenal of common experience, I may seem foolhardy in offering a third counterargument: that the students still rarely imagine themselves in that status. So far my only support is the comparison of first-week essays, with changes that suggest that a certain vital flux has continued to operate since sophomores and juniors entered college as freshmen. But there is a sleeper of a finding buried in a small cluster of observational studies that have tried to fathom the inner motives and attitudes of college students about writing. The finding is that even those students who might be labeled "backsliders" with the most justice rarely think of themselves as such. Instead they envision themselves as surviving, adapting, growing. James D. Williams and Scott D. Alden, for instance, isolate a subgroup of University of Southern California students, about a third of all students at the end of their freshman composition course, who hold the most strongly extrinsic motivations for writing. These students would not have taken the course had it been an elective, do not enjoy writing, write only if required for courses and mainly for grades (although they assume grades for writing are totally subjective), write papers only at the last moment and revise them only once if at all, rarely place a high value on writing well, and generally believe that writing cannot be taught. Yet as writers, these students see themselves as "relatively better" than other students, even as "highly proficient." They feel they have "already mastered" writing (110–11).

Dave, a student whom Lucille Parkinson McCarthy observed from his freshman into his junior year, judges college writing in the crassest terms, as mere show of academic competence. From his elevated rank as junior, he would give freshmen this advice: "First you've got to figure out what your teachers want. And then you've got to give it to them if you're gonna get the grade" (233). Since he seems to take writing assignments in new courses as totally "unfamiliar academic territories," McCarthy demotes him to a "stranger in a strange land." Yet this phrase, it is worth remembering, originally belongs not to Robert Heinlein's hero but to the young Moses, self-exiled from Egypt, where he had committed premeditated murder. As a wanderer in the upper lands of Academia, Dave has the same lack of guilt and the same excess of self-confidence. A junior now, he feels he has with him the necessary companion skills: "Writing is no problem for me" (261).

If any student deserves the earmark of recidivist, it is Mark, Stephen M. North's case. He is a senior taking a freshman-level philosophy course, an upperclass student "doing a bit of intellectual slumming," as North puts it, a master of "an academic patter" (252). Every one of the ten sections of Mark's journal, written entirely in capital letters and, as he puts it, "off the top of my head" (247), has to be resubmitted to meet the grader's standards. By comparison, one of the two freshmen studied along with Mark has to resubmit four sections, the other just one. Yet, though Mark thinks he has wasted his time in the course, nowhere does he question his inner resources of writing. In his journal he sees himself as a successful combatant, bold and honest, never writing "what the professor wants to hear" (231). Mark and Dave hold opposite notions of the proper strategy students should take in writing to what their teacher "wants," yet both show the same faith in their capabilities as strategists.

Are these students just self-deceived? One value of ethnographic research is that it takes the self-perceptions of students seriously. If, so far, the approach has found that students rarely imagine their status as nonlearners, as nongrowers, the students, I submit, have a certain right to their view. What looks like recidivism from our perspective may be growth from theirs. When the students of Lange elected to pay less attention to surface errors in their sociology papers, what looks like a decline in skill may have been a reasonable rhetorical decision. Under normal circumstances would their sociology teacher have noticed? When Dave forgets about a paper a year after he wrote it, the action may appear to be carelessness, but it may have been craft. It was written for an assignment poorly conceived by his teacher. "I have no need to remember it" Dave says. Even if sophomores and juniors try to psyche out their advanced-writing teacher by concocting dumb diagnostic essays, what appears to be a betrayal of writing skill may rather show loyalty to a rhetorical acumen that adapts to the situation. These are all changes in writing behavior, but, in the way of all youthful change, they probably are growth in some sense. Even the surreptitious countertalk in the back ranks of a writing class may be a sign of writing growth. More often than we assume, as the ethnographer Robert Brooke found out by joining the back row, such talk is following up ideas introduced by the teacher: "The students are developing their own stances towards class activity, not whispering about unrelated subjects like parties and dates" (144). In 1983, when twenty-three hundred seniors from eight colleges were asked if they felt they had made "substantial progress" in their ability to write, from half to four-fifths (depending on the college) responded positively (Pace).

Discovered in the middle of a journey, on the alien ground of the advanced course, the college student records a tale that may appear archaic, an Anglo-Saxon fragment about a bird flying through a strange mead-hall out of winter into winter or about a wanderer equipped only with doubts and undauntedness navigating a river that can never be stepped in twice. But the tale is not necessarily one of losses. Student change implies growth, which implies learning, which entails a new status. Advanced students do not begin the course as beginners, and to treat them as such may be a pedagogical mistake, denying them the status of learners.

For a teacher to treat advanced students with the old freshman standards may be equally a disaster. Clearly, for the new sophomores and juniors the values of writing have shifted with their status. But should the values of the teachers therefore also shift? We are left with the question of whose standards should rule. "Interpretation is not an isolated act," writes Frederic Jameson, "but takes place within a Homeric battlefield, on which a host of interpretive options are either openly or implicitly in conflict" (13). In the writing classroom, the clash between student and teacher standards has been waged largely in secret. I intend in the next chapter to bring it more into the open.

CHAPTER 2

Three Interpretive Tales of Growth

IT IS THE SECOND DAY OF CLASS, AND THE ENG-lish teacher and advanced-writing students face each other across the field of the "diagnostic" essay. That battlefield—or ball court, if you will, or discipline—extends to the whole semester and, as we have seen, much further. We have glimpsed the way the students size up the new course, an evolving set of expectations that may make the teacher into something of an opponent to outfox or an authority to follow, something of a maze to thread or a puzzle to solve. All these imply different interpretive systems. But what do the teachers make of the older students? Their own varied systems can oppose and inter-act with the systems of the students and make the classroom arena less a battlefield and more a funhouse of facing distorted mirrors. "Frame organizes more than meaning," says Erving Goffman, "it also organizes involvement" (1974: 345).

The situation, though, is no carnival. Interpretive ways of the teachers have a real impact on the student, beginning with their evaluation of the first-week essay and continuing on through the course that the diagnostic prognoses. Just like students, of course, individual teachers run in interpretive modes that are highly complex and idiosyncratic. They make their own sense of growth. The three modes I will isolate in this chapter rarely work in isolation. But when one of them holds sway, the consequences are anything but illusions.

The Ungrounded English-Teacher Vision and the Tale of Holistic Assessment

Most teachers in an "advanced" writing course have already taught, and many no longer teach, a "beginning" course. In part for these reasons, they probably entertain a right to expect the first-week performance of the students in the second course to differ from the first-week performance in the first course. And in part because they have been reared in the collective discipline of English, the teachers expect the performance to differ in specific ways. We all know these English-teacher ways well. They cohere under an interpretive vision that this book will give an unfamiliar name: "ungrounded." It does so from the angle of its own vision. Although the English-teacher vision applies a value system in a way that creates a simulacrum of change—discovering what it calls improvement or regression— that set of values levitates free of solid developmental ground. It reflects course learning, not developmental learning.

Here is part of the ungrounded vision. The teachers will expect the first-week essays of the older students to be longer and to have longer paragraphs. They will expect more of the essays to own titles. They will expect the organization to be better boxed and trim, with logical compartments divided by paragraphing and explicit transitions. They will expect, in fact, more transitions everywhere—between paragraphs, sentences, independent clauses—a change in cohesion that, along with a greater control of introductions and conclusions, will show a clearer awareness of purpose and audience. They will expect a more direct and verbal style, with fewer passives, fewer verbs of state, less elaboration of nouns, fewer nominalized participles and clauses and infinitives, less inflated diction. They will look for the "advanced" sentence to continue to distance itself from the school sentence, from what the 1974 National Assessment of Educational Progress called a "primer-like style"—to show more dependent openings, more subordinate clauses, and fewer coordinate conjunctions. They will expect a reduction in solecisms of spelling, punctuation, syntax, and predication. Above all, they will expect more concreteness: more examples, more allusions, more specificity of subject. All these expectations teachers base on an idealized platform of "good writing." They taught it in freshman composition or they assume someone should be teaching it there, they saw those students move toward it, and they feel older students ought to continue toward it at least from where they left off. In short, their students find themselves inserted into an interpretive tale so basic it takes on a fairy-tale simplicity: the student acts in one way; the teacher holds up a magic mirror empowered with a vision that reflects the student ideally, out of current time, by the light of an unknown past or unachieved future; the student uses the visionary image to act better.

In the English-teacher mirror of "good writing," there are more items than the ones I list above, of course, such as greater sensitivity to style, willingness to revise, sense of rhetorical context, and so on. I can speak directly only to the part I have outlined. What we can now say is that advanced-writing teachers are unlikely to find that part. According to Essays F and J, and the group styles sketched by the measures of the Sample, the only item teachers might reasonably expect to see in place is more conventional introductions and conclusions. None of the rest.

Within such an idealized interpretive tale, of course, a *right* to expect does not mean truly to expect. Indeed some of the teachers who have taught advanced composition long enough may expect their expectations to be dashed—a perversity they may be allowed because, like the students, they too are human. The teachers act much as the art critic Leo Steinberg says the

public has always interpreted vanguard art, as if they were seeing a "sacrifice" (33). They note only absences. The first view-
ers of Georges Braque saw only the nonpresence of values they
cherished, such as perspective and story, not the presence of
new accomplishments in wit and juxtaposition of color. Teachers too may see only what the "advanced" diagnostics have sac-
rificed, missing what the essays have succeeded in doing. This
is the back side of the ungrounded English-teacher vision, the
black of the mirror hinted at by the etymology of the word
expect. To expect one thing is to neglect another.

The situation holds an irony with a serious allegation. The
very effort of English teachers to keep good writing in sight
tends to blind them to, or at least discount, the changes the older
students manage in their writing, for instance those changes
catalogued in the previous chapter. The irony, of course, does
not necessarily question the ultimate validity of the standards in
the value set of English teachers. Fully accomplished writing
probably is more concrete than student writing. But the allegation does question the teachers' abilities to carry out their professional obligation to read student writing with acuity and
fairness. The teachers have seen one valuable thing, say a lack of
concreteness, and failed to see another, say a presence of complex ideas. The allegation begs for backing. Unfortunately, the
Sample can provide it, with a certain uncompromising clarity.

The evidence emerges from a particular telling of the ungrounded English-teacher tale. Involved are fourteen young
university composition teachers whose task was to assess the
Sample essays by means of a system of holistic rating. They were
not inexperienced, averaging two and one-half years teaching
composition in college and two years in the schools. They were
all in their twenties and full of enthusiasm and empathy for
student writers. They had an admirable priority of values,
shown by a separate analysis of their rating of similar student
writing, in which they put content and support as the most
important ingredients of writing, followed by organization,
sentence structure, diction, and mechanics, in that order. An

admirable priority, as I can say, since it is pretty much my own—and loosely an assignment of values that researchers have found young teachers acting on elsewhere. But in this particular telling, that good-intentioned priority has an unhappy denouement. It did not reflect, within the framed mirror of the holistic rating, any of the changes the sophomores and juniors made in their diagnostic writing. On a one-to-eight scale (eight representing top quality), the teachers awarded an average holistic score of 4.0 to freshman essays, 4.2 to sophomore, and 4.2 to junior. (Discount the slight rise. It does not even approach statistical significance.) This is not a passing, fireside tale. It expresses in pure form an interpretive act that is eager to occur and, I think, usually does occur in one way or another whenever a teacher picks up a new piece of student writing. As such, it bears close study.

Always, in trying to interpret an interpretation, one needs to ask what happened. Initially the teachers professed a common priority of values. But profession, even if professional, is not application. There the set may easily be reversed. Teachers may agree most in their independent assessment of mechanical mistakes and agree less and less up to content. Other reversals in the professed order of importance will show up in the critical weight the teachers apply when they actually evaluate essays, as researchers now well know. With these human biases in mind, the holistic system explicitly forced the raters through a systematic framing of values to correct skewing and create a better concordance. It trained the teachers to give equal weight to set components such as support, organization, diction, and mechanics and to cling to anchor essays holding levels of achievement for each component. Typing and anonymity of the essays squelched other cryptic inclinations that might lurk behind the teachers' profession of values, factors such as handwriting, gender, age, and academic class. The system meant to make the final value judgment of the teacher-raters more objective.

And the system worked. Worked, that is, in creating a concordance of scores (inter-rater reliability was .93). But did it make the English-teacher vision more objective? Yes, if we take *objectivity* to refer to similarity in independent judgments, where the assumption is that two judges agree because they must be setting aside individual biases and attending solely to the object. No, if we take *objectivity* to refer to qualities in the object itself, independent of human subjectivity or judgment. It should not be forgotten that the systematic frame of a holistic scheme does little more than tidy up, regularize, the subjective. More to the point, behind its formal shape and method lies the ungrounded English-teacher vision. In both the ungrounded and holistic act, raters hold each piece of writing up against the magic mirror of their idealized rubric of writing components. Historically, in fact, the components now used in holistic schemes—support, organization, diction, etc.—were derived by factoring impressionistic English-teacher responses to student writing. (There are no beginnings to the interpretive circle.) High concordance among raters may be a sign that the holistic system forces each of them to set aside individual subjective values and attend solely to the English-teacher vision— which the rating system urges because it is the one value set all raters hold in common and therefore can agree on. In its effort to prioritize the object, the holistic may legitimatize the vision.

In short, it is possible that this particular holistic project failed to mirror one particular object, the older students' essays in the Sample, because it tailored its system to a vision unfriendly to that object. The possibility is supported by an assessment of the assessment. The statistical procedure of multiple regression identified the part in the fourteen teachers' holistic rating played by those twenty-one measures marking changes accomplished by the post-freshman writers. It was about 2 percent. Of the twenty-one traits, the largest contribution to the teachers' vision was sophistication of vocabulary. The degree of logical complexity of the organization had no influence, for good or bad, on the rating. All the changes in syntax—in sentence length, amount of free modification, placement of nominal modification—accounted for less than 1 percent of the rating. Out of the full battery of eighty-four measures, what accounted for the largest share of the teachers' holistic appraisal were staples of the ungrounded English-teacher agenda: length of the essay, correctness of spelling, size of main clauses, and number of examples. Yet these are all features of writing in which older students show little interest as they grow from their freshman ways (Haswell 1986a; Haswell 1991 arrives at the same conclusion with a factoring of the eighty-four measures).

These results are not surprising. They accord with the growing body of research into the critical judgment of writing teachers—a sometimes highly technical but compelling reading. The one consistent finding is that syntax and logic account for little, while length, error, vocabulary, and concreteness account for nearly all. What has been little documented, though it has been suspected, is the ominous way writing performance (status), critical judgment (standard), and developmental growth (change) fail to interact. The failure, however, suggests a reinterpretation of another common research finding: that impressionistic judgment of teachers finds no difference in writing from different academic classes of undergraduates. Andrew Kerek, Donald Daiker, and Max Morenberg paid juniors to rewrite a topic they had written as freshmen, and the average junior rating, on a six-point scale, did not show a statistically significant growth, from 3.7 to 3.9. As freshmen, the students of Charlene Eblen wrote essays averaging 3.4 on a five-point scale, and as juniors—volunteers this time—they again averaged 3.4. Aviva Freedman and Ian Pringle had graduate students in English holistically rate papers written by high-school seniors and college juniors for courses in literature, history, geography, and biology, and they found junior papers no better unified, organized, supported, or made coherent (1980b). It has been argued that since holistic assessment does not record developmental change in areas such as syntax, those areas may not play a significant role in development (Faigley 1980). But just as the engagement between teacher and student works as a set of facing mirrors, so does the confrontation between holistic appraisal and writing sample. It is development in writing that may not play a significant role in holistic assessments, if raters lack the necessary sensitivity to the nature of writing growth.[1]

If the holistic is simply a version of the English-teacher vision writ large, or writ neat, then it is ultimately teachers, not just raters, who may lack a valid system of assessment. As Freedman and Pringle argue, "awareness of how writing abilities develop has not yet been assimilated into evaluative structures" of the "'current-traditional' rhetorical framework" (322). What I call the ungrounded vision connects with the "current-traditional" approach, as opposed to a process or ethnographic or developmental approach, in that it operates from absolute, de-contextualized standards. It tells a paradoxical tale like that of *The Picture of Dorian Gray,* which Oscar Wilde subtitled *A Moral Entertainment.* It tries systematically to entertain writing free of questions about circumstance and status. "There is no such thing as a moral or an immoral book," says the ungrounded vision, along with Wilde in his preface. "Books are well written, or badly written. That is all." But the teachers discover, dismayed (as Wilde was after he published *Dorian Gray*), that they have written a story with a moral after all. As a result, two images clash: the self-image of the student projects healthy growth, while the portrait painted by the English-teacher perspective reflects moral stagnancy or loss.

---

[1] Although the holistic system trains raters to give equal weight to each component of writing, it cannot keep them from unconsciously emphasizing one component over others or allowing one to influence others (the halo effect). For further reasons why holistic assessment is inept in capturing developmental change, see chapter 14. An especially convincing illustration is Betty Bamberg's 1983 reanalysis of essays written by thirteen- and seventeen-year-olds for the National Assessment of Educational Progress. NAEP's holistic rating of coherence found a 39 percent improvement with age. Bamberg's analytic count found a 51 percent improvement. Actually, all kinds of formal assessment have trouble measuring individual growth in writing (see the valuable survey of the problems in Ruth and Murphy: 203–35).

The clash spells pedagogical trouble. What should be common ground between teacher and student, a unified field of performance and evaluation, is almost disjunct. The result can be seen directly in the way the teachers measured Essays F and J. On their scale, where a score of eight was high, the freshman essay received an average rate of 5.0, the junior 4.3. Whatever else that substantial difference says, it certainly tells of one set of traits (extracted by the assessment procedures of the teachers) overriding another set of traits (implicated in the changes in writing of students during the first two years of college). I guess the features of the freshman essay that dominated were the cultural allusions, however badly misspelled, the novelistic words <u>ludicrous</u> and <u>sinister</u>, the appearance of controlled structure with the five paragraphs and with the list of examples, and above all, the concrete support. One can hardly underestimate this last. In Thomas R. Newkirk, Thomas D. Cameron, and Cynthia L. Selfe's enlightening survey of forty-one weaknesses perceived by college teachers in student writing, failure "to provide supporting details" comes in first. In Freedman and Pringle's essays, "supporting detail" was the trait influencing teacher grades by far the most. The last thing that the English-teacher vision will see is a countervision to support, for instance Richard Ohmann's elegant demonstration that textbook advice to "use definite, specific, concrete language" often "closes off analysis" and subjugates students to immediate experience by withholding from them "the language that might be used to understand it" (1979: 391, 396). What might be taken as an effort not to be subjugated—Essay J's increase in generality of reference and in complexity of logical organization—did not stand a chance.

If the teachers' holistic assessment of Essays F and J, and of the freshman, sophomore, and junior essays as a whole, reflects a common reading of advanced-student writing, and if the advanced-writing teacher succeeds in making that reading prevail over the students' reading of their own performance, then we can assume a common and unfortunate occurrence: advanced-writing courses invalidated on false grounds from nearly the first day. The older student's growth in writing (which is there) teachers cannot see, the growth teachers expect (which is not there) they cannot find, and therefore the evidence needed to sustain a belief in their teaching or in their department as a working organization, evidence of sustained learning in the students, they find missing. The course may even be taught by a teacher who, to avoid self-incrimination, has taken these images of loss or absence in student writing as signs of a generational assault or a cultural collapse or otherwise of evil times. In that case, we have one interpretive tale, the ungrounded English-teacher vision, supplanted or heightened or saturated with another of quite different color.

The Legend of Deterioration

The moral entertainment of the English-teacher vision seems to miss or misread evidence for growth in student writing because initially it images the object by means of a frame that is static and abstract. This may be why, at one extreme, it simply erases the student and considers only writings: the age of the author of an "A" essay has no bearing on the "A." At another distasteful and fortunately rare extreme, it portrays students in absolutes that reject any notion of learners in midstream: they "can't write," "don't know what a sentence is," are "illiterate." In contrast, what I will call the legend of deterioration operates from an interpretive frame that expects students to change. Yet it has more difficulty in seeing the evidence of growth because the change it expects is a kind of academic entropy. The postsecondary version of the legend has a striking plot: left unattended after freshman composition, the writing skill of students rots. An early but essentially complete telling can be found in a *College Composition and Communication* review of Albert R. Kitzhaber's 1963 study, *Themes, Theories, and Therapy: The Teaching of Writing in College:* "Kitzhaber's report that student writing actually deteriorates, rather than improves, after the freshman year, should not be surprising, for it is given every opportunity to atrophy. Not until writing becomes a central pedagogical tool in every discipline will Freshman English begin to enjoy the achievement it ought to" (Robbins: 61). The plot is tragic, and could be reasonably drawn with Gustav Freytag's classic pyramidal diagram of rising action, crisis, and falling action in dramatic tragedy. Indeed, two decades after the review, in 1984, *College Composition and Communication* offered a diagram Freytag himself might have drawn (see figure 2). "We all know studies," Eugene Hammond explains, "like the Dartmouth study reported by Albert Kitzhaber in *Themes, Theories, and Therapy,* which show that college students' writing skills follow [this] path. . . . Once students leave their freshman course, their skills gradually fade because they are too infrequently asked to practice them" (1984: 217–18).

It is crucial to follow up these citations of Kitzhaber. He is the authority, often the only authority, used to sanction the tale

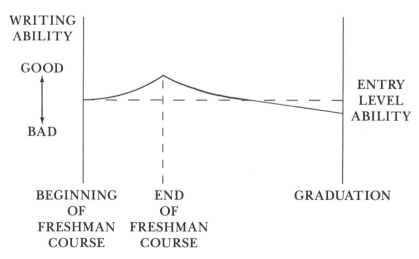

Figure 2.   Deterioration of student writing during college. The diagram is from Eugene Hammond 1984: 218. (Copyright 1984 by the National Council of Teachers of English. Reprinted with the permission of the publisher and the author.)

of deterioration. Supposedly his 1963 study provides the hard data, the research footing, to support the image—now fact—of unattended writing skills fading away during college. Kitzhaber has to be revisited anyway because his book stands as the main predecessor and, at least on the surface, as the antagonist to this one. As it turns out, a close look at Kitzhaber finds more of a father than a foe. It also discovers less grounds for atrophy of student writing skills and more grounds for atrophy of information when research is appropriated by legend-makers.

Kitzhaber's work emerged from a vague, committee-room charge, widespread during the cold-war years, that college students suffer a post-Creation fall. In 1954, for instance, the Conference on College Composition and Communication had officially assumed "a general falling off in composition after the freshman year" (Hackett). According to Kitzhaber's own faculty at Dartmouth, "Once freshman English is completed, many students appear to fall back into their old habits" (Kitzhaber: x). The faculty commissioned him to direct a study of undergraduate writing at Dartmouth, which he undertook from 1960 to 1962. Probably the most concrete of his findings, and certainly the most remembered, is his comparison of errors made in the writing of first-semester freshmen, sophomores, and seniors. This was no hasty count of misspellings and punctuation. Kitzhaber used a tabulation of eighty-two separate errors in these and other aspects of writing, in "focus and structure," "material," "paragraphs," "sentences," "words," and "grammar." The resulting figures, as he puts it in his usual mild way, "look discouraging." End-of-the-course freshmen score better than sophomores, who score better than seniors, who score worse than beginning-of-the-course freshmen—in all eight aspects. Converge Kitzhaber's eighty-two counts of error into one graph and you have Hammond's tragic plot.

The trouble is that one cannot with fairness turn Kitzhaber's figures into such a plot because they do not mean or measure the same thing at one end as they do at the other. The points in Kitzhaber's table record quite different attempts on the part of the students and quite different methods on the part of the assessors. The freshmen were writing essays for their composition course—essays read and marked by their teachers as usual. Sophomores were writing commentaries on three books from a required list in a general-reading program for no academic credit—commentaries read by "college-educated women of the community," who returned them for rewriting only if marked "Unsatisfactory." Seniors were writing journal entries for a year-long "great issues" course of scattered lectures and discussion sessions—journals read and judged by a panel of graders as "Distinction," "Credit," or "Unsatisfactory" and returned to be rewritten if the last. Shades of the students of Phil Lange, shades of Dave and Mark! Given the motivations of the writers, Kitzhaber's table and Hammond's graph much more likely plot an increase in the undergraduates' grasp of genre and audience than a deterioration of their writing skills. Add the fact that for his record of sophomore and senior errors, Kitzhaber counted those he himself found in their writing yet for the freshman figure counted only those errors the teachers had marked, and one has the makings of a legend indeed.

Kitzhaber, however, does not write the legend, only provides the stuff for it. Nowhere in *Themes, Theories, and Therapy* does the word *deteriorate* appear. Instead, Kitzhaber explicitly interprets the "ill-written" commentaries and journals as a natural outcome of the writing conditions, for instance of the fact that upper-division students received no credit for the general-reading program and that the "great issues" journals often were read so perfunctorily that they were taken by students "as something one could slap together in a couple of hours the night before they were due." It is Kitzhaber's main point, in fact— and a point that makes his work remarkably contemporary after a quarter century—that the "increasing carelessness" of the students occurs only "when permitted to" and that the main "therapy" called for is to put "steady pressure" (52, 121, 151) on the student throughout the four undergraduate years by installing "disciplined practice in writing in courses other than freshman English" (154) or, as we would say today, across the curriculum. Kitzhaber certainly feels that student "indifference" and "cynicism" and even "hostility" lead to writing *performance* that is "reprehensibly slipshod," a "backsliding," but he never suggests that the writing *competence* of the students decays in college. It is others who find that decay in Kitzhaber's account.

It is useful to consider the subsequent history of the legend because it illustrates the point, made at the beginning of the present book, that interpretive acts, even ones as innocuous as the reading of student essays, are bound to disciplinary communities within larger social and political movements. The word *deteriorate* appears the next year in the major reviews of *Themes, Theory, and Therapy,* as though that were the only available receptacle to hold Kitzhaber's new data. Then follows more than a dozen years when the study seems to have gone the way of similar professional investigations—into oblivion. But at the tail end of the 1970s, Kitzhaber suddenly reappears, redivivus, wearing even more legendary clothing. Frederick Crews promotes the strong form of the legend, referring to "the Kitzhaber effect, whereby students' writing skills actually deteriorate in the course of a typical undergraduate career" (62). Richard Lanham promotes a softer form: "The Kitzhaber effect: if students didn't continue to write, they were right back where they started as freshmen" (159). Kitzhaber's table of error is hypostatized into a natural law, a kind of Doppler effect, where from the perspective of way-stationed freshman-composition teachers, the students rush toward and through their course at a rising pitch and, without stopping, depart at a falling one.[2]

The timing of Kitzhaber's return is not hard to fathom. His original study was written in the early 1960s, in happy days

---

[2] See also *Teachers College Record* 65 (Feb. 1964): 470; *Educational Leadership* 65 (Apr. 1965): 530; *College English* 25 (Feb. 1964): 327; *WPA: Writing Program Administration* 4 (Spring 1981): 12; *Teaching Writing* 9 (Fall 1987): 1.

when the only "crisis" in composition circles was how to get literature out of the freshman-composition course and get writing into it. Few questioned the literacy and writing competence of students; in 1963 the SAT scores were the same as they had been since the tests were initiated. A year later Kitzhaber himself, as the president of the National Council of Teachers of English, argued that the preparation of students entering freshman composition was improving so fast that "many English departments are now faced, or soon will be, with the prospects either of upgrading the course or getting rid of it" (Squire: 456). Then in 1966 the SATs started falling, and the literacy crisis gradually became a national concern and an educational embarrassment.

Into the habitual expressions for that "decline" in the language skills of American youth entered the visceral feeling of "deterioration," with its deep imagery of entropy, disease, and direction downward: the generation was "spoiled," the hippy cult "degenerate," commercial language "polluting," creative teaching a "waste" of time, structural linguistics a "breakdown" of the rules; the English language was "decaying," the ability to use it "withering," the ability to read it becoming "impaired"; the standards were "crumbling," the values "eroding," the students "rotting" their minds out with TV; and the educational system was on the verge of "collapse." This imagery, of course, was already mildly familiar to language teachers, who traditionally spoke of broken rules, weak verbs, faulty commas, and split infinitives. But now they proposed "curing" the "drop" in literacy with "functional" sentences, "tough" standards, "foundation" courses, and "rising" junior exams. Culturally and professionally they *felt* the deterioration of skill and by 1975 were asking, along with the readers of *Newsweek*, not only why can't Johnny write but how does one "stop the rot" (Dec. 8: 61).

For college composition teachers at the end of the 1970s, the crisis now was how to revitalize writing skills in the seniors who were leaving college "semi-literate," "functionally illiterate," or just "illiterate" and entering appalled law schools.

The crisis was how to stop the Kitzhaber effect. It is no accident that Kitzhaber's figures became a law of nature at just about the same time that writing across the curriculum arrived in the United States.

By this time, the legendary tale of deterioration was well enough established to be able to swallow data much less amenable to it than Kitzhaber's figures. At the end of 1977, Dean K. Whitla, Director of the Office of Instructional Research and Evaluation at Harvard, made available his final report of a study of 347 undergraduates at Harvard-Radcliffe and four unnamed colleges. As at Dartmouth, the intent was to find what students had learned in four years, but unlike Kitzhaber, Whitla matched freshmen with seniors (and some sophomores) by high-school standing and SAT scores and gave subjects the same basic research tasks. Apparently also unlike Kitzhaber, Whitla expected positive change, as did the others directing the research, including well-known developmental theorists such as Lawrence Kohlberg and William Perry. As Whitla later reported to the *Chronicle of Higher Education:* "Those of us who had worked with college students have seen marked changes in them. . . . It seemed to me that the whole thought process of seniors was different from that of freshmen and that we ought to be able to document the change" (Jan. 9, 1978: 5). And, in writing skill, positive change they found. As noted in their summary statement, repeated by both the *Chronicle* and the *New York Times:* "Students' abilities to present an organized, logical, forceful argument increased dramatically over the college years. Except for the natural science concentrators, seniors also have a greater ability to write effective, lucid prose than do freshmen" (Whitla n.d.: 35). Overall, seniors both at Harvard-Radcliffe and at the other colleges even recorded fewer mechanical errors. It didn't look much like deterioration.

But a legend does not need much. It can simply forget, as did Malcolm G. Scully, who ten months after quoting the above finding for the *Chronicle* went back to describing "the writing crisis," which had been "widely publicized over the past three years" (Oct. 30, 1978—a double hypostatization, since it was Scully himself who regularly publicized it during those years for the *Chronicle*). Or the legend can raise the ante. The president of Harvard, Derek Bok, in his annual report to the board of overseers, cited Whitla's findings of growth in the basic skills of writing and mathematics and then added, "Despite the overall improvement, many students showed no improvement." He concluded, "Our studies suggest that basic intellectual skills need continued application throughout the college years if substantial improvement is to occur" (13–14). Or the legend can focus on the exception. For instance, the Modern Language Association's *Profession '83* seizes on the fact that a minority of Harvard seniors, the science "concentrators," scored worse on one writing test than their freshman counterparts. The report concludes, with the now formulaic expression, "It is possible to train freshmen to a certain level of skill in writing ability but . . . such a skill, if not used, can deteriorate during a student's college career" (Kinneavy: 14).[3]

The conversion of Whitla's findings of growth testifies to the deep-seated feelings that empower the legend of deterioration. When Richard Ohmann published his courageous *Chronicle of Higher Education* piece in 1976, "The Decline in Literacy Is a Fiction, If Not a Hoax," pointing out the existence of statistical evidence that student language competence was actually improving, a correspondent to the *Chronicle* promptly reaffirmed the truth of the "literacy crisis": "We don't need statistics to prove there is a problem" (Nov. 15, 1976: 17). Actually, what that reaction seems to reaffirm is a charge Ohmann made in his essay: that the myth of decline has roots in a political conservatism blind to certain facts and opposed to mass education and open admissions. And perhaps certain elements of the

---

[3] An initial report by Whitla, who studied 254 students—including some from Boston College, Brown, Texas Tech, and the University of California at Santa Barbara and Irvine—apparently most of whom were later dropped, did not find that natural science seniors regressed but rather "did very little better than their freshman counterparts" (1981: 6).

legend we have been describing do fit a conservative reading of history, especially the hard version of deterioration, which erects a natural law of depravity pulling older students to a level even below that achieved by the institution of freshman composition and which calls for further institutionalization in composition courses as a solution (see Shor: 1–29 and Daniels: 117–45 for conservative readings of the parallel legend involving the "deterioration" of national test scores from 1975 to 1983).

The softer versions, however, fit what most will admit is an ideological orientation more common in English departments, a gentler radical-anarchism that occasionally may yearn for a legendary golden age when students entered college better prepared but that more often looks ahead to solutions calling for a renovation of existing institutional structures. Here deterioration of skill is taken as evidence for failure of the established method and for immediate need of a new one, usually envisioned as uprooting instruction from the English department and seeding it across the curriculum. Indeed, if we accept Hayden White's analysis of the way ideological beliefs typically "emplot" themselves in historical "writings" (that is, readings) of the past, we would expect the radical-anarchist to mold the academic history of composition students in post-WWII America into the genre form of tragic-romance, shaping tales not much different from the ones of deterioration we have been listening to (22–29). To my mind, if the composition "emplotment" has an affinity to any traditional forms, they are those romantic "legendary tales" read today by no one outside of English departments but by everyone in England two hundred years ago—Northumbrian tragedies of young Elfridas and Oswalds who begin virtuous and happy, fall thwarted and self-deceived, and languish betrayed and friendless until their death and reward in heaven. The youthful writing skills thrive in freshman composition but thereafter, through lack of self-will or reinforcement, fade away until they find their just due in life after college—or find their rehabilitation in lands on the other side of the curriculum.

Whatever the ideological promptings, the pragmatic effects on any midcourse composition class look discouraging, right from its start. Teachers do not face learners really, but learners manqués, students with a "history" of failure who will be therefore inclined to fail again. As with the ungrounded English-teacher vision, the legend of decline tends to solder closed the interpretive circle at an especially destructive and self-perpetuating mode, with feelings of frustration and patronization on the part of the teacher and guilt, resentment, and resistance on the part of the student. There is, of course, no way out of the room of mirrors that is the classroom. Teachers have to confer some sort of status on the people sitting before them and some sort of value on their performance; students react to that status and value. The question is whether a different tale can interpret student growth in a way equally adequate to the facts but not as destructive as the ways just chronicled.

A Tale of Growth

Many teachers do not believe in the legend of deterioration. As long as SAT scores continue stable (as they have for the last fourteen years) and the literacy crisis keeps fading into the past along with the cold war and the counterculture, it may be the legend itself that is on the wane, a twice-told tale relegated to faculty coffee-room mutterings about incompetent TAs and illiterate engineering seniors. But then again, not many teachers voice the contrary belief, what I will call the tale of growth. Here, however, is one, John Calabro, who describes the advanced composition program at West Point Academy, where cadets are required to wait until they are juniors or seniors before taking a second writing course. Calabro does not see teachers of this advanced course facing a loss of competence or skill—just the opposite.

We have gained in terms of what our students bring to the course. They not only possess a good deal more knowledge than they did when they were second-semester freshmen, but they return to us with at least a year and a half's worth of further experience with writing itself. They have written papers and essay examinations in their history, literature, philosophy, political science, and economics courses; and they have made a modest use of prose in lab reports and exams for chemistry and physics courses. This experience has made them more fluent, better able to manage complex subjects, and familiar with various disciplines' conventions for form and substance. (82)

The interpretive tale informing these observations may look simple and even self-evident. On the surface, it may seem to be "no tale" at all, like Wordsworth's portrait of Simon Lee in the *Lyrical Ballads,* merely a flash of understanding across a gap of generation and experience. The implied narrative behind Calabro's picture of the upper-division student needs to be extracted ("Perhaps a tale you'll make it") before the radical implications for the teaching of English can be seen clearly.

The tale Calabro tells (like Wordsworth's) looks incomplete because it begins and ends in medias res. The focus is on protagonist rather than on event, but the plot is not static and picaresque. It is progressive. The students enter the scene, first as freshmen and later as juniors, obeying and enjoying an innate capacity for change. They are impelled by four main drives: restlessness, curiosity, venture, and acquisitiveness. As a result the story they create, over and over, moves in four main directions: toward the new, toward the interesting, toward the challenging, and toward the enriching. Skill has been steadily gained through a day-by-day focus on immediate interests, needs, and self-trials. Some course learning has been kept and some rejected, but what has been retained has become broader in quality. It has been kept because it has proved useful. It has become more accessible, more adaptable, has expanded to new external contexts and accommodated to new inward strategies. In Calabro's words, the students are further "experienced," more "knowledgeable" about social tasks, more "familiar" with conventions, more "fluent" with skills, better "able" to put to "use" or to "manage." In Wordsworth's phrase—no one else has described this tale better—what they have kept is "knowledge not purchased with the loss of power." In a word Calabro does not use, the students record a tale of *growth,* of ordinary complex creaturely experiential growth.

This is the baseline interpretation of the college writing student that this book will promote. In effect, chapter 1 has already viewed the tale of growth from the student's side. The next two chapters will elaborate and embody the tale with learning and developmental theory and so transfigure it into a more powerful and useful vision for teachers. What is worth showing here is how this perspective of growth, as yet crude and unelaborated, can still radically alter the instruction of writing in college, alter even the most honored and stubborn practices. The three interpretive frames isolated in this chapter obviously project quite different pedagogies in a writing course, but what may not be obvious at first is that only the last recommends practices that we would be startled to discover in actual operation in the classroom next to ours.

The Impact on Evaluation and Content

Consider two activities that most dramatically show the writing teacher's hand: evaluating a piece of student writing and deciding on course content. I have argued that an act of learning is understood as such when teachers apply a change of standard to fit a change of status in the student from experienced to more experienced. The vectors are change, status, and standard. The moral entertainment of the English-teacher vision is characterized, we now can see, by a decontextualized centering on standard to the exclusion of status and change. Students have a face-value status of neophyte, judged by whether they can perform the rites correctly. The legend of deterioration centers on standard and change, to the denigration of status: the harder, conservative forms confer that status of recidivist on the writing student, imagining some negative inner bent that veers toward social peccancy, while the softer forms, although removing the guilt from the learner and placing it more squarely on institutions, confer a status of weakness or passivity on the student, imagining some internal flaw that will not or cannot allow control over external circumstances.

Both these interpretive tales severely compromise the engagement between teacher and student, since in some essential way they distrust the full act of learning. Since the interpretive frame of creaturely growth is more open to an equal interaction among all three of the vectors, it regains a certain potential of teacher-student work otherwise lost. Faced with the image of a changing student inquisitive and acquisitive by nature, an image better reflecting the self-image of the student, the teacher will need to attend closely to standards to find those that best intrigue and challenge. Faced with a teacher also inquisitive and acquisitive, the student will be pushed to reach for new status.

Evaluation. One immediate result will be a teacher more likely to see the accomplished changes in sophomore and junior writing and therefore to read more positively and react more constructively to a first-week effort such as Essay J. Take the rhetorical movement from the penultimate to the last paragraph: The best of all posible worlds. . . . The ungrounded frame would see absences and mark them with a preemptory "TR," "Cliché," and "SP," acting on the principles of numbers 27, 46, and 82 of Kitzhaber's "Error List": "Lack of or faulty transition between paragraphs," "Triteness," and "Misspelling." The tale of deterioration would see not only an absence but also a previous superiority, contrasting this junior effort with performance typical in freshman writing, say the assistance to the reader that Essay F provides in *its* movement to its last paragraph: If all the facts are put together a theory like this comes into grasp. . . . The tale of growth detects in the junior piece a presence the other two frames miss. It is precisely between these

two paragraphs that this junior was engaged in a process of logical thinking more complex than that betrayed by the typical
freshman: a re-visioning of the static contrast described in the
first two paragraphs (beneficial and harmful effects of codes of
conduct) and a forging of a progressive resolution to it (recommending moderation to let a creative spirit act around these
codes as guide lines). How long the writer sat at his classroom
desk generating this dialectical mediation can only be guessed,
but the longer he thought, the less likely he was to remember, as
he started to write his last paragraph, to connect his idea to the
previous material with some clever cohesive tie. A perspective of
growth is aware that as new trials are essayed, old concerns may
be left unattended, and it is not surprised to discover that as a
group, the junior essays here achieved their increase in complexity of logical organization with a decrease in explicit logical
transitions. Arguably, from the viewpoint of growth, logical ties
can even hinder logical thinking. On second look, the If all the
facts are put together of the freshman essay records a ceremo-
nial gesture that may appear to announce an inductive leap but
that actually disguises, perhaps from the writer himself, a failure of all the previous data to fall under the final claim (his first
paragraph mentions President Carter's fate as evidence that if
voters come to dislike a politician, in their eyes his appearance
will change from good to bad, whereas the theory in the final
paragraph claims that if politicians have a certain style, grace or
good physical appearance they can win votes). The teacher
might well decide that using a negative marginal comment to
make the writer of Essay J conscious of a lack of logical transitions might be a mistake and that a better action would be to
cheer on the attempt at dialectical thinking: "Excellent progression of ideas here. Expand."

On the level of style, the frame of growth operates just
as radically. Take the following junior sentence: Codes of conduct restrict the individual to where in many cases one feels
he/orshe can not function in the way they wish. The English-
teacher vision seizes on the comic complication of pronouns and

the solecism to where. By way of emendation or explanation, this vision might rewrite the passage as two sentences to eliminate to where, with the pronoun one maintained throughout the second sentence to solve the problem of agreement. The frame of deterioration circles the entire sentence and asks marginally if the student has forgotten everything learned in freshman composition about consistency of pronouns. The frame of growth rejects these two reactions as vying with the changes we have already identified in the writing of postfreshmen and as misjudging the status of the writer. Recommending two sentences would block the impulse of older students to embrace more ideas within one sentence, and accusing the writer of memory loss about pronoun choice would strip the student of any positive impulses that may have produced the pronouns in the first place, such as an attempt to avoid sexist language. The growth frame looks for stylistic goals more amendable to shifts in techniques that the student's peers have already shown some feeling for. Even limited to the twenty-one changes of chapter 1, a teacher would have a wide choice. Cutting out short relative clauses, for instance, supports the tendency in older students to try longer sentences and postnominal modifiers, and incidentally bypasses the problem in pronouns: "Codes of conduct, in many cases, are so restrictive that the individual feels an inability to function in the way desired."

That may not sound like the ultimate in stylistic felicity (I would not write it), but the growth frame looks more toward steps than toward ultimates and does not take felicity as the only criterion. Writing goals are promoted that best enhance the possibility of changes at the present turn in the student's growth and that may even reduce possibilities in one area of writing in order to allow growth in other, more active areas. Actually, out of the infinity of possible writing recommendations, the growth frame will find ones that blend with undergraduate development without traducing a teacher's personal taste, no mater how fixed or outré. If The best of all posible worlds seems an insufficient bridge to J's last paragraph (I find it tolerable), one can always recommend better setting up, in the introduction to the essay, the logical frame implied by the phrase, a technique J's peers have shown some clear affinity for. Still, Hamlet's advice to composition teachers—to absent them from felicity awhile—so alien to the ungrounded English-teacher vision, will be taken seriously by the vision of growth. It follows from the one home fact established so far: undergraduates do change their writing. If they change, they must have motives for the change, and pedagogy will do best to use these motives. For teachers, the ultimate criterion will be learnability.

Course content. The teacher's evaluation of second-day Essay J is chronologically only the first of many acts taken as a consequence of interpretive frames. Consider what happens to students under the first two frames. The expectations not found in Essay J, the "failures" to provide a title and isolate the introduction and provide examples and so on down through the essay, will be found in the next papers in the stack—generalized, normalized, prioritized. The older students' shift toward different forms of logical organization and syntax may go unnoticed. Their turn to a more learned vocabulary may be labeled as inflated, their interest in broader generalizations as vague, their speeding up of their writing with fewer logical transitions as incoherent. Their success in simply maintaining levels of some writing skills despite these new changes, skills such as spelling and predication and punctuation, will be "rewarded" with the red marks of old, or with redder ones out of irritation. What students have not done will be the topic of the next class meeting.

And the next. In terms of course design, the failure to find change or the success in finding deterioration in midcurriculum leads inevitably to a notion of the "advanced" course as essentially a repetition of the "beginning" course. The ungrounded vision contrives a course to counter the sacrifices seen in the first-week essays. Much of it will repeat freshman composition because what is seen within the frame of course learning is only those lessons the student did not retain. The legend of deterioration even more surely leads to a repetition of the first course, though it takes several forms. For the advocate of writing across the curriculum, a decline proves that isolating composition in the English department does not produce a lasting cure and suggests a continuous dosage of intensive writing courses to prevent future relapse. For the "current-traditional" English teacher, the decline in writing makes the freshman instructor into a convenient straw man to elevate the advanced teacher and to initiate weeks of "review" followed by a syllabus that emphasizes practice of old skills. For the administrator of English departments, a decline offers a solution to another decline of greater emergency: drop in enrollments and entitlement. In a 1982 issue devoted to this emergency, the *CEA Forum* argues that the departure of students from college with poor writing skills, "for all practical purposes, illiterate," in conjunction with "the diminished status of an English faculty which has the major responsibility for teaching these skills," is as hard to justify as if the United States, faced with an energy crisis, "capped its remaining oil wells, closed the coal mines, and recalled all field explorers in from the search and discovery missions" (9). Here the legend of decline may end in a remarkably confined or blind circularity, recycling older students from advanced courses back into basic courses by means of some "rising junior" competency examination.

The ungrounded vision and the legend of decline generate a situation of unpleasant ambivalence in which important distinctions are always on the verge of decay. It is hard to reject the darker motives lying barely beneath the surface of these rationales—for instance, the need to demean one course to justify another, or the need to bring in a crisis to solve a crisis, or the need to brand some students as minimally incompetent in order to congratulate others as competent—and at the same time to approve of some of the action the rationales call for, such as writing across the curriculum or Kitzhaber's strategy of "steady pressure." The trouble is that decline itself is so ambivalent. As Karl Mannheim long ago pointed out, one person's decline is another person's growth. A drop in enrollment in English departments is a rise in other departments, a drop in exiting high-school SAT scores is an increase in the base of female college-student population, a reduction of "competent" writers in freshman composition is an increase in the percent of students who will benefit the most from the course, a decline in juniors putting full effort into an advanced-composition "diagnostic" may be an increase in experienced writers aware of audience context. In such a metamorphosing Lewis Carroll dream-terrain, genuine change in course content can be forever postponed.

The tale of growth offers a perspective affording some stability. It sets aside unlearning as a rarity and orders the landscape into a simpler map with one basic direction. Consequently it imagines a radically different design for course content. Whether beginning or advanced, a writing course will assume that students are midway headed somewhere and that the syllabus had best take them up *at that point* and carry them on. It will also assume that individual students may arrive in class at different points in growth, and it will be less likely to subjugate the entire class to the same set of conformist norms. It may recognize the dialectical organization of Essay J as a late and exceptional one, and think twice about teaching it even to all juniors. The frame of growth generates, then, two major curricular premises, diametrically opposed to assumptions of the other two frames. It assumes that a second course will be different from the first and that the second course will be in sequence to the first, changed just as the students are changed to meet and abet that growth. From these two premises, part 5 of this book will derive a method of evaluation (truly diagnostic) and an undergraduate curriculum (truly developmental).

But that is far along in my argument. At present, an essential question immediately arises. Is the change adopted by the students a change in the right direction? Up to this point, I have avoided words implying that the natural development of students is necessarily a change for the better, words such as *advancement, progress, improvement.* Growth may not be unlearning or deterioration yet may still be warped or misguided, the students mislearning. Essay J may be different from Essay F, and worse written—junior writing different from freshman writing, and less profitable. The standards of students and teachers may clash, and both may be wrong. Part of the radical nature of the frame of growth is that it sets aside the ethical frame of better or worse. But teachers cannot set that frame aside. Growth alone does not establish standards, which change with learning but remain standards. Teachers are paid not to help students grow but to grow up.

In one word, evaluation and course content should be based not on the growth but on the *maturing* of students. John Calabro does not hesitate to interpret upper-division change in such a light: "Finally, our students are at least one and a half years older. Most have matured. And this in itself improves their writing" (82). It is time to test this assumption.

PART II

The Standards of Maturity

I love a public road: few sights there are
That please me more—such object hath had power
O'er my imagination since the dawn
Of childhood, when its disappearing line
Seen daily afar off, on one bare steep
Beyond the limits which my feet had trod
Was like a guide into eternity.
                          —William Wordsworth,
                          The Prelude XII (1805)

CHAPTER 3

Maturing

CLEARLY WE HAVE TO DEAL CAUTIOUSLY WITH the concept of maturity. With its establishment of set standards, it takes on the guise of establishments everywhere, takes on a compelling or coercive interpretive power. In this chapter we will look at some cultural evidence that sets certain standards of maturity, those standards in turn allowing us to judge whether the growth of the junior students in the Sample could be termed *maturing*. The danger for the teacher in this procedure I will take up at the end of the chapter. But the procedure does not much specify the nature of the growth that might achieve such standards. That specification will continue to evolve through the next two chapters. Here I would like to stake out some preliminary ground.

A Continuum: Learning,
Maturation, and Maturing

As I define the term, *maturing* is a kind of growth situated roughly between two other kinds. I am only following a host of developmentalists who name these two *learning* and *maturation* and who picture them at opposite ends of a continuum of maturing processes. *Pure learning* is change, independent of age and dependent on environment, toward values set by human culture. Learning standards are therefore highly manipulable, as abstract or removed from the inner life of a student as the instructor wishes to make them. Students can learn gerunds from some fusty workbook. Or they can achieve fairyland institutional objectives, like that of the New York public schools administrator who told a teacher, "We don't like to see kids reading books: we're trying to bring up the scores around here."

At the other extreme, *pure maturation* refers to inner human change, dependent on age and independent of environment. Instead of a cultural base, maturation reflects a biological base, and the term often is used synonymously with *epigenesis,* suggesting that growth is effected by inner, sequential, emergent forces (Richard F. Kitchener). The standards set by maturation wait inside us like blueprints in an architect's office and include such evolutionary plans as a greater differentiation of muscle coordination, a more capacious short-term memory space, a capability to reproduce sexually, a need to resolve the Electra/Oedipus complex, or an outgrowing of the middle-age crisis. Maturation has an advantage over learning in that it is never abstract, locked as it is into biological imperatives. But that is also its disadvantage. The student can evade learning, but not maturation.

Maturing. Despite the clear opposition between pure learning and maturation, many developmentalists today are reluctant to separate the two. In the first place, they find it technically impossible to divorce the effects of the two in the vast majority of cases of human change. A fourteen-year-old runs away from home, or her forty-five-year-old father does. Did they learn this or did they act on epigenetic urges? It is highly unlikely that at age ten the author of Essay J would have organized his thoughts about conduct codes dialectically, but no experiment so far devised can tell whether his ability to do so at age twenty (or his probable difficulty in learning to do so at age ten) is due to learning or to development. In the second place, current developmentalists do not believe learning and maturation should be divorced. They tend to conceive of the two as a unified field, "dynamically interactive." Inner and outer forces, nature and nurture, simultaneously allow each other and together effect human change (Lerner 1978). The author of Essay J would not have managed a dialectical arrangement of his ideas through maturation (cognitive or otherwise) without certain learning experiences (school or otherwise), nor would he have learned such an arrangement without that maturation. Loosely, developmentalists call any behavioral change that is slow and spontaneous *maturation,* and any change that is rapid and formal *learning.* Beyond that, most envision what one of them, Sidney Strauss, calls "the middle ground," a social arena where growth may take place with the help of both inner and outer promptings and within both biological and cultural constraints (1987). In this middle-earth dwells what I call maturing.[1]

Within that middle ground of learning-maturation, developmentalists also distinguish between quantitative and qualitative changes. In the first, the learner merely accumulates knowledge, storing it by means of cognitive or affective structures already developed. In the second, qualitative change, those structures themselves develop. Piaget, of course, called the first *assimilation* and the second *accommodation.* I prefer to

---

[1] The locus classicus for this unified view of human growth is Vygotsky's essay "Interaction between Learning and Development," published posthumously in 1935 (1978: 79–91). For excellent discussions of the debate over learning and development, see Brown 1982, Brown and Reeves 1987, and Liben 1987b: 121–29. Writing researchers tend to excuse themselves from the debate. Kellogg W. Hunt, after 154 pages of the fullest description available of syntactic change in student writing, categorically purifies his findings of learning: "This study provides no justification for teaching some structures early and others late" (1965: 155). At the beginning of a study of equal weight, describing age changes in the psychology of writing production, Carl Bereiter and Marlene Scardamalia take the opposite step and purify their findings of development: "It has seemed advisable to adopt merely as a working assumption the position that all adult-child differences are due to learning experience" (28). But what are confounding variables for the researcher are founding concerns for the teacher (see Kroll).

call the second *generative learning,* after Chomsky's familiar notion that a limited number of deep linguistic structures give speakers "generative" power to produce an unlimited number of novel utterances. Most learning is assimilative, to be sure, but I am after, and I imagine most writing teachers are after, bigger game. To teach students to assimilate a new method of forming introductions is worth a class hour. To help them generate a new conception of audience, which will thereafter alter everything they write, is easily worth a whole semester. As Strauss says, change becomes truly developmental when it involves a reorganization of internal frames (1987: 133).

This gives us, then, a new working definition for a conception of human growth appropriate for writing instruction: maturing is generative change, at once nurturable and natural, toward cultural standards. For writing teachers, the interpretive frame of maturing can be salubrious. It retains the idea of ductility that lies in the core of our word *education,* defining growth as something that can be shaped and is not merely driven. It rejects a naturalistic tale of students helplessly caught along in some maturational trajectory, in what William Kessen calls "a ballistic biological or pseudobiological force" (8), whether that force be Darwinian or Gesellian or Kitzhaberesque. By the same token, it provides a way to question naive modes of instruction, looking, for instance, with great wariness upon the English-teacher vision and asking if its standards are realistic given maturational constraints and if they truly match the going or mature competencies of our cultural world.

Novice and Expert: A Tale of
Two Consciousnesses

Once given that definition of maturing, we have to ask what those worldly competencies are. As it turns out, the way one goes about finding the standards by which writing maturity will be judged is not as obvious as it looks. Scholars have debated the issue for a couple of decades, not without a certain unscholarly acrimony (for some of the calmer thoughts, see Christensen, Joseph M. Williams 1979, Susan Miller, Faigley 1980, Odell, and Carter). Ten years ago the lament was: "We still have no agreed-upon definition of what it means to be an able adult writer" (Miller: 119) or of "what adult competence in writing consists of" (Faigley: 293). Since then, rapid strides have been made toward the goal of establishing mature competencies. This fact has not been much noticed. We have awarded so much acclaim to the shift in compositional studies from a product method to a psychological or sociological method that we have overlooked as radical a shift in the discipline's method of value making, a shift from relying on its own traditions and textbooks to taking in practice and texts outside the discipline.

The most common methodological approach to the question of maturity has been the direct comparison of student or "novice" with "experienced" or "expert" writing. The approach respects writing processes and situations, and it challenges conventional pedagogy by redesigning the shape of mature writing competence for teachers and replacing the exhibit of models of good writing for students. The utility of such novice-expert studies is evident from the Sample, where despite the growth discovered in postfreshman writing, teachers can make nothing definitive of it without the clear end of mature performance, without a terminus ad quem. The possible use of such a comparison, which was made, will occupy the rest of this chapter. Evident utility, however, does not mean interpretive simplicity. The perspective of maturing, with its inherent comparison of less and more experienced, requires at least one distinctive and difficult interpretive step. That step will lead, as we will see at the end of the chapter, to a problematic question about the role of teachers and the very utility of the method itself.

The distinctiveness of the viewpoint of maturing finds a memorable expression in the second book of *The Prelude*. Wordsworth has just recorded a typically vivid and sensuous memory, from childhood, of him and his friends romping in the village night before being sent to bed "Feverish with weary joints and beating minds." The memory rouses up a disturbing thought, that of the wide distance between his present and his past life.

> The vacancy between me and those days,
> Which yet have such self-presence in my mind
> That sometimes when I think of them I seem
> Two consciousnesses—conscious of myself,
> And of some other being.

More than mere memory or consciousness directed from the present toward the past, this point of view simultaneously turns about and looks from the past to the present. It produces a double or stereoptican image possessing a startling three-dimensionality because it superimposes two different minds, "two consciousnesses," of equal concreteness. The effect is exactly that of another well-remembered description of human change: "You cannot step twice into the same river." This fragment by Heraclitus also records two consciousnesses, both sensuous and singular: the river that swirled around the ankle with the first step and the river that swirls around the ankles with the second. In both passages, the forced yoking of two heterogeneous images—eidetic and concrete—exposes a third image as too abstract, the idea of River with Heraclitus and the idea of Life with Wordsworth.

The interpretive frame of maturing, with its implied comparison of novice and expert, projects the same twofold, concrete vision, exposing a third perspective as abstract. For composition teachers, it superimposes one actual writing performance, what a less experienced writer writes, on another actual writing performance, what a more experienced writer writes, and thereby dispels the hypostatization of Writing. In this it differs from the ungrounded English-teacher vision, which sets a piece of student writing against a magic mirror of Perfect Writing. The author of Essay J did write: in many cases one feels he/orshe can not function in the way they wish. To judge the line as wanting, the English-teacher vision does not need an actual version that is perfect—all it needs is a vision of perfection. By contrast, before judging the student performance as "immature," the frame of maturing has to overlay it with the actual performance of another, more experienced writer, as if the two were a palimpsest.

Study of mature performance is fraught with complexities. If pure moral entertainment is an idealization that will not long stand pragmatic scrutiny, the particularized double consciousness of Wordsworth and Heraclitus is difficult to achieve and even more difficult to sustain. Perhaps this double consciousness itself stands as an idealization (see chapter 7). The maturing frame, in fact, cannot deal forever with particulars. Soon it must derive generalized standards from more experienced performance, must delve beneath the surface of particular cases and extract general competencies as touchstones for less experienced writers. And even to set aside the comparison and to generalize about competent writers is not as easy as it seems. As the particularistic nature of the maturing frame warns us, the contexts of experienced writing vary greatly. There is a bewildering choice of mature writers to study, from acclaimed authors honing their work for the slicks, to workaday journalists pounding at newsroom PCs, to lab technicians jotting on clipboards. The variety itself, of course, stands as the first questioning of the entertainment of Perfection, but it also warns how easy it is to conduct student-mature comparisons that look like attempts at revision but that are no more than attempts to find support for a preestablished position. The circularity is especially deceptive: a particular ideological ground will include a notion of "mature writing," which will apparently restrict the selection of experienced writers for study, who will then, independently it seems, validate the original grounds.

Those grounds, as we have seen, are historical as well as ideological. In the 1960s and early 1970s, mature writers were usually conceived of as "experts," perhaps as a counter to the feeling that student writing was growing more and more uncultured, or as a reflection of the great gulf between the unwashed and the washed. Student writings, often in-class essays, were compared with belletristic essays published in the *American Scholar, Harper's, Atlantic Monthly,* the *New Yorker,* or the *Saturday Review of Literature,* giving the experts a good deal of a head start, not to mention a battery of editors. Beginning in the late 1970s, with the writing-across-the-curriculum movement and the legitimation of technical writing courses, maturity became identified with "professional writers," and comparisons were made with journalists, editors, and anonymous academics such as speech and composition teachers. Since much of the interest lay in writing processes and involved interviews or videotapes or think-aloud protocols, the models of maturity tended to be less often paragons of their profession and more often whoever was near campus and willing. The writing tasks, though artificial, were usually the same for student and older writer.

In the 1980s, with a new interest in social context, mature performance has been envisioned as "nonacademic writing," and researchers have left the ivy towers to observe real-world writers in the wild. Ethnological (one is tempted to say ethological) studies, however, make evaluation of student writing problematic, since they cannot make a direct comparison. It seems unreasonable to make students write a case report or an action memo.[2] In the historical drift toward the pragmatic, clearly the point has been reached where one has to question the value of the observations for erecting standards of writing. If it seems unfair to judge students by the talented and renowned *Harper's* and *Atlantic* authors Kellogg Hunt talked into rewriting "Aluminum," it seems unprofitable to compare students with his second group, "adult writers," namely Tallahassee firemen who had never been to college (1970). Or what about social-services caseworkers or midlevel banking executives, to mention two other research groups?

---

[2] It has been attempted only in dissertations. But the reverse (as in this study), where professionals are persuaded to perform a student writing task, was tried once by Sarah W. Freedman (1984), with results that make her piece one of the most informative—and iconoclastic—readings for teachers of writing.

With these problems in mind, I attempted a compromise in my selection of a *terminus* or "target" (the word is Hunt's) to judge the student writing of the Sample. Following a recommendation of Lee Odell, I chose "adults who are not professional writers but who frequently write as part of their work" (111). I simply chose the kind of writers we can reasonably hope our students will become and tried to have them write the same kind of essays under as similar conditions as possible. Since many of the remaining chapters of this book rely on the material I gathered, I will describe this matured group in some detail.

The subjects were thirty-two employees, representing a wide variety of occupations. They were all college graduates, thirty years old or older. I will call them simply "employees," since to call them "adults" strikes me as patronizing the freshmen, sophomores, and juniors of the Sample. The employees wrote impromptu for fifty minutes on the same choice of topics and with the same understanding that their essays would be evaluated by a university teacher. They were chosen for this task by their managers and supervisors, who were asked to pick one of their staff who was not a superfine writer but was a worker whose writing on the job, in whatever form it might take, could be called "competent," no worse but no better.

The result was a group of writers with a certain appeal of motley. Among others, it included a technician in radiological sciences who composes his own reports, a secretary for an arbitration firm who cleans up her boss's letters, a legal assistant who generates contracts and publicity material, an art gallery manager who prefers to use the telephone when he can, a salesman in the aerospace industry who has his secretary edit his memos, an architect who lacks a secretary and who wants only to "get his message across" in his proposals and disregards "where the commas go," a YWCA coordinator, a geologist, an assistant director of nursing, a field sales manager in signs, and a personnel director of a hotel chain. Collectively, the sixteen women and sixteen men embody, I hope, an argument of force. They are where many of our students will end up after graduation, in professional or technical jobs spending (according to surveys) a quarter or more of their time writing and likely holding a hard-nosed, unworshipping attitude toward it. One of the employees added a note of apology to his essay, saying his wife always "fixes up" his writing, yet he was an assistant bank manager who had a reputation for blunt, effective letters.

The employee sample was hard to get. The working world has as little free time to donate to essay writing as students have. We can assume that some of the employees wrote with an eye toward getting it over, perhaps with some irritation that the boss had asked them to write at all, certainly with some frustration and resignation over the topic and time allotted, and in at least two cases with express complaint about distracting noise in the room. These misfortunes of the writing situation are fortunate in that they qualify the sample as a record of what working-world writers do under similar pressures and confines as faced by students. There is not a paragraph that I can read without my hand assuming its reflex editorial grip. On the other hand, though the sample may not have picked the kind of college graduates who, when freshmen, caused teachers to give thanks to the god of good student writers, it did select individuals whose writing skills satisfy the idols of the agora. That success asks for a certain respectful attention. It demands that before we condemn the writing as below our expectations, we first ask if perhaps our standards are not elitist or unworkable.

That attention is sharpened by a finding totally independent of the supervisors' prejudgment of "competent." The objective measures confirm a massive and multilateral difference between postgraduate and undergraduate. In forty-four of the eighty-four preset measures, there is a statistical difference ($<.05$) between the essays of the employee group and those of one or more of the student groups. Just as these measures offer a way to revamp our notion of status and standard in the growth from freshman to junior, they offer a similar revision of our notion of the road that wends from regular progress as student to mature competency as employee.

Change in Performance:
Evidence from the Employees

As it turned out, we have another support for the supervisors' judgment of "competent," again entirely independent. In fact, it is found in an arena as far removed from the agora as can be imagined. Mingled with the student essays holistically rated by the fourteen English teachers were these thirty-two working-world essays. To say that the mean rate of 5.7 earned by the employees was significantly higher than that of 4.1 earned by the undergraduates understates the difference in quality. Only five freshman, five sophomore, and three junior essays earned a higher rate than the *median* workplace essay. The teachers found the majority of the employees better writers than all but a few students. Since we are dissecting the impressions of teachers, their vote of confidence may appear less a help than a finding in need of further study, but it is uplifting to know that two groups so distant from each other, humanities teachers and entrepreneurial supervisors, may find common ground in their intuitions about writing.

This median essay offers one way to judge the employee competency and to exercise a trial of Wordsworth's "two consciousnesses." We must superimpose a concrete piece of mature writing, perhaps familiar enough to stand as a kind of "self-presence," upon our knowledge of immature writing, perhaps vivified by our recent memory of Essay F and Essay J. Since the median employee essay lacks a title, I will call it Essay M (see page 76). Unimpressive? As representative of the employees' skills—half of them produced essays rated better—it will still serve to illustrate the major differences between the workplace and the student performances. What follows is only a sketch, fleshed out in chapters 6 through 11.

Essay M

The author of this questionaire makes the assumption that, in fact, codes of conduct do exist, although he/she makes no statement concerning the origin of such codes. Since the field is left open to interpretation, I will focus my effort on my personal code of conduct and why that personal code of conduct was created and maintained.

First, what is a code of conduct? To me, a code of conduct represents guidelines for behavior that keep me performing in a manner consistent with my purpose in life. The function of those guidelines then is to provide a framework that keeps me aligned with that which I have decided is most important to me.

Life consists of a seemingly infinite series of moment-by-moment problems to be solved. Without some code of conduct, how do I choose my response to each of those moment-to-moment events?

I know what it is that I want to achieve in life. In my case, I want to contribute to the well-being of those around me, to create more love, health, and satisfaction of those I come in contact with. In order to achieve that I must channel my energy and activities into alignment with those goals. A personal code of conduct then becomes the roadmap for traveling in the direction of contributing to others' well-being, and some of those elements of that road map are trust, co-operation, support, keeping agreements (including societal laws), being consistent in thought, word and deed, being honest, sharing myself with others fully, acting in a positive manner, being loving and caring, and being good-humored. So the first part of the answer to why are codes of conduct created & maintained is to provide guidelines of behavior for the purpose of keeping me moving in the direction I want to go in life.

The second part of the answer to that question is that it works. Having a set of groundrules works. From an experiential level I have definitely proved for myself that when I am consistent with the rules of any given situation, the focus given by my being aligned with those rules gives me clarity of thought, satisfaction and creates positive feelings for myself about myself and about others, resulting in my being more willing and eager to participate with others and share myself, creating value for myself and for them. The result is then in alignment with my purpose, which was to contribute to the well-being of those around me.

In summary, why have codes of conduct? First, to provide guidelines in alignment with purpose. Second, because they work. It's actually quite simple.

Organization. The older writers prefer logical patterns that are open-ended. Unlike the students, they avoid organizing their essays with schemes setting up closed systems, such as a chronology or a comparison or a division into parts. The employees turn more to incremental patterns always ready for the evolution of further logical points, patterns provided by inferential arguments, dialectical progressions, or choice among options. Essay M is typical. The third paragraph establishes a problem to be solved but presets no particular solution: how do I choose my response to each of those moment-to-moment events? Despite current-traditional assumptions, these open-ended structurings help the older writers create superior introductions. Since the introductions are open too, and lack a thesis-like forecast of the essay's conclusion, they generate more compelling, suspenseful motives for the reader to read on. They more often create a sense of controversy or a need for discussion, leaving the field, as Essay M's introduction puts it, open for interpretation. The employee essays also resist the often taught method of writing a conclusion as a restatement or summary. Their final paragraphs more often function as the last logical step of their argument. Essay M ends more simplistically than do most of the other employee essays, but still its last sentence, It's actually quite simple, establishes a new position quite distant from the initial position of the piece: Life consists of a seemingly infinite series of moment-by-moment problems. In sum, the open-ended movement of the employee essays asks whether current teaching about organization does not encourage essays fated to stodginess from the start (see chapter 10).

Specificity. Despite using a more complex movement of ideas, the older writers are able to endow their essays with more specificity. But again they do so not in the ways many writing teachers foster. The employees do not use more illustrative examples, or more often restrict the focus of their essays, or deal less in high-level abstractions and generalizations. But they are more apt logically to restrict the subjects of their sentences to the unique or close to unique (the author of this questionaire) or or to the once-modified substantive (<u>positive manner</u>). They have fewer qualms about making the first-person the subject of their sentences, and the I in particular—sometimes banned outright by teachers—spreads like ivy (Freedman 1984 found the same tendency in her professional writers). They also use an exact and idiomatic vocabulary carrying with it whole chunks of technical fields, as with <u>personal code</u>, <u>societal laws</u>, or <u>groundrules</u> in Essay M. Above all they achieve the effect of specificity, or at least solidity, simply by writing longer essays—about one hundred words more, or a third longer. The median essay above is almost exactly the average length of their essays. Since all writers had fifty minutes to write, we can assume that the employees were disregarding teachers' common advice by writing faster and revising less. Although individual acts of revision could not be measured exactly from the copy, the workers' drafts show fewer changes than the students'.

Coherence. Further differences signal the presence of a more rapid writing style (see chapter 8). The employees express more nouns as pronouns, saving time and easing flow. They start more of their sentences with simple subjects, neither compounded or modified. And they expand their sentences more with simple coordinate logical connectors (such as *and*) and less with complex ones (such as *rather than*). This rapidity of production seems to enhance coherence in the mature essays. They actually use fewer of the explicit devices of cohesion often recommended by textbooks, such as word repetitions, synonyms, and logical transitions (*on the other hand*), and instead turn to tacit or implicit means. While they let the content of their subject provide coherence locally, they take pains to help the reader connect larger sections globally, for instance when they move from one paragraph to the next; they clearly link the first sentence of a new paragraph with the previous paragraph 95 percent of the time, compared with 61 percent for the students. Here their devices of cohesion are usually explicit, even crude (<u>First, what is a code of conduct?</u>)—although they also find implicit means, such as the question and answer that binds the third and fourth paragraphs of Essay M (see Haswell 1989).

Diction. Perhaps another reason the older writers could write more is that their vocabulary range is broader and more sophisticated. They almost double the students' rate of using "unusual" words, such as alignment and channel in Essay M. They apparently have forgotten their teachers' admonitions about noun adjuncts (personality development, sex roles) and generate a third more. They often produce a style that would have made George Orwell wince, but in return they probably were not breaking their flow of thought as often with word searches.

Syntax. Not only does vocabulary move away from the kind of Orwellian simplicity and directness that teachers love, but syntax does too. Three times as often, the older writers construct long series of three or more items, such as in the second and fourth sentences of the fourth paragraph in Essay M. This growth in syntactic complexity is pervasive. Their sentences, T-units, and clauses are all longer, not flatly so, but with an increase in variety and emphasis. In number, the weight of extralong sentences (thirty-five words or longer) doubles with older writers, but so does the punch of extrashort sentences (such as the last sentence of Essay M). The sentence skill of the older writers achieves one especially telling statistic: their variance of sentence length increases over that of the students' by a third.

Counter to much textbook advice, the employee sentences are more noun-centered, less verb-centered (see chapter 9). They record a substantial growth in nominal modification, both bound and free. Their increase in bound modification of nouns is expressed, for instance, in clumps of a size and logical complexity hardly ever seen in student papers, such as Essay M's a seemingly infinite series of moment-by-moment problems to be solved. Equally substantial is the increase in nonrestrictive modification, with students using a free modifier about once every two sentences, older writers three times every four. Nearly all of the increase comes at the end of structures. The employees put more words in final free modification than in initial, more in postnominal modification than in prenominal. And as for that one most pervasive trait of the technical (or learned or pretentious) style, a fifth more of their words are packaged in prepositional phrases.

Mechanics. The working-world writers, in fact, sometimes do disregard where their commas go. Their essays are by no means error free, with a par of three or four words per essay misspelled, one sentence out of every twenty-five a run-on or attachable sentence fragment, and every fifth possessive misformed. Yet these "competent" writers are not ignorant of the rules. Compared with the students, they are substantially better at parallelism, spelling, apostrophe use, pronoun agreement, and exactness of predication. But by and large, the evidence shows them reversing the priorities sometimes seen in teacher practice, setting correctness as less worthy of their time and attention than matters such as production and flow. They are using the five minutes before the bell rings for things other than proofreading.

Gifts for the Student from the Employees: New Standards, New Status

Such, in rapid review, are the main differences between experienced and more experienced writers elicited by this particular task and sampling. Can a perspective of maturing convert the differences into teaching standards? The previous chapter found the idea of growth qualifying the ways teachers evaluate student writing. It looked vertically at the student's milieu, suggesting somewhat loosely that teachers ought to handle stylistic infelicities with more lenience and find rhetorical challenges and interests closer at hand among the writer's cohorts. Here the maturing frame stretches horizontally to more distant goals, across the "vacancy" between studenthood and employment, and finds rhetorical skills and competencies of considerably more definition. These are not new to the traditional rhetorical whatnot but rather are seen from a new angle and therefore given a different luster and priority. As it turns out, there is an unexpected further payoff, a new and more positive interpretation of the student's status.

Concision. Efficiency, the primum mobile of workplace style, the awareness that words are time and time is money, fosters one obvious overriding standard: compression. In surveys asking the working world's criteria for good writing, concision perennially places among the top three. Some techniques of the older writers—for example, syntactic series and tacit coherence—may have been developed under the constant pressure in the working world to save space.

Productivity. Compared with the students, the older writers wrote not only more compactly but also more. Much current writing pedagogy cautions against haste and mere length, recognizing one danger, slovenliness of language and thought, but neglecting another, waste of time. The older writers, who on the job probably average one or two writing tasks a day, here outproduced the students by over a fourth. Their extra paragraph or two simply allowed more facts and more ideas, a final qualification making a position credible, a final logical step making an argument seem practicable (as with the fifth paragraph of the median essay). Combined with the evidence from process studies of working-world writers, who tend to compose quickly with little revision, the evidence from the competent writers here argues for increased fluency as a permanent goal for writing students throughout college.

Flow. Fluency, which strives for rapidity of production, must take special pains with cohesive flow, which helps readers follow shifts in thought. The employee essays suggest that maintenance of flow, not installation of preset formats, operates as the major competency handling the rhetorical problem of organization (which again the working world puts among the three most important criteria). Implied is a modification of the traditional standard of coherence, which sometimes deals exclusively with explicit means that often add unneeded words. The employee essays recommend a standard integrating efficiency (concision and production) and therefore, for instance, encourage tacit means.

Expandability. The way the employees handle the problem of flow overlaps with a pervasive cluster of techniques allowing expansion. One of the deepest differences between students and employees is the preference of the latter for open-ended structures. They like problematical theses, logical plans open to incrementing, and syntactic structures that permit adding on, such as interrupters, series, postnominal modifiers, and free modification in the terminal position. When Sarah Freedman's professional writers took on her student writing task, they generated more parenthetical expressions and more "unconventional" organizational patterns (1984: 339–40). No doubt these were patterns not fitting the tidily packaged systems of textbooks. The traditional classroom concern for order and pigeon-holing needs to allow for the workplace concern for thinking and organizing on the run.

Maneuverability. A more important competency may be the ability not only to increment but also to change, backtrack, hesitate, and qualify, in fact to do anything language allows, at any point in the writing—midessay, midparagraph, midsentence, midclause. Notice how readily, at the last sentence of the fourth paragraph of Essay M, the writer assimilates an unforeseen second part to his reasoning: So the first part of the answer. . . . Better, look at the previous sentence. Not only must the writer have plunged into it without a clear notion of where it would end, but he must have been perfectly at ease in maneuvering around as he went—adding an afterthought in parenthesis, switching to gerunds when he could not quickly find suitable nouns. Students rarely produce that kind of sentence. To write such takes confidence in the malleability of language and practice in letting that malleability record whatever quirk or jump urged by reason or imagination. Maneuverability is not a familiar rhetorical standard. Studies of professional writing have found the term for this basic competency: *flexibility* (Halpern: 24; Freedman 1984: 346; Hammond 1979: 9). The word renders well the fluid constraints and situational nature of the workplace, whose tasks often force writers to "rewrite as they write" (Sommers: 384).

Adaptability. Flexibility, of course, in itself does not run counter to the competency of handling formats. Indeed, the supervisors of the employees must have selected these employees as "competent" writers in part for their success in handling technical forms. The author of Essay M says that he must write reports and specifications. Other employees mention medical summaries, court documents, audit reports, marketing analyses, advertising copy, proposal evaluations, user manuals, patient data, procedure guidelines, and so on. On the other hand, neither the engineer who wrote Essay M nor any of the other thirty-one employees responded to the set topic with any of these set formats. Instead, they sat down and, without the least evidence of distaste or unease, wrote informal and usually personal essays, creating on the spot an original organization adapted to topic and audience and progressively shaped to their ideas. More basic than the ability to follow a given format (as taught in courses that emphasize academic writing) is adaptability, because it includes the skills of recognizing what particular format is required, intuiting the requirements of an unfamiliar format, and finding or creating the proper space within any format to allow for the unique shape of the subject at hand. Adaptability transforms the traditional pedagogical skill of following conventions into something more creative and shrewd, an ability to meet an unpredictable variety of future rhetorical situations, to which applies, if one word can, the Heraclitan image of *flux* (see Knoblauch: 156, and compare Susan Miller's concept of *virtuosity:* 121).

These six competencies are only a few for which my particular analysis shows direct evidence. Other maturing comparisons involving other rhetorical tasks have indicated other skills, though usually with a similar discontinuity with skills traditionally taught: to tell the truth, to express more emotion, to imagine a varied audience, to collaborate with co-writers, to accept subjects as problematical. But all studies of matured writers have two findings in common, findings not hypothesized by the researchers nor much mentioned by them afterward. The first is a tendency for the matured competencies to attract students. Compared with many current-traditional skills, they tend to be more graspable, more in tune with the students' understanding of their culture, more a part of their vision of their own success in it. As competencies to train for, being productive and adaptable look better than being decorous or emphatic.

The second finding, related to the first, is more surprising. It finds competent mature writing closer to student writing than one expects. This is certainly true in the present study, despite the forty-four statistically significant differences. To begin with, there is simply the paucity of gain in some of these traits. The employee sentence averages only two and one-half words longer than the freshman sentence, the employee clause only one word longer. Employees put only 5 percent more words into final free modification. Four of the freshman essays are free of spelling errors, but the employees increase that number by only eleven. More telling are some of the ways employees do not significantly differ from the students. They qualify no more assertions than students do, provide no more examples or allusions, write no longer paragraphs or introductions or conclusions, use no more active verbs, and produce no more dependent clauses or parallel structures.

These facts match the findings of every other study that compares student writing with older, more competent writing, and together the results hand teachers one of the more useful and pleasurable gifts of empirical research. The more pragmatic and equivalent the writing task, the less far, it turns out, students have to change their writing habits to achieve cultural standards of competency. Typically, students will have to change some of their ways but not others. Banking executives do spend a fifth of their time writing but rarely compose any-thing other than a first draft that needs only minor revisions (Van Dyck). Technical writers do examine their drafts for logi-cal progression but rarely refer to preset ordering techniques (Mair and Roundy), and they do develop an ear for their copy but do not read it aloud to themselves (Cooper and Odell). Journalists, editors, and academics do revise more in terms of the whole piece, but most changes are still on the sentence level (Sommers), where professionals make fewer changes than stu-dents do (Faigley and Witte) and where they can detect no more errors than students can (Flower et al.). Professional writers are more conscious of paragraphing, but they start only 13 percent of their paragraphs with a topic sentence (Braddock). They generate longer and syntactically more complex sentences, but they avoid explicit transitional markers (Sloan: 184) and relish the first person (Freedman 1984: 340), the passive (Warfel), and the indefinite "this" (Roberts).

I could go on, but the point is made: the revision of writing standards by study of ordinary mature writing performance has had one largely unappreciated effect, to elevate the perform-ance status of ordinary students. The father of the novice-expert comparative method, Francis Christensen, put it neatly, after showing that the student use of sentence openers was ex-actly like that of famous highbrow authors (a finding duplicated by the present study): "Susie, in her innocence, writes like the professionals" (Christensen and Christensen: 68). Only I would not say innocence, but rather experience.

A Second Elevation of Status

Susie was a freshman. Do sophomores and juniors write even more like professionals? We can now answer the question posed at the end of the previous chapter: whether the growth displayed by the sophomores and juniors in the Sample can be construed as maturing. The response is another gift to teachers from empirical research, perhaps of even greater value. The students are not only growing but are growing more competent. Despite Kitzhaber and the ungrounded intuition of unlearning, they are maturing rhetorically.

Using the employee performance as a measure and viewing the older students from the freshman end, we find that where the junior or sophomore essays differ significantly from those of the freshmen, nineteen of the twenty-one traits lie in the direction of mature competence. Where postfreshman writing changes, it changes largely toward—not away from—older, working-world writing. Viewing the growth from the other end affords an even heftier affirmation. As we have seen, the employee group differs significantly from the student groups on forty-four traits. Of these forty-four, the junior writing shifts from the freshman in the direction of the employee in thirty-five. Here, of course, many of the shifts do not reach statistical significance, and some are minute, but an assumption of random movement from freshman to junior would hypothesize around half of these differences to favor the juniors, and instead we get nearly 80 percent. No doubt a different set of traits under a different writing context would result in a different proportion. But the set here does pretend to broad coverage, and I doubt other traits with an equal coverage would alter the general picture: in early college writing, there is a massive maturing shift, certainly not unilateral but certainly gravitational, toward matured levels.

Other sets of traits, as it turns out, add support to this finding. The research is piecemeal and scattered, and it is best taken up separately as it applies in later chapters. But wherever writing growth during the college years has been studied with care, wherever measures are analytical and not holistic or impressionistic of entire essays, and wherever those measures depict real-world rhetorical needs, more evidence has been found of maturing in writing than of stasis and none of deterioration. College writing teachers, who do step twice in a river, the first step when they teach beginning composition and the second when they teach advanced, are going to find the waters healthy and flowing.

The effect of the maturational frame is to alter twice all three factors of the act of learning. It again elevates the status of the older students. Measured by mature standards, they not only have a shorter distance to go than we thought, but are already on their way there. And they have been traveling on their own, *acquiring* the skills rather than just being taught them (to use Stephen Krashen's vital distinction). That change of status then alters twice the teaching standards. From traditional notions, the criteria are revised through the inclinations of the competent employees and then secondly through the willingness of the majority of students to pursue them. And that modification of standards twice alters the expectations we have about change, first that students ought to be changing in certain ways and second that they ought to be doing so at a certain pace.

All this sounds complicated. As in most field models of learning, it is complicated. But that model also suggests that interpretive focus on just one of the factors will probably effect changes in the others. A shift to a maturing perspective may not come as hard as it seems. After a semester of analysis, zeroing in on just a few of the nineteen traits showing employee maturing in postfreshmen—logical organization, degree of topical specificity, explicit and implicit coherence, relative infrequency of vocabulary, syntactic placement of free modification, sentence length—the fourteen teachers reapplied the holistic assessment, rating the Sample essays they had not rated before. The freshman Essay F, initially earning an average rate of 5.0, dropped to 3.7, whereas the junior Essay J rose from 4.2 to 4.7—a model case of students teaching their teachers.

The Tale of Zeno's Stasis: Loss of the Teacher

But how are the teachers going to teach the students? The question brings us back in a nasty circular way to our new definition of maturing as lying between maturation and learning. It may be that on their path to maturity, humans are not

87

riding exclusively an inner-ballistic trajectory. It may be that they are shaped, not driven, toward that cultural-biological goal. But if culture and biology are the shaping forces, what hope can a mere teacher have to change such powerful, sovereign ends? The evidence of maturing comparisons seems to film college students caught up in a slow, swarmy migration toward preferred writing but not necessarily toward the kind of writing preferred by many composition teachers. What if the teacher disapproves of organizational open-endedness, sloppy proofreading, jargon, tacit cohesion, sophisticated vocabulary, noun adjuncts, the nominative style?

I have mentioned how easy it is for researchers to exclude the preferences of workplace culture by setting up comparisons that in a circular way discover the standards the researchers want to find. But do not more valid comparisons draw an interpretive circle potentially as vicious and exclusionary—putting the teacher beyond the cultural pale? Certain older writers are taken provisionally as mature. Their writing performance sets criteria by which student writing is interpreted as maturing. The fact that students are changing, perhaps despite their own awareness, toward the older writing then validates that older writing as mature. Or the circle can begin with the students. The ways they change are provisionally defined as maturing. Then the people they eventually change into, older writers on the job, are taken as exemplars of maturity, and the way *they* write is confirmed as standard for the kinds of change sought in the students. By this question-begging, the mere facts that student sentences grow in length during college and that, after college, sentences written by engineers grow even further prove not only that big sentences are better but also that students are on the right track. Students, says Joseph M. Williams, "do not have to be taught to write long, complex sentences. They will, willy-nilly" (1979: 604). The exclusion of the English teacher from all this is evident.

We must not avert our gaze from the deeply felt resistance among some teachers to novice-expert comparisons. It is related to the equally strong distaste for developmental theory in general, as we will see. There is good reason for the resistance. Regardless of how exhilarating Piaget can be when he writes comments such as "Every time we teach a child something, we prevent him from discovering it on his own" (cited by Case: 389), he can't prevent teachers from discovering the obvious implications for their discipline. The growing child and the encircling culture form an embrace that may include teachers but shackles more than enfranchises them. Teachers must reenter this self-admiration society yet at the same time become free of it. They have to have the ultimate freedom from cultural values to be able to say: This may be the way students write and the way engineers write, but it is bad writing.

The natural impulse, therefore, is to reject the long-distance view of maturing because it makes a teacher feel culturally outcast or helpless. I believe such rejection is premature. To begin with, taking a long interpretive perspective is always the first step toward resolving such cultural confrontations. We have already seen how a vision of growth dissipates the clash between a notion of unthinking decline in writing ability and a notion of willful refusal by students to meet abstract standards, suggesting that both notions are, each in its own way, illusions. Similarly, a vision of maturing can dissipate a related phantom, what might be called the Zeno illusion. Zeno of Elea, it will be remembered, opposed Heraclitus by denying the existence of change. Zeno did so by standing very close to motion, arguing that no matter where you are on the road to a goal, you are never more than halfway there. Peer close to the flight of an arrow, and you see that it is always half the distance to the target. Peer close enough, and you see that it never reaches the target. The short-distance view, in other words, leads to another kind of despair: that no change is possible.

So there is Zeno's stasis, and there is Wordsworth's sense that the "vacancy" between maturing and matured cannot be completely traversed even by the matured—a doubly negative impasse that can be resolved many ways. My argument is that the best resolution will not reject the fact of maturing but rather will look for a better theory of maturing, one that will bring the teacher back in. We need to turn our inquiry now from the vector of standard and look more closely at the vector of change, and in particular at the mechanisms that make human change possible. Only through an understanding of the process of change can teachers work best as changers of change—which role, after all, earns their most privileged status in culture.

The next chapter will loop back to consider two of the most familiar tales interpreting the way people mature, namely through models. I believe both accounts fail to envision a fully credible mechanism for change and a vital role for the teacher. Then, following Bruner's recommendation that "theories of development require a meta-theory of values concerning the cultivation of the good man and the good society" (1986b: 27), chapter 5 will take an even wider loop, through the philosophy of Habermas and Gadamer. The plan is to devise a more useful and more defensible tale of maturing, one that I can call genuinely developmental. This excursion through theory may seem tedious, and perhaps some readers may wish to skip ahead to the last section of chapter 5. But I hope this last turn will return the writing teachers to the maturing process of students, this time armed with an understanding that will make teachers a legitimate part of the process.

CHAPTER 4

Interpretive
Tales of Maturing

THE WRITING MODEL IS A SECOND BATTLE-
field or field where teacher and student motives clash. Early
in most composition courses, typically just after the first
"diagnostic" trial and the handing out of a syllabus, students are
assigned some reading. The source of the material ranges
widely, on the wings of the teacher's expectations, from an-
thologies of classic essays, to collections of occupational or academic exempla, to copies of previous student writing, even
perhaps to a selection from the class's own first essays. Whatever the expectations, the teacher intends to provide students
with writing they can appreciate, learn from, imitate, "role
model" their own writing on. Behind the intent lies a clutch of
interpretive stories with a common assumption: that the act
of learning from models affords teachers access to a tried-and-
true mechanism by which members of the culture grow toward
maturity.

Tried, for certain. But how true? How much of a role
do writing models play in the actual writing development of
students? The essential criterion of modeling, of course, is its

lasting effect on the student, not its traditional favor with us teachers. Do we have a realistic understanding of that effect? My intuition is that even more than with the diagnostic essay and its tacit classroom war of evaluative strategies, conflicts operate on the sly with models of writing. Students generally hide their true reactions from teachers, and teachers generally fail to communicate their expectations to students. Here, if anywhere in the teaching of writing, we find a darkling plain swept by confusion, struggle, and flight.

I assume, as before, that a teacher's choice of models for writing will be conditioned by a habitual interpretive method. Since a student's productive use of models requires the reading of them, that too will be conditioned by strategies of interpretation. The question is how well the methods and the strategies accord, accord with each other and accord with a reasonable account of general writing development. Of the plethora of interpretive frames to consider, I begin with one traditionally voiced by English teachers, residing toward the learning end of the developmental spectrum. Then I turn to a less cited but equally well known tale lying toward the maturational end of the spectrum. In brief, this chapter asks how well the common use of writing models fits the two basic images of maturing in writing identified by Joseph M. Williams (1989): a route traced by an outsider entering the pale of a discourse community, and a graph recorded by a natural growth in weight or height.

The Tale of Imitation

The assignment of some reading—say King's "Letter from the Birmingham Jail," or Welty's "The Little Store"—is both a traditional event, occurring hundreds of times a day across the land during the school year, and a serious one. Teachers admire these essays. They believe they represent model discourse, written with clarity and probity in contrast to the mass of inept, slant, and often dishonest writing produced by our culture. The assignment may be handed to students under the aegis of tradition

("You all know Martin Luther King, you take a day off in his name"; "You may not have heard of her, but Eudora Welty is sometimes thought to be America's finest living author"). But the pedagogical act is deeply radical. Teachers present these pieces in an Arnoldian spirit, as actual touchstones of an ideal culture, as the best that has been written and the models of what should be written. They trust that through an act of imitative reading, the student will enter and help perpetuate that ideal culture, learning to write better by copying their traits, adapting their strategies, pursuing their high accomplishments.

How intuitively the teacher narrates this imitative learning process may be both vague and varied, but the "protonarrative," in Frederic Jameson's sense, takes the romantic form of an initiation in which younger protagonist learns from older. Generally it will follow one of three basic variants: of a successful *emulation* of hero (childe and knight), of an epiphanic *conversion* to the true light (neophyte and enlightened), or of a gradual *accumulation* of good advice (apprentice and master). Essentialized, these teacher tales may appear fanciful, but they express very real, even pedestrian beliefs. We imagine students so impressed by King's heroic life, ideas, and style that they want to copy his ways, just as they used to emulate Wonderwoman or Batman. We imagine—doesn't it happen?—students coming up after class with a wondering shine in their eye, new converts, their text open to Welty. In less sanguine moments, we still imagine that a semester of acquaintance with such fine writing will somehow accumulate or rub off.

Now if the imitative tale maintains an existing tradition of pedagogical hope—and the giant market of "readers" with titles like *Prose Models* and *Patterns for Exposition* proves that it does—this is also a hope under heavy indictment by all the current theories of composition. In essence, the theories say that the tale of imitation is foolhardy, that the students simply won't learn to write better that way. Advocates for an epistemic purpose to writing argue that the discovery of ideas has little to do with outside circumstance and everything to do with inner conditions. Advocates for information processing minimalize the presence of modeling in the act of composing. In their flow charts (ironically called models), they confine encounters with readings to a single peripheral loop through a value box labeled "discourse knowledge," and this at the planning stage, with no representation at the generating or revising stages. Entire articles synopsizing the theories of revision, invention, and social context lack any reference at all to the use of models in natural writing acts. In another ironic switch in usage, the modern *disposition,* a concrete inner condition of the individual, has replaced the classical *dispositio,* an ideal outer arrangement provided by tradition. As C. H. Knoblauch and Lil Brannon say, there is "no ideal text": "Operational purposes rather than idealized aims are what really motivate writers to make choices while composing. These purposes exist in writers' minds as dispositions to communicate particular information to particular readers in specific situations" (28).

Current theory tends to upbraid teachers who put the imitative tale into practice, accusing them of perpetuating a dead tradition. "Operational purposes," to continue with Knoblauch and Brannon, debunk "the ancient habit of looking at existing texts, a collection of venerated works by poets, tragedians, great orators, and others, and then describing their characteristics in ways which implied that other writers should produce similar-looking discourses" (28). Modeling, if it teaches anything, will just get students to produce chimerical or superficial forms that are not truthful, appropriate, or sincere, papers (not essays) exhuming some eighteenth-century mode such as description, some nineteenth-century arrangement such as comparison and contrast, or some twentieth-century pedagogue's fantasy such as the five-paragraph theme. The real irony, then, is that current theory, as we have seen in the last chapter, often holds the same image of novice-to-expert growth or initiation that lies behind the imitative tale, without offering an explanation of how that maturing may come about (but see Michael Carter's pathfinding essay).

A developmental approach argues that although the tales of hero worship, conversion, or accumulation describe maturing, they do not accurately specify the mechanism of that change. They gloss over or assume a chain of steps, most of which are belied by current knowledge about the process of learning to write. Fully converted to Burke's condition of temporality, the act of imitation turns out to be not as simple as it looks. Consider the steps—each a necessary link—that students will have to take to be positively influenced by reading King or Welty.

Step 1. They will have to recognize the writing traits to be imitated or at least become conscious of them.

Step 2. They will have to appreciate the traits well enough to want to make them their own.

Step 3. They will have to abstract each trait from its rhetorical context without destroying its efficacy and convert it to paradigm form so that it can be used later to instantiate original text without committing plagiarism.

Step 4. Subsequently, they will have to be writing in a context appropriate for the traits.

Step 5. They will have to call the traits up, probably consciously at first.

Step 6. They will have to be capable of producing the traits.

Step 7. They will have to want to borrow somebody else's rhetorical success.

Step 8. They will have to like the borrowing well enough to repeat the production often enough to insure that it becomes a permanent part of their writing repertory.

None of these steps are beyond demonstrated human capacity, but then none of them occur easily or frequently, so much so that taken together, they tell a tale that becomes as unlikely as the discouraging research into the transfer of writing traits from school-assigned texts would lead us to expect. As an example at hand, consider the odds against each of these steps were a teacher to assign Essay M as a model for freshmen to imitate. (It is a reading assignment not without a certain plausibility, since it would avoid the difficulties of persuading students to learn from King or Welty or other masterworks such as "Marrakesh" or "Grant and Lee: A Study in Contrasts."

Step 1. How easy will it be for a freshman simply to recognize traits in Essay M that a teacher might admire? Take its easy use of a vocabulary empowered with the ambience of established technical disciplines: <u>author</u> of a questionnaire, <u>field</u> of interpretation, <u>focus</u> of an effort. Lacking this kind of vocabulary, how will the student recognize its distinct quality and become aware of it? The skill needed to make something conscious for learning is the skill to be learned. We will return to this catch-22 in the next chapter, as the center of Gadamer's insights into the growth of knowledge. Gadamer shows that the basic act of understanding a text requires a previous understanding, a "fore-knowledge." Since language is "the reservoir of tradition and the medium in and through which we exist and perceive our world" (1976: 28), the reader must somehow share the tradition or "horizon" from which the text was written. Gadamer's analysis is important because it takes us down to the ground reason why students often do not learn writing tactics. It is not that they lack the skill or desire to copy the tactics, it is that they do not see the tactics. This hypothesis has begun to find backing from research into the unique language knowledge of students. Freshmen often do not recognize clichés as clichés (Olson), do not detect any difference in character or authority of the author in passages written syntactically at high-school and professional levels (Raforth and Combs), do not recognize the difference between discourse spoken impromptu and discourse composed with pen and paper (Means, Sonnenschein, and Baker).

Step 2. If students were somehow helped to see the mature traits in Essay M, would they still appreciate them? The question of the literary taste of students has only recently been taken as a legitimate one by research—as if researchers have only recently been able to see *it*. But the few studies have produced results that may startle composition pedagogy. Of the paragraphs that Means, Sonnenschein, and Baker typed to disguise the circumstances of composing, college teachers preferred the written, students the oral. Olson's students *liked* the clichés, perhaps because they sounded familiar or because they were easy to comprehend. Just as Kellogg Hunt's college freshmen rewrote up the kindergarten syntax of "Aluminum" to suit their taste, Stephen Witte's freshmen rewrote down a passage from a linguistics text, cutting the average length of T-units by a third (1983). When Thomas Newkirk gave two essays for college freshmen and graduate teaching assistants to read, two-thirds of the students preferred one, and four-fifths of the teachers preferred the other. The students liked obvious facts and familiar content, explicit organization, elevated register, noncommittal stance toward the issues, and objective tone. In contrast, the teaching assistants liked new facts and content, implicit organization, less pretentious diction, and passionate engagement with the topic. The two readings, Newkirk explains correctly, do not show one taste inferior to the other but rather "two equally plausible ways of viewing text" appropriate—in Stanley Fish's concept—to "distinct evaluative communities" (1984: 298). My evidence shows that teachers preferred Essay M to Essay J, but the above research into comparative taste argues that students would reverse that evaluation. They easily might dislike the most "competent" or mature features of Essay M: the open-ended organization, the implicit cohesion, the long sentences, the specificity of subject (The author of this questionaire), and the personal and engaged stance (I know what it is that I want to achieve in life).

Step 3. But once somehow seen and in some way appreciated, will a trait worthy of imitation, not yet part of the student's repertoire of rhetorical skills, be remembered for later use? Here is perhaps the most mysterious passage in this interpretive tale. Yet it is also a point where a number of different disciplines—philosophical hermeneutics, information processing, learning and reading theory, sociological frame analysis—all converge to offer the same hypothesis. Long-term and accessible storage will not occur unless the student already has the right knowledge frames, the cognitive and affective prototypes that match the structures of the text. No matter where the investigator looks along the route from text read to text produced, functional framing operates. In short-term comprehension, in long-term recall, in memorization, understanding, paraphrase, and transfer of trait to self-instigated text, production improves as frames are shared.[1] *Headfitting* is one current term for it. I prefer Gadamer's vivid imagery, "the fusion of horizons," because it evokes better the sharing and the intimacy that occur when a reader truly absorbs text, both standing, as he puts it, within the same "living tradition." "We do not conceive of what tradition says as something other, as alien. It is always part of us, a model or exemplar" (1975: 250).

If students lack the frames making sense of the mature features of Essay M, how will they construct those features to mature their own writing later? Take the characteristic way Essay M proceeds by means of an open-ended series in which set topic precipitates question (First, what is a code of conduct?), question impels answer, and answer precipitates new question (how do I choose my response to each of those moment-by-moment events?). Students cannot imitate such an organization, based as it is on "problem-finding" systems of reasoning that require stepping outside the system, if they have available only a "problem-solving" system of reasoning that is intersystemic (Arlin). Or take the long sentence of the fifth paragraph:

> From an experiential level I have definitely proved for myself that when I am consistent with the rules of any given situation, the focus given by my being aligned with those rules gives me clarity of thought, satisfaction and creates positive feelings for myself about myself and about others, resulting in my being more willing and eager to participate with others and share myself, creating value for myself and for them.

---

[1] This book assumes the hypothesis of language frames. For excellent introductions to frame or schemata analysis, see Anderson in language comprehension, Spivey in reading, Flower and Hayes 1984 in writing production, Brown in learning.

How are students to construct a sentence with this peculiar, spiral, unfolding effect without an internal model of this kind of complex causal sequence, where the final effect simultaneously effects the initial cause?

Step 4. Even if students were armed with the appropriate frames, they would still need the right motivations matching the right circumstances to reproduce the original rhetorical effects. The whole weight of the discipline's new knowledge about psychology and context questions the odds of that happening very often. The realistic "operational purposes" of Knoblauch and Brannon require "dispositions to communicate particular information to particular readers in specific situations" (28), and the vacancy between a college freshman and a working engineer (not to speak of a Welty or a King) is too wide to hope for the only luckiest hit. To note one instance, the author of Essay M wants to express his personal code of conduct. Yet most eighteen-year-olds are just beginning to form their own individual codes, hardly ready to formulate one they already have built. They are more interested in learning the established social code. It is true that study of social context has mollified the somewhat narrow limitation that schema theory seems to set to transference of skills. Children, for instance, can successfully perform tasks involving concrete and formal operations sooner than Piaget found if a friendlier environment is generated, and a change in home environment seems to prompt reading and writing sooner than does educational intervention based solely on language-frame theory. But environmental factors end by setting their own limits to what a student can or will do.

Steps 5 and 6. Given the right motivation and organizational frames, will the student be able to take advantage of them? Here we could delve into an area recently of great interest to learning theorists, one loosely called "production deficiencies." It is clear now that learners have many accessible capabilities that, under production constraints, are not accessed. The reasons are both obscure and complex, but the situation is not counterintuitive. Just as it is perfectly natural for us to admire Welty and regret being unable to write like her, it is natural that students may comprehend and admire the sophisticated vocabulary of Essay M without being able to reproduce it. At all age levels, writing skill lags behind reading skill. At the college level, little has been done to discover what the differences between the two levels are, but one consistent finding in school-age students can be generalized safely. When reading, children use more top-down strategies, such as getting at meaning and generating implications, than they do when writing, which involves more bottom-up strategies, such as choosing words and worrying about correct form. Not surprising, what schoolchildren transfer from model readings to their writing are discrete elements rather than global ones. The findings fit the general learning theory that the knowledge of novices is more "welded, or tightly wired" than the knowledge of experts (Brown: 106). New knowledge can be applied or transferred only piecemeal.

Steps 7 and 8. Research is hardly needed to establish the poor probability that students will take the last two steps. Only determined practice will set a mature writing trait firmly enough to last much beyond the final essay in a course. Given the questionable respect typical freshmen pay an anonymous engineer, given the questionable yen typical eighteen-year-olds will feel to pattern themselves after anyone outside their peer group, what are the odds they will engage in the eager repetition of trials needed to make any complex skill one's own? Imitation is deep-rooted in emulation, or it is soon dead.

Is the teacher's fond tale of imitation also dead? Perhaps, at least these versions of it. My rather formal demythologizing should not obscure the brute reality of students, classrooms full of them, responding to the teacher's esteem for King and Welty with averted gaze, averted mostly from the text open in front of them—students responding to concepts like "concrete" and "sincerity" with concrete and sincere incomprehension, students leaving a fifteen-week course unable in two more weeks' time to reproduce any particular stylistic accomplishment of any of the famous stylists, sometimes unable even to recall any of their names. It is a reality from which the imitative tale seems to avert its gaze. And if students will be unable to imitate Essay M, toward which the measuring of the Sample indicates they show some propensity, then the teacher who wants to challenge that novice-expert tradition with models of better writing (like King and Welty) has even less chance of succeeding.

This does not mean that modeling itself, as a universal means of learning to write, is dead. There are reasons to maintain that modeling has always worked, reasons which the next chapter will revive. The most obvious, however, is the simple fact that students do end up writing like their elders. As we have seen, freshmen, sophomores, and juniors are on their way toward the particular writing accomplishments of the employees, who once were underclass students and no doubt wrote much like them. How do present students move toward that maturity without, somehow, using it as model? My formal demythologizing operates too much like Zeno's sophistic procedure of denying motion, logically halving and halving into such fine steps that the living deed is minced out of sight.

The long-distance frame that development casts on modeling, to which I now turn, at least avoids the Zeno illusion. But the essential question will remain, whether the new interpretive tales are better "mechanisms-of-change stories," offering better ways to help teachers choose effective and defensible models and helping them free themselves and their students from compulsive routes toward an unworthy maturity.

The Formative Tales

A common historical pattern holds wherever we survey modern theories of human development, whether in psychology from Freud and Erik Erikson to Robert Kegan, in cognition from James Baldwin and Piaget to Klaus Riegel, in learning from Gesell and Bruner to Ann Brown, or in information processing from Pascual-Leone to Robbie Case. Generally the older theories situate themselves closer to the maturational end of the spectrum of development, in terrain farthest from learning and therefore most hostile to teachers. It is only in the last decade or so that theorists, such as Riegel and Brown and Case, have constructed theories that allow postsecondary teachers a reasonable and humane role in their students' process of maturing. The essential trouble with the early theories of development is that they indeed extend the tale of interpretation, extend it with a vengeance, stretching it so far into the biological or biographical past that it finally stands beyond the conscious reach of teacher and student too.

It is equally essential, however, to consider their tale—in part because it is outdated and in part because it is not. On the one hand, it is these established theories, such as Freud's and Piaget's, on which is based much of the composition teacher's antipathy to development. On the other, much of the theory still maintains and cannot be cast away. That is why it became established. For example, it would argue that not employee Essay M but junior Essay J would function as a more effective model for the eighteen-year-old author of Essay F. Such a position must grate against the opinion of the typical writing teachers who rated the essays, since they saw Essay M as much better than Essay J, and Essay J as worse than Essay F. Yet although recent developmental theory will modify much of the older position, I think probably it would still basically agree that Essay J would serve as a more productive model. A certain essence of the developmental perspective has not changed since Freud and Piaget and remains deeply radical in its pedagogical implications.

That essence is as follows. Human change proceeds by means of a vital interaction between inner and outer. Outer forces—such as parentage and culture and vicissitudes of the environment—prompt, shape, and to a certain extent schedule inner change but cannot alter its constitutive constraints or reorder its basic sequence. That sequence is hierarchical in that the preceding step lays the necessary ground for the subsequent step. Each step carries with it an endogenous organization and therefore a characteristic way of interpreting and dealing with the world. The child is father to the man or is mother to the woman by experiencing in proper order the inner lives of one's life, no life being totally left behind but each having its own maturity, its own raison d'être.

Where the early theory differs is in its assigning to development a larger share of biological, genetic, or evolutionary origins. It holds as its central defining image the incontrovertible biological truth about maturation: that humans turn into pretty much the same adults despite enormous differences in diet and vicissitude. Therefore it tends to see the successive perspectives by which the human views the world as essentially of its own construction. Inner growth is "auto-regulative," impervious to direction from forces other than its own laws of formation. This is why I label the early theory "formative." Of course, within the parameters of formative developmental theory lie a wealth of different and often antagonistic schemes. I am deliberately conflating theory from many different fields—among them psychotherapy, psychology, sociopsychology, epistemology—in order to extract some general lay notions of maturing. I want to show that much of the formative developmental perspective is still familiar, operating behind the daily understanding of most English teachers, even those who resist Freud and Piaget the most consciously. Each of the following three kinds of formative theory has a characteristic interpretive tale intuitively sound and appealing.

Since the human imagination, even of diametrically different camps, runs in familiar patterns, the three formative tales parallel the three forms of the imitative tale. In the imitative tale of hero worship, the maturing subject finds an object with admirable qualities and pursues them as ends. What I will call the formative tale of *identification* turns this tale outside in and relates how the subject finds the subject admirable. With Freud, for instance, identification is the essential mechanism of psychic growth. It is the way the ego gradually assumes control over psychic energy, the way unrealistic attempts of the id to gratify instinctual wishes are replaced with realistic methods of the ego. For Freud, that replacement stands as the healthy development of both individual and civilization. Originally, the infant id cannot discriminate between its images of the self and events of the world and constructs a perspective of pure wish (identity). But the world thwarts the wish, and to adapt, even to survive, the mediatory ego forms. As maturational forces impel the self through new stages (oral, anal, phallic, latent, genital) and as family and culture generate new and increasingly complex demands, the ego takes over more and more libidinal energy from the id to adjust the id's wishes to reality (identification).

The formative tale of identification is thus a radically interpretive one, in which the self sees the world in terms of its own growth. This route toward maturity follows a familiar ancestral trail where, at crucial turns, the heroine (as in Jane Austen's novels) or hero (as in D. H. Lawrence's) first lacks control over outside powers not understood and then takes command when he or she recognizes those powers as ones possessed all along. The model to emulate simultaneously challenges from without and arises from within. The process of identification is slow, but gradually emergency—a time of crisis such as toilet training or puberty or courtship or leadership—will be met with emergence, a rising up of old knowledge in the form of wishes, dream images, unconscious attachments—old identities assuming the form of new identifications. The technical term for such emergence is *epigenesis,* but the tale itself is lay. We resort to it as English teachers whenever we imagine students discovering in the most grown-up piece, such as Welty's "The Little Store," images and skills they greet with a "shock of recognition" and eventually identify with.

In the imitative tale of conversion, a radically new event from outside causes the learner to experience a sudden change of view, an insight. What I will call the formative tale of *restructuring* again inverts the process. It locates insight internally, converts it to in-sight. The subject's perspective on the world alters because the inner mental organization or schema undergoes a significant change. The main theory follows the idea of knowledge frames, which we have seen casting doubts on the functionality of the imitative tale. But developmental restructuring adds an additional turn. New structures build stage-like on previous structures. Elements reintegrated and forming a novel internal organization are not new but rather have been constructed via previous restructurings. So in Piaget's theory of cognitive development, the structural view he calls "formal" allows the growing self to understand the interrelationship between two variables, say the amount of weight on a balance beam and the distance of the weight from the fulcrum of the beam. But such a relationship requires a previous structural perspective ("concrete") allowing the child to conceive of the properties of any one variable as reversible, for instance, to be able to predict that the beam will return to its previous position when a weight is removed equal to that which had been added. Of course, such moments when "the scales fall from the eyes" are familiar stuff of autobiography and Bildungsroman, from Augustine to Proust. When teachers imagine a student suddenly breaking out of an inner cloud, exclaiming, "Oh, I get it," they have revived the pivotal event of the plot. An internal apparatus, prepared in advance, waits until suddenly and mysteriously it rearranges itself, and everything outside changes.

The imitative tale of accumulation, of gradual acquisition of skill, also takes an inward turn with what I will name the formative tale of *expertise*. Development is envisioned as a sequence of internal capacities, slowly enlarging to be able to handle tasks of increasing complexity. The tale may imagine the sequence of this enlargement as invariant in that certain capabilities will depend on the expertise of other capabilities, but early tellings did not hold to a notion of structurally distinct stages. For instance, the information-processing model of development advanced by David Klahr and J. G. Wallace pictures the subject growing more efficient in the management and execution of intellectual problem-solving. The mechanisms are basically internal. The subject can encode larger amounts of information by organizing them with more and more complex schemata ("chunking"). The store of goals and plans grows, and the internal routes accessing them become more accessible. Certain executions become automatic through use, allowing attention to a wider array of strategies. In its view of a gradual and rather mechanical acquisition of skills, this formative theory lies closest to behavioral theories of learning, but it departs from C. L. Hull and B. F. Skinner by imagining a vitally active machine, processing input in ways always unique and human. The tale it tells is of the sleuth, the mental adept who solves a problem by first sharpening her or his own wits. It is a tale we all learn through popular initiation stories, of naive protagonists who pass the final test only by learning as they struggle with it. The largely apocryphal anecdote of Louis Agassiz, the student, and the fish, a tale beloved of composition teachers, renders the essence of the formative tale of expertise.[2]

These three narrative abstractions are rough and simplistic. Actual theories of formative development overlap and mingle these tales with a richness of concrete speculation and observation that, later, will prove more useful than these synopses. But one fact has emerged. Compared with the ungrounded English-teacher vision and with the behavioristic imitative tale, this formative conception explains the natural, creaturely growth promoted by chapter 2 as a much more powerful drive toward a more substantial kind of learning. Identification, restructuring, and skill acquisition are basic, adaptive, even survival techniques that involve generative changes in inner being,

---

[2] Apparently Agassiz, the great Swiss naturalist, once forced new students to observe and study the anatomy of a fish for a week without any help. The story passed down from the separate recollections of two students—Nathaniel Southgate Shaler and Samuel H. Scudder—to Lane Cooper, to Ezra Pound, and thence, altered considerably in the process, to numerous textbooks of writing. The genesis of this interpretive tale is told wonderfully by Robert Scholes (129–44). The original participants in the tale were not all as enthusiastic as later narrators of it. Shaler said, "The incident of the fish made an end of my novitiate."

permanent alterations in the construct of mind and affect allowing much more than course-learning of isolated facts.

Consider our question of the odds that freshmen might learn to write better from reading Essay J or M. Psychological identification provides the most reasonable motives and mechanisms for such an imitation. Students could become attached to either essay in a number of ways. They could see it as an object representing a part of their ideal self, that image of upperclassmen or professionals lying buried inside freshmen (narcissistic identification). They could value Essay J as the achievable effort of a member of a peer group (goal-oriented identification). They could want to assume from Essay M the characters of a desired person, parent or teacher, who has been lost or withheld (object-loss identification). They could even assume the duty of imitating the pieces out of unconscious fear of authority reprisal (identification through the superego). Restructuring and skill acquisition may locate the method of modeling even more deeply within the natural history of human learning. For Piaget, imitation is the instinctive behavior that most purely reflects a need to restructure ("accommodation"). Children engage in carefree play merely to adapt outer impressions to inner schemes ("assimilation"), but they turn to imitation (as early as the first four months of life) when conflicts between inner needs and outer forces require structural adjustment. For the information-processing theorist, imitative behavior or "tutor proneness" is unthinking and compulsory whenever humans need to acquire technical expertise. Witness the rapt attention of the six-year-old watching his older sister ride a bike or of the eighteen-year-old athlete watching a professional game on television.

But if the formative is encouraging in its view of the ways learners learn, it is discouraging for teachers looking for ways to teach. As I have said, the tale stretches back to the instinctual and evolutionary, to chthonic centers of maturing change not much open to conventional classroom or conference methods. To begin with, all these formative changes occur nonrationally.

By definition, the promotive role of the id and the prohibitive role of the superego are totally unconscious, and the executive decisions of the ego are often motivated by emotion. Cognitive restructuring, it seems, cannot be consciously willed. And all the major steps in skill acquisition lie in that intangible arena usually called, for lack of a better term, the intuitive: automaticity, invention, discovery, insight, solution. To imagine how their crucial third tier of mental problem-solving functions when new information (Tier 1) and known strategies for dealing with it (Tier 2) are reprocessed by a new and more efficient system, Klahr and Wallace have to imagine a review or "replay" operation taking place during a time of mental disengagement, such as sleep. In short, if the formative view finds nodes of potential maturing—attachment, role-modeling, problem-solving—they all lie in that tricky, underwater world of the inner. How is a teacher to maneuver with any sure success in that distorted land of displacements, compensations, defense mechanisms, instinct transformations, projections, sublimations, rationalizations, and repression?

From the teacher's point of view, each of these powerful "endopsychic mechanisms" looks more like a constraint than an impetus. The cognitive side betrays this focus on limitations especially well. Accounts of information processing are thick with adversarial terms warning of ultimate barriers to human activity: "task difficulty," "information overload," "limits of capacity," "attention span," "short-term memory bottleneck," "executive buffers." The study of problem solving in composition counts errors and analyzes pauses and hesitations, and the standard picture of this resistance, apostatized (or essentialized, as Kenneth Burke would say) into a map of the human "processor," is a flowchart with vectors limiting direction and route to and from closed boxes. Pascual-Leone named his sine qua non of cognitive growth "mental power" (or, more dramatically, "M-power"), but it turns out to represent the maximum number of schemata a person can activate at one given time and is supposed to increase at a slow, steady rate from one at birth to seven at about age fourteen. George A. Miller's famous parameters of adult short-term memory, the "magical number seven, plus or minus two," seems more like black magic than white. No wonder college teachers prefer to hope that the major stages of cognitive and affective growth are over by the college years, giving them the liberty to assume the working hypothesis that there is finally a limit to the limits of what students can learn.

In the end, a sort of doggish conservatism haunts formative theories. The bête noire whose sleepy hug they cannot escape is fixation, the human tendency to stick at an immature point in development because it is safe and easy. Formative interpretations prepare the bed for fixation. Piaget argues that growth in thought is impelled by cognitive discrepancy, where new information needs an accommodation of inner structures to explain it fully. But the learner can always achieve equilibrium by assimilating conflicting information in the light of existing structures. The six-year-old first thinks that water poured from a squat container into a tall and thin container grows in volume because it becomes taller, then thinks it shrinks because it becomes thinner. Piaget thinks that the child resolves the contradiction by creating a new theory (conservation of matter), thereby progressing toward a more mature conception of the world. But the child could achieve equilibrium by seeing the event either as no contradiction at all (believing contrary states can exist simultaneously) or in terms of knowledge structures already possessed (assuming the water grows just like babies, taller and skinnier). It seems Piaget's mechanism of change— equilibration—can operate as a mechanism of fixation. Similarly, in information-processing theory, skills are acquired as humans wrestle with new problems. But the very drive toward solutions may encourage the learner toward the most efficient one, which is to interpret the situation as not being problematic. Freudian analysis of development, from which we get the term *fixation,* tenders an ominous definition that later formative theories have never exorcised. Fixation is a defense mechanism arising from anxieties associated with the fear of change itself.

From the formative perspective, fixation is a reasonable developmental adaptation deeply antidevelopmental.

In sum, formative theories contain a profound bias against teaching. They end up arguing, for instance, that a freshman would be highly unlikely to learn anything from reading employee Essay M. From the static, anxiety-suffused perspective of a typical eighteen-year-old, the progressive, open-ended organization of both thesis and sentence, for example, would look either like a mess or like a simplistic stacking up of items (first one question and then another). In fact, the essay most likely to be appreciated by a freshman is none other than Essay F simply because the authorial model it presents (peer), the information it offers (stock ideas about political image-manipulating and stock examples of Carter and Eisenhower), and the problem it poses (how to achieve political success) can be readily identified with, assimilated, and solved with internal mechanisms the freshman already has. It seems that the formative theories of maturing take us full circle back to the educational bind that the idea of maturing wants to escape, back to advanced-composition students preferring freshman composition over again because it is a course they have already had.

The long-distance view of the theories easily dispels the Zeno illusion of ungrowth (by age eighteen, the former eight-year-old has certainly become a different creature), but its situating of the vital mechanisms of growth within the inner expels the teacher to a Wordsworthian vacancy. The formative finds students changing through models, but they are choosing the models for themselves. The formative lacks and a teacher needs what the philosophy of social action of Jürgen Habermas calls a "regulatory idea." That is a kind of "model" (1971: 226) operating under the control of a mentor, not of the learner, administered from the outside, not emerging from the inside. A teacher needs not only an explanation of change, which the formative tales give us, but also a theory by which change can be effected, which the tales do not give us.

Teacher Frustrations, Teacher Dreams

Furthering an argument with a long tradition in Marxist critique, Frederic Jameson says that culture produces narrative form—artistically or not—as an ideological act "with the function of inventing imaginary or formal 'solutions' to unresolved social contradictions" (79). He means "contradiction" in the Hegelian-Marxian sense of internal conflict. By this argument, the clash of interpretive tales such as we are extracting here would reflect "irreconcilable demands and positions of antagonistic classes" (85). The tales of imitation and self-formation, as applied by teachers to explain the classroom fate of writing models, would be taken as wish fulfillments escaping a real-life dilemma. In this case I would argue that the unresolved clash is between students and teachers, or more exactly between the experience of being a student and the experience of being a teacher. They are two horizons that finally just do not fuse: the students' view that they are learning; the teachers' view that the students are not learning. These particular tales arise out of teacher frustration. They are teachers' excuses.

But as narrative expressions of frustration, the imitative and the formative are contrary enough to suggest the presence of two opposing camps within the teacher class and consequently the presence of internecine warfare. Consider the antinomies of the imitative and the formative tales. The imitative assumes that the student begins with a status of novicehood or incomplete knowledge, the formative that the student begins in a status of equilibrium or completed stage of growth. The imitative imagines the student meeting the ideal text as an outside model from an older, more skilled generation, the formative as an inner model objectified by a peer-group piece. The imitative sees learning from the model as a conscious imitation into established, adult ways, the formative as an unconscious self-discovery of potentiality already lying within.

These antinomies do not align very well with conjectures of social clash within the teaching profession. The imitative may lend itself more to a teacher-centered than a student-centered—or more to a product-oriented than a process-oriented—curriculum, but as we see, both the imitative and the formative tend to diminish the role of the teacher, and both, as interpretations of the act of modeling, focus on product. Barry Kroll's division of composition camps into interventionist and maturationist may come closer to the contradiction here, although his resolution of the clash into an "interactive" approach shows that his division does not quite coincide with ours, since the formative is already deeply interactive.

The way out of any dilemma is just that, to step outside of it and view it from an alien system. The dilemma created by Zeno's paradox, proof by logic contradicting what we know by experience, can be erased simply by standing far enough back, about as far as was Burke's wont, to recognize the two distinctive perspectives of the human involved: logical abstraction (essence) and physical experience (temporality). The first lies outside time, the second within. So in terms of physical doing, there is no paradox: while the thinker is mentally dividing the distance to the target, the arrow has already struck the target. The one act does not stop or any way affect the other. Conversely, infinite divisibility is a fact of mental abstraction: it is what humans can do with imaginary pen and paper (or imaginary computers with a binary code) and does not affect what arrows do.

The paradox of modeling is that students do not seem much to appreciate the teacher's writing models and the mature standards of the discipline reflected by them, yet in the end, the students' writing ends up moving toward both models and standards. The way out of this paradox is to stand back and recognize that there are not two but three maturing perspectives involved in modeling: the mentor, the student, and the culture. From the essential angle of the teacher, as in the imitative tale, the students have no convincing way to be changed by models. The tale reflects a dream about students relishing the kind of writing the teachers like. From the temporal angle of the student, as in the formative tale, students on their own have little reason to be changed by the models that teachers give them. The tale reflects a dream about students independently taking to models without the coercion of teachers. But what is the cultural tale of modeling? It must lie somewhere between the extremes of maturation and learning, and its dream must somehow reflect less of a divorce between student and teacher. It will therefore help resolve our teacher dilemma and solve the model paradox. More important, it will create a new image of writing development that combines and synthesizes Williams's graph of natural growth and path into the discourse community.

The next chapter makes an effort to stake out that "middle ground." To do so, it will turn to Habermas and Gadamer, two of the most eminent contemporary philosophers of cultural change. The issues they take consummately as their own—social change in the case of Habermas and historical evolution in the case of Gadamer—will give the distanced perspective to help interpret recent theories of development, providing the outer frame (such has always been the benefit of philosophy) to mold them into a central interpretive tale for composition teachers, a tale that will apply to more than just models. The present chapter and the next chapter, then, in a maneuver not entirely playful, form a unit that models itself after the dialectical organization of Essay J.

PART III

The Changes of Development

He allowed himself to be swayed by
his conviction that human beings are
not born once and for all on the day
their mothers give birth to them, but
that life obliges them over and over
again to give birth to themselves.

—Gabriel García Márquez,
Love in the Time of Cholera

CHAPTER 5

A Transformative
Tale of Developing

LET'S STIPULATE SOME TERMS. *GROWTH* IS A one-dimensional interpretive frame defining human change relative to its own past. A habit of using more nouns as a junior than one used as a freshman reflects a writing skill that we judge simply as having grown. *Maturing* is a two-dimensional frame that interprets *growth* in terms of a fixed standard for the future. Only if we take a certain nominal style as a proper goal will we see the above growth as maturing. If we take George Orwell as a standard, we will judge that growth as regression or deterioration or some other perversion from maturing. *Development* is a three-dimensional frame that interprets *maturing* in terms of its own potential or—ultimately amounting to the same thing—in terms of culture. Only if we take growth toward a certain nominal style as a maturing grounded in previous maturing and headed toward possible future maturing will we see it as development. If the goal of Orwell's verbal style does not work as a turn in a student's past and future maturing or, by extension, in the culture's past and future maturing, it is antidevelopmental. Likely it will not be achieved, and if it is, it will not be retained.

Growth brings in the student, maturing brings in the teacher to direct the student's growth with standards, development brings in the culture to qualify the teacher's maturing standards with its actual past and potential future. This concept of development imagines student and teacher working together within their particular domain or educational orbit of society toward the common shaping or development of all three. Development includes but cannot be confined to *maturation,* which here would be interpreted as a form of maturing where standards are fixed by nature. As Bruner points out, "Theories of development require a meta-theory of values concerning the cultivation of the good man and the good society." Bruner speaks from the latest position of developmental thought, which recognizes much of development as culturally molded and which consequently recognizes the dangers of forgetting that it therefore is moldable. Otherwise, "developmental theory will risk serving as the mindless handmaiden of implicit beliefs in the culture rather than as a vigorous participant in the debate about the next generation" (1986b: 27).

The task of this chapter is to shape an interpretive tale of writing development consonant with this general conception of development and applicable to teaching. For its "meta-theory of values," it centers on the element of development that is most problematical, not only to writing teachers but to developmentalists themselves: the mechanisms of change. It looks to Habermas and Gadamer for a philosophical exposition of social change or the means by which the good citizen may be cultivated. Philosophically, the two are at odds. The ends of Habermas are change in political action and social learning; the ends of Gadamer are change in personal understanding and experiential learning. I argue, however, that their meta-theory of change merges into a common plot of value to any theory of development.

The procedure of this long chapter will be to stand back from development per se, establish a meta-theory of values concerning human change, use that meta-theory to construct a theory of development (in the above sense), support that theory with recent studies and speculation about development, and then show how such a theory creates an interpretive tale that writing teachers can use. The chapter ends with a brief application to student writing, although the rest of the book constitutes the full application.

Meta-Tales of Change: Habermas and Gadamer

One way to view the famous debate between Gadamer and Habermas is as a radicalized argument over the question of social change. How do people change, thereby altering knowledge, custom, political structure, and other forms of tradition? Gadamer seems to express the ultimate foundationalist answer, arguing that change proceeds through traditions, most centrally through the tradition of language: our very understanding of life is "historicized." Habermas offers the ultimate radical answer, arguing that change proceeds through the breaking of traditions: it is the peculiar nature of language that allows us to emancipate ourselves from those very social forces that curtail change. The debate obviously encloses the imitative-formative dilemma over the pedagogical use of models, whether they are subversives or vehicles of culture and whether they can alter the maturing of young writers. But, as I say, the views of Gadamer and Habermas will go far beyond the issue of modeling and will enlighten us on all the problematical questions about generic, human change, of which learning and development are just two species.[1]

---

[1] Both Gadamer and Habermas are students of human knowledge systems, but Gadamer is essentially concerned with questions of how we know, Habermas with questions of how we should act. Gadamer is a hermeneuticist of the school of Heideggerian ontology, Habermas a Marxian sociologist of the Frankfurt school of social critique, whose earlier members most familiar to American readers are perhaps Erich Fromm and Herbert Marcuse. A balanced account of their long public debate, which began with a criticism of general hermeneutics by Habermas in 1967, is hard to find, though in getting

I take up Habermas first because he shares most directly the fear of teachers that learning unconsciously obeys cultural changes so powerful and pervasive that the classroom may be as ineffective in changing the student as it is the culture. Habermas sees individuals as subject to forces that dominate through ideology, which he defines as any irrational, freedom-limiting system of belief so deeply entrenched in our lives that we are not aware of it. He also sees that ideology deceives chiefly through a debased use of language, through "systematically distorted communication." Ideally, the nature of speech acts could allow a communication perfectly free of force, but ideology inculcates a "pseudo-communication" where deception or domination remains undetected because it has the authority of a concrete social behavior absorbed naturally from birth.

Herein lies Habermas's intuition that theoretically he has a major opponent in Gadamer and his discipline of philosophical hermeneutics. For Gadamer believes that the crucial step of communication, understanding, cannot occur without already held belief systems ("fore-knowledge"), which in turn are shaped by traditions of natural language use. Culture provides the only medium by which culture can be understood. Just as the teacher has to ask how a student can imitate the feats of a model essay if the student doesn't already possess those facilities of language that convey the feats, Habermas has to ask how ideology can be changed if the only tool to change it, understanding through language, is fashioned by it.

Habermas's answer, in effect, is to create an alien language system, a nonnatural one taking the form of a theory of what

to the essentials, Paul Ricoeur's assessment must be praised (1981: 63–100). Gadamer presents his position best in "Scope and Function of Hermeneutical Reflection" in *Philosophical Hermeneutics* (18–43), and Habermas in an astonishing piece, "The Hermeneutic Claim to Universality" (1980: 181–211). The impact of Gadamer's analysis of language (*Truth and Method:* 345 ff.; *Philosophical Hermeneutics:* 59–94) and of Habermas's (e.g., *Communication and the Evolution of Society:* 1–68) on composition and rhetoric has hardly begun (but for Gadamer, see Louise Wetherbee Phelps).

could be (an "anticipatory regulative idea"), and to use it as critique. The theory questions, makes aware, and debates in the hope of starting self-reflection, escaping from the domination of ideology by becoming aware of it, and ultimately revising the natural socialized system. The most radical way of putting Habermas's notion is to say that one can escape the false consciousness of ideology through critique because critique is non-factual.

That claim can only put a "general" explanation (not yet an "instrumental" understanding) up for debate: "It is only the formal anticipation of an idealized dialogue, as the form of life to be realized in the future, which guarantees the ultimate supporting and contra-factual *agreement that already unites us;* in relation to it we can criticize every factual agreement, should it be a false one, as false consciousness" (1980: 207). The phrase I have italicized has its roots in a premise of Habermas's that separates him perhaps most definitively from Gadamer: his belief that critical theory stands essentially separate from other forms of social interaction. It has its source in a primary motivation of all humans to free themselves from social constraints ("the emancipatory interest"), as distinct from the motivation toward communication and other forms of socialization ("the practical interest").

Can critique work? In some of his most compelling analysis, Habermas replies that it already does, in the instance of psychoanalysis. The classical technique of Freudian therapy provides Habermas with an exemplary or interpretive tale of emancipation through critique of ideology. The main turns of the plot ("processes in a drama," 1971: 259) are as follows. They form Habermas's meta-tale of social change.

1. *Self-deception.* The patient, say an adult male, arrives for therapy in a state of personal development that has been interrupted in that he is no longer able to communicate freely *within himself.* Perhaps because the patient has internalized neuroses fostered by culture ("the mutilated text of tradition," 1971: 216), or perhaps because his ego weakness has generated,

through repression and censorship, an internal language that is misleading and unconscious, he can offer the therapist only "symbols in which a subject deceives itself about itself" (218). The patient resides in a state of "systematically distorted communication," just as does the citizen who self-perpetuates false ideology.

2. *Theory.* The therapist does not speak to the patient in the patient's own distorted language but counters it with a different system, in this case Freud's theoretical vision of an ideal uninterrupted development and his explanation of the normal causes of deviation from it. By necessity, the therapist's analysis is guesswork, not a specific instrumental method but a "general anticipation of the schema of disturbed self-formative processes" (1971: 259). The therapist can offer the patient only a "model" that proposes, not any natural law that disposes (226).

3. *Dialogue.* The therapist's office is removed from family and work and other possible sources of domination and therefore allows unforced conversation. It is an alcove of "sheltered communication" (1971: 252), where the therapist freely proposes explanations and the patient fully considers them. The therapist's "regulative ideas" do not control the patient but lead to self-reflection. Therapy is "a dialogical process of enlightenment" (1980: 201) in which the physician "instructs the patient in reading his own texts, which he himself has mutilated and distorted" (1971: 228). Basically, the therapist reconstructs the patient's past by anticipating an ideal future, and the patient creates a future change by recollecting a repressed past.

4. *Emancipation.* With success, the theoretical schema or "narrative background" (1971: 259) provided by the therapist allows the patient to fill in his missing past, freeing himself from self-deception and restoring healthy development. But regardless of the results in changes in the patient's social behavior, the genuine success will be on the level of what Habermas calls "communicative action." In this situation, the action is self-awareness. The essential way the patient's self-formation will be changed is in his understanding of it. It is a meta-cognitive

act, where self-formation is textualized or turned into "life history." Self-reflection in fact, *is* the proper next step in his self-formation. "In our own self-formative process, we are at once both actor and critic. In the final instance, the meaning of the process itself must be capable of becoming a part of our consciousness in a critical manner, entangled as we are in the drama of life history. The subject must be able to relate his own history" (259).

With this insistence, we see how entrenched is the idea of emancipation in Habermas's philosophy of social action. No way free of ideology is truly free for the self until the way proves a "path upon which it constituted itself" (260). In psychotherapy, unlike in medicine, the doctor cannot cure the patient, who must be the instrument to cure himself. This fact also holds in sociotherapy. For Habermas, there is no way to emancipation other than through a self-change, and that can be effected only through self-reflection, the only truly free act a human can make. Habermas sums up this end of individual development in a word that holds a vital message for our particular concern with the development of writing: *Mündigkeit* (1971: 198, 206; 1980: 206). *Mündigkeit* means the state of being of legal age and hence of having earned the responsibility for one's own acts. But its etymology (*Mund,* mouth) adds the idea of having achieved language competence and the responsibility for one's words. And historically it connotes, as every German schoolchild learns, the freeing of oneself from lazy ignorance or dependence on others for knowledge, for in a famous essay Kant used the word to answer the question "What is Enlightenment?" "Enlightenment is man's emergence from his self-imposed immaturity [*Unmündigkeit*]." For Habermas, *Mündigkeit* is mature competence, that stage of development achieved when people free themselves of ideologue, therapist, or teacher and, through linguistic self-reflection, gain control over their own development by making their understanding of development part of development. It marks the point when the self gains the power of self-critique "to the extent that it becomes transparent to itself in the history of its genesis" (1971: 197–98).

Gadamer responds that the self is never truly free in that its genesis never becomes totally transparent to itself. The self is unable to relate its own history fully. Whereas for Habermas genuine change—any human change, psychological or social, that tends in the direction of autonomy and freedom—finally has a meaning that resides in the knowledge of it, for Gadamer meaning itself, by nature, can never be fully manifest. He compresses this radical divergence from Habermas in one laden sentence: "Meaning can be experienced even where it is not actually intended" (1976: 30). Gadamer may or may not ascribe to Freudian psychotherapy, but it is clear he believes that no reflection by the self about the self will ever fully enlighten the forces that operate unconsciously there (Freud, in fact, believed the same).

Gadamer's ideas on change take the form of an intense study of the processes by which humans understand and interpret the world (hermeneutics). But if these processes sometimes occur without conscious intention, then Gadamer has to ask Habermas's question in a new way: How can misunderstandings and nonunderstandings be changed if the only tool to change them, understanding through language, is fashioned by forces beyond the interpreter's reach? For Gadamer, these forces can be summed up in the word *tradition,* which in some ways stands directly opposed to *Mündigkeit* (the Enlightenment libertarianism of Kant took the two as enemies). Gadamer sees tradition involved as predispositions in every act of understanding. The prejudices and codes and beliefs of culture, the endowment of history, the constitutive structures of language—all are before us, are ineluctably given to us. "We stand always within tradition, and this is no objectifying process, ie we do not conceive of what tradition says as something other, something alien. It is always part of us, a model or exemplar, a recognition of ourselves which our later historical judgment would hardly see as a kind of knowledge, but as the simplest preservation"

(1975: 250). Notice that Habermas's "model" acts to change understanding from the outside. Gadamer's "model" maintains understanding from the inside. Gadamer's question is how humans can grow in knowledge if everything is interpreted by such familiar "models." Won't any alien experience be interpreted as familiar, in effect be noninterpreted, with understanding fixated and tradition fixed? Gadamer's models and exemplars, of course, embrace the information processors' knowledge schemata or Piaget's *structures d'ensembles,* and the question repeats, on a more general scale, their inquiry into the mechanisms of developmental change.

Gadamer's answer is exact and deeply thought out (and deeply Heideggerian). Behind these given predispositions lies an even more basic one, residing as the very ground or condition of our being: the expectation of meaning itself. And if people look for meaning, they must look for newness. For when people let life simply make sense through given prejudgments, understanding does not occur. "Without the assumption of meaning, failure of understanding would not be noticed, which leads to an attempt to understand" (1975: 262). Consequently, the human search for meaning is an "orientation to the world as the *atopon* (the strange) [literally, the other place]" (1976: 25). Gadamer makes the startling point that lack of understanding would occur only if we *had no* prejudgments. Only by what we already know do we know that we need to know something new. In its most radical form: it is *by* prejudices that we learn.

Since tradition consists not of things and institutions but of individual acts of understanding, tradition has to be in constant change. The "horizon" of tradition, its perspective or "range of vision" (1975: 269), is ever encountering the alien perspective of new experience and fusing to form a new horizon. "The heart of the hermeneutical problem is that the same tradition must always be understood in a different way" (278). With the merest understanding of the world, there is a dialectical process in which a live being, endowed by nature with "expectation and readiness to hear the new" (1976: 9), first discovers that *atopon* by means of preconceptions and then, by means of the *atopon,* alters those preconceptions retroactively or reflectively. "The prejudgments that lead my preunderstanding are also constantly at stake, right up to the moment of their surrender—which surrender could also be called a transformation. It is the untiring power of *experience* [*Erlebnis*] that in the process of being instructed, man is ceaselessly forming a new preunderstanding" (38). Tradition is preserved only through change.

If there ever was an interpretive meta-tale, a tale underlying or prerequisite to all other tales, it is Gadamer's. "To understand," he says, "is itself a kind of happening" (1976: 29), and lying at the heart of understanding is a story of experience with distinct turns. Gadamer takes *Erlebnis* as a cornerstone of his philosophy much as Habermas does *Mündigkeit.* He finds a word also with a genealogy significant to him, in this case with origins in two nineteenth-century philosophers of experience, Hegel and Dilthey. In using their neologism *Erlebnis* instead of the familiar *Erleben,* Gadamer means by *experience* not just something that happens but something that happens creatively with a productive aftermath. It is the difference between having the "experience" of a year in the dorms and finding dorm life an "experience," roughly between living experience and learning experience. Some remarkable pages of *Truth and Method* (there are many others) analyze the narrative structure of *Erlebnis,* this "process of being instructed," and from them I plot what might be taken as Gadamer's meta-tale of learning change (1975: 310–25).

1. *Openness.* The learner does not enter into an experience with expectations to make sense of something, that is, with an investment in a "method" or a frame of technical knowledge that looks to *explain* unmet events, but rather with expectations not to make sense of everything, that is, with an interest in "truth" or a frame of mind that looks to *understand* future events. It is a state Gadamer simply calls openness. It is characterized not by an openmouthed naiveté but by a tough-

minded acceptance of one's lack of fully sufficient methods, a "skepticism in action." "Openness to the other includes the acknowledgment that I must accept some things that are against myself, even though there is no one else who asks this of me."

2. *The atopon.* There is no such thing, Gadamer surprisingly argues, as a positive experience. *Erlebnis* is always negative. Whether in reading unfamiliar texts or visiting strange locales or meeting new persons, experience somehow upsets the generalizations formed from old experience. True experience requires the alien or strange, the *atopon.* To have the same thing happen again, to have previous experience confirmed, is not to experience but to know or to see through. Gadamer's *Erlebnis* is like Heraclitus's river that can't be stepped in twice: "Strictly speaking, we cannot have the same experience twice" (1975: 317). The negativity of experience, then, is generative because it alters one's way of understanding and creates a new predictive power.

3. *Dialogue.* This "logical structure of openness" or negativity endows generative experience with a "dialectical" progression. The basic movement is inner → outer → inner. "The experiencing consciousness has reversed its direction, ie it has turned back on itself" (1975: 325). This act of consciousness may be instantaneous or reiterative or long delayed, but the dialectical movement of self-reflection is there. "The experiencer has become aware of his experience, he is 'experienced'" (317). Gadamer sees this movement as a process of questioning and answering that responds to the essential ground of humans to seek meaning. It is a "dialogue that we are." But it is easy to misunderstand the way this dialogue proceeds. It is not a search for answers to questions we have of life, but a search for questions life has of us. Understanding begins when the learner tries to answer questions that the text, the locale, the stranger asks. For to ask a question of the world will only reveal answers that will not negate preconceptions.

127

4. *Application. Erlebnis,* then, results in the learning self applying the event to itself. Just as the final step in theological hermeneutics is the application of God's word interpreted from the Bible to specific cases and in juridical hermeneutics is the application of the law interpreted from the legal code to specific cases, in generative experience, meaning is applied to immediate, unique circumstances. This application has the cast not of a ruling but of a decision, just as a judge must decide whether to apply equity or a musical performer must decide how to interpret a piece. The lessons experience teaches are characterized by freedom of choice and situational inductiveness, an "unprincipled universality" (1975: 316). In a conclusion typical of the philosophy of meaning in general, with its deep attraction to the hermeneutical circle, Gadamer states that the end of experience is more experience. At heart, what experience teaches is an openness to new experience. This is why Gadamer says that the most universal application, the "truth-value" of experience, is a meta-cognitive one: the knowledge of one's finitude, the awareness of the limits of one's knowledge, the limits indeed of all human expectations. "True experience is that of one's own historicity" (321).

The dialectical or dialogical relationship between preconception and experience operates as the same relationship between lesson and learning, text and interpretation, culture and behavior. Since most broadly it is the relationship between tradition and understanding, we see how deeply and paradoxically tradition is rooted in Gadamer's conception of human change. Tradition, always present, does not loom as an inescapable mortmain, preserved forever to reach from the past to smother human change. Tradition is an evolving, self-generating force for change. "Tradition is not simply a precondition into which we come, but we produce it ourselves, inasmuch as we understand, participate in the evolution of tradition, and hence further determine it ourselves" (1975: 261). Tradition understands itself and thereby shapes itself, destroys itself in order to renew itself. Tradition (*traditio:*

paying of tribute) is a "surrender" that could also be called a "transformation."

Habermas and Gadamer United:
A Tale of Developmental Change

The encounter between Habermas and Gadamer over cultural change parallels the clash between the imitative and the formative over educational change. Habermas's regulatory "model" allies with the imitative "ideal writing" model, Gadamer's preunderstood "model" with the formative inner "ego ideal." Gadamer fails to answer Habermas's charge that by itself hermeneutical experience cannot correct a state of unknowing misknowledge—just as the formative fails to explain how self-formation can unfix fixation. Nor can Habermas answer Gadamer's contention that the primary human interest of emancipation does not stand outside the interest of understanding because interest itself is conditioned by preunderstandings provided by culture—just as the imitative cannot explain how a model for writing can be appreciated without a previously learned inner model. This philosophical debate suggests that the "contradiction" within our profession may be a battle over whether teaching should proceed by critique or by experience. But the debate can lead further than that.

The Habermas-Gadamer encounter, in which each tries to outflank the other with arguments that his view is more universal, has been of long interest to the French philosopher Paul Ricoeur. He certainly has gone further than anyone else in trying to resolve it. Ricoeur argues that logically the issues constitute a true dilemma or vicious circle but that pragmatically the aporia can be mediated to a "living circle." His arbitration of the impasse encourages each side to recognize dependency on the other. The dialectical emergence of new values ("transvaluation") cannot proceed without a beginning in given cultural institutions or without a theoretical projection of emancipation (1973: 165). Tradition survives by critique, and "critique is also a tradition" (1981: 99). Ricoeur's dialectical resolution is a goal I will pursue, although I will take a different route (see Phelps: 183–201 for an application of Ricoeur's "third way" to resolve the clash between theory and praxis in composition methodology; her "theory" and "praxis" compare—but do not equate—with Habermas's "critique" and Gadamer's "experience").

I will argue that though philosophically Habermas and Gadamer operate at levels difficult to integrate (epistemology and ontology), and though politically they may stand poles apart (critique of ideology and defense of tradition), on the level of interpretive action they describe a natural, human process of change with a common narrative base. Their parallels with the imitative and formative antinomies actually further my hope to render a pedagogical scheme that teachers of all camps may find somehow central. Even more hopeful is the way Habermas and Gadamer cross over in relation to our teaching tales. On the one hand, Habermas has affinities with the long-distance perspective of the formative and with the rationalistic techniques of the imitative, and on the other hand, Gadamer adopts the closeup perspective of the imitative and the intuitive premises of the formative. Any deep-level fusion of the horizons of Habermasian critique and Gadamerian experience has to have a predictive power of some promise. I designate this Habermas-Gadamer plot as *transformative*.[2] Supported and fleshed out with recent advances in developmental theory, it will be my best offering as a learning-developmental explanatory frame that, whether it stands before us in a recollective way as "prejudice" or in an anticipatory way as "regulative idea," teachers may use

---

[2] *Transform* seems the one verb most shared among current advocates of a postformative theory of development as both sequential and recursive, where "the higher concepts in turn transform the meaning of the lower" (Bruner 1986a: 73): e.g., Gould; Feldman 1980: xv; Brim and Kagan; Brown: 102; Gergen. *Transformation* melds a long tradition of outer social change (Marx) and inner psychological change (Jung). Significantly, "to transform" is the customary translation of Hegel's crucial verb *aufgehoben*, by which he referred to the dialectical act wherein a term is "raised up" and "out" of a contradiction to a higher synthesis.

to interpret, predict, and promote individual acts of maturing in student writing.

In gist, the transformative tale relates how an initial state of internal instability is shocked into a kind of self-reflection that learns a new knowledge or skill by unlearning and revising old knowledge or skill. So it is a mechanism-of-development story based on a scheme less formative than *trans*formative. Following the trail of my analysis of Habermas and Gadamer, I divide it into four salient turns.

1. *Self-contradiction.* An act of generative learning-development begins in medias res, with the concrete structures of previously formed frames. But though concrete, the structures are not solid. Both Habermas and Gadamer show they do not form the naive nescience of the imitative or the satisfied equilibrium of the formative. They are unstable in that one structure tends to destabilize or deconstruct another. The external signs of this self-contradictory inner state may be the energetic restlessness we have seen in college students in chapter 2, or in the anxiety and neuroses of Habermas's patient, or in the "openness" of Gadamer's experiencer (not a void but an expectation to be changed), or in the yearning of the apprentice to become adept, or in the sulking unhappiness of the growing adolescent caught in epigenetic emergence. Internally, superego identifications clash with id identities; the wish that one's prejudgments provide security clashes with the anxiety that one's prejudgments are finite and limited; the fear that one is unskilled clashes with the satisfaction that one is already skilled.

2. *Alienation.* Such internecine warfare will not resolve itself. Instability will just become sublimated and fixated. It takes an encounter with something outside the self to precipitate change. It may be as socialized as a freshman's hearing comments by a junior, as adventitious as a startling experience (the *atopon*), as prescribed as a therapeutic analysis, as electric as a new-level internship task (you go ahead and write the advance), as natural as a Piagetian balance-beam problem for a

seven-year-old. But as Habermas and Gadamer insist, this other does not first appear positively to the learner as an imitative model or as a formative identification. It contains something alien and threatening, a direct challenge to the self and, more important, to *both sides* of the contradiction within the self. Habermas's "principled claim" challenges both the primary interest in socialization that fell for ideology and the primary interest in emancipation that deceived itself into thinking it was free of ideology. As Gadamer points out, every new experience will change the whole of tradition, not just part of it.

This is why I choose the term *alienation* instead of a friendlier one such as *novelty, surprise,* or even *atopon.* I want to emphasize the profoundly disturbing implications to the learner of this step in a generative learning process. *Alienation,* of course, is the old term for insanity, and still the legal one, a remnant of the medieval belief that the rightful self of a mad person has been usurped by an alien being. *Alienation* also means the transfer of property from oneself to another. For Hegel and Marx, *alienation* describes an even more disturbing transfer, one where the self unconsciously strips itself of its own capability, which it then imagines as a power lying outside of itself, as an other or alien to which it is slave. The workers confuse their skill with the products of their skill and then labor to "earn" them. Finally, the contemporary sense of *social alienation* describes the feeling of being estranged from one's own group. All these senses of the word enter into this step of the learning process. Unlike in the formative or the imitative tales, in the transformative, learners confront a new experience or idea with some feeling, even of the mildest, that they are being threatened with loss of self, whether they identify that self with their own views, their own property, their own skills, or their own social group or culture. Educators who take on the responsibility for encouraging learning must resign themselves to be seen at first as alienists—stealers of parts of the cherished psyche—and as alienors—legal fences of stolen property.

3. *Re-action*. Both the imitative and the formative tales prefer to look ahead, the first toward new accomplishments in skill, the second toward new phases, stages, or levels of inner growth. In contrast, both Habermas and Gadamer insist that no step forward can be taken without a step back. "Self-reflection" (to escape from ideology) and "reflection" (to adjust the pre-judgments of tradition) both entail a return to the already learned. But it is a return with a difference, not just a rebound off of the alien. That difference is awareness—consciousness of the self's previous position. This is the most radical departure of Habermas and Gadamer from the customary way of viewing learning and development. Learning involves a change in what one knows or can do *as well as* a change in what one knew and could do. The two changes, rather, are the same change. But a major means-effect of this reactive process is not only the shaky acquisition of new knowledge or skill but also the balky revising of old knowledge or skill. Again, both Habermas and Gadamer concur that this process of gaining new *understanding* of the old while acquiring a *capability* of the new can happen only through dialogue, or a free exchange between self and other, competence and model, past teacher and present teacher.

Dialogue might be a better name for this turn in the transformative tale, or *reflection*, or simply *reflex*. But just as Habermas and Gadamer want to commemorate their intellectual roots with their terms *Mündigkeit* and *Erlebnis*, I repay my debt to Wordsworth with *re-action*. I am thinking of the famous passage in the 1800 preface to the *Lyrical Ballads* where Wordsworth analyzes the process of creating an original poem, narrating how an old emotion is first "recollected" and then "contemplated" until a "kindred emotion" is gradually produced "by a species of re-action." By "re-action" Wordsworth could not have had in mind any automatic response to stimuli, since that meaning did not appear until the end of the nineteenth century. He must have meant a more active sense of the word, something akin to four older uses of the word: *reagency*, as in a chemical reaction; *reversal,* as in a political reaction; *resist-ance,* as in the Aristotelian notion of physical reaction (where it is the natural property of things to resist force directed against them); and *replay,* as in a dramatic re-action (a meaning current in 1800 but since dropped from the language). All four of these meanings combine in my sense of transformative re-action, where response to the new takes the form not of automatic re-buff but of a half-resistant, half-yielding recursion to modify and transform previous notions.[3]

4. *Appropriation.* And this is from Ricoeur, who traces to Heidegger his meaning of the word as the "terminal act" of understanding (1981: 113). For Ricoeur, appropriation is the end of genuine acts of interpretation, when readers leave the text having been changed by it, having made it their own (*proprio:* one's own): "To appropriate is to make what was alien become one's own" (113). I myself appropriate the word here to name that last turn in generative acts of learning, when learners are permanently altered. They are not just informed as in the imitative or newly formed as in the formative, but are transformed, their initial self not just instructed but recon-structed. Generative learning always entails self-learning. As Ricoeur explains, appropriation "culminates in the self-interpretation of a subject who thenceforth understands him-self better, understands himself differently, or simply begins to understand himself" (158). This is the same insistence of Habermas when he argues that the self must be emancipated so it can forge the "path upon which it constituted itself" (1971: 260), and of Gadamer when he argues that as humans, we are free to "participate in the evolution of ourselves" (1975: 261). All three argue that in the long run, a true act of learning is not proven subsequently by any coerced act. The writing of a "passing" essay to exit from a writing course does not prove that

---

[3] Wordsworth's rich meaning of "re-action" in the preface has not been inves-tigated by Wordsworth scholars, but his notion of a dialogic and dialectic, inner-outer play of consciousness has received much profitable attention: e.g., Geoffrey Hartman, M. H. Abrams, Don H. Bialostosky.

a skill has been genuinely learned. That is shown only when students are willing to apply that skill on their own. The only sure sign of learning is development itself.

The transformative tale of maturing has been told many times in fictional form. It is the story of second sight, of the protagonists who can't go home again (Zora Neale Hurston's *Their Eyes Were Watching God,* Doris Lessing's *The Summer before the Dark*), who return at the end from a journey into the alien future (*Gulliver's Travels*) or into the familiar past (*Remembrance of Things Past*) to find their beginnings irrevocably changed. It is the story of Huck Finn, who escapes from self-conflict, sallies into the alien, engages in free dialogue with Jim and others, and finds in the last chapters that he cannot step twice into the river of his life, that in the re-action Tom and Aunt Sally may have remained the same but he has changed. I am tempted to take as prototype the spiral form of *The Prelude,* that description of beginnings endlessly revised as Wordsworth got closer and closer to his end. But I will offer another work of Wordsworth's as more condensed: "Resolution and Independence." In a state of anxious self-contradiction, both proud and fearful of being a writer, the speaker suddenly is faced with *atopon,* "a some-thing given," the strange figure of the leech-gatherer. To the speaker, the man is as alien as possible—in age, health, afflu-ence, philosophy, and social class. Yet after the outer-inner dia-logue with the stranger, he appropriates the old man as a part of himself, a revision of his old image of himself in a feared future: "Solitude, pain of heart, distress, and poverty." Now that self is objectified, converted into prejudgment or regula-tive idea. That the event has been a generative act of learning is proven by the fact that the speaker is freely narrating the tale. As Habermas says, "He is able to relate his own his-tory." Or as Gadamer says, the experience is "historicized." In Wordsworth's own terms, *Resolution* and *Independence,* the speaker has resolved his self-contradictions by becoming more resolute, which act is also freedom or in-dependence from both self and other. That is the essence of developing.

From the Transformative Tale to Recent
Developmental Theory to Axioms for Teaching Writing

As a synthesis of Habermas and Gadamer, the transformative interpretation of human change offers a resolution to the pedagogical battle over critique and experience in the instruction of writing and to that extent offers independence from that obdurate stalemate. The contradictory movement of *alienation* and *re-action* requires both the outer agency of teacher critique and the inner agency of student experience. As an underlying protonarrative for John Flavell's "mechanisms-of-cognitive-development stories," the transformative also suggests resolutions to the running skirmish in composition circles between developmentalists and antidevelopmentalists, between, for instance, Janet Emig, who argues that it is indulging in "magical thinking" to reject the developmental finding that "writing is predominantly learned rather than taught" (140), and Ann Berthoff, who argues that it is an instance of "developmental models uncritically deployed" to derive from them a writing program that "does not require instruction" (749–50). What I am now going to argue is that recent, post-Piagetian developmental theory itself resolves most of this skirmish, and does so because so much of it supports the transformative tale of maturing as opposed to the formative. Much of teachers' opposition to the idea of development is, in fact, based on theory that either has been superseded or was never truly advanced by developmentalists like Freud and Piaget in the first place.

The transformative tale defuses some of the more common charges leveled against a use of developmental theory in the teaching of writing in college: that the theory applies only to the "formative years" and not to college-age adults, that it devalues the role of language in learning and creating thought, that it is empirically based (Habermas and Gadamer, in fact, are deeply united in their belief in the limits of natural-science methodology), that it rejects the influence of environmental or social or cultural contexts, that it is behaviorist and cannot deal with reflective or meta-thinking, that it believes change is strictly linear, that it fosters universal or mechanistic or automatic or preset programs for instruction, that it rejects interactive or dialogic models of learning, that it is simplistic and reductive of human complexity, and that it creates an unreal, lockstep and age-bound ladder of growth that can be unfairly used as a deficit model to tag some students as backward or even permanently deficient (I am summarizing Berthoff, Kogen, Rose 1988, Dixon; a brilliantly clear rebuttal to many of these arguments is Hays 1987a). Recent developmental theory shows that much of this attack is now directed at a straw man. Compared with the formative telling of Freud, Piaget, and the early information-processing developmentalists, present theory extends development far past the college years, adopts a constructivist and meta-cognitive notion of knowledge, accepts the deep implications of language in human evolution, embraces interaction between self and environment as intrinsic to growth, and takes as normal all sorts of recursions, variance of scheduling, and other departures from the universal and linear. In short, recent theorists have applied the same antidevelopment criticism to their own discipline. No one believes any more, with Gesell, Hull, and Skinner, in a "species-indifferent, activity-indifferent, and context-indifferent" model of development (Brown: 99). And everyone, in one way or another, has shifted the notion of development much farther along the spectrum toward the learning end.

This is not to say that an older monolithic one has been replaced by a recent monolithic one. The variety of contemporary theorizing—not to speak of the astonishing volume of it—is nothing short of inspirational, the extremes ranging from those who believe, with Donald M. Baer, that developmental learning has no relation to age, to those who believe, with Bernard Kaplan, that it has no relation to maturational constraints, to those who argue, with David Feldman, that it lies entirely outside people and only within disciplines, to those who argue, with C. J. Brainerd, that it has nothing to do with stages but is purely accretionary, to those who follow the social phenomenologists Gubrium and Buckholdt and assume that developmental change exists only in what people make out of it through discourse and action. In fact, the plurality of "stories" has inspired a certain despair that perhaps there are no universal developmental patterns, that inquiry is doomed to find an "essential messiness" (Kessen: 15). I do not intend to get lost in this attractive wilderness, nor even to attempt a survey (for that, see Lerner and Busch-Rossnagel, Brown, Case, Brown and Reeves, Liben 1987a: 237–52). Rather, I will attempt two steps at once, both pertinent to my main argument that the transformative tale provides a reliable guide for writing teachers: first, that its major turns are supported by recent theory from a variety of fields, and second, that the tale and theory together generate recommendations teachers can apply directly to writing situations.

Self-contradiction. Begin again with the initial state of a learner. It is important to see that Piaget's theory that humans progress through cognitive stages has fared worse than his postulate that a main spur for progress is disequilibrium, by which he meant a state when mental organizations are not sufficient to assimilate novel information. Current theorists have expanded the notion of disequilibrium, making it more of a permanent and more of an internal condition where, as in Habermas's conception, one part of the self conflicts with another, usually unconsciously. So in the formulation of the late psychologist and historian Klaus Riegel, human change is neither open (merely accumulative) nor closed (characterized by sudden, stage-like reorganizations) but is dialectical, a complex, open-ended, ongoing striving toward a state of inner-outer stability ("coordination"), a striving in which four main continua—the two inner ones of the biological and the psychological and the two outer ones of the cultural and the physical—are always interacting and yet separately progressing at different rates, producing, when they fall out of coordination, confrontations that lead to new coordination (1972, 1979; see Wozniak for a history of this position). Others may visualize the inner contradictions differently. Heinz Werner, otherwise very similar to Riegel, sees a battle when the organism's innate need to grow more and more differentiated tries to integrate a growing number of tasks requiring competencies arising from different, interactive levels of development (an important concept labeled "embeddedness," Lerner 1984: 24–25). Robert Kegan, generally following the lead of Erik Erikson, sees a constant tension between an already constructed world view (a "holding environment") and a new one encouraged by interaction with a changed social environment, the encounter characterized on one side by a drive toward self-independence ("autonomy") and on the other by a drive toward social acceptance ("inclusion"). Sidney Strauss sees a clash between sets of conceptual tools, for instance between a spontaneously acquired method of numerical counting and a school-taught one based on sets. Carl Bereiter sees the clash between automatized and not yet automatized skills, Jane Loevinger (1976) and James R. Rest between more liberal intellectual knowledge and more conservative affective ties, Joanne Kurfiss (1977) between areas of interest more advanced in expertise and areas of ignorance less advanced.

For teachers, this emphasis on internal conflict means that *instruction does not have to wait helpless until the student grows some inner state of "readiness."* (The now classic rejection of readiness is Bruner 1963: 33–54.) The student will already be in a state of self-contradiction, always more or less ready to make that inner shift of perspective that prompts generative learning. If a student does reside in a condition of self-satisfaction and hence unteachability, that occupation is brief compared with time living in the unstable and hence ductile transitional periods between such periods (Flavell 1977: 246–47; Feldman 1980: 73–85; Salkind: 194). *Student writers are not as fixed in their present stage as even they might imagine.* This also means that self-contradictory performance is a normal outcome of learning. Early on, skill building is always characterized by a patchiness or "hard-wiring." Subskills are weakly integrated, automaticity uneven, routines poorly accessed. *Teachers should expect a piece of writing from a student to be uneven in quality.* This is why holistic evaluation does not assess developmental progress very well. It is the even piece of writing that, like Blake's standing water, should be avoided as poisonous, warning that the writer is least ready to learn or has failed to have advanced. It follows that *teachers may have as much reason to encourage unevenness as to demand the "perfect" or "well-rounded" essay.* A reasonable teaching goal may be "induced instability" (Heath: 175) or "calculated incongruities" (Hays 1983a: 141).

Alienation. Recent theory, then, sees the evolving self not as fully open to experience as in the imitative tale nor, on the other hand, as helplessly closed to experience in a formative stage awaiting inner epigenesis, but somewhere in the middle, at best maintaining a momentary "evolutionary truce" (Kegan), with "a mind both unified and fractionated" (Fischer, Hand, and Russell: 57). Consequently, the theory tends to picture the learner confronting new experience, with both hopes and fears, "both exhilarated and anxious, excited and troubled" (Feldman 1980: 83). This picture of a divided, restless self allows the generative role of outer influences. Four of the developmentalists whose theories have had the most influence since Piaget give more due to the environment as a force in inner development: Erik Erikson, with his tale of major cultural thresholds, such as weaning, schooling, courtship, marriage, and work, precipitating inner crises; Lev Vygotsky, with his tale of social communication gradually internalized to become part of the inner language vital to further development; Jerome Bruner, with a similar tale of increasingly complex, culture-specific representational systems (enactive, iconic, symbolic) helping to develop increasingly complex cognitive capabilities; and Klaus Riegel, with his tale of the evolving history of a society altering the inner evolution of an individual who has by chance been born into that history. At its mildest, this trend toward contextualism has qualified Freud's system by pointing out that it may fit pre-WWI bourgeois Vienna but not necessarily other societies, and has loosened Piaget's cognitive stages by showing that the time (though not the sequence) of the stages is considerably altered by altering the variables of culture, schooling, and experimental situation. At its strongest, this trend argues that some of the changes our culture regularly sees in humans and therefore assumes are biologically given are not seen by other cultures—changes such as formal operations, adolescent rebellion, mid-life crisis, and senile memory loss. Of course the argument that theories of development are value-laden (for instance, that Western "theories of moral and social development have been ethnocentric, logocentric, and phallocentric," Bernstein 1986: 9) does not argue that development is all a fiction or is a nonessential factor in education but just that a valid interpretive map of development will lie further from the determinism and universalism of the formative and closer to Habermas's vision of freedom to change through reflective critique and to Gadamer's vision of the "inner historicity of experience."

The implications for the teacher are significant. On the one hand, if developmental lodgments are also class, social, and cultural lodgments, attempts by the teacher to dislodge will be taken by the student as some sort of alienation. "Es ist so bequem, unmündig zu sein," wrote Kant. "It is so convenient to be immature." The situation recommends a teaching strategy that Bruner has described as "inductive to the margin of anxiety," a strategy that he argues many cultures apply traditionally (1972). The inner developmental state of students is necessary but not sufficient to prompt most learning. *The teacher can and should intervene for change because such intervention is the way generative change occurs socially.* On the other hand, to the degree lodgments are cultural, they also give students leeway to change and hence legitimize this intervention. That leeway is limited by developmental constraints, both social and biological, but it exists. It can rightly be called teacher space, the area shaped by the difference between what students will learn on their own and what they can learn prompted by a teacher. Conceived in such a developmental frame, teacher space was first seen clearly by Vygotsky. It has turned out to be one of his most fruitful concepts. He termed it the "zone of proximal development," but whether called by that name or another ("plus-one modelling," "bandwidth," "optimal level"), it has been the one area most productively explored by developmental educators (Brown and Reeves, Wozniak, Strauss 1987). To reduce the resistance from the learner's sense of alienation, *teachers should be aware of developmental constraints in order to know and teach within constraint leeway.*

For teaching, constraint leeway is more productive than restrictive. For instance, it stands as the best source for writing models. They will not so much attract emulation, as in the imitative tale, or awaken identification, as in the formative, as they will arouse some reaction in between, perhaps a sense of curiosity, part admiration, part envy, part self-accusation. *The best model will be what learners sense they can do but know they have not yet done.* (The role of imitation in development has enjoyed a revival, with Vygotsky as its guru: Brown and Reeves: 1976; Case: 268–69; Bruner 1986a: 106–8.) Another instance is the "dynamic interaction" (Lerner 1978) between individual development and culture. If culture is necessary for change, then in the end that change can never be against culture. For culture is not given by nature but is created and maintained by people. It itself develops. It develops itself. Change modifying culture may be harder for a teacher to induce than change maintaining it, but not so much harder as one would think. Students know less what they may change into than what they are, and their sense of alienation may be much the same whether the *atopon* they face is or is not culturally respectable. Our uniting of Habermas and Gadamer argues that *the pedagogical means for furthering development will be the same whether the ends are foundational or radical.*

Re-action. The new theory views the student as not on one learning track ("single sequence model") but simultaneously on several ("multiple sequence model"). In what I take to be the new position most significant for writing teachers, the theory further envisions a "complex sequence" (Riegel 1972). The difference is that multiple levels of being not only interact with the environment at different paces but also interact with each other ("embeddedness"). As a result, skill-level A in one area may not merely serve as a foundation for skill-level B, as in Piaget, but may undergo modification or even substitution by B (Flavell and Wohlwill). With embeddedness, the progression is not merely hierarchical in a building-block way. It is genuinely dialectical, where previous blocks have to be destroyed, reshaped, rearranged to form the new structure. Change then proceeds as much backward as forward, is re-active to be active. In Perry's scheme of developing ethical cognition, the adolescent position that our authorities are right and their authorities are wrong ("dualism") is a useful learning step to the next position: that neither our authorities nor theirs can be proven wrong ("multiplistic"). But it is a step that has to be unlearned to get there. Such a developmental dynamics has been worked out by Case in information processing. But it is in theories of psychological development that a dialectics of "complex" or re-active sequencing holds most sway, perhaps on the precedence of Freud's therapeutic notion that old fixations must be destroyed to release healthy development. As Erikson puts it, the individual has to "take chances in the next stage with what was most vulnerably precious in the previous one" (1985 [1950]: 263). For instance, the validation of ego identity needed by the adolescent has to be in part surrendered by the adult to achieve intimacy with another person (see Rest: 52–67 for a full defense of this complex model over simpler models).

Now in all fields this action of modifying previous embedded positions consistently takes three forms, all extremely insightful for the writing teacher who wishes to help students achieve generative change. (1) It is revisionary. It requires a deliberate return to and confrontation of old positions, usually in some sort of Gadamerian mode of retesting the adequacy of what one knows to find out why one cannot answer a question. Such recursion may take the form of a search over old problem-solving procedures (as in the "hindsight" of Langley and Simon), or a reassessment of the self to find ways to meet a changing environment (as in Kegan's "renegotiated balance"), or simply a retreat or deflection or escape from the alien, an "alienation" itself that turns out to be somehow a necessary hiatus preparatory to change ("a space of meaninglessness between received belief and creative faith," Perry 1981: 92). For the writing teacher, recursion means that the new techniques or understandings of writing will be learned only by active comparison with the old. *Learning is as much a revision of old practices as a trial of new ones.* The pedagogy, it must be emphasized, refutes the standard idea that writing skill proceeds stepwise and that to rise to a new step, the student must brace one foot securely on a solid lower step. *Re-action is not review,* which if anything aids only assimilative learning. *Generative advance in writing proceeds not only by acquiring new frames but also by breaking old frames.* The writing discipline's recent replacement of a linear conception of the writing process with a "recursive" notion runs, of course, parallel with developmental theory. The metaphor of change is no longer stairs (the favorite image of Piaget and other formativists who took as their model biological epigenesis) but an ascending spiral or helix (Werner: 137; Perry 1981: 97; Langer: 95–96; Kegan: 108 passim; Chickering 1969: 8; Hays 1987a: 13).

(2) Re-action is regressive. Viewed horizontally, as along a time line, the spiral shows not Joseph Williams's growth chart but a rightward moving cycle of rise and fall. An up-close, partial, Zeno view could easily see only one phase, something like Eugene Hammond's graph of Kitzhaber's findings. An even closer shot might see only a decline. Regression, in fact, features as a medial outcome or logical step in nearly every major study or theory of developmental learning in the past thirty years. In Jonas Langer's blunt developmentalist translation of *reculer pour mieux sauter,* "The first step toward progress

is regress" (95). Regress may take the quid-pro-quo form of internal give-and-take, where one subskill suffers so that another can advance (Feldman 1980; Loevinger 1986: 71–72), of a "starting anew" where the confrontation with novel tasks encourages a search for old creative grounds to "utilize the primitive" (Werner: 129), of "functional regression" (Kohlberg) or "fallback strategy" (Fischer, Hand, and Russell) to handle novel situations with an established though inadequate structure (Langer: 93–95; Riegel 1973: 365), of misapplication or overgeneralization of a newly learned rule or procedure (Keil 1984: 89; Bever 1982), of slips in attempting more difficult skills (Freedman and Pringle 1980b: 323), of incomplete automaticity or internalization on first learning a new skill (Vygotsky 1978: 89–91; Bereiter: 76), of loss in handling of detail when new and poorly instantiated frames replace old frames (Labouvie-Vief 1981: 205–9), or simply of a perspectival distortion, where because different areas mature within individuals at different rates, one area appears to backslide when another advances (Riegel 1972: 98; Perry 1981: 89). *It is to be expected that advance in writing skill will not be unilateral but will be accompanied by regression in some skills.* Teachers who aim to effect generative acts of learning, not short-term course learning, must resign themselves to the unrewarding labor of planting the seeds without often seeing the material harvest.

(3) Re-action is reflective. Habermas's contention that self-reflective knowledge is an essential step toward genuine change is widely confirmed by recent developmentalists. Information processing has theorized and detected a variety of reflective procedures, not only the behavioristic "feedback loops" that allow the learner, usually unaware, to appraise results and thereby modify procedures, but also much more self-aware techniques, "recognition mechanisms" (Langley and Simon: 369–70), conscious monitorings that abstractly consider problems and executive choices: "understanding feedback, figuring out how to act on feedback" (Sternberg 1984b: 166).

These meta-procedures are paralleled by acts of meta-consciousness in the psychological arena and meta-cognition in the cognitive (Brown). For Perry "meta-thought" is "the most critical moment in the whole adventure for both student and teachers" (1981: 85), when the learner uses reflection to break free from an old automatized and hence unconscious frame. As far as I know, only Bruner has approached stating the notion as a hard-and-fast rule (1986a: 73), but a survey of experiments and theory suggests the axiom that all generative acts of developmental learning must entail some reflection or objectivization of previous positions. *For writing to advance, old and less mature procedures must be made conscious.* And though it is not always so, the main mechanism for achieving this act of self-reflection appears to be language, the all-purpose instrument in Bruner's "cultural tool kit" for achieving lasting personal change, "the most powerful means we have for performing transformations on the world" (1968: 109; see also Vygotsky's notion of "internalized speech"; the "school-based symbol-systems" of Strauss 1972 and Feldman 1987; and Wozniak's argument that linguistic information about the object is necessary for Piagetian accommodation: 234). *The assigned task of writing teachers is to achieve progress in the one skill —language use —that holds the key to progress in all other advanced skills.*

Appropriation. A final major shift from Piaget has been the verification and study of a phenomenon he discovered but treated more as aberration than rule: that learners do not necessarily apply a structural frame they have learned in one situation to other situations, even where it obviously fits ("horizontal décalage"). Children may conserve volume but not weight; adults may think formally in school about a math problem but not at home about a tax issue or may view literary taste multiplistically but religious beliefs dualistically. When it comes to appropriation, the final proof of developmental change, the dictum of Ann Brown, has been confirmed over and over: development is "not species indifferent but domain specific" (99). *Writing teachers should never expect that a skill, once performed, will naturally transfer across the board.* On the other hand, the mass of evidence coming in from studies of learning in specific domains, from map drawing to ethics building, shows little evidence of the loss of generative skill or knowledge once it is gained within that domain. As we have seen with Kitzhaber's study, what looks like decay of skill probably is just the result of testing under new contexts (Keil 1984). Yet confirming Gadamer's analysis of human change in general, meta-cognitive acts of appropriation in all domains have been shown to allow the learner "reflective access" to the learning rules themselves. *Each turn in writing development helps, even if infinitesimally, writing development itself to mature.*

This theorem underscores a final way recent theory supports the transformative and in so doing continues to depart from the formative. Development hands teachers and students an arena full of constraints. But few of those constraints are biological. The great majority are specific to discipline and culture, falling under Gadamer's notion of tradition and liable to Habermas's charge of ideology. The constraints themselves are then finite in Gadamer's sense and changeable in Habermas's. From cognition (Labouvie-Vief) to ethical judgment (Gilligan) to ego formation (Kaplan) to skill learning (Bruner), the trend of developmental theory has been to recognize that human development is deeply free. Every developmental act transforms the constraints that constituted the domain *as* developmental. "Only those beings," Kaplan insists, "who could be construed as capable of utilizing means for the attainment of invariant ends could be said to have the possibility of development." The rest is mere change (55). It's not only that writing teachers should be aware of developmental constraints for successful teaching; *they should be aware that every time they are successful in teaching they have helped create a developmental constraint.* This is the final turn where development spirals back upon itself in order to transcend itself. *A teacher of writing faithful to human development will help students alter and thereby escape that very development.*

So to the degree that contemporary developmentalists recognize that they are describing a "probabilistic" (Lerner 1984:24), disciplinary, domain-specific, cultural and historical artifact, they tend to be aware of the danger of fooling themselves that they are describing something else, something nature-given, and hence are witlessly perpetuating ideology, not furthering what surely is the original evolutionary or survival benefit of human development: to alter when it alteration finds. To circle back to Bruner's passage, if developmentalists "fail to examine their value presuppositions while hiding behind the naturalistic fallacy, developmental theory will risk serving as the mindless handmaiden of implicit beliefs in the culture rather than as a vigorous participant in the debate about the next generation" (1986b: 27). Habermas and Gadamer have already told us the kind of participation the writing teacher should take in that debate: dialogue. *A course in composition should be neither merely a selling of nor merely a critique of culture but rather an open dialogue between teacher and student, the goal of which is the development of that culture formed by the unforced future writing of the student.*

I end this rough survey by stressing two ways recent theory has continued to uphold the formative tale of Freud, Piaget, and the early information processors.[4] These ways recommend two working rules that teachers of writing cannot afford to discard as passé. First, whether studying children or adults, whether observing the solving of balance-beam problems or the construction of moral frames, researchers have continued to find invariant sequences. Movement along the sequence may lack

---

[4] Here is as good a spot as any to apologize for the way I have made these original and complex thinkers themselves appear immature. I would not like to be a part, for instance, of what Bruner calls the "vulgarization of Piagetian theory" (1986a: 23). In Piaget's fertile works can be found expressions of nearly every one of these transformative advances on Piaget. One quote will have to make amends, in which we find Piaget ridiculing the very belief in the epigenetic, time-bound, lockstepped, stage sequence he is so often ridiculed for holding: "Let us suppose that the structural variations of the child's thought are determined from within, bound by an immutable order of

sureness, uniform front, dependency on age, or regular tempo, and individuals may appear sometimes to manage two turns forward at once. But observers have rediscovered over and over Piaget's insight that in the acquisition of a particular skill, certain turns require prerequisite turns. *In the learning of writing skills, there are sequences that teachers contravene only to the loss of time and gain of frustration* (see chapter 12). Second, the theory has generally maintained Freud's operating belief that individual acts of change at any age occur embedded in a field governed by three basic developmental movements: broad ontogenetic change spanning years and even decades, brief assimilative learning experiences taking place even in the space of seconds, and therapeutic or pedagogical change needing anywhere from a conference period to a few months. Therein, in Sidney Strauss's "middle ground," the learner-developer can achieve lasting reorganizations of affect and knowledge. *The term or semester is ample time to further genuine developmental change.* The first of these two points maintains Piaget's and Gadamer's vision of prior constraint, the second Freud's and Habermas's vision of free critique. Both are held in uneasy and gravid synthesis in the tale of transformation.

Appropriation of the Transformative by the Writing Teacher

So far this book has forced together, like opposite poles of magnets, the contradictions of several popular pedagogical narratives: the English-teacher moral entertainment, the legend of deterioration, and the simple country tale of natural growth;

---

succession and an unvarying chronology, each stage beginning at its appointed moment and occupying a precisely ordained period of the child's life; suppose, in a word, that the development of individual thought is comparable to an embryology obeying strict hereditary rules, then the consequences would be incalculable for education: the teacher would be wasting his time and his effort attempting to speed up the development of his students, and the problem would simply be that of finding out what knowledge corresponded to each stage" (1970: 167).

the close-up of Zeno and the distance shot of Wordsworth. It has re-acted the more sharply contradictory classroom practices of the imitative and the formative frames and endured the alienation of a swing outside English-department territory through the theories of Habermas, Gadamer, and recent developmentalists. Home again from such a lengthy interpretive circuit, it is time to see if the experience has transformed our view of college writing instruction in concrete ways, has developed a critical or regulative idea that as teachers we can appropriate and apply. That inquiry will occupy the rest of this book.

By way of preview, and completion of business still on the table, let us take up again the finding of chapter 3: that undergraduate writing in the Sample shows a pervasive trend or tropism toward working-world competence in writing. The bracketed question was, Does this particular noctambulation allow anything for teachers to do? With that query unanswered, we have no compelling reason to stop the teacher who, I understand, on leaving a presentation on college-age development, said, "I prefer to think students can be taught." Indeed, at first glance both trajectory and target of the Sample's ballistic flight seem to map teachers outside the course of action. But that is from the angle of the imitative and the formative. The perspective of the transformative draws teachers back in. It integrates a course in writing with the Sample's course of development.

Consider again, one last time, the Monday-morning question about teaching the junior Essay J and the employee Essay M to freshmen. The transformative unrolls a generous list of possible actions for teachers: to know and use long-term developmental trends common in the culture; to know and use short-term developmental trends manifested by the writing discipline; to determine and work the students' "growing edge" of competence, the proximal zone of development where teacher space lies; to detect and attack immature presuppositions by sounding and bringing contradictions to the surface; to seek and respect regressions and interactions in subskills; to choose and foster writing goals with an understanding of developmental facts, treating accordingly those goals that are cultural and those that are anticultural. Contrary to its reputation, development here locates a trove of ways students can be taught.

Here is a representative pick. Despite the initial English-teacher disapproval of Essay J in comparison with Essay F and despite the current bad odor of imitation generally as a teaching technique, the transformative recommends the junior piece for freshmen. It argues that the essay will not teach itself but, in fact, requires a teacher's "loan of consciousness" (Vygotsky 1962) to guide beginning students to upper-division accomplishments. One such achievement is the dialectical structure of Essay J. Age-span studies have shown dialectical thinking under slow acquisition during the college years (Perry 1981; Basseches 1989), and the writing discipline offers some evidence that older college students argue dialectically in compositions somewhat more often than do younger (Hays and Brandt). Only one of the sixty-four freshmen essays in the Sample was organized dialectically, but six of the sixty-four sophomore and junior essays were. Given this history of reluctant inclination, the transformative suggests a rather stout intervention. Instead of describing dialectical thought in the abstract (thesis, antithesis, synthesis), the teacher would make freshmen aware of those presuppositions that keep them from seeing things dialectically. Using two entry-level positions in ethical thinking identified by Perry, the teacher could show first how each of the contraries in the first two paragraphs of Essay J can be defended, then second how they negate each other (the structure of social codes is both beneficial and an entrapment; what some people expect, others do not wish). Freshmen would first become aware that they have been rejecting positions that have some legitimacy and then that they have been accepting positions that logically contradict, making them more likely to see, like, and appropriate the next logical and developmental step: the resolution of contrary positions.

The transformative defends this focus on the structural achievement of Essay J because it is supported by human development in general, which proceeds generatively to the degree underlying frames are altered. The focus would also be supported by that small band of writing teachers still convinced of the pedagogical value of imitation, since typically they argue that modeling techniques succeed to the extent that they cue students to underlying forms rather than to surface features. But surface features are empowered by their own surface structures, and developmental information will help teachers make choices there as well. On the level of the sentence, the Sample backs up Joseph Williams's contention that students will lengthen their sentences "willy-nilly," and adds that they will be doing so already as freshmen and sophomores. Knowledge of particular trends, however, will help teachers shape and direct that tendency rather than leave it to carry students off. If teachers like the way mature writers pack sentences with information, then they may use the fact that both sophomores and juniors show a strong advance in final free modification. The rhetorical effect of the following sentence of Essay J might be singled out for study or imitation: <u>This type of restraining is not always the case and is usually found where codes of behavior have been strictly enforced, to the point of near entrapment.</u> On the other hand, if teachers prefer good sentence dynamics over mere sentence length, they can work especially hard with freshmen to develop the syntactic maneuvers that the juniors do not pick up on their own but that the matured writers clearly develop: parallelism, simplification of nominal subjects, and mixing of extralong and extrashort sentences.

This sentence illustrates the potential for teachers in understanding developmental regressions. Compared with the freshmen behind and the employees ahead, the juniors in the Sample fall back in two statistically significant areas, specifically in nominal coordination and generally in all kinds of syntactic parallelism. Instead of treating this as a fallback demanding correction, the formative takes it as a fallout from growth elsewhere. The juniors, for example, expand their logical grasp of hierarchical class relationships. This they naturally express with syntactic complication of nominals. They do so not through coordination but through modification—a developmental advance in the sense that the matured writers carry such modification further. Here the transformative perspective shows the teacher first the quid-pro-quo interdependency of these two syntactic forms and then a normal sequence of developing them in undergraduates, indicating that teaching freshmen better syntactic parallelism may take extra effort and might well proceed after attention to logical modification. It also predicts that instruction in parallelism may well lead initially to an increase in comma splices and run-ons and probably to an awkward placement of coordination toward the front of the sentence. Consequently, it recommends a certain lenience on the teacher's part toward these forms.

Through such developmental interactions, the transformative opens up diagnostic entry to a storehouse of unsuspected teaching space. Take the connection of free modification and logical qualification. Essay J's one clear instance of final free modification (to the point of near entrapment) occurs in a sentence expressing a double hedge. By contrast, Essay F has no final free modification at all. A second look at the essays discovers that J qualifies often, whereas F is characterized by many absolute expressions: perfectly, nothing special, just because, simply portraying, didn't know the first thing, only have an I.Q. of 50. Unlike the quid-pro-quo relationship of sentence faults with sentence length, here we have a supportive relationship of syntax with argument, where instruction in one may well advance the other. The transformative perspective, in fact, often transforms negatives into positives, or absences into presences. It is easy to see the absence of concrete specifics in Essay J, but the transformative sees the maturing junior's advance in inferential thinking, in strong conclusions, in variety of T-unit length, in more sophisticated vocabulary—all possibly aided by the presence of high-level generalities.

The power these mysterious conjunctions of subskills lend teachers stems from the way they tap transformative currents. Teachers learn and lead from the strengths of students, the instincts of the novice combining with the knowledge of the tutor. On the one hand, the teachers rely on the intuitions of undergraduates, watching their almost litmus sensitivity to what the culture will expect of their writing outside of college. Before automatically condemning the juniors' growth in noun adjuncts, unstated transitions, or homophone errors, teachers might ask why competent employees share those predilections (following chapters will find good reasons). On the other hand, the teachers rely on their own intuitions. Better than anyone else, they can make sense and pedagogical use of developmental interactions and transformations, deciding where instruction should be focused and how much energy will be needed to make a difference. Trends in the Sample argue that little time need be delegated to convince freshmen that the first-person singular or plural pronoun is the easiest solution to the gender imbroglio in Essay J's sentence: Codes of conduct restrict the individual to where in many cases one feels he/orshe can not function in the way they wish. Historically, that is a solution students themselves find. But those teachers—including myself—who would like to sensitize freshmen permanently to the dangers of using euphemistic catchphrases—such as Essay J's considerable role, individuals interacting in society, day to day situations, creative spirit within us—will have to sustain a forceful strategy of instruction, since that language is fostered in a thousand ways by our culture, as the undergraduate trends and the employee performance show full well.

Constraints, Freedoms, and Wishes

Enough examples for the moment. The essential point is that the transformative perspective does not reduce the teacher's options but informs them. This book began with the generalization that learning involves standards, change, and status, to all of which, it is true, the transformative has added certain specifications. It has recognized the continued presence of developmental constraints in the growth of postadolescents—constraints in cognitive processing, in stored knowledge, in psychological bent, in cultural sequencing, perhaps even in a few remaining postadolescent biological upthrusts. But—to adopt the philosophical distinction of Alfred North Whitehead—these constraints involve antecedents, not subsequents. They help define what students are, not what they may become. The constraints themselves undergo change. It is not paradox but *doxa,* the basic transformative law, to say that constraints are freeing: they serve as the instrument of generative change for whatever end teacher and student together negotiate.

It is a remarkable irony that the fact of human development, which experts cannot distinguish from human learning, should be taken as an enemy of teachers. The transformative role of the educator is not just the honorable propaedeutic one of midwifery. It is also hermeneutic, a Hermes-like or tutelary trickery of students into an experiential genesis of new knowledge out of old. And it is also therapeutic (*theraps:* servant), an honest seneschal-like or advisory persuasion of students into the critical replacement of limiting frames with better ones. In one word, it is *creative.* The "set" *standards* that initially we took to define an act of learning are preset only if that is what teachers and students together want to develop.

The transformative, then, also further specifies our initial vector of *change,* as this chapter has taken special pains to show. It defines genuine learning—again in one word—as *self-actualizing.* The term, of course, is Abraham H. Maslow's, designating a peak flowering of personality so rare and late-blooming that after a survey of some three thousand college students, he had only one clear exemplar and no more than two dozen potentials (150). Charlotte Bühler, Jane Loevinger, Arthur Chickering, Robert J. Havighurst, and other life-span theorists have proposed awareness of limitations, conscientiousness, self-adjustment, and other effects of

155

self-actualization as midcareer culminations. But in a less demanding sense, self-actualization can be taken as the basic quotidian fact of development: maturity defines and creates itself only by its own acts. The fact applies from birth to death, across the board in art, science, language, and individuality. "Poetry," says the poet Allen Ginsberg, "is what poet's write" —not what critics say it should be. "Literature," agrees the critic Northrop Frye, "shapes itself." Traditions, Habermas tells Gadamer, can be altered by critique, but critique itself, Ricoeur reminds Habermas, is an evolving tradition. The notion that traditions are exploded by science, Karl Popper reminds scientists, is itself exploded when we recognize that science progresses only by generalizing its own traditions and exploding them in turn: "Science advances by the tradition of changing its traditional myths" (130). After building one of the most influential theories of cultural development, Bruner reminds himself that theories of cultural change themselves change culture, and he puts the central transformational fact in one pregnant sentence: "A culture is constantly in process of being recreated as it is interpreted" (1986a: 123). To the extent that concepts of maturity themselves mature and that interpretation is creative, writing teachers are free of developmental constraints. "Each day," as that original father of the transformative, Heraclitus, put it, "Each day the sun is new."

But teachers are not free of the mechanisms of development and, through them, the responsibility to the student. For the *status* of the student also grows in specificity under the transformative. Students are not just learning, informing themselves of knowledge and accumulating skill, nor just growing, performing some epigenetic migratory destiny, but are transforming and developing in the transitive sense of the verbs. As a nation develops its resources or a community develops plans for a park or painters develop their art, writing students act as agents of their own transformation. And as subagents of that transformation, as subdevelopers or architects of that development, writing teachers share that development but also take on the responsibility of the hierarch to mind ahead and the burden of the servant to remind behind. The instructor helps society construct the student and helps the student construct society.

They take on as well the frustration of teachers. If the imitative and the formative tales are narrative wish-fulfillments arising, as Frederic Jameson would imagine, out of the contradiction between what teachers hope students are learning and what students feel they are learning, then the transformative tale must express a comparable sublimation of thwarted desires. The difference, I would hazard, is that teachers who project themselves into some kind of transformative tale sense less the failure of students to learn and more the failure of students to learn as much as they might. The contradiction arises not out of issues involving particular lore but out of those involving time. Such teachers suffer from a Wordsworthian double consciousness, of students unaware that they are wasting their time and of teachers unable or unwilling to reach across the "vacancy" to help. The teachers' frustration partakes of Habermas's anger that society will not free itself as soon as it can from ideological oppression and of Gadamer's sadness that people do not sooner open themselves to the true generative nature of experience and tradition. Whether the transformative tale is more or less of a wish than the imitative and the formative remains to be seen.

No doubt each widespread protonarrative has its own truth. I would like to imagine, however, that the transformative transcends the other tales by performing that aboriginal act of transformation, by ingesting them. Doesn't it partake of the formative yearning for inner change, the imitative approval of teacher action, the deteriorative relish for regression, Zeno's love of minute increments, Wordsworth's fondness for mountaintop prospects, even the English-teacher trust in standards derived from the discipline? But that thought probably lies somewhere beyond mortal wishes.

There is, however, the unquestionable fact that study of the transformative has circled back to English-teacher traditions. Far from excluding composition teachers, as chapter 3 feared, development embraces them as adepts, transmitters, and shapers of their own domain's tradition of maturing, although it asks that they integrate this tradition with other, more universal patterns of maturing. It follows that the ultimate source of freedom and power for the teacher comes from specific knowledge of developmental trends, all kinds. Following David Feldman's advice that teachers should look first to the maturing patterns in their own disciplines, the next six chapters will extract transformative recommendations from a rather Zeno-like dissection of the writing in the Sample—before standing back one last time in part 5 to consider how a Wordsworthian or, in today's jargon, a life-span prospect can further form and transform the transformative tale into practice.

PART IV

Style and Development

God to Mephistopheles:
Until Faust stops living
That long you may do as you will.
Humans keep stumbling as long as
they keep on striving.
—Johann Wolfgang von Goethe,
prologue, *Faust*

CHAPTER 6

Tales of Style:
Nomothetic and Idiographic

A USEFUL VARIANT OF THE TRANSFORMATIVE
tale of maturing is told in a short story by Jorge Luis Borges. It
bears the gnomish title of "Undr." An eleventh-century Ice-
lander, Ulf Sigurdarson, hears that the poetry of a southern
people called the Urnos consists of one word alone. Ulf is an
aspiring bard and understandably wants to learn the word. He
finds his way to the Urnos, who turn out to be a dwindling and
barbaric tribe living in the lower reaches of the Vistula River
near the Baltic Sea. Unfortunately, during the one chance Ulf
has to hear their poetry sung, he fails to catch the word, whose
meaning the Urnos themselves have lost. Nor will an old skald
living among the Urnos, Bjarni Thorkelsson, tell the word to
him. "Nobody can teach anything," Bjarni says. "You will have
to find it yourself." Ulf leaves the Urnos, and after many adven-
tures—as slave, bandit, lover, betrayer, murderer—he returns.
This time because Bjarni is dying, the old poet sings the word
for Ulf. It is *undr,* which means, as the contemporary Argen-
tinian retelling this story puts it, *maravilla:* marvel. In Bjarni's
song Ulf now hears the sound of his own poem about his own

life, and he picks up Bjarni's harp and sings. But he does not use *undr*. He sings to a different word. "You have understood," says Bjarni.

It is not hard to glimpse in Ulf's novitiate the matrix spiral of our own tale of transformative maturing. Caught at first in self-contradiction, yearning to act as his own bard but following a faulty prejudgment that poetry has only one language, Ulf fails to understand the art, suffers through the alienation of travels and experiences elsewhere, returns and re-acts his old desires to be an expert skald, and in a successful act of transformation, appropriates the craft, makes it his own.

Those of us preoccupied with the contemporary craft of writing, however, can also see in "Undr" an implication of the transformative that I have held in abeyance so far. That is the approach it takes to the question of student writing and personal style. Gadamer would say that "Undr" maintains the belief (or perhaps illusion) of Friedrich Schleiermacher, Alexander von Humboldt, and other Romantic philosophers of language that writing can convey the unique life and personality of each individual. Habermas might say that the story reflects the human potential to escape the prison of pseudocommunication by inventing one's own life story. Literary historians will recognize "Undr" as one of the several protonarratives of Jorge Luis Borges expressing the modernist concept of literary voice. According to that still tempting idea, a fully developed writing style is the signature of the writer. Like any marvel, personal style does not recur; it resists imitation, defeats the hope of perfect translation. In measure that style has been merely taught, it is only stylish, artificial. To help students develop a genuine *undr*, teachers can only encourage them to set out on their own.

This vision of personal style stands as one of the fructifying centers of twentieth-century literary consciousness. And yet as we near the end of the century, it stands under siege everywhere—no more so than in composition studies, where the expressivist paradigm of a Ken Macrorie or a Richard Young looks dim and medieval compared with the shining new social-contextual paradigm of an Elaine Maimon or a David Bartholomae, a standard whose ends of academic or technical writing direct students to master the accepted style of established groups—the proper format for a biochemistry lab report or the going jargon of an architectural grant proposal. Given the impersonal voice required by some of this writing, and the group voice underwritten by all of it, the teacher's task seems less to help students find their own *undr* than to help them hide what vestiges of it they might still retain. This new social-contextual paradigm, of course, is in turn under attack from resurgent forces who question the ethics of a pedagogy encouraging the cultivation or enculturation of a style defined as more acceptable the nearer it approaches anonymous submergence into whatever institutions happen to be around. Currently, Borges's fantasy leads straight into the middle of the discipline's best candidate for a real-life, hands-on ideological battle.

And therefore it leads into a pedagogical bind, one locked not only into the profession but within every teacher, whenever he or she speaks from a majority or conventional position. That is most of the time, of course. Choosing models for writing, constructing placement-exam rubrics, penciling in surface emendations, the teacher takes sides in a mute conflict over stylistic rights. That Bakhtinian struggle between the individual voice and the group voice lies at the center of any inquiry into the best sequence of instruction for apprentice writers in our craft (see Fulwiler). Therefore it should be an issue informed by a developmental perspective. Does that approach side with Ulf or the Urnos?

Style, Development, and the Nomothetic and Idiographic

In part it depends on the particular developmental standard one wishes to hold aloft. Especially the formative perspective, or perhaps more accurately the "vulgarization" of it, has been charged with a tendency to disregard uniqueness of persons. Composition specialists defending the personal voice accuse formative stage theory of providing simplistic schemes for teachers who want to package or slot students by means of some sort of apparatus for socialization, "levelling rather than elaborating individual differences" (Rose 1988: 294). Most of the developmentalists during the first six or seven decades of this century, from Gesell to Jung to Maslow, were also trait psychologists or differential psychometricians, yearning to find and describe human universals. They wanted to begin with a general law (say, normative performance on the Minnesota Multiphasic) and then describe and advise the individual in terms of it, a procedure now termed *nomothetic*. But the nomothetic operation ends up moving in the reverse direction, away from the individual. As that tireless defender of the individual, Gordon Allport, put it in a famous lecturing of his fellow psychologists on the dangers of the nomothetic, they consider "Sam," the single case, only "long enough to derive some hypothesis" and then spring "like a gazelle into the realm of abstraction" (1968: 82). The hankering after the nomothetic, of course, can reflect the most altruistic motives for Sam. William C. Crain ends his 1980 book, *Theories of Development,* with a peroration on "Universals." "Developmentalists, like humanists, are trying to show how, at the deepest levels, we are all the same. . . . Hopefully, an appreciation of the positive strivings that we all share can help in the building of a universal human community" (265).

In conscious opposition to the nomothetic procedure, many current developmentalists aim to show how we are all different. Their goal is to describe the unique combination of traits that distinguish each person, a pursuit aptly termed the *idiographic.* [1]

_____

[1] The newer theories of development, says Mark Freeman flatly, are "more conducive to the idiographic than the nomothetic" (15). The term *idiographic* was coined by the German life-philosopher Wilhelm Windelband from the Greek *idiographos:* signature or, literally, one's own sign. Its application to a notion of personal style, then, seems fortuitous, as is its equivalence to the Latin etymology of Ricoeur's term *appropriation.* Windelband's

As Allport expresses it, "Sam, to be sure, has many attributes characteristic of the human species, and many that resemble his cultural fellows: *but he weaves them all into a unique idiomatic system*" (1961:15). This position becomes more credible the more external factors are assumed to influence human development. Given the variety of changing human environments—historical, cultural, and physical—and given the host of arts and crafts with their diverse ways of apprenticeship, the question is no longer whether Ulf and Sam, and Mary, have a personal voice, but which of the infinite *undrs* available to them they ought next to develop. David Feldman ends his 1980 book, *Beyond Universals,* with a peroration on "Individuality." "The desire for individual expression is a part of the heritage of every human being." It is not only a desire but a realistic goal: "All of us can contribute our best efforts to our work—whatever it may be—in a way which carries the stamp of our own individuality" (172–73).

The developmental paradigm I call the transformative extends a tentative offer of conciliation to these two interpretive factions. On the one hand, it describes a nomothetic process of learning in which individuals necessarily begin, over and over, with cultural understandings, which they then revise through experience to generate personal understanding. On the other hand, it describes an idiographic process of self-actualization in which individuals, through unique experiences, help transform the culture. Such a conciliatory position is inevitable, given the way the transformative embraces both Habermas and Gadamer, each of whom tries to place human change in a framework of individual within culture yet each of whom tries to respect the integrity of individuals and cultures—Habermas

---

opposing term, *nomothetic,* derives from *nomothetes:* lawgiver or law enforcer, taking us back to the English-teacher vision of moral entertainment. I like the terms because they reflect that conflict between individual and law so vital to the history of Western culture, during which, for one instance, the Greek idea of the inviolately personal, *idios,* was pejorated in English into *idiotic.*

with his argument that a "principled claim" (such as the concept of ego) makes the individual aware of his or her true uniqueness (1979: 90–91), Gadamer with his argument that genuine experience, an understanding of new and unique events, requires cultural traditions (such as one's language) as a start (1975: 278–305, 397–414). In one sense, the transformative does not take a side in the battle—it is merely an interpretive frame that suggests methods to help teachers further the development of their students toward either a group or an individual voice. In a more accurate sense, the transformative rejects the battle as being fought on false grounds. It argues that any genuine utterance, whether of student or not, expresses the voices of both group and individual, univocally.

The transformative approach, then, will not resolve the writing teacher's bind concerning the question of style. It may, in fact, bind the dilemma more thoroughly into the daily fabric of the teacher's professional life. But the approach does, I believe, offer humane ways of handling issues involving style. Above all, it offers correctives to the present tendency in the discipline toward the erasure of individual gesture. First, understood correctly, it offers (idiographically) frames of action for individuals to try rather than (nomothetically) categories by which to try individuals. In the vocabulary of Habermas, it offers general interpretations rather than explanatory laws. Second, it has a strong bent to return to Ulf, the single case. We ought to remember that the case-study approach, lauded today for its refusal to be lured by the call of the nomothetic (North), was begun by developmentalists. To read most of them— Freud, Jung, Erikson, Laing, Perry, Gilligan, Labouvie-Vief— is to meet subject after individual subject, lovingly described with a sense of human singularity and roundedness found elsewhere only in history, journalism, and fiction writing. Third, current developmental science carries with it a sense of culture as an ever possible threat to individual human growth. It is true that the ranks of developmentalists have always displayed a full political spectrum—with the maturationalists, behaviorists, and information processors providing most of the examples of conservatism. But lately the majority consider seriously Freud's embittered observation: "Every individual is virtually an enemy of civilization" (1928: 9). The tale they tell, in varying degrees of complexity, is Freud's late parable of the "first epic poet" who, like Ulf, in a progressive resistance to the collective myth of the primal horde, invents the heroic or personal myth, "by which the individual emerges from group psychology" (1955: 135–37). Fourth, developmental theory, following its own teaching, tends to develop its own nomothetic pronouncements in the direction of the idiographic. It did not take long before the male-biased schemes of Kohlberg and Perry were transformed to include female realities, as we will see in a minute.

Beyond this ideological bent to take the individual rather than the group as the center of gravity, the transformative has an interpretive virtue for teachers of writing. Frames other than the developmental interpret style in their own way and recommend their own brands of instruction. The writing-across-the-curriculum approach tends to hold what Louis T. Milic (1965) calls "the theory of ornate form": that ideas may be expressed in different ways (style is the dress of thought). Therefore the approach tends to encourage students to "exceed their idiolect" (1971: 80)—to practice different styles and learn to choose between different language options and adapt to different registers, jargons, and formats required by the conventions of different groups. The feminist approach tends to assume what Milic calls the "individualist or psychological theory": that both ideas and expression reflect the unconscious and habitual slant of personality (*le style est la femme*). It tends to look for ways to free students from established or conventional language in order to find their true voice. The developmental, I believe, tells a different tale of style and recommends pedagogical action that may not be readily found through any other interpretation.

Comparing Distributions: A Developmental
Way from the Nomothetic to the Unique

Consider the style of this paragraph from the Sample, written by an entering freshman whom, following Allport's lead, I will call Sam. What is the best course of instruction for Sam? (The slashes marking ends of clauses are mine.)

> Some people don't respect anybody. / I have always been told that / to respect myself I have to respect others. / I find that true in many circumstances. / This respect also means other things besides people. / It could also mean the law. / The law is made up so that / people will live by a standard / to which everyone can live by. / Its made not to put anyone down or to put anyone ahead. / It's trying to benefit all instead of one. / Anyone one who breaks the law / is just being selfish. They're only out to benefit themself. /

Seeing that the rest of Sam's essay modulates this style not one whit, we hardly need guess the ungrounded English-teacher advice, all of it standard in Kitzhaber's thirty-year-old arsenal: to specify the logical connections between the first and second and between the fourth and fifth sentences ("Lacks subordination"), to lengthen some of these monotonous clauses ("Unemphatic"), to combine some of the sentences ("Choppy"), to expand with ideas and support ("Inadequate development"), to untangle the prepositions in the sixth sentence ("Ungrammatical"), and to fix other mistakes such as the missing apostrophe in <u>Its</u>, the extra <u>one</u> in the penultimate sentence, the <u>themself</u> in the last sentence ("Needs attention to mechanics").

This advice could be extended indefinitely, and that is part of the trouble. What of all this should Sam work on first? Ungrounded in developmental realities, the advice does not distinguish effects due to immaturity and effects due to misapprehension, misdirection, sloth, circumstance—or the writer's distinctive personality. The developmental looks for ways the teacher can make these distinctions. One way is with a double-flanking, nomothetic-idiographic maneuver. First, novice and expert performance is compared, as in chapter 3. Take Sam's remarkably short clauses. How remarkable are they? Clauses average 7.1 words for the paragraph and 6.8 for the entire essay of four hundred words, in which the longest clause, of 13 words, happens to be the seventh sentence here. Both the Sample and other research samples show that in impromptu, non-narrative writing, college freshmen average around 9 words per clause and expert writers around 10. Judging by both peers and elders, we see that Sam's production of clauses is far from normal.

Then the idiographic counters these group norms (that stock nomothetic weapon) with individual norms. It asks whether a person, even a person labeled "student," doesn't have the right to make a 7-word average part of a "unique idiomatic system"? In Wendell Berry's *The Unsettling of America* there are stretches, far longer than the usual student essay, that average 2 words less a clause than do the impromptu essays of Kellogg Hunt's high-school seniors. The crowd huddling together around the median may not produce such short clauses as Sam's, but what about those individual eccentrics whom statisticians call "outliers"?

A partial answer to the question can be found by comparing the frequency distribution of average clause length for the Sample's 128 undergraduates with that for the employees (see figure 3). One virtue of frequency distributions is that they disperse the weight of central-tendency figures like group mean and medium, depicting the whole range of individual scores and therefore allowing speculation on the way extreme performances relate to the rest of the crowd. When the distribution of scores from competent writers is set against the distribution of scores from novice writers, as in figure 3, with both performances achieved on the same writing task, then specific teaching advice for particular Sams begins to emerge. The fact that both distributions of clause length are skewed with a tail toward the right, for instance, suggests that more room for stylistic experimentation—more permissible eccentricity, so to speak—lies in the direction of greater clause size. It is possible, of

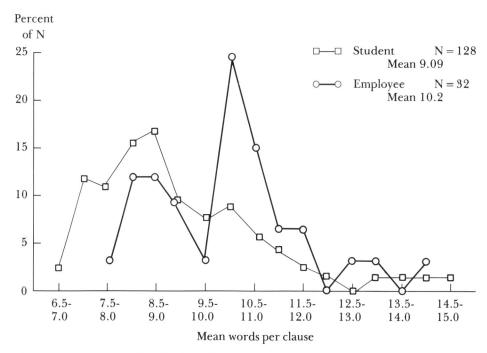

Figure 3.   Frequency distribution of mean clause length per word for undergraduate essays and for employee essays.

course, to generate syntactic English with average clause length at 2 words ("Respect nobody? Others may. Not me. I care."), so apparently somewhere around 6 words per clause enter pragmatic constraints. There is a limit at the right as well, at around 15 words per clause, but the gentler slope in that direction indicates a more elastic barrier, perhaps including contextual factors such as the difficulty of building complex clauses under time pressure.

Compared with the student distribution, the left-hand half of the employee distribution shifts as a whole to the right. That suggests clause length may be a developmentally mobile trait for many students—a useful notion the ungrounded vision does not consider. Yet, as the overlapping of the shift also shows, the trait may not be mobile for everybody. The twenty students in the Sample who write between 8 and 8.5 words per clause are writing no differently—in whatever words-per-clause measures—than four competent, successfully employed college graduates. A teacher cannot tell whether the style of these students is maturing or already matured. Sam and eighteen other undergraduates, however, are writing below 8 words a clause, outside the pale of older competence entirely. A teacher can advise Sam to lengthen clauses, not on the dubious nomothetic ground that those on the bandwagon don't write that way but on the more pragmatic ground that not one of thirty-two competent writers did.

One trait does not a style make. At first, further comparisons bolster out intuition that Sam is an exceptionally immature writer. The extreme syntactic monotony of the essay is developmentally backward, and Sam joins the 10 percent of the undergraduates whose standard deviation of T-unit length fell below that of the lowest employee's performance. Of the sixty-one clauses in Sam's entire essay, only seven are longer than 9 words. The standard deviation of clause length is 2.2, which is to say that clauses picked at random from the essay would average out to little more than two words distant from the mean of 6.8 words—not a feat easy for a mature writer to achieve deliberately. Similarly, the lack of development of ideas looks immature. One bit of syntactic evidence shows Sam, and eighteen other undergraduates, generating no final free modification in their essays, whereas every employee produces some. Even more eccentric is Sam's fixation on simple nouns. The essay modifies nominals less than did all but one other of the 160 essays in the entire Sample (that other was written by another freshman).

So far these novice-expert comparisons have, in an ominous nomothetic way, managed only to distinguish Sam's voice by typifying it, associating it with a group of student outliers whose home ground lies in the opposite direction from the shift toward matured writing. But as we continue with the comparisons, a curious idiographic turnabout occurs. We begin to see

171

that this pattern of traits "weaves," to use Allport's word, with other traits that counter the typification. We begin to find exceptions to the freshman norms, exceptions pointing toward the direction of maturity. It is a tendency of the employees, not the students, to leave logical connections tacit or to express them with coordinative rather than subordinative transitions, as Sam tends to do also. Sam's mis-scribing of <u>Its</u> reflects another characteristic of the employees, who tend to confine their misspellings to common homophones (notice that the <u>It's</u> in Sam's next sentence is correct). Sam's essay is over four hundred words long, near the employee average and one hundred words beyond the freshman average. These three developmentally positive traits (and others) begin to mix with the counterdevelopmental traits. Plural traits begin to form a singular *Sam:* a strong-willed and emphatic thinker, writing rapidly to keep to a rather stubborn and stern train of thought, simplifying perception of entities (<u>people</u>, <u>the law</u>, <u>anyone</u>) in order to focus on actions (<u>respect</u>, <u>mean</u>, <u>live by</u>, <u>put</u> . . . <u>down</u>, <u>benefit</u>, <u>breaks</u>), immaturely omitting complexities of life and audience and maturely letting the push and flow of the argument have main sway.

Developmental comparison of just two groups—undergraduates and competent graduates—and application of the transformative principle that cultural skills among and within individuals mature at different rates have begun to uncover the fact that Sam's essay, though hastily written, still projects a unique voice. Interpretive movement from the nomothetic to the idiographic slowly develops a negative into a positive voiceprint. Paradoxically, Sam's signature grows with the authority of a distinct individual the more it can be interpreted as belonging to legitimate groups. That distinctive voice will sound even more clearly as we are able to locate it in other developmental trajectories—that of engineering majors, perhaps, or music hobbyists, or white western Americans—groups whose privileges Sam feels are genuinely hers.

Development, Gender, and Style

Yes, hers—Samantha's. Which leads to a second instance of group privilege: the right of one's sex. It is a perilous instance, illustrative not only of the way the perspective of development helps isolate individual voices within groups but also of the way the transformative approach leads to heretical questions. Does the writing of males and females develop differently enough to affect a teacher's advice for Sam?

Take a different trait, bound prepositional strings, such as through the imposition of the parent's values on the child (written by an employee). The Sample finds the amount of total words writers choose to put into these strings to be both highly developmental (students about 12 percent, employees about 21 percent) and significantly gender-specific (undergraduate females 10.7 percent, males 13.4 percent). As comparative distributions show (see figure 4), the gender difference is entangled in the age difference and extends to the outliers. Of the ten students below the lowest employee performance, seven are female. Of the twenty-eight students equaling or bettering the employee mean, twenty are male. Both the undergraduate males' skew and their overall achievement point more strongly toward the employee "competence." When it comes to that stylistic trick of stringing together self-modifying chains of prepositional phrases, so characteristic for instance of formal prose, the male students seem to have a head start on the female.

The gender difference in the prepositional-string distribution curves may map a geologic slippage running very deep. Lesley M. Morrow found the conversation of boys as young as six years of age scoring higher than that of girls on a syntactic-complexity formula that counted prepositional modification. Kellogg Hunt's 1965 data shows an increasingly greater use of prepositional phrases in the writing of boys at grades four, eight, and twelve. The gender predilection continues beyond the college years. Analysis of teacher talk in the classroom found

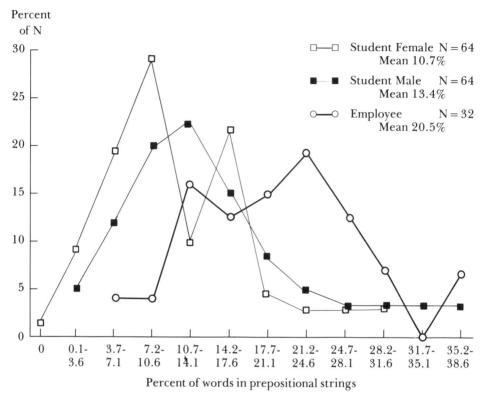

Figure 4.   Frequency distribution of mean percent of words in prepositional strings for student (female and male) and employee essays.

male teachers using three times as many expressions of instrumentality, manner, and source—all three grammatical cases most often expressed syntactically with prepositional phrases (N. Barron). A similar analysis extending the population to the twenty- to fifty-year-old general public found that men used more prepositions and females more verbs in formal talk, in part because the men preferred expressions of measure, location, and spatial relationship (Gleser, Gottschalk, and Watkins).

Sexual dimorphism in language uncovers bedrock issues. To take Sam's essay as nothing more than a freshman diagnostic blatantly in need of work in sentence combining, logical transitions, and expansion of ideas is to rive student style from its foundation in some very complex social realities. The bimodal shape of the employee distribution in figure 4, for example, reflects a disturbing underlying cause, a deep chasm in the female employee essays, with half of them using prepositions quite differently than do the other half. Figure 5 shows that gap prefigured by the female undergraduates. Are we looking at the gradual foisting of a masculine style on the female population, a marginalization of a natural feminine style, which college writing teachers may promote unwittingly?

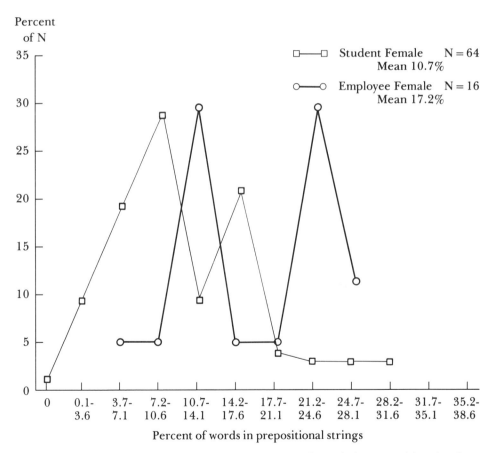

Figure 5.   Frequency distribution of mean percent of words in prepositional strings for student female and employee female essays.

Compare Sam's paragraph with a letter from a British woman writing a dissertation for her male advisor. The letter is quoted by Dale Spender (the slashes marking ends of clauses are mine).

> My supervisor is constantly telling me / what an awful writer I am. / He says / I let my imagination run loose / and I have no style. / He insists on looking at my work / before I send it off anywhere. / He always keeps it for weeks (very frustrating, particularly / if you have a deadline to meet) / and it always comes back covered with red pencil cross outs. / Am I such an awful writer? / It really is beginning to worry me. / (230)

Despite her advisor's opinion, this Ph.D. candidate has a style (including no prepositional strings and an average clause size of 6.4 words), which we now suspect as developmentally akin to the style of our eighteen-year-old Sam. We can only imagine the kind of unnatural voice this graduate student was coerced into assuming in her dissertation, or the voice that Sam, ten years older as a graduate student, might become coerced into assuming. At least one of the female employee essays, I believe, may show us what that forced voice or Habermasian pseudocommunication might look like:

> From [For?] all the codes that have been created in order to keep justice, order, a flow of things running smoothly, are part of a natural born instinct of man, that is somehow created from a sense of this is the way things should be. There will be those conduct codes that are broken, and in a way, that would have to happen, because of the balance of how things should be. If you can imagine or think back to the beginning of man, the order of how things were done in order to find food, a sense of conduct codes were set as to what the men were to do, and what the women's responsibility was.

Is this a naturally verb-centered idiom wrested into the kind of nominal, instrumental, long-breathed style the woman writer felt the male researcher wanted? Is this one-half the "bilingualism" that gender linguists say women develop in our culture?

Sam's fumble with prepositions (so that people will live by a standard to which everyone can live by) reads like a dark and eerie foreshadowing of future gender duress.

In more than prepositions is Sam's paragraph implicated with a long-lived stylistic gender split. Of the fourteen research measures recording a statistically significant difference between all undergraduate males and females, twelve hold fast with the older writers. The employee women still produce not only shorter clauses and fewer prepositions and prepositional strings but also more synonyms, fewer identical ties, fewer subordinate logical connectors, more infinitives, a higher rate of correctly spelled words, better-rated introductions and longer conclusions, and longer and better-rated essays. Later analysis found several other trends. The women use more contractions and possessives, prefer the generic pronoun "we" over "you," and have a higher ratio of verbs of psychological mood to those of physical state. This analysis also found perhaps the most comprehensive stylistic difference: a higher ratio of all predicates—both finite and infinite—to words. The two undergraduate gender differences erased by the employees were the student female use of more cohesive ties of all kinds and of shorter T-units of just one clause.

The issue here is not whether females or males are superior writers. The research format does not allow an answer to that question, since the teacher-raters were influenced by dubious traits such as essay length and conventional spelling, since the impromptu classroom task may have hindered the formal or nominalized style favored by the men, and since the two topics—on public codes of conduct and standards of appearance—may have been more interesting to women. The issue is whether these traits do not federate into a style developmentally natural for females. How is that gender style received by contemporary American culture? How may that reception affect the higher language apprenticeship of students such as Sam? Certainly these gender traits have been linked by researchers to usage somewhat more prevalent in the

language of Western females. Shorter clauses are preferred by
girls as early as the eighth grade (Hunt 1965). A greater reliance on the predicate has been found in females from age six
to adulthood (Lee). More logical coordination has shown up
repeatedly, for instance in oral jokes, first-year college descriptive writing, and professional nonfiction. The mix of easy
contractions, elegant synonyms, stative verbs of affect, correctness of spelling, and more accommodating introductions and
conclusions connect with the well-known edge females have
over males at nearly every age in sociability, conversational
facilitation, and acquisition of nonvernacular forms (Belenky
et al.; Coates). In the Sample, these differences are minimal,
with nearly every measure quite a bit less than the difference
between the employees and the students as a whole, close to the
quarter of one standard deviation that typifies the gaps reported between the sexes in all kinds of verbal functioning.
The differences are not sex-exclusive but sex-preferential. But
do not natural preferences add up to a deep-set proclivity that
might alter the way a teacher should interpret and instruct
Sam's writing?

Let me indulge—aware of Louis Milic's warning about
typologizing styles—in a nomothetic moment of stylistic law-
enactment. Sam's essay could be said to exaggerate almost
every ingredient of a definable style composed of the feminine side of these gender differences: fluency, contractions,
short clauses, conventionality of surface form, verbs over
prepositions, synonyms over identical ties, syntactic coordination over subordination. This style overlaps with other established styles, such as the conversational, the affective as
opposed to the scientific or dispassionate, the informal, the
"casual" of Martin Joos. But it does not quite identify with any
one of them. I will call it the Laelic, after Cicero's famous
praise of the speech of Laelia, his mother-in-law, who maintained the way her parents and grandparents spoke, *recto et
simplici:* without ostentation, directly, naturally, simply (*De*

Oratore, 3: 45).[2] The Laelic is allied to Virginia Woolf's "psychological sentence of the feminine gender," which she argued the woman writer has had to create for herself, a sentence "that takes the natural shape of her thought without crushing or distorting it." The traditional sentence, chiefly made by men, is "too loose, too heavy, too pompous for a woman's use" (48).

The Laelic style, of course, has also been brilliantly appropriated not only by Wendell Berry but also by Jonathan Kozol, Paul Goodman, G. K. Chesterton, Charles Lamb, Jonathan Swift, Robert Greene, and—to nip off an endless list with Cicero's own example—Plautus. Nor is brilliance a prerequisite for freshman Sam's appropriation of the Laelic to form her own *undr.* The point is that the style may allow an easy and natural access to those aspects of the human that operate as a characteristic center of women's lives and often as an object of fear and devaluation among men: access to the intimate, the affective, the everyday; to the conversational, sensual, narrative, practical, concrete, attached, and growing; to the personal and interpersonal. If so, then Sam's teacher may have to reinterpret Sam's motives in writing her diagnostic essay. If she had a desire similar to that expressed by the college women interviewed by Mary Field Belenky and her colleagues, to engage in "real talk" as opposed to "didactic talk," then a teacher's efforts to make vital aspects of her style more mature—to lengthen clauses, to stiffen the formality, to eradicate the first-person or the contractions, to make explicit "higher" logical connections

---

[2] In a chapter justly ridiculed by analysts of gender differences and full of pronouncements about feminine style subsequently supported by neither my data here nor anybody else's, Otto Jespersen typifies Laelia's style as characteristically female—a step, incidentally, that Cicero did not even imply. Jespersen perpetuated many myths, including the Victorian figment that the feminine style was good for only particular social situations, such as tea-table chitchat. But we ought to allow him the insights that have held up, for instance that men tend toward hypotaxis and women toward parataxis (251).

—may be met with more recalcitrance and feelings of offense and emotional retreat than innocuous instruction in style might seem to warrant. No doubt the Laelic is as prone to distortion from immature enthusiasm or inexperience as any other style, but not all styles may be as intimately attached to gender. The teacher may be repeating the act of ethnic violation of Dale Spender's dissertation advisor, declaring null ("no style") a vitality that just happens to be not so much youthful as other.

The Laelic shares a similar ground with so-called cognitive styles, whose endemic nature poses such a threat to instruction (and whose threat to a developmental pedagogy will be discussed in chapter 8). Unlike cognitive styles, however, the Laelic may lend Sam's individual voice some of its tonality (some of its very meaning, as Gadamer would point out) from its historical status as a group style fighting for legitimacy. Sam's teacher can take that status as both a caution and a boon. Sam speaks from two groups—females and students—in jeopardy of having their dialects overridden by the styles of more powerful groups. The caution is against trying to develop Sam's style by having her imitate or play around indiscriminately with a variety of different styles, or teaching Sam too early and too imperatively the need to learn the right register for the right audience. Both these instructional procedures, advocated by Richard Lanham and a host of others, have the laudable aim of making Sam's style more versatile and persuasive, but they run the risk of deceiving Sam into thinking, incorrectly, that the unique voice never sounds in occupational or institutional prose and that an individual does not further the development of group styles with her own idiosyncratic development. This caution may be especially apt in Sam's case. Several of the very strengths of Western women's language proclivities as documented by sociolinguistic research—their adeptness at dialect switching and quickness in acquiring prestige forms—may push Sam on to relinquish her own rightful vernacular.

The boon for the teacher is that once the group affiliations of Sam's style are recognized, then her progress takes on some of the purpose and appeal and historical destiny of the group. The legitimation of feminine style in many social realms is a just and growing cause—good reason, say many teachers today, why it should begin in the writing classroom. There a knowledge of the normal development of that style will help reduce the neon beckoning of possible courses of instruction that can dazzle student and teacher alike. Even the little we know of the way college women tend to mature will help. According to Belenky and her coauthors, college women more often advance out of a dualistic position of unthinking acceptance of authority (where Sam seems to reside) not by confronting multiplicity and conflicting facts, as William Perry's Harvard men usually did, but by questioning authorities who have been merely received rather than identified with. Instead of asking Sam to deal with the empty abstractions in her paragraph by adding contradictory evidence (what are examples of these <u>many circumstances</u> and <u>the law?</u>), she could be asked specifically to consider what she means by <u>respect others</u>, <u>live by a standard</u>, and <u>being selfish</u>. Or Sam could be asked to pursue her statement <u>I have always been told</u>, by means of reportage or autobiography. That advice uses Marcia B. Baxter Magolda's finding that college women develop a preference for concrete experience over abstract conceptualization more readily than do college men. The advice also follows Carol Gilligan's observation that college women tend to mature morally by letting their devalued feelings of personal integrity reemerge rather than by setting one abstract right against another, as Lawrence Kohlberg found college men tending to do.

This instructional advice for Sam derives nomothetically from the typical development of a specific group: women college students. Adding the developmental evidence from the employee groups pushes my analysis of the Sample about as far as it will go. In terms of syntax, for instance, Sam's proximal zone of development seems to include much more variance of sentence length and free modification and more—but not much more—use of prepositions and bound modification of nouns.

Sam, however, may not take to any of these forms. Above every-thing else, the transformative perspective requires that the writing teacher first sit down with Sam and find out what and whom she would like to write like. She might objectify her own style (clause slashes are only one means) so that she can re-act meta-cognitively her current *undr.* And following Edith D. Neimark's suggestion that modification of cognitive styles is better accom-plished by imitation than by direct instruction, Sam should be given some new stylistic experiences. But the options should be presented to her fairly, as developmentally "probabilistic." If she has aspirations to be an anthropologist, her models should not be only the stuffy formality of Alfred Kroeber but the Laelic ease of Theodora Kroeber as well (*Ishi in Two Worlds*); if a historian, she should be shown both the conventional uniform of a Ruth Milkman and the unconventional gown of a Barbara Tuchman. If, following the conclusion of chapter 3, models developmentally closer to Sam are needed, they can be pro-duced easily. Cuttings from the employees' essays, quoted later in this book, might convince her that even in impromptu writ-ing, the Laelic style can blossom into prose of great mobility and incisiveness—or might not. It is up to the teacher to know stylistically where Sam has developed from and where others have gone from there but not to know where Sam will go. Like Ulf, Sam has to find that for herself.

Three Interpretive Tales of Style: Expressive, Ornamental, Transformative

A look at the style of one student's paragraph has led to some rather long thoughts about "human possibilities and per-sonal choice in the psychological development of men and women." The phrase (a prepositional string) is the subtitle to a book whose spirit lies close to this one's, Leona E. Tyler's *Individuality.* For her peroration, after a concluding chapter on "The Plural Individual," she succinctly voices the basis of the transformative approach to style: "Individuals create themselves. To understand a person completely, we would need to trace the road he or she has taken on one occasion after another. It is development we must study, but the development of the shaper rather than the shaped" (233–34). The transformative takes style as neither exclusively expressive nor exclusively ornamental but inextricably both, as an immediate act of a person's ongoing and creative lifework. Style simply develops along with other aspects of that unique construction that is a changing person journeying through a changing world. Kept honest, the style of students will transform both the institutional and the individual voices into one voice, both intelligible and distinct. Students should not have to acquire some preformed style nor find their own style. They are always in the act of rewriting the one they already have.

The next five chapters will focus rather tightly on specific teaching techniques suggested by this definition of style. Here I would like to outline, in a kind of pre-peroration, some general responsibilities of teachers who take up the mantle of instruction tendered by this approach. One responsibility is to disillusion and keep from illusioning Sam about the idols of pseudocommunication set up by groups with which she aims to share allegiance. An obvious instance is the false tales spread by men and women alike about the way women do and should use language ("folklinguistics," the linguist Cheris Kramer calls them). "It would be a thousand pities if women should write like men," wrote Woolf, but a thousand more if they should be encouraged to write the way people say women write, with verbosity, pretty and excessive adjectives, superfluous adverbs, dangling sentences, home-bound vocabulary, obsequious hedges, tag questions, ultracorrect and ultrapolite forms. (No evidence was found for any of this in the Sample, nor has evidence been found in any research carefully controlled for gender and task.) Another instance is the notion that the academic style is so privileged that it serves for all occasions. Setting the academic as a target style can be counterdevelopmental even in the context of the academy, as Maurice Scharton found with postfreshmen students, who suffered a Kitzhaberian decline because they attempted an impersonal "dry academic tone" for an interpersonal rhetorical situation. More common and tempting are the siren songs of writing practices in the world outside of college, some of which are listed and exposed above in chapter 3. But the most common pseudocommunication, and closest to what Habermas meant by the term, are those duplicities and leverages powered by institutional styles of every kind, which general semanticists once warned us about and which teachers still ought to warn student writers about. Required at this point is a Habermasian critique that appeals to communicative claims beyond style, applying interpretive schemes such as truth, truthfulness, accountability for one's words, and free access to information (1979: 1–68).

Another responsibility is to respect a student's present style. It is easy to interpret Sam's style by what it does not do, to describe it as "limited," "vulnerable," "placid," "hobbled," "impoverished," "shallow," or "insecure." Sandra Schor, whose knowledgeable essay on students and style provides these characterizations of beginning college writing, argues that a student's writing is "singularly out of touch with the personality of its writer." She would not be surprised to see Sam show up at her office as a "dignified" and "interesting" young woman, "with considerable personal grace and enough presence to get through a conference with a professor" but whose adolescent lacks—lack of ideas, writing experience, language control, and ability to handle stress—result in a diagnostic that must lack a style (206). The transformative disagrees. It argues, first, that these "lacks" must devolve from some previous life and, second, that vulnerability, insecurity, difficulty with self-autonomy, and poor communication with one's personality in fact *are*—according to Freud, Erikson, Jane Loevinger, Karen Kitchener, and other students of ego development—genuine components of the adolescent personality. This argument would not improve Sam's rating in a placement exam. But instead of reading her essay negatively as a verbal *dis*placement, unable to express uniqueness of individuality, the argument would separate out traits that are normally developmental and interpret the rest positively as an expression of singularity, in Sam's case perhaps as unusually "succinct," "pellucid," "forthright," "strong."

In teaching, the all-too-common attitude toward style, namely that student writers have none, derives from the assumption that students as yet belong to no group giving them the authority of a voice. They are put in a limbo state of stylistic nescience, allowed only a vacuous "student" idiom characterized by, if anything of significance, a sort of protoplastic latency. Such a state fits well into the two most common interpretive tales of style. The expressive imagines beginning students as *unmündig,* not responsible for the law that language must reflect personality, since their identities have not yet come of age. They are not yet licensed for a personal voice, though they are in training to "acquire" one. The ornamental imagines students as apprentices who must first learn to use and care for the tools before they can handle a professional assignment. They may have the inspiration or spirit, but they are not ready to project a personal voice because they do not yet have the techniques down. (We might add a third tale of style, the ungrounded moral vision, which projects somewhere over the horizon one stylistic law for the lion and the fox, a perfect way of expressing any idea in language—although it is difficult to say that this represents a concept of style at all.)

The transformative tale of style asks the teacher to expect that a writer, at whatever age, already has a style. Ulf's mistake is to think he does not have the right word to sing. Once teachers begin to look for personal styles of students, they will find them, as diverse and eccentric as those of thirty-year-olds. The present case study of these 128 individual acts of lower-division college writing discovered them, though perhaps it took, along with a developmental eye, a hand analysis of individual traits, essay by essay. Sam's essay displays no clause longer than thirteen words; another essay has clauses that *average* fifteen words. One essay has no participial constructions of any kind;

another has participials beginning a third of the sentences. Essays that have no qualifiers, or no sentence openers, or no relative clauses, or no words more than nine letters long—and there were such in the Sample—have styles with body and distinct individual voice. If such achievement seems precocious for college freshmen, note that Anne H. Dyson found individual styles in first-graders.

Dyson found them, of course, by appraising not one but a plurality of features, an approach she calls the "orchestral vision of writing." The transformative also judges writers in terms of more than one normalized trait and avoids thinking a student immature if his mean T-unit length falls below Hunt's "adult" norm of twenty words or if her rate of errors rises above Robert J. Connors and Andrea A. Lunsford's college-freshman norm of two and one-fourth per one hundred words. Instead, the transformative looks for Saul Rosenzweig's "idiodynamics" or Allport's "idiomatic system," the unique way an individual "weaves" traits together.

The developmental approach to style asks teachers never to forget the ultimate relativity of most of their writing standards. Always tempting is the hope of para-stylistic virtues with fixed rhetorical ends such as variety or euphony or readability or conventionality. But the inherent "plasticity" of the transformative says there can be few such universal rhetorical laws. In a famous passage, Coleridge said he would recognize a certain sentence of Wordsworth's should he meet it running wild in the deserts of Arabia. But whatever trait identified the style as Wordsworth's must perforce violate the canon of variety, since it must operate pervasively, in a nonvaried manner. In his turn, Wordsworth said he could provide the two models on which all of the sentences of William Robertson were framed, as if that were a sufficient damnation of the Scottish historian's style. But what if such monotony, or such loyalty to the two models, forms an essential part of Robertson's *undr?* There is just no rhetorical virtue exempt from stylistic appropriation. Look at what Thorstein Veblen does with euphony and Loren Eiseley with clarity, or what Isak Dinesen and William Burroughs do with convention-ality of punctuation. Had the educator Thomas Arnold taught his son Matthew a normal rate of identical cohesive ties, he might have eradicated what was to become a key ingredient in a brilliant and effective style.

And perhaps another responsibility of the teacher is to think twice about rebutting this argument with the familiar plea that few students have the genius of these literary greats or the contention that even the greats had to learn the ground rules first. These pleas may be forms of the expressive tale that "students have no style" and the ungrounded tale that "students can't write"—at source, perhaps, a cryptic form of class nega-tion. Style is usually attached in some way to identity develop-ment (Erikson 1968: 49–50), and historically the denial of inner growth has played its role in the suppression or control of group destinies, from the trust of white settlers that Ameri-can Indians had no sentimental attachment to land, to the cur-rent academic myth that young professionals must make a publishing name for themselves in an impersonal, scholarly vein before they can enjoy the idiosyncratic stylistic liberties of a Clifford Geertz or a Lewis Thomas. There are ways to get established other than to ape the establishment and ways to be verbally distinctive other than to be great. Nor does the trans-formative deny the usefulness of instructing students in the rhetorical game-rules of our culture in recommending that teachers also instruct students in the ways those conventions can be an enemy to the individual.

As I have said, such gravitation toward the idiographic characterizes the transformative. Its home request is for courage to keep from enforcing, nomothetically, one group style over another. In the end, Ulf uses his teacher Bjarni's harp. But it is not to sing to an *undr* Bjarni had taught him. Both Ulf and Bjarni, it is worth noting, are strangers in a strange land. The spiral frame of the transformative asks teachers to save, out of an old allegiance to their own past development, developmental space for the rhetorical growth of subcultures, of dialect groups, of personality types with minority ways of knowing and habits of composing, of groups so powerless that sociologists call them "mutes," and of social outliers whom the linguist William Labov called "lames," all the way down to the idiographic base of the individual in the middle of a self-actualizing journey from unique origins to, we hope, a distinct maturity.

The developmental point about style is that the spiral evolves. It is a point that Borges is making in "Undr" but that, at one point, the English translation of his story slights. When Ulf listens to the poetry of the Baltic Urnos, he is hearing part of the Indo-European heritage of his own eleventh-century Icelandic tongue (the word *undr* appears in Old Norse). Ulf's wisdom is to realize that although *undr* has served as a communal expression of the Urnos, it cannot serve as his own personal expression. Borges's wisdom is to imagine that Ulf will take his personal invention back and, through his function as community bard, will add it to the common language, assisting a universal process of language evolution. In this and similar ways, *undr* will spawn cognates in many Germanic languages, for instance the Old English *wundor,* the Old High German *wuntor,* and the modern English *wonder.* The last is how the English translator of Borges chooses to render *undr.* From the angle of Borges's own vowel-rich and Latinate Spanish, "Undr," of course, looks as foreign as possible, and when his fictional narrator translates the word from the eleventh-century Saxon document as *maravilla* ("My Spanish version is not literal," he says), he is repeating Ulf's final act of appropriation and is illustrating on his own the marvelous way language simultaneously transmits and transforms its communal self through creative individual use. "To everybody life gives everything," says the teacher Bjarni to the student Ulf, "but most people miss it." A thousand pities if writing teachers should forget their responsibility to make sure students do not miss that wonder of language.

These transformative responsibilities will not free the teacher from the paradoxical bind between writing instruction and writing style. But, as the following five chapters hope to show, it can offer concrete ways to further the writing development of students caught in their own bind between the overlapping range rights of individual and group. It can help teachers to deal with the multitudinous ways students break the prevailing rhetorical game-rules (chapter 7), to advise students caught in what looks like a self-destructive cognitive style of composing (chapter 8), to identify stylistic tolerances distinguishing immatures and outliers and to find ways to tolerate them (chapters 9 and 10), and to create sequences of practice for different writing subgroups (chapter 11). The transformative offers a rough survival guide for teachers operating inside the spiral that translates back and forth between nomothetic rule and idiographic character, between the developmental ends of socialization and individuation, between the rhetorical means of cultural communication and individual *undr.*

CHAPTER 7

Solecisms:
Mistakes and Errors

IN 1819 THE FOUNDER OF MODERN HERMENEU-
tics, Friedrich Schleiermacher, was calling the nomothetic
the *grammatical* and the idiographic the *psychological*. For him
the terms identified two contrasting procedures by which one
interprets or makes sense of unfamiliar discourse. The grammatical procedure sets new language within the bounds of conventional usage. The psychological reads through language to
the singular ideas of the speaker. Schleiermacher wrote, "Just
as every speech has a twofold relationship, both to the whole of
the language and to the collected thinking of the speaker, so
also there exists in all understanding of the speech two moments: understanding it as something drawn out of language
and as a 'fact' in the thinking of the speaker" (Palmer: 88). One
of Schleiermacher's lasting insights was that grammatical understanding is essentially negative because in that "moment"
the interpreter sets the new utterance against an established
language system. The grammatical "merely indicates the limits
of understanding," explains Paul Ricoeur. "Its critical value
bears only upon errors in the meanings of words" (1981: 47).

The subject of this chapter is blunders in language—in the narrowed sense of solecisms appearing in apprenticeship writing—and the way teachers can avoid interpreting them negatively. Another of Schleiermacher's insights also will prove valuable to our inquiry. He took the positive goal of interpretation to be the grasping of an author's unique thoughts and individuality. This requires both grammatical and psychological procedures. Yet he saw that the two "moments" cannot occur simultaneously. To attend to the general language system means to disregard the writer; to comprehend the writer's novel thought means to abandon the language system. This is Schleiermacher's variant of the hermeneutic circle, and it is not mere abstruse Germanic Idealism. When Sam writes of <u>a standard to which everyone can live by</u>, the reader can wrestle "grammatically" with her unconventional syntax (is it English to say one "lives to" a standard?) or search for her thought (does she mean "a standard toward which people strive and at the same time manage to live by"?). Yet it is impossible to do both at once. Schleiermacher's point is that ordinary language interpretation entails a Wordsworthian "double consciousness," much like the either/or bind in which the human perceptual system finds itself as it confronts an optical illusion. The disturbing feature of the Necker cube (figure 6) is not that a viewer can perceive it two different ways or even that one can flip the perspective back and forth at will. It's that a viewer cannot see both perspectives at once.

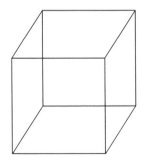

Figure 6.   The Necker cube.

Schleiermacher's two basic "moments" of discourse understanding partly explain the two divergent and sometimes antagonistic ways teachers generally react to formal solecisms in the writing of students, the way they interpret aberrations from conventional punctuation, spelling, grammar, syntax, and format. Some tend to see the "grammatical" perspective first and the "psychological" second—others reverse the sequence. In either case, the act of interpretation is inevitably narrative. The subsequent tales teachers formulate to explain solecisms, or the pedagogical steps they take to treat them, need not repeat their initial sequence of understanding, but they often do. The developmental tale cannot replace the basic hermeneutical optical illusion. But it does intervene between the initial understanding and the interpretive tale and offers its own explanation of the natural role of blunders in writing growth and its own recommendations for teaching.

The Interpretive Order of Solecisms: First or Second?

Certainly the most common reading of formal solecisms is "grammatical." In the very act of marking, teachers usually see misformation first, thought second (just glance at the content of the running comments in contrast to the end comments in a set of composition papers). Some of the priority assigned to surface errors may owe to the fact that they are just that, on the surface, hence seen first and easily. But the effect on a teacher's appreciation of other rhetorical matters can be powerful. Measures of error—usually misspellings—usually end up among the top three predictors of quality judgments by teachers of student writing, along with vocabulary and essay length. Bennett A. Raforth and Donald L. Rubin compared the way teachers reacted to pairs of essays, one version mechanically perfect and the other identical except for fourteen surface mistakes. On a general impression scale, the flawed essays dropped 40 percent from the unflawed ones. Worse, they dropped 23 percent on an assessment of ideas and 16 percent on an assessment of organization, although neither ideas nor organization suffered any change.

Behind this largely unintentional primacy assigned to error probably lies a pedagogical tale of almost gossip simplicity. Removal of blunders will better writing: SOLECISM REDUCTION → IMPROVEMENT. Solecisms take on a causal priority. The writer errs, the errors are corrected, the result is a better essay and maybe a better writer. Kitzhaber assumed this causation, counting "errors, infelicities, weaknesses" (42) to measure long-term advance in the writing of students. Students too assume the causation, perhaps absorbing the notion from their teachers. Just as teachers mark "weaknesses" first, students then often revise them first, and sometimes only them. Sometimes students simply equate instruction in writing with emendation. In Robert Stiff's experiment manipulating teacher commentary on essays, the students who received fewer comments complained that they had not been given "full correction," although they advanced during the course as well as did the other students. In sum, both teacher and student assume that the health of composition is naturally measured by what Ken Macrorie called Kitzhaber's "Errors Approach." It made Macrorie "sick" (267).

The "psychological" reading of solecisms, traditionally a maverick position like Macrorie's, has made rapid gains in respectability since Kitzhaber, at least in theory. It looks through surface "infelicities" to rhetorical acts deemed more important than the meeting of language dress codes. When it studies blunders directly, as in miscue analysis, it treats them as secondary or symptomatic, worrying not about the effect but the causes. It often sees blunders as produced by writers out of positive needs—to free up creativity, to get inspiration on paper quickly, to attend to thought, or simply to be human (teachers like Kitzhaber make error out to be a vice, wrote Macrorie, but "the virtuous often err"). From this angle, truly psychological factors can be proposed, such as the possibility that some intractable misspellers may be "strephosymboliacs," beggars for attention who will leave off the style when teachers deliberately do not react to it (Lavers). The most positive psychological reading of solecism reverses the grammatical, arguing that stumbles have to accompany learning: IMPROVEMENT → SOLECISM PRODUC- TION. The theory is not as counterintuitive as it may seem at first. Mistakes are seen as mis-takes, mis-steps or wrong turns made when new tactics are attempted, as natural as the fumbles of a musician trying out a piece for the first time.

Although the developmental will tend to approach sole- cisms psychologically, it does not reject the grammatical en- tirely. After all, meeting the dress codes is a skill that develops too. Compared with the students, the employees committed fewer faults in orthography, predication, and syntactic paral- lelism. Only a third of the student writers remembered to provide a title to their essays, but half the employees did. Ulti- mately, as with style, the developmental tends to collapse the distinction between language and thought, form and motive. For instance, writers themselves often operate grammatically, reading the language forms they have just written or are about to write *as* form. They may think of the piece they are writing as belonging to a genre requiring a title (or not). This operation requires a self-reflecting meta-cognitive process that, as we will see, itself continues to grow in writers during and after college. Schleiermacher's distinction does not quite provide what could be most useful, a way to distinguish solecisms that result from development itself.

We get nearer to that goal with S. Pit Corder's distinction between *mistakes* and *errors*. According to Corder, mistakes are due to performance factors or chance circumstances. They are stumbles in haste or distraction, slips of the pen, memory faults, misunderstandings of the assignment, applications in good faith of bad teacher advice. Errors are due to what Corder usefully calls "transitional competence" (10). They are "re-creations," generated as all novel expressions are generated by developing writers, through restructuring and transference (93). They arise not out of incompetence but positively out of the writer's current knowledge or concept of language. The competence happens to be transitional because it is still moving toward social, pragmatic standards. Mistakes, then, tend to be unsystematic, errors systematic. When Sam spells "it's" wrong in one sentence and right in the next, she probably has made a mistake, a solecism not characteristic of any particular phase in the acquisition of writing. When she writes a standard to which everyone can live by, her nonstandard fusion of an infinitive phrase ("a standard to live by") and a prepositional phrase ("a standard by which everyone can live") is probably an error, due to a transitional rule she has created that overextends the customary ways function words may be elided when syntactic forms are combined. That it is an error is indicated by the fact that Sam creates two similar forms in her essay: I treat my parents now as equal and they to me and This comes mainly from being between in ages of two boys. We probably are looking at steps, including mis-steps, that Sam is taking toward a more mature use of prepositions.

Faulty parallelism with prepositional phrases, of course, is not confined to Sam but pesters college writers everywhere, and even seems to get worse. If so, then the trouble may be construed not only as evidence of transitional competence but more specifically as a sign of transformative development. Such errors naturally follow when new skill and knowledge frames replace old ones, reflecting the self-contradiction, unevenness, unstable alienation, and re-active give-and-take of generative learning.

Of all the signs of error in transformative learning, the most telling is regression. It is the phase that is graphed in the classic "U-shaped growth curve" (Strauss 1982), where for a while later skill appears to perform worse than earlier. The paradox, much studied, has produced some of the more fascinating phenomena of normal human learning. Ten-year-olds can recognize upside-down photographs of acquaintances 90 percent of the time; twenty-year-old college students only 60 percent (Carey 1982). When two cups of water are identified as equally cold and then combined, three- to five-year-olds tend to say the mixture is the same temperature, eight- to twelve-year-olds that it is twice as cold (Strauss 1987). Language acquisition is attended by regression nearly from the beginning. "I made that fall down" occurs earlier than "I fell that down" (Bowerman). Three-year-olds make more mistakes than do two-year-olds in acting out the sentence "It's the horse that the cow kisses" (Bever 1970). In all these cases, worse results are momentarily produced in a self-contradictory way by better but newer knowledge frames. Strauss's eight- to twelve-year-olds reason incorrectly about the water temperature because of their ability to add. Bever's three-year-olds misinterpret the direction of the kiss because they have acquired a syntactic forestructure, the actor-action-object sequence canonical in English.

Regression continues as long as language competence continues to grow, and transformative types can be found in college-age writing everywhere. Rules are extended beyond their customary range ("overregularization"), as when students put quotation marks around block quotes. Old frames are applied to new situations ("transference"), as when they spell, and probably read, "beatify" as "beautify." Previously learned coding systems interact with new ones, as when they write incorrectly what they then correctly read, or scribe mistakes that they later cannot find by proofreading but can correct once found. Isolated rules are learned in a new system but not their internal relationship, as when they mix registers. In a quid-pro-quo or interactive way, some subskills lag so that others can advance ("embeddedness"), as when they mispunctuate a novel syntactic form such as appositives. During points of stress or indecision, retreat is beaten to previously acquired strategies ("fallback"), as when they write, the future of work, marriage, and to be a good parent. Relics of old systems hang on, getting in the way of new ("fossilization"), as when they place an oral-language way to form possessives on top of a more formal way: the appearance of a friend's.

In written language, only a few developmental regressions have been clearly identified.[1] Misspellings should be expected to increase from the first to the fourth grade and then decline to the eighth (Taylor and Kidder). There will be an increase in lapses in pronoun reference with eleventh- and twelfth-grade students (Freedman and Pringle 1980a), probably as they are trying to write more complex sentences. When college students lengthen clauses and T-units through sentence combining, they probably will make more embedding errors (the students of Elaine P. Maimon and Barbara F. Nodine doubled their rate). And in a finding with far-reaching implications, as college students advance in intellectual or ethical ideas, their argumentative papers may regress in coherence and focus (Hays et al.). I will hypothesize a few more developmental regressions in the following brief effort to interpret errors in the Sample from the angle of transitional competence.

Eight Solecisms under Development: Errors or Mistakes?

The Sample did not find a blanket or Kitzhaberian "backsliding" in either mistakes or errors. (As we have seen, neither did two other studies of undergraduates, Whitla and Graham). For the eight common solecisms analyzed, the general picture is of total blunders remaining level from freshman to junior, at thirty-six to thirty-eight per thousand words (compare Connors and Lunsford's rate of twenty-three for out-of-class writing). Since improvement took place in other aspects of composition, the few glimpses of developmental regressions are of the quid-pro-quo sort, where a plateau or setback in a particular skill seems to assist successful advance in another.

---

[1] Specialists with a developmental leaning, however, have well argued the need for teachers to be generally aware of similar regressions: Freedman and Pringle 1980b; Miller; Kroll; Bereiter; Newkirk 1984; Kutz; Onore. For an especially insightful developmental analysis of student errors in logical reasoning, see D'Angelo 1983.

Misformation of possessives. The rate possessives are used remains stable from freshmen through employees. Sophomores and juniors, however, jump from misforming a third to half. One reason may be that, compared with freshmen, they form a third more of their possessives from abstract, pluralized, or otherwise generalized nouns, burdening themselves with the problem of making possessive such words as "societies" and "women." Twice as many of the sophomores' possessives involve plural nouns, and four times as many of the juniors'. Another context leading the older students to misformed possessives is their increase in amount and complexity of nominal modification, as in <u>the present day countries practices</u>. The employees have learned better to integrate syntax with punctuation. They continue to increase the complexity of nominals yet cut the freshman rate of misformed possessives in half, although they still misform about one in every five they attempt.

Faulty predication. The employees cut a stable undergraduate rate by nearly a fourth. Collette A. Daiute's miscue analysis of impromptu freshman-placement essays shows that some common types of faulty predication tend to follow complexly modified subjects, as in her example "The recent outbreak of riots are upsetting," or, from the Sample, <u>The wife you marry may often result from your concept of beauty</u>. Students, who are making their nouns more general and more complex, put more than half of their compounded nouns in the subject slot, whereas the workplace writers put there less than a third of theirs. Interposing structures between subject and predicate also must hinder accurate predication. Twice as many sophomores and juniors attempt appositives in their essays as do freshmen. Also the greater use of "unusual" words by sophomores and juniors may also momentarily block their way toward better predication.

Faulty pronoun reference. The trend is for pronoun-antecedent agreement in number or gender to worsen with sophomores and improve with juniors. Part of the sophomore slump has to do with their yearning for high-level abstractions (the effects of which we have just begun to see), for they show a sudden increase in third-person pronouns, where trouble with pronoun reference almost always occurs. The advance in syntactic complexity that Murray F. Stewart and Cary H. Grobe saw influence a rise in faulty reference among high-school seniors continues among college undergraduates, most broadly in their push toward longer sentences. Again one thinks of interposing structures, here between pronoun and antecedent—not only nominal modifiers and appositives but also final free modifiers, which grow in length and nearly double in frequency from freshman to junior.

Misformed syntactic parallelism. Here is another sophomore regression. Statistically it is only a trend, but two changes in context support it. First, compared with freshmen, sophomores make a third more of their parallel structures not simple coordinations (with "and," "or," etc.) but comparatives and other noncoordinative forms (e.g., "not X, but Y"). Juniors and, surprisingly, workplace writers show less favor for these complex formations. Second, juniors in fact disfavor syntactic parallelism of all kinds, one of the few upper-class deviations from the direction set by the employee essays. The junior push toward other kinds of syntactic complexity, especially toward modification of nominals and greater sentence size, may carry with it liabilities. Perhaps juniors are reluctant to attempt forms, such as parallelism, that can give trouble. Daiute's study found that sentences without error average 17.9 words, with error 20.3.

Mispunctuation of final free modification. Readers proceeding from the freshman to the sophomore essays will find twice as many mispunctuated final free modifiers. But this is because the sophomores attempted the form twice as often. Juniors and employees continue to favor the form but gradually improve the punctuation. It is a particularly clear instance of a common developmental priority, correctness of form waiting on experimentation with form. Compare the *initial* free modifier, with which the majority of writers have stopped experimenting by college. Its production remains steady all the way through the employees, while its punctuation steadily improves.

Sentence fragments and comma splices. With undergraduates, fragments decline and splices rise. Both trends may reflect the impulse toward writing longer sentences, splices lengthening and fragments shortening them. Another positive motivation for the errors may be sentence variety, which shows such a clear advance in the employee essays. Donna M. Kagan's analysis of run-ons in college writing, for instance, finds the strongest mis-cue to be the juxtaposition of a long, complex T-unit with a short, simple one: "Because he had lost the money he did not buy a gift he arrived empty-handed" (130). Such long-short combi-nations almost always reflect a healthy rhetorical flow. Another likely motivation is final free modification. Of the forty-four undergraduate attachable sentence fragments, forty-one were free modifiers of the previous sentence, a clear support of Muriel Harris's warning that brute red-inking of the mispunctu-ation will stunt the growth of that "late-blooming" form (177).

Misspellings. The trend from freshman to junior is mo-lasses-slow improvement. But when these errors are considered in the context of vocabulary, the situation appears less of a plateau and more of a transition. As we have seen, sophomores and juniors double the freshman rate of unusual words such as "emphasis," "flare," and "nuisance." As with free modification, only after experimentation with use comes improvement in form, and the older students and the employees show increasing success in spelling such words correctly. Interestingly, the older writers seem to have increased trouble spelling common words. The portion of all misspellings that are correctly spelled com-mon words, for instance where "are" is penned and "all" in-tended, continues growing through the workplace writing, from about one-fifth with freshmen to one-half with the em-ployees. The portion of misspellings caused by dropping suf-fixes also grows steadily, from around a twentieth to a quarter. It seems reasonable to interpret this misscribing of common words as a fallout from improvement in other techniques, among them a greater concentration on content, a more auto-matic scribing of all words, a more rapid rate of production—

and perhaps a decision that in the impromptu writing situation, time should not be wasted on proofreading. In sum, misspellings in the Sample illustrate what is, on second thought, an obvious developmental postulate: that as a skill matures toward competence, mistakes will increase in proportion to errors.

Blunders and Benefits

Can Corder's "transitional errors" approach, in replacing Kitzhaber's "Errors Approach," make a difference in the way teachers habitually react to solecisms? I think so. It has the immediate benefit of lending a reasonable explanation to what otherwise will seem to be uncalled-for blots cluttering up student papers. A junior writes, Children who have been ridiculed for their appearance, often grow-up thinking of themselves as different, and most times becoming some what excentric. It helps the teacher read the author as a bona fide learner to interpret some what as a production mistake and excentric as a word the student may be attempting for the first time in writing and a reasonable overregularization to boot (how many words begin "exc-" and how many "ecc-"?). It helps to know that the two ambiguous commas signal structures (postnominal modifier and final free modifier) that juniors typically are still actively acquiring. The approach simply encourages the positive psychological reading, which inquires into the causes of all kinds of student goofs. It may turn out that ridiculed is a reasonable slip of the pen because the author is majoring in Spanish (cf. *cualidad*).

The etiology of student solecisms, of course, is bound to be very complex. Students blunder with language for many reasons: because the wrong form is set in and difficult to erase, because the complex rules governing conventional expression have been forgotten or misunderstood or partly understood or mislearned or mistaught or simply discarded as too involved and too trivial, because most teachers—at least outside of freshman composition—have paid attention to mistakes with little or no difference on grade, because an impromptu and timed writing situation sets other compositional priorities first, even because a diagnostic essay is taken as a chance to see how the teacher will react to surface mistakes. Students may commit solecisms that ought to be defined neither as performance mistake nor developmental error because they issue from second-language or psychiatric or learning-disability problems. Obviously, one benefit in sorting out any of this tangle of causes is being able to isolate treatment.

The distinction between mistakes and errors has the added benefit of recommending a fairly simple axiom: to concentrate first on treating mistakes. Errors should be treated only with care and with an open and re-active understanding of the student. Unthinking or wholesale instructional tactics to squelch errors may squelch only the growth in writing that precipitated them. The worst case of error in the Sample is not the junior essay with seven comma splices but the two essays with no commas at all. The error was committed by past teachers who persuaded these two writers not to venture, with who-knows-what loss to normal development. In "On Education," John Milton calls tasks forced prematurely on students "preposterous exaction." He means (with his customary attention to etymology) pedagogical acts wherein the posterior is put first, with the result that "proficiency" is cast "so much behind." To interpret error grammatically, as source rather than symptom, may be preposterous exactly in Milton's sense, at least if we take true proficiency in writing as having to do more with maturity of thought than maturity of surface form.

The developmental also counters the most common interpretive tale of the "Errors Approach," which takes error to be the simple negative of some positive skill. If there are "stringy sentences"—at least Kitzhaber counted them—then the rest must be nonstringy, or in that respect correct. The trouble with this reasoning is that it leaves no possible motives for the production of error except ones that are also negative. Why else should students create error but out of stupidity, rebellion, orneriness, or laziness? Moving grammatically from language first to thought second breeds such Imp-of-the-Perverse stories. Viewed from the angle of development, correctness is not opposed to error, just as a cause is not opposed to an effect. Error and correctness are no different from other features of writing, such as clause length or audience appeal. They have no opposites, just quid-pro-quo connections with other rhetorical features.

The tale of error told by the developmental tends rather to assume the positive motives that chapter 2 found in that counter-tale to the myth of deterioration and to the vision of moral entertainment, that simple country tale of creaturely growth with its motives of acquisitiveness, curiosity, restlessness, and venture. To these virtues we might add practicality. Especially in impromptu writing, more attention on correctness means less attention elsewhere, just as, quid pro quo, more concentration elsewhere may mean more mistakes. Undergraduates know that while composing, they should think about their own writing psychologically, at least that there should be a limit to time spent thinking grammatically. During the writing pauses investigated by Gary M. Schumacher and his associates, upper-class students thought no more about "surface elements" than entering freshmen did, but the older students did think more about content, planning, support, ideas, and other nonformal factors. Holding ground with mechanics means gaining ground elsewhere.

The truly negative sign would be if the students were holding ground with their knowledge frames. From the philosophical perspective of human change, Gadamer and Habermas agree that the primal error is self-deception that forestalls learning. With Gadamer, it is the "tyranny of hidden prejudices" (1975: 239) or a self-closedness that keeps people unaware they are misunderstanding and therefore blocks new experience. With Habermas, it is a self-alienation in which an internal pseudocommunication, a "corrupt text," keeps one from gaining new ideas through reflection and instead generates "scars" or Freudian-like slips (parapraxes) that one is unconscious of and that no one else will notice "as long as they fall within the conventional limits of tolerance" (1971: 219). Such experiential or intellectual stagnancy is less likely to precipitate mistakes and errors than will efforts to learn. It is the student paper free of error that should sound a pedagogical alarm.

It follows that if teachers truly wish to help the student gain ground in writing, they will, as chapter 2 recommended in evaluating Essay J, absent themselves from felicity awhile and deliberately flip the Necker cube of solecism from its correctness face to its learning face. The ideal is Wordsworth's hope for "knowledge not purchased with a loss of power," by which he (and Augustine, Dante, Milton, Bunyan, Goethe, Proust, and every other writer whose vision of biography is still respected) means the opportunity to learn without the opprobrium of loss of face. That developmental ideal recommends a direct and simple pedagogy: make the student aware that mistakes and errors are secondary, and keep them that way.

CHAPTER 8

Production:
Slow and Swift

AS IF RISEN FROM FREUD'S COUCH, A DEEP-
rooted frustration of student writers emerged in a spoken protocol elicited by Linda S. Flower and John R. Hayes (1981).
Thinking out loud about his writing, one student suddenly con-
fessed to an envy of other students who can compose rapidly.
"Why can't I do that? Why can all these other people do that?
They just pick out their little topic sentence and then they write
their paper. If I just stuck to the topic sentence, maybe, and I
just let the topic sentence govern all my thoughts and let that
dictate what I was gonna talk about . . ." (48). It is one of the
primal motives of writers everywhere—to get the words out
and down in good time. Fluency. Not fluidity, which characterizes the way few humans write, as Flower and Hayes themselves
have shown. Perhaps water and sewage and, according to Heraclitus, everything else flow, but not words, whose normal composing pace is one of fits and starts. This student is lamenting
not loss of tempo but loss of time, that in the end not much has
got done. He is a slow writer, who does not produce at the going
rate. For teachers, his question is the essential one: Why *can't* he
do that?

Cognitive Styles and Production Styles

Writing teachers do not have ready answers. Despite the profession's growing interest in writing for practical purposes and despite the clear call from outside the university for the understanding of unprofitable composing habits, teachers can cite few explanations for unproductive writing. Although Peter Elbow and others offer excellent therapeutic activities to help blocked writers, only a few scholars have pursued causes. Compared with our information on slow reading, our understanding of slow writing looks embarrassingly immature.

I can propose two reasons for this. One is the profession's ambivalent attitude toward swift writing. We assign minimum pages on writing assignments and at the same time lecture on length-envy as a hazardous motivation that leads to padding and sloppy thinking. Unconsciously, in holistic assessments, we award the speediness that produces the longer essays; publicly, in textbooks, we promote that other form of efficiency, economy. Theoretically, in articles, we praise the time-saving skills of coherence and automaticity and the time-consuming habits of incubation, planning, revision, and proofreading. We may hesitate to question the causes of slow writing because questioning itself would define it as a problem.

We may also hesitate because of our intuited answer to the question. We suspect that the causes of sluggish writing have largely to do with fixed temperament or set cognitive style and so stand beyond our instructional jurisdiction. This suspicion seems to be justified with the seven "cognitive components" Robert Boice found in his survey of the research on writing blocks. The six most cited components are familiar emotional sets: apprehension about the task, procrastination, negative emotions ("dysphoria"), impatience, perfectionism, and anxiety over the reaction of readers. Only the least common component, reliance on maladaptive rules for writing, describes a habit an English teacher would know how to treat better than would a psychologist. Further justification for the fear comes from

James D. William's study of the connection between writing quality and the most famous of cognitive styles. He identified his first-semester freshmen as field dependent or field independent. Only 5 percent of the impromptu essays by field-dependents had identifiable topics, compared with 65 percent of the essays by field-independents. The finding is both plausible and threatening. The original formulator of the cognitive style, Herman A. Witkin, says that field-dependent individuals tend to have difficulty with problems "where the solution depends on taking some critical element out of the context [field] in which it is presented and restructuring the problem material so that the item is now used in a different context." The frustrated writer of Flower and Hayes may be a field-dependent who feels as frustrated trying to pick a thesis from the essay prompt as he would trying to discern shapes in the embedded figures test used to measure field-dependence—and feeling as envious of others who can find them easily and quickly ("They just pick out their little topic sentence and then they write their paper").

Mike Rose, who quotes the passage from Witkin, comments that although most composition teachers "could think of linguistic-rhetorical problems that might fit Witkin's description, it would be hard to claim that it characterizes rhetorical activity and linguistic production in any broad and inclusive way" (1988: 275). I would like to claim that too, but I find it hard to discard decontextualizing and restructuring of critical elements as an insignificant part of writing. And if field-dependence is not a liability for students who need to produce some writing fast, what about other known cognitive styles? They relate readily to problems writers have always had in producing at the going rate. Scanners (opposed to focusers) cannot weed out irrelevancies except by constructing more and more narrow constraints; sharpeners (opposed to levelers) hesitate to put new information in familiar categories; reflectives (opposed to impulsives) are slow to categorize items because they look for analytical rather than functional relationships; constricteds (opposed to flexibles) tend to be distracted by new information. If character is somewhat fate, are these cognitive types somewhat fated to be slow writers?

Current developmental theory, at least the brand of it I have called transformative, agrees wholeheartedly with Rose's main argument that uncritical acceptance of cognitive temperamental or style sets will too narrowly categorize the true diversity of our students. It also agrees with Rose that we ought not shut our eyes to such possible personality constructs and continue blindly to teach on in the hope that they will make no difference. Developmental theory has long wrestled with the question of fixed attitudes, temperaments, values, or styles. Out of a love-hate relationship with them it has evolved an interpretive approach amenable to teaching. The approach suggests some reasons why Flower and Hayes's student cannot write faster and some ways teachers might help him deal with his problem, if that is what it is. Most of the approach has already been indicated in chapter 5. In the present chapter I will do little more than summarize that theoretical outlook and then use it to decontextualize from the Sample some advice for slow writers, handing it over to teachers in the field to restructure for their own courses.

Perspectives on the Development of
Personality Styles: Constancy, Change, Continuity

In the past, the developmental handling of the issue of personality styles has seemed trapped in a circular relationship between change and constancy. For developmentalists, there would be no general subject to study were there no change in human lives, and no study to be made of change were there no human constancies in it. The paradox extends beyond the discipline. Intuitively, we all concoct a notion of a self that has changed during our life yet has somehow remained integrally the same (precisely that notion is Erikson's definition of personal style). Indeed, objective study of life histories finds people periodically and unconsciously rewriting their pasts to maintain a sense of autobiographical consistency. Socially, we all recognize that although everyone adapts to life, the degree of adaptation ranges and that at either extreme lie psychopathologies and moral pathologies: multiple personalities and sycophancy at the overly mobile end, fixation and dogmatism at the overly fixed end. Experimentally, longitudinal studies of personality traits and cognitive styles show the same mixture of change and constancy. Test-retest scores for social extroversion and introversion, for instance, correlate as highly as .84 even after thirty years (Costa and McCrae), yet IQ has proven so unstable that most schools no longer give the test.

As we have seen, the recent dialectical approach to development has reformulated this constancy-change circularity into a more hopeful concept of plasticity (Gollin; Lerner and Busch-Rossnagel). Plasticity does not deny set antecedents but does deny set consequences. It tells the student of Flower and Hayes that he can't compose like some other students because of past familial and social and maybe even genetic influences, but that he can use those forces to continue constructing his personality. As Paul B. Baltes (1984) puts it: "The malleable and the unmalleable travel together. They are bonded to each other not like the opposite sides of the same coin, but like forces that give shape to each other" (x). The plasticity or modifiability of human nature that has turned the student of Flower and Hayes into what he is can allow him to turn himself into what he would prefer to be.

Let's say the student indeed tests out as a strong field-dependent. What can he then do about his writing problem? The transformative has a number of answers, introduced in chapter 5. First, the test may state certain present capabilities of the student but can only hazard statements about future capabilities ("probabilistic epigenesis"). No test-retest for field-independence, or any other trait, has ever shown perfect correlation among any population, and the presence of individuals making both gradual and sudden changes from the past is also a constant. Second, the student probably will not suffer from the problems associated with field-dependence under different writing conditions. Less than a third of both children and adults use such conceptual styles consistently (Tyler: 160). Third, it is unlikely that the student will demonstrate field-dependence, or some similar performance, at every level of his self ("embeddedness"). If he was given a prompt dealing with an area in which he had physical expertise, he would probably not suffer the same problems in constructing a topic. He could then use one level to help develop other levels. Fourth, certain qualities of the personality are less stable and more changeable over time than others. The most consistent traits tend to be vocational interests and self-reported cultural values such as honesty or cheerfulness; the most changeable are social attitudes such as authoritarianism and intellectual styles such as reflectiveness-impulsiveness or abstraction-differentiation. The student's intellectual problem with finding topics seems a good candidate for betterment.

Fifth, developmental adaptability itself can develop. It is a fact seen all across the evolutionary spectrum: "The processes that contribute to an organism developing plasticity and to its final level of plasticity may themselves be considered plastic" (Lerner 1984: 6). The student can train himself to use different cognitive styles (see Witkin and Goodenough's concept of "mobility") and can be taught to find or create writing contexts in which his problem does not apply or even becomes a virtue ("self-actualization"). Finally, in what turns out to be the most agreed-upon fact of recent longitudinal studies, the truly enduring dispositions of humans are not compulsive iterations but open-ended coherencies, not characteristics that keep cropping up but characteristics that keep becoming something else (see Loevinger and Knoll's review of "heterotypic" change: 209). A fear of rejection in high school evolves into hypochondria in middle age, or perhaps into success as a politician. A loner becomes submissive at age eight, anxious at age fourteen, perhaps autonomous at twenty-five. The student's field-dependence can't be turned into a silk purse but can be turned into a lot of other things, probably more useful. The race may be to both the swift and the slow. As Gadamer and Habermas show on the level of experience and social action, development finds a way out of the vicious constancy-change circle via transformative continuity.

Unlike the closed structure of pure constancy and the structurelessness of pure change, the modifiable architectural design of continuity gives teachers a role. "Because there is plasticity," says Lerner, "there is always a potential for intervention" (1984: 147). To personality dispositions that affect writing, teachers can bring a knowledge that works horizontally and vertically, as it were. They can know patterns of continuity, using the common history of a particular style to propose viable proximal zones of development. And they can identify which aspects of a current style tend to be fixed to personality and which tend to be free to change. The second is a very difficult but important critical identification, for which several specialists have recommended a distinction in terms between *cognitive style* and *cognitive strategy* (Messick: 6; Tyler: 160). Perry suggests how a teacher might distinguish the two. Cognitive style is "the relatively stable, preferred configuration of tactics that a person tends to employ somewhat inflexibly in a wide range of environmental negotiations." Cognitive strategy is "a configuration of tactics chosen or constructed from an array of available alternatives to address a *particular kind* of environmental negotiation." Perry argues that even styles can undergo rapid change and can then change strategies and conversely that a strategy can consciously overrule a style (1981: 106–7). Obviously, horizontal knowledge about the histories of particular styles will help make this distinction.

But so far in both areas, the formal knowledge teachers have to go on is slim. I know of no study that attempts to describe how individual writing styles develop over time. No one has taken the trouble to trace the history of students such as the slow writer of Flower and Hayes.

Hints for Novice Slow Writers from
Expert Slow Writers

Although the present study is not longitudinal, the circumstances and findings of the Sample offer a small instructional entry, and I will try to infer a patch or two about the development of slow writers. Both employees and students had the same amount of time to respond to the same prompts. So with some leeway for writers who quit early, we can judge different rates of production by sheer length of essays. The results of such a simplistic measuring are surprising. At the same time that the thirty-two employees were writing better and longer essays, they were producing a wider range of production rates than did the ninety-six students. (Actually this is consistent with an often repeated finding of longitudinal studies: that as people grow older, the differences between them increase; see Baltes 1979.) The distribution of the employee essay lengths shows at the short end a rather isolated group of ten who wrote so little that they can be called blocked even by the standards of student writing. Yet they had been deemed, along with the others in their group, competent writers on the job, and they fared not much worse than did their more rapidly writing group-mates on the holistic rating. In short, there seem to be employee writers who have never shaken the habit of composing very slowly but who have developed the temperament style into competence.[1]

This fact lets us look for special writing strategies or, in Perry's phrase, a "configuration of tactics" that the employee slow writers display and that could benefit those apprentice

---

[1] In fifty minutes the ten wrote essays ranging from 209 to 324 words long. This averages out to 275 words. The students Mike Rose identified as "high blockers" averaged 272 words in a sixty-minute impromptu. The essays of the remaining twenty-two employees ranged from 377 to 821 words long. The student group of fourteen whom I identify as slow writers wrote essays ranging from 94 to 216 and averaging 174 words. Five were freshmen, five sophomores, and four juniors, suggesting that slow writing is a trait that neither changes much with time nor much affects academic success in college.

writers who are blessed with the same disposition but are still saddled with troubles in appropriating it. The transformative first requires that we find out where the students are. Certainly, apprentice slow-writing style shows some strategies that must have contributed to the meager 100 to 200 words they produced in nearly an hour of work. Compared with the average undergraduate, who generated 300 to 400 words, and with the speediest students, who generated 500 to 650, the slow writers tend to organize their essays around complex, thoughtful schemes rather than easy, partitional ones (see chapter 10). They pursue formal, highly generalized ideas almost exclusively, avoiding particulars, examples, and the first person. They extend this formality to diction and syntax, tending to use more "unusual" words, infinitives, and syntactic parallelism, resulting in longer and more complicated clauses. They do not take as much advantage of some small labor-saving tricks, such as relying on pronouns, contractions, abbreviations, and substitution cohesive ties (e.g., "so," "do," "one," "the same"). They like adjectives and identical ties, the use of which slows down production, according to research. They prefer to begin sentences directly with complex, heavily coordinated or modified subjects, or indirectly with "it" or "there" inversions, and to follow up that heavy subject with fewer active verbs, fewer nominalizations, less verbal and clausal coordination, and little free or bound modification. Studies of speech and writing pace have found all these forms attracting extralong hesitation.

Many of these characteristics can be seen in the following typical slow essay, entitled "The Beauty Burden":

> The role of physical appearance is much to significant in our lives today. We spend an astronomical amount of time, money and energy on becoming beautiful. We are socialized in to thinking that beautiful is better. Television, newspapers, infact all forms of the media are constantly bombarding us with beauty aids, youth creams, and fad diets. There are more calories used in making the container for your diet pop than are in the diet pop itself. All this waste of energy for beauty.

It is sad that many are so consumed with the exteriors they neglect to either develope an interior of their own or look for the interior in others. If you could wear your inside face on the outside then there would be a reason to be beautiful; but in real life the outside is rarely a true reflection of the inside.

It is important to see that, compared with the undergraduate writing as a whole, some of this strategy of student slow writing lies closer to the competency of the employee writing, and some of it does not. For instance, the employees also eschew partitional organization, prefer tacit transitions, use a more sophisticated vocabulary, and make longer clauses, as we have seen in chapter 3. So it is misleading to think of the student's slow style necessarily as a deficiency. Put positively, it is an apprentice strategy of writing that in some ways is more mature than other apprentice strategies, and rather than ask if a temperament naturally conducive to such a style can ever be changed, it is fairer and more productive to ask what changes in the strategy more mature writers have made. Have they also made changes in the temperament?

Here is one of the shortest of the employee essays, whose stylistic affinity with "The Beauty Burden" will be evident. Notice in particular the ungracious opening, the fondness for unstated logical connections (parataxis), the aversion to dependent sentence openers, the marmoreal texture of the sentences, the absence of short clauses, the stubborn repetition of certain words (wildlife), the formality of diction and sentence structure, and the progressive emergence of one thought from the previous.

> It is acceptable to kill wildlife in our society.
> It is acceptable to kill small birds and animals on a whim, to vent anger or experiment with a weapon. Young persons are encouraged as hunters to graduate from small to large animals, from helpless species to predators. Trophy hunters are photographed taking large "game" in inaccessible environs.
> The reasons for taking the lives of wildlife range from instinctual (that is the human animal's quest for survival), to sport (a contest

216

between the hunter with weapon and the natural abilities of the bird or animal to detect and avoid the hunter), to slaughter or elimination of a species for a variety of reasons.

Wildlife holds a low position in our societie's values. It is seen as expendable and often the only protected species are those favored for sport hunting. Consequently it is viewed as no great loss when entire areas of land used as habitat for wildlife are cleared and paved.

Wildlife could be seen as an indicator to the wellbeing of our planet. A robust, healthy mix of wildlife indicates a natural system that both supports wildlife and human life. It is a system that supplies food and water fit for human as well as wildlife consumption. As humans, a compassionate view of wildlife could mean a concern for natural systems and for the future of mankind.

I will call this piece "Wildlife." I am guessing that it is the kind of writing the author of "The Beauty Burden" might naturally produce twenty years later. Even her willingness to spend time crafting compact understatement occurs here, and There are more calories used in making the container for your diet pop than are in the diet pop itself finds a family resemblance in often the only protected species are those favored for sport hunting. Such a maturing would not be a bad fate. One thing we can say about "Wildlife" that we cannot yet say about "The Beauty Burden": it reads as competent. Ideas and tactics mesh and move to set forth a brief but lucid and controlled statement. As an essay, it may sound just begun, but I for one trust the author's ability to be able to finish it well. I believe its competence earns it the right to stand as touchstone or milestone for the author of "The Beauty Burden." Here is a sample of strategies, and only a sample, she might entertain as especially fitting her temperament and its natural verbal development.

Filling in the gaps. Logically there is as much distance between the second and third sentences of "The Beauty Burden" as between the first and fourth paragraphs of "Wildlife." Both writers travel from socialization to the effects of socialization, but the student forgets to describe the journey. In part this is to note that "The Beauty Burden" is a whole essay, not a piece of one, and that what is missing lies in between. The gap after the second sentence does not betray an incoherence, and the writer, consciously or unconsciously, must have traversed some of the logical bridge that got her to the third sentence. This is also to note, however, that whatever this bridge consisted of— value judgments, other causations, examples, particulars, counterparticulars—would be better put down than left out. Just as the student of Flower and Hayes does not sound blocked when thinking out loud, so the author of "The Beauty Burden" might be encouraged meta-cognitively to re-act her thinking on paper. Of a thoughtful temper to begin with, she probably would benefit from the kind of "cognitive modeling," or verbalizing of thought processes, which has been found to advance "self-regulative" or self-actualizing aspects of temperament (Bandura: 221).

Letting particulars lead. Given her reflective nature, it is not surprising that three of the four times she approaches particulars, she arranges them neatly in the logical form of an exhaustive or completed analysis: time, money and energy; Television, newspapers, in fact all forms of the media; beauty aids, youth creams, and fad diets. Especially the last is cleverly conceived. The slow-writing employee also shows a predilection for closed categories (small birds and animals; wildlife and human life), along with a similar absence of first-person experience, descriptive detailing, background, and helpful specification. The configuration again suggests a common personal style. Field-dependents also would have trouble extracting background particulars from the context. Several times, however, the employee leaves a series of examples open-ended, which then generates new ideas. In the second paragraph, the reference to predators expands into the detail about the trophy hunters, and the final example of elimination of a species at the end of paragraph three leads to the final idea about the wellbeing of our planet. The thoughtful student slow writer might be persuaded to indulge in the recording of particulars to see what ideas evolve from them.

She might note that it was her detail of <u>fad diets</u> that probably prompted her next sentence, which is the best sally of her essay.

Using tropic sentences. Nevertheless, she will probably be intent less on the exploration of particulars and more on the construction of generalizations. Here I find especially revealing the vexed comment of the student of Flower and Hayes on how rapid writers "just pick out their little topic sentence": "If I just stuck to the topic sentence, maybe, and I just let the topic sentence govern all my thoughts and let that dictate what I was gonna talk about . . . " This is all appealingly ambivalent. The topic sentence confers the gift of length by taking away freedom of thought. His insight into the contrasting natures of fast and slow writers is supported by the Sample, which finds student swift writers willing to be "dictated" or "governed" by familiar, partitional schemes. Slow writers may avoid these traditional forestructures because they prefer the liberty and interest of progressive thinking. Half of Mike Rose's high-blockers expressed a distrust of "plan" as limiting spontaneity (1984: 93).

But the student of Flower and Hayes makes a mistake characteristic of slow writers—who often view composing as a backward-thinking process—when he assumes that swift writing sticks to the topic sentence, as Lot's wife to Gomorrah. Perhaps the classic topic sentence does have this effect, but there is another kind of head sentence, which assists both production of words and release of thought, better named a leading or tropic sentence. It serves not to dictate the ground that the following stretch of discourse will cover but only to point the direction and perhaps the method of travel the writer intends to pursue—a rubric not of topos but of tropos. The third paragraph of "Wildlife" begins tropically with <u>The reasons for taking the lives of wildlife range</u>. . . . At this point the reasons are not topically qualified, and how far they range is not yet known to the reader or, probably, to the writer.

With their yen to develop thought rather than detail, student slow writers might use an early awareness of the kind of thinking they intend to pursue in a stretch of discourse. Once announced, the thought process would both guide the reading and facilitate the writing. The author of "The Beauty Burden" would have benefited from a tropic sentence like the one leading into the body of an employee short essay: <u>This warped beauty value system that seems to plague me, what caused it?</u> Then all along, tropic boosts could push the writing on: "But why do people spend so much?" "The causes must lie deeper." Besides effect → causes, other progressive routes of thinking also serve as conduits of idea production: alternatives → choice, problem → solution, opposition → concession, backing → conclusion. These are all basic organizational patterns increasingly used by students and, as we will see in chapter 10, used almost exclusively by the employees to keep production free of intellectual bogs. "Singling out of parts," said Francis Bacon, "is the life of dispatch" ("Of Dispatch"). The employees have also learned what Bacon immediately adds, that as bad as not dividing at all is dividing too much.

Breaking down the sentence subject. Just as premature definition of the essay or paragraph topic slows production, so does premature definition of the sentence topic. When the author of "The Beauty Burden" begins her fourth sentence with <u>Television, newspapers, in fact all forms of the media</u>, she has wrapped up a box before filling it. "Wildlife" illustrates the simple technique of placing such coordination after the predicate and keeping the subject relatively simple with pronouns or nouns lightly modified (<u>Young persons</u>; <u>Trophy hunters</u>). It also illustrates the standard exception, when a complex subject serves as an interim summary of previous material, as in the second and fourth sentences of the last paragraph.

Unstopping the end. "Wildlife" remains faithful to what may be a deep-seated bent with slow writers: a tendency to visualize life essentially (as Burke would say) in a series of isolated, nominal-like nodes rather than narratively in action strings. But it shows the author of "The Beauty Burden" two ways her method of visualization may be broken down a bit for easier comprehension. One tactic uses "it" and "there" expletives to put new information toward the end of the sentence, ready for easy expansion. So the second sentence of "Wildlife" does not read "To kill small birds and animals on a whim [the new information] is acceptable," but rather It is acceptable to kill small birds and animals on a whim. . . . This allows the writer to continue the sentence with the second tactic, free modification in the terminal position: . . . to vent anger or experiment with a weapon. The nominal focus of their style may discourage both of these slow writers from using many dependent sentence-openers. The employee, however, shows that a dependent structure attached to the end of the previous sentence can serve the same purpose. Francis Christensen first noted the tendency of professional writers to attach new information after simple sentence subjects, and he recommends making free modification terminal. What he did not mention was that the final free modifier of one sentence often carries the theme of the next when that old information is complex and when the rheme, the new information, is simple. The technique is illustrated by the second and third sentences of the second paragraph in "Wildlife." Student slow writers might well practice free modification by putting it wherever it seems right. "Wildlife" shows, for instance, that with a style investing heavily in subject sentence-openers, a few dependent openers can serve admirably to signal logical transitions of major import, as with the Consequently of the fourth paragraph and the As humans of the last.

Forward revision. Despite the oxymoron, the phrase refers to a common and quite reasonable language maneuver. Studies of revision do not mention it because they count only instances when writers go back to alter words already written. In forward revision, writers simply write in the revision as they proceed, as in this passage from one of the employee short essays: We separate these two behaviors as moderation and overindulgence. I should say "society" separates these two behaviors. Revision backward would strike the second sentence and change the We in the first to "Society," thereby eliminating words but also some coherence and emphasis and, of course, good writing time. The author of "Wildlife" possibly took recourse to a variant of forward revision when he came to the word <u>instinctual</u> in the first sentence of his third paragraph. Realizing that the word alone would not bear the weight of his intended meaning, he added the explanatory parenthesis rather than revise back of the word. This set a pattern of postmodification for the next two nouns in the series, prompting ideas he would not have had otherwise, perhaps. "Wildlife" shows forward revision working in concert with two structures slighted in "The Beauty Burden" yet according with its spirit: postnominal modification and logical concession.

Forward revision is also allied with techniques of speech, where changes have to be made incrementally, through repetitions, backtracking, and self-repairs. Teachers are tempted to recommend that blocked writers loosen up and try some of the oral-language strategies utilized by speedy writers of all ages—colloquial diction, brief clauses, few adjectives, contractions, the first person, and such. But that may strike too close to the temperamental heart of the slow style. As much as possible, instruction will respect the developmental ground of the writer, as this short sample of tactics has tried to do. The teacher should be out to make the slow style more efficient, not turn it into the Laelic or any other style.

Benefits of a Developmental
Approach to Production Styles

As an investigation of production styles, this analysis of impromptu writing may appear to be wasted time. It would seem better to ask how students and competent employees write under unforced conditions. That question would respect quality, show what a writer *can* do. But in its own way, the present question of what a writer can do in an hour does show this. "True dispatch is a rich thing," Bacon wrote, characteristically intending the second adjective as no metaphor. "For time is the measure of business, as money is of wares." As practically any sociological study of occupational writing will show, quality and efficiency of production are rarely separated in the world of work. The often maligned, unrehearsed impromptu may be the student writing exercise that comes closest to that most common occupational form of writing, the letter or short memorandum occupying less than a page of space and less than twenty minutes of composing time. One of the employees in the Sample was identified as "competent" because of the "blunt" letters he wrote for the bank he worked in. All the working-world writers of the Sample probably respect brute productivity in writing and know their personal formula for it well. The fact helps explain not only their significant increase in length over the students' essays but other differences too—their increase in additive connectors or in pronouns, objective coordination, question-clause nominalizations, homophone misspellings, and postpositioning of both bound and unbound constructions. All aid or reflect rapid writing.

What an investigation of production style truly needs are approaches that go beyond the formal analysis here. If the maturing of temperament is an important factor in writing, then the motivation for writing effects has to be studied, as well as the effects themselves. Consider pauses in the act of writing. At a normal transcribing speed of twenty-five words a minute (idiosyncratic differences in scribing rate will be minimal), slow writers in the Sample spent about forty-three minutes of the fifty *not* writing. What did they do with this time? Stephen Witte's speak-aloud study of "pre-text," the amount of text that writers produce in their heads before they start putting words down on paper, found wide variation in writers. Perhaps slow writers are mentally composing entire sentences before scribing. Ruth, one of Mike Rose's high-blockers, "believed that every sentence she wrote had to come out grammatically correct the first time around" (1984: 15). Such elaborate pre-texting might explain the tendency of student slow writers to start sentences with complicated subjects containing new information, and might recommend writing exercises that would increase their trust in their ability to carry off midsentence improvisations. Studies measuring reaction time and subvocal activity (reflex movement of the articulatory musculature) suggest that some writers have a concentration problem and tend to stop composing when they stop scribing. Gary M. Schumacher and his associates had writers analyze videotape of their writing. Juniors and seniors paused as frequently as summer-orientation freshmen, but for shorter durations, during which (they say) they engaged more in writerly activities such as planning and rescanning and thinking about strategy. Apparently, writing done while not writing can also develop. Unfortunately, none of these studies look at slow writers per se. How they spend their time remains unknown, although some techniques for finding out are now available.

The teaching profession also could use longitudinal studies of personal styles. Beyond finding out nomothetically how writing changes with time, we need to know idiographically how particular styles develop—what of a style changes and when, what remains stable over the years despite the variety of tasks and the changes of circumstance (Perry's *style*), what can be adapted or negotiated for temporary needs (Perry's *strategy*), what tends to develop in sequence with other styles? Such studies can model themselves on already achieved longitudinal programs that have found ways to look at the transformative development of temperament. These programs study outer historical and cultural changes, inner universal changes, and self-regulatory changes in interaction between personality and environment.[2] Without such information, the teaching of any

---

[2] Especially the studies that follow subjects over decades make fascinating reading, e.g., the populations of the Fels Research Institute (Kagan and Moss) and of the New York Longitudinal Study (Thomas and Chess), Terman's gifted individuals (Sears), and the students of Jyväskylä, Finland (Pulkkinen), the University of Michigan (Mortimer et al.), and the University of Stockholm (Magnusson). A 1980 review of such investigations is Moss and Susman. There is only one comparable longitudinal study of writing, Loban's following of schoolchildren from kindergarten to grade twelve. The farthest that the writing of college students has been followed is *two years:* Jewell et al.; Maimon and Nodine; Kerek, Daiker, and Morenberg; Eblen.

stylistic writing strategy will remain ungrounded and moot. What should we teach students about something as simple as the first-person pronoun? Half of entering freshmen have been told never to use "I" in their writing. *Yet* historically, "I" and "we" are acquiring respectability in professional science publications. *Yet,* although half of the thirty-two professionals in the Sample felt no qualms about using the first person, only two of the ten who were the slowest writers did so, and Herman Witkin describes research that finds field-dependents reluctant to refer to themselves in speech and writing (1976: 67–68). *Yet,* as we will see, age-span researchers found college-age people—women more commonly than men—generally moving toward a surer recognition that the unique self holds its own privileged position in questions of morality and knowledge. Amid such circling among cultural standards, personal temperaments, language-processing constraints, and maturing trends, the teachers' simple rhetorical advice sounds like whistling in the wind. An understanding of the way some common personal styles develop would not hand a teacher a panacea, but it would help.

Among other benefits, it would help reject blanket pedagogies. The maturing of different styles and sets asks for a certain amount of instructional tailoring. Judging by the progress of the employee slow writers, the author of "The Beauty Burden" could well use exercise in free writing to fill in logical gaps and to give her confidence with midsentence alteration. A Christensen program in generative sentence and paragraph expansion would give her the practice she needs in the syntactic reflex to add to any structure being written, instantly, any idea that arises unpredictably out of it. But an O'Hare program of sentence combining might do no more than exaggerate the kind of compression that she is already skilled enough at. Student swift writers have different needs. Free writing would review rather than re-act the present developmental phase of a writer whose nimble five-hundred-word essay reads from beginning to end like this:

As stated earlier in the paper fast food chains have really picked up, *BUT,* have you noticed that there are many health food restaurants, delis' & cafe's popping up everywhere. Food in the stores is becoming more natural, you see signs "no preservatives added" or nutrisiously grown" etc. Also all kinds of spas & gyms & joggers are coming out of hiding.

Here it is sentence combining that might give the writer a needed push toward more variety and more point. Above all, the transformative approach cautions against setting one temperamental style against another, against asking slow writers to attempt a fast style, or frugal to imitate profligate, or thoughtful to yearn after impulsive. It does not recommend any immature style to seek after any particular mature style but rather after its own mature style.

The approach would also help pacify, or at least comprehend, the free-for-all of interpretive tales concerned with temperament and the act of writing. The tales teachers tell about production alone are so familiar that they need only listing to show how they contradict. Good writers craft slowly, like sculptors in marble—good writers use tape recorders if necessary to catch the flow. Good writers wait until the moment of inspiration—good writers force themselves to compose something every day at the same hour. Efficient writers plan ahead and scan behind—efficient writers follow their impulses and "shape at the point of utterance." Good writing can never be produced under impromptu conditions—in-class essays are frequently better than out-of-class essays because the latter are overwritten. Behind this interpretive mishmash lies one certainty left behind from the spate of investigation into cognitive and temperamental styles during the 1950s and 1960s: that people of one style or set tend to understand more easily and evaluate more highly the communicative strategies of someone else of the same style or set (Witkin 1976: 63–69).

To that we can add the transformative certainty that mismatches will occur even between people sharing the same style if they stand at different points in the development of that style—teacher and student, for instance. In sum, it would help if teachers would recognize their own role in those genuine differences in temperament, developmental turn, historical change, and composing habit and would adjust their interpretation of student writing accordingly. Teachers tell students that good writers sense the audience in order to adapt their style to it, but teachers often forget the corresponding principle of communication: that good readers sense an author's peculiar style and adapt their reading strategies to it. Slow writing often requires meticulous reading, rapid writing often needs swift reading. What happens when fast-reading teachers meet slow-writing students? (For one thing, the five-hundred-word essay cited above receives a better holistic rating than either "The Beauty Burden" or "Wildlife").

One has to read slowly Edward Hoagland, Edward Dahlberg, Emerson, Hazlitt, Sir Thomas Overbury, and Francis Bacon himself. To place "The Beauty Burden" and "Wildlife" in that Theophrastian tradition is not to set them up for failure or ridicule but to set them in their own proper personal history, for success. It is not to try them under the formative law of change, that everybody goes through the same stylistic stages, or to test them by the English-teacher moral entertainment of constancy, that there is one best or universal style for everybody. Instead it is to apply the developmental "regulative idea" of continuity, that people grow best by leading from the strength of where they are.

CHAPTER 9

The Sentence:
Studio and Free

ENGLISH TEACHERS USED TO DEFINE THE SEN-
tence as a complete thought or as a grammatical structure complete in itself. Those definitions were doomed once William
James had routed the rationalist fancy that "a single idea" could
be "a definitely outlined thing" and replaced it with the psychological notion that a thought must be "a mental field" or "a wave
impossible to define" (190). Of course, the sentence did not die
at once, not in institutions, such as composition courses, that
have a certain stake in grammar and outlines, but its demise has
been reported more and more often. Today the sentence almost, but not quite, has joined *point, simplicity, theme,* and other
quaint terms of language analysis now past their prime.

Researchers were some of the first to doubt the sentence.
Since it could not be defined structurally, discourse analysts
stopped using it in speech transcription. Since there are regressions in the linear match between length of sentence and
age of writer (sixth graders compose shorter sentences than
fourth graders), composition researchers replaced it with the
T-unit or clause—those researchers who had not given up

measuring syntax altogether. Teachers gradually followed suit. They retired workbooks requiring students to name underlined "parts" of speech or to "complete" sentences by "filling in" blanks with the correct form, and they substituted workbooks requiring students to dissolve and "combine" someone else's sentences into their own. Many teachers even questioned sentence combining as putting the formal cart before the rhetorical horse, and focused instead on the invention of ideas and the appeals of argument. Certainly many doubted the usefulness of data showing "age trends" in sentence features, as we have seen in chapter 3. Professionals may write longer sentences than students, but the fact is a moot point for teaching, or if not moot at least precarious, since some of the most appalling extravagances, with which we ought to alarm rather than to familiarize apprentice writers, take the form of long sentences—State Department documents and legal contracts and the like.

Precarious or not, the trends *are* developmental and need to be faced here. The employees write essays both with a better holistic rating and with longer sentences—significantly longer than the junior sentence, which is significantly longer than the sophomore and the freshman. In short, the Sample repeats the finding of nearly every comparison between experts and students regarding sentence size: given similar writing tasks, experts will construct sentences from 10 to 20 percent longer. This chapter asks three basic questions about this growth in sentence size. What formal components contribute to it— changes in syntactic structures, in cohesive devices, in dictional choices? What developmental shifts in ideas or affect lie behind these formal changes? And what do these two changes together imply about a shift in the rhetorical sense of the sentence? This last question will bring us to a central paradox in the maturing of sentence strategy: although the competent employees are preferring longer sentences, they are, in their own way, undermining the independent status of sentence.

The approach in this chapter (and the approach to essay organization in the next) will be a return to the nomothetic. I argue that general population trends in development do help teachers decide on course procedures applying to the entire class. The argument bears on the major decisions about composition and "sentence-work"—whether teachers should have students spend time with the Christensen-like or the O'Hare-like exercises mentioned in the last chapter, whether they should have students meta-cognitively study techniques of obfuscation or obscurantism in "systematically distorted discourse," whether they should proceed top-down from the larger forms of the paragraph or the essay to the smaller ones of the sentence, whether they should put content before form or vice versa.

A quarter of a century ago, Kellogg Hunt's advice for researchers was to study subsentence structures: "It is time for sentence length to be superseded" (1965: 48). The message the competent workplace writers send teachers is to return to the sentence. It hasn't died among writers, who know that it is still the elemental rhetorical unit. They do not *write* in morphemes, phrases, clauses, or even T-units. The way to tell this is to note the command that is exercised by the sentence and that these units lack. Sentences are like knights in chess, the first piece that can move backward as well as forward. You cannot make a clause out of any shorter element, whereas you can make a sentence out of a dependent clause ("Which brings us to another point"), a phrase ("A final introductory point"), a word ("Done"), even part of a word ("Wh____?"). These have been called "minor" sentences—an unfortunate name, since they are full grown. The sentence is something better than "a single idea," a "definite outline," or even a "mental field." It is a rhetorical gestalt. Writers make conscious decisions about their sentencing, just as they make conscious decisions about their paragraphing, specifying, exemplifying, arguing, and so on. There will always be more to be learned, by teachers and students, from a study of sentences than from a study of words, clauses, or T-units.

Why the Employees Need Their Sentence

The employee sentences average three words longer than the sophomore, one word longer than the junior. Although this may not seem much of a change, the top of the distribution shows the difference. Three-quarters of the employees and only a third of the students make sentences thirty-five words long or longer, 22 percent of the employees and only 2 percent of the students make sentences fifty words long or longer. How do the older writers handle these longer sentences, and what prompts them to do so?

The evidence suggests first that they are willing to use and require the reader to use more short-term memory. This shows up in what Victor H. Yngve calls "sentence depth," or roughly the amount of delay a sentence forces on readers in bringing its words to fulfilled grammatical sense. With the phrase "a large, expensive, new house," readers must hold the article in mind for four words before its sense is completed with "house," whereas in "a new house both large and expensive," they must wait only two words (460). The employees construct more two-part and three-part prenominal adjective series, as in this first example, as well as more interruptive appositives and medial free modifiers, which also can increase sentence depth. Developmentalists in information processing have documented a highly systematic increase in short-term memory capacity up to about age sixteen. Eight-year-olds generally can hold in storage and then apply a set of instructions up to three information bits long, sixteen-year-olds up to seven (Case: 34). This growth, however, depends on familiarity with the task and willingness to use the capacity (Fischer, Hand, and Russell), and teachers may well expect sentence depth to continue growing on through college as writers become more and more accustomed to and sure of their writing and their ideas.

Maturing writers require greater memory capacity partly for their push toward more complex nominals. One need not be adept in the intricacies of Yngvian analysis to see the reading and writing memory requirements of a noun cluster such as a̲ brief overview of a selected frame of time. In nominal restriction the Sample shows a highly consistent rise. Juniors devote 6 percent and employees 10 percent more of their words to it than do freshmen. That makes a weighty and quite noticeable difference. Older writers do not spread this additional bound modification around but concentrate it in larger and larger clumps, a trend astonishingly regular, beginning with fourth-graders (Hunt 1965: 114–15). The example above has four levels of restriction, as shown in figure 7. As we move from freshman to junior to employee essays, we encounter a larger and larger portion of nominal restriction appearing in each category from two-level to eight-level clusters. As John C. Mellon argues, such packaging of nominal units reflects an obvious developmental change in the way people order their ideas into increasingly complex classificatory hierarchies. He called the ordering "naming" and associated it with Piagetian decentering. It has been shown, however, that the ideas people use and comprehend keep requiring a grasp of more and more complex or "higher-order" ideas through and beyond the college years, not only for formal, Piagetian class-inclusion operations (Moshman and Franks) but also for critical thinking that is analogical (Sternberg 1984a), dialectical (Basseches 1984), relational (Sinnott), and epistemic (Karen S. Kitchener 1983).

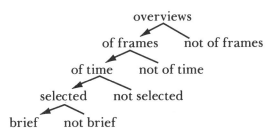

Figure 7.

233

As Yngve's analysis makes clear, the depth of a sentence does not necessarily depend on its length. In managing their longer sentences, the employees actually *decrease* Yngvian depth. Their need to express or name a more complex world is accompanied by the need to make the naming of it readable. For instance, they use more gerunds and question-word nominalizations, where a predicate and its attendant adverbs can enliven an especially sluggish restricting apparatus. As we have seen in their short essays, they avoid balky, heavily modified subjects, which require readers to hold complex information in mind until the predicate. When their subject has to be complex, they are more likely to resort to the "it" or "there" inversion or to pronouns that carry with them previous modification. They place only a fourth of their nominal compounding in the subject slot, students around half.

All this entails moving information to the end of structures. That tactic describes a deep developmental trend, highly consistent, already apparent in the student sentence. With the postfreshman writers, this can be seen in an increase in final free modification (but not in initial), in posthead nominal modification (but not in pre-), in coordination of objects (but not of subjects), and in prepositional phrases, which usually follow noun heads. Meanwhile, the employees' number of words put up front in dependent sentence openers is exactly the same as the students', as other novice-expert comparisons have found (Riley, Christensen, Gebhard). This developmental trend toward postpositioning can be of great diagnostic use to teachers. Readable English, of course, has only so much room in front. Modification need not increase in complexity much at all before even students can hear that it—or part of it—must be placed after the structure modified. Construction of postplaced or "progressive structures" (Yngve: 456) is the classic way of reducing memory load.

In the last chapter, we saw that postpositioned or open structures also assist production, which leads to another, less obvious reason the employees write longer sentences. It saves words. The explanation can be seen most readily in the finding that employees use fewer explicit devices of coherence. They show a lower rate of pronouns, demonstratives, comparatives, repeated words, and logical transitions such as "on the other hand" and "for example." Synonym rate remains the same. Only the rate of simple coordinative connectors increases. I have pursued the pedagogical implications of this odd finding at length elsewhere (Haswell 1989), but here I will repeat two developmental facts of special help to teachers. First, grammatical relationships within sentences provide writers with their most economical means of generating coherence. In the following employee sentence, notice how the conditionality of a dependent clause and the progressive order of a nominal series express a coherent chain of causes: If there weren't the constant pressures of changing styles, the economy would suffer and lag, unemployment would rise, and those who are out of jobs would not be able to continually adapt to the new ideals themselves. Any attempt to chop this into smaller sentences requires the addition of explicit and potentially confusing ties: "Styles are always changing. *This* creates a constant pressure. Without *that pressure,* the economy would suffer. *As a result it* would *then* lag." And so on. Compared with students, Kellogg Hunt's professional writers rewrote the information in "Aluminum" with longer sentences and fewer words (1970). Maturing writers intuit what discourse analysis has just begun to affirm and explain: that long sentences tend to be easier to comprehend than short ones.

These same grammatical structures abet a popular choice of older writers among the various means of coherence: collocation ties. Collocations are those tacit connections that inhere in conceptual frameworks of shared knowledge and experience. In the above sentence, a knowing reader collocates (co-locates) the words economy, lag, unemployment, rise, and jobs as parts of a familiar politico-economic system and needs no explicit verbal bridge when the next sentence begins As long as the free enterprise system is desired by the majority of society. . . .

Collocations or unstated cultural frames underlying discourse are a small, unexplored realm in the study of development, but there can be little doubt that as writers mature they rely more and more on collocations (Bamberg; McCulley) and that the lesser use of them accounts for some characteristic behavior of apprentice writers—their slowness of production, awkwardness of flow, thinness of content.

That there is an intimate bond among grammatical structures, cultural frames, and production rate can be surmised from research into writing pace. Ann Matsuhashi found that writers pause less before collocation ties than before repeats. Writers also tend to pause longer just after function words than they do around content words. That may be an unexpected finding, but it is easily verified with a moment's listening to impromptu speech and is perfectly reasonable on second thought. Function words name syntactic structures, and usually we take less time grabbing a syntactic cart than selecting the groceries to put in it. Observe the longest pauses in the following sentence, taped by Ann Matsuhashi and Karen Quinn. The student is in the act of writing about a collaborative writing group: "Once we had everything figured as to [10.0 second pause] what we wanted to do [7.5], [8.6] there was now [9.1] the matter of researching this remarkable man" (330). The structural decisions to follow "figured" with a prepositional phrase and to shape the main clause as a "there" expletive obviously were determined before the exact verbal expressions used to fill these slots.

Such syntactic framing acts as a kind of propulsive mechanism for expression, but also as a possible semantic trap. Here the writer pulls out two boxes to hold substantives ("as to," "there was") when he wants to fill them with action. In an interview later, the writer explained that he got trapped in the middle of the sentence with his "as to" preposition because he could not find a way to jump from motivation ("what we wanted to do") to means. But notice that he also failed to follow up on the "once . . . then" syntactic frame he began with. Clearly, a cultural frame appropriate to the syntactic frame would have allowed quicker expression, for example, the familiar scenario attached to the concept of *strategy* and expressed with a complete "once . . . then" structure: "Once we set our goals and settled on our strategy, we could begin our research." Teachers can help maturing writers develop their fund of these cultural-syntactic frames in variety and accessibility.[1]

The final major difference in the longer employee sentence is free modification. In some ways it conveys more developmental motives than any other formal element. Cynthia Watson found its increase from senior high-school to upper-division college writing to be the only syntactic change present across three different rhetorical aims—expressive, explanatory, and persuasive. In the Sample the rate at which free modifiers appear jumps from about one every two sentences (undergraduates) to three every four (employees). Compared with freshmen, sophomores and juniors put more than half again as many words into final free modification. Employees double the freshman rate. In some ways the most compelling figure of all is that more than a seventh of the students used no final free modification in their essays at all, whereas all employees used some. The figure supports Christensen and other novice-expert studies (Gebhard; Wolk; Broadhead, Berlin, and Broadhead) and seems to say that a certain amount of free modification, especially at the end of sentences, is almost obligatory for mature writing. Why?

---

[1] The location of function words at the head of the frames makes English a "look-ahead language" (Kimball: 21). That production, comprehension, and remembrance of language rely on these frames (usually of about the size of a clause) is a fact thoroughly documented by discourse analysts. One of the pioneers deserves a note, since he is often forgotten: John A. Van Bruggen. In 1946 he published an account of a laborious study of writing flow, in which an observer copied the scribing motions of subjects on a motor-driven roll of paper, just as a human electrocardiograph. Van Bruggen's eighth- and ninth-graders already show the classic post–initial structure hesitation (each period marks a pause of .3 seconds): "Surrounded . . by tackle and . . . hooks I cast my line into . . . . the water . . and sat waiting . . . . . for the first . . bite, which, . . . I . . . felt confident, ... would come in . . . a few minutes" (145).

The answer seems to be that the form serves a plethora of mature rhetorical purposes, more than just the function of commenting that Christensen assigned to it. It has been noted that Christensen's attractive examples of final free modification almost all come from descriptive narration, arguing that the form may not be crucial to nonfiction. I think it can be argued that indeed the form has a narrative base, but a base underlying a number of intellectual maneuvers essential to mature nonnarrative discourse. I will call this base *incrementation*. Consider this final free modification from an employee essay on the adverse personal effect of artificial standards of physical appearance:

> It is a shame too, you know, the way I was saying those Woody Allen things in my head about my underdeveloped friend Gordon last summer, *only to find out recently that Gordon has had 5 operations for brain tumors.* He's slight, he's stooped, his face is drawn in lines of pain, that's what!

The final free modifier, in my italics, describes a moment of enlightenment dispelling misconception and leading to reconception. It is incremental because it both repeats and adds: without the earlier illusion, there would be no new insight.

Notice what happens when this free modifier is converted to a bound construction: " . . . those Woody Allen things in my head about my underdeveloped friend Gordon last summer that were dispelled by my discovery recently that Gordon has had 5 operations for brain tumors. He's slight. . . . " This unwieldy nominal contraption ("things" is restricted seventeen times) sits like an overelaborate tank without treads, only vaguely aimed in a direction. By comparison with the original, we see the most common service provided by final free modification: to simplify the comprehension of a complex nominal by freeing and singling out those parts the writer will follow up.

Like other syntactic relationships, final free modification also saves words. To convert the form into a separate sentence usually requires added words if the full meaning is to be retained: "It is a shame too, you know, the way I was saying those Woody Allen things in my head about my underdeveloped friend Gordon last summer. Only, to my chagrin, I found out recently that Gordon has had. . . . " The phrase "to my chagrin" must be added because originally the free modification performed two operations at once. It related two ideas together as a sequence and as equal forces. It split the action in two (first the denigration of Gordon's appearance and then the discovery of his operations) but spread the *shame* equally over both. Its diplomatic ploy is to emphasize the first syntactically by making the second dependent on it and to emphasize the second rhetorically by placing it last. Writing the version as two sentences forfeits this ploy. Sentence length will be shortened but wordiness increased.

Final free modification, then, is the optimal form for two ideas, both fairly complex, of equal weight, with the second incrementally rising from the first—a kind of dialectical doubletake. This describes the minimal instance, and the form allows chaining of such doublets. The point is that incremental progression of ideas characterizes forms of thinking that intuitively we feel to be mature and that apprentice writers are actively acquiring during the college years—concession, refutation, justification, qualification, irony, and other recursive forms. Here are a few examples from the employees.

Concession:

Roman literature by Cicero and medieval literature by St. Thomas Aquinas all recognized the significance of physical appearance in determining the acceptability of a politician, *although not to the same degree as in Greek literature.* It was during the Renaissance that ideas of beauty or handsomeness became a dominant factor.

Concession followed by reaffirmation:

[Arguing that politics have always been influenced by physical appearance] Queen Elizabeth I, whose suitor, Sir Walter Raleigh, was known as handsome, was herself a model of stately beauty. On the other hand, the kings of France were considered effete, *in part due to their decadent life-style, but also due to their physical appearance and dress.* More recently . . .

Rebuttal of expected criticism:

In other words when I look at a person I believe I can look past his dress, hairstyle, manner of talk, and appreciate his or her beauty, *even though she or he may not appear to fit my perceived standard of good looking.* In other words . . .

Redefinition, the second causally related to the first:

Standards provide a sense of direction, *a norm for action that a majority of some identifiable groups accept.* As a result, a standard provides direction, security, and structure.

Repetition with increment in emotion:

It was the decade of the "Me Generation"—*the beautiful "Plastic People"—the product of too much Madison Avenue.* We were sold a bill of goods.

Explanation, with increment in implication and emotion:

Young persons are encouraged as hunters to graduate from small to large animals, *from helpless species to predators.* Trophy hunters . . .

Ironic revision:

But something happened several weeks ago that rather rattled me. It was the woman who sat down next to me in church, *of all places.* She was the type I couldn't just glance at.

Summary of equal but progressively related points:

The reason, then, that Codes of Conduct are created and maintained is for educational purposes, *which hopefully limit those loss of dollars that come about from those costly nasty indiscretions.*

This last sentence concludes its essay, and helps explain why so many employee essays end with a final free modifier.

Two more examples of free modifiers make a last, important point. Most students would conceive and write the following employee sentence without the commas: At the same time women ate healthier foods, *with fewer refined sugars and animal fats.* This helped prevent skin blemishes as well as excess pounds. As Christensen says, the comma signals the addition of a comment on the main idea, but in this case it is a comment of a characteristic nature. The comma warns that the subject, what women ate, is going to be reclassified—as it turns from a final cause (the food will make them healthier) to an efficient cause (it is composed of less refined sugar and saturated fat). Free modifiers are aptly named in this central ability to escape the bounds of their neighboring classification.

The ability serves especially well in the middle of sentences and explains why the employee use doubled the student use there. From an employee essay: The clothing industry for kids, *especially in the junior high age,* can be a real rip off for parents. The key signal, especially, suddenly creates, as if in midair, a new logical system, free of the preceding chronological classification in the sense that it may relate to that classification in any number of ways. Will cost, style, or psychology explain the prominence of the junior-high years? As we will see in chapter 12, a willingness to make these kinds of jumps from one hierarchical or classificatory system to another, and to relate them, is a major factor in the intellectual and affective age-span shifts from late adolescence to adulthood. Such system jumping is the key to dialectical thinking (Riegel; Basseches), contextual thinking (Gilligan), meta-cognitive thinking (Karen S. Kitchener 1983; Birnbaum), and metaphorical thinking (Arlin), as well as to awareness of self-limitations (Viney), to growth in empathy (Benack), and to escape from the personal or the institutional to the interpersonal (Kegan). Again it argues that developmental growth in syntax reflects important inner growth.

A Sense of the Sentence: Student, Employee, Teacher

In one of the few process studies of writers constructing sentences, David S. Kaufer, John R. Hayes, and Linda Flower show how six professionals fashioned longer ones than did graduate students. Basically the professionals proceeded much as we have surmised the competent employees did. They advanced largely in a "progressive" or left-to-right way, rarely thinking backward to use an idea they had not used earlier. And they advanced largely in chunks—phrase by phrase or clause by clause. Their pauses show the classic hesitation after function words. The researchers conclude that the fluency of expert writers depends "on a large body of sentence pattern knowledge acquired through thousands of hours of practice" (127).

Despite this conclusion, however, the researchers' flow-chart model of the composing of a sentence has writers "choose meaning" before they "select surface form" (139). Their idealized sequence may reflect a contemporary pedagogical disillusionment with the imitation of form, as we have seen in chapter 4, and it may reflect a cognitive-processing tendency to put inner mental activity before outer community conventions, as Patricia Bizzell would argue (1982). But it does not exactly reflect their own findings or a great deal of contemporary thought on the way language works. Both Habermas and Gadamer would point out that to "choose meaning" *is* to choose form. The part of experience humans wish to communicate is a "symbolically prestructured reality," as Habermas puts it (1979: 10). Or in Gadamer's equally radical formulation, "Language pre-forms thought" (1975: 491).

Perhaps with this issue it is not necessary for teachers of the language to take the high philosophic road, but it is important for them to keep in mind a certain fundamental interaction between meaning and form. Of course, approaches can emphasize one or the other, can stress language use as debate or as game. Habermas, for instance, emphasizes meaning in his analysis of the way people arrive at a "consensus" through the action of speech, and hence he focuses on such nonformal "validity claims" as comprehensibility, truth, trustworthiness, and suitability (1979: 1–68). Gadamer emphasizes given linguistic structures in his analysis of one individual's understanding of another through "language games," and hence he focuses on the way language "draws the players into itself and thus itself becomes the actual subjectum of the playing" (1975: 446), the way for instance "people conversing are far less the leaders of it than the led" (345). But the teacher of competence in the use of language might well balance emphasis on form and meaning. Anyone who has had to learn and use a foreign language knows how the lack of syntax stymies the expression of mature ideas and how the lack of a situation for meaningful communication retards the acquisition of syntax. As Kaufer, Hayes, and Flower show (flow chart aside), the process of composing inevitably marries meaning and sentence form, and teachers probably ought to try to develop one along with the other.

We can surmise that not only has the form of the sentence generally developed with working writers, but their working sense of it has changed as well. Compared with the students, they seem to seize the sentence as something less self-contained, more a part of the larger discourse flow, more sensuous than sententious. The sheer length of some of their constructions suggests that they sally into sentences less often with an exact notion of where they will end. In the middle, their fondness for post-positioned structures suggests that they are more aware of readability. At the end, their use of free modification suggests that their gaze is already partly on the next sentence. No doubt their amazing jump in T-unit variance holds for their sentence as a whole, and they have a better sense of rhetoric effect achieved by contrasts in size with surrounding utterances. They produce not only more outstandingly long sentences but more emphatically brief ones too. Only a tenth of the students wrote sentences of three words or less, as opposed to nearly a third of the employees.

Whereas the students grasp sentences as something simpler and neater, and can afford to express them in a thinner yet more definitive manner, the older writers apprehend the sentence as something more complex, and almost out of necessity have found ways to express it more densely yet more openly.

243

Students are more likely to intuit the sentence as a finished whole, the older writers as something fluid, without clear boundaries, or at least with a terminus more like a breather than a finish line, more of a step than a stop, less a "definitely outlined thing" and more a part of a "mental field." Heterodox as it sounds, I imagine that students sense sentences more clearly than the older writers do, more as handbook exempla— sharp and bounded like the aphoristic Renaissance "sentence" or like sentences from the bench, isolated dooms. They have not yet learned what George L. Dillon calls the "Snippet Paradox": "a readable snippet is a bad discourse chunk" (10). Matured writers apprehend the sentence more as a sentience, their sense of closure weaker. Often, matured sentences can be cut up or recombined without loss of effect, but this is less often the case with student sentences.

What then do these writers want with the sentence? The students want to get the sentence down right, as if they were spelling a long word. The competent writers want the sentence to get them on with their argument. The student sentence is stiff and studied, like a studio piece, self-aware of fingering and the threat of mistakes. The older sentence has internalized technique, is now freer to attend to effect and interpretation.

And what is the typical writing teacher's sense of the sentence? That is not easy to locate. The occasional ungrounded mutter that "students don't know what a sentence is" seems to reflect an interpretation nearly the opposite of this chapter's. In fact, it seems to write large the student notion that sentences are self-contained atoms whose internal rules have no bearing on surrounding sentences. Another common interpretive angle on sentences still takes the Errors Approach (which always seems to get more charged as it nears the smaller rhetorical particles). Teachers who want to believe the myth of deterioration find plenty of evidence left by students experimenting with sophisticated forms new to them. In an opposing camp are teachers who apply the quite defensible theory that sentences should be left unattended in favor of heftier rhetorical agents such as tone, thesis, and argument. Finally, there are teachers just insensitive to sentences. Lorraine Neilsen and Gene L. Piché once fabricated versions of student essays radically different in the way nominal heads were modified. One version read, "The short, straight spurts of warm air that came out." The other read: "Warm air came out in spurts. They were short and straight." The two styles had no apparent influence on teachers. Yet as I have shown here and in chapter 3, and as Hunt, Mellon, Gebhard, and others have shown, nominal modification plays a developmental role, as do many of the other syntactic maneuvers teachers downplay. I can argue only that generally teachers could use a greater sensitivity to the common development of the sentence.

That sensitivity would simply make more reasonable some of the sentence quiddities of students hitching and winding their way to rhetorical maturity. Here a junior is wrestling with the relationship between aging and conceptions of beauty.

> The second aspect of age is how old mentally, assuming the person is normal and chronological age equals mental age, is the judge of beauty. If he (since I don't know how female children think, the judge is male) is a child he would probably think the most beautiful girl of his age level is abhorent and something to be avoided. If he, turning his attention to teenage women or young adults, were to judge them, a different standard would be used: that of his mother or sister, if he has any. Here he would probably not show any real interest in beauty either because of his age.

Nearly every one of these syntactic lurches is positively associated with ordinary development. Older writers indulge in long parenthetical comments like these. But they no longer automatically put everything up front. They are attracted to the shifts in perspective reflected in the concept beautiful in the second sentence. But they would avoid the confusion with a final free modifier: "he would think any girl of his age level abhorrent and to be avoided, no matter how beautiful." They like the kind of meta-cognitive aside in that sentence (Erving Goffman calls it a shift in "footing" [1981: 125–57]). But they would put it in its customary way and place, at the beginning or the end of the paragraph: ("I have made my example male, since I can't pretend to know how female children think"). In general, the developmental perspective would recognize that most of the sentence problems here are rooted in a budding intellectual relativism, common in most college students, that struggles to make sense out of several separate but interrelated systems: mental aging, physical aging, gender differences, and authorial bias. The syntactic missteps reflect as much a "transitional competence" as does the word <u>abhorent</u>, which is spelled both incorrectly and reasonably.

To deal with these kinds of sentence problems, the developmental perspective would look with special favor on the techniques offered by the employee practice and supported by other novice-expert comparisons: simplified subjects, modified nouns to convey complex hierarchical categories, medial and final free modification, postplacement of elaborated ideas, cultural framing to keep cohesion tacit, series to order complicated detail, and—let's admit it—longer sentences. The majority of undergraduates could use practice in these tactics, although individual tailoring should be maintained. Based on the transformative principles, a teaching sequence would first locate immature structures that writers are overusing, then meta-cognitively draw attention to them (perhaps by showing self-contradiction when the structures are carried to an extreme, as with overloading of prenominal modification), then allow selection from fitting and more mature tactics, and finally encourage practice until the tactics have been absorbed with some automaticity. And based on the principle of generative learning, teachers might do well to advance these specific *tactics*—which, as Perry points out, will be appropriated eccentrically for different personal styles—in tandem with the more general underlying *strategies* of the mature competence: reducing short-term memory load, trusting midsentence creativity, maintaining variety, respecting given-new order, balancing economy with readability, attending to the flow of surrounding sentences.

In all of this, syntactic regression should be expected. It will show up in comma splices, anacolutha, Kitzhaberian "stringy" sentences, and other aberrations—an exuberant mélange of guises. Just as old syntactic maneuvers have been "hard-wired" or otherwise learned to excess (e.g., medial free modification and the "if" clause with the above junior writer), at first new ones will be exaggerated as well. It is true enough that all of the mature sentence traits of the employees take special form in some of the worst professional language perversions, not the least being pretentious and barely readable long sentences. But that is no reason to reteach *Unmündigkeit,* however "convenient" that would be for teacher and student. Since William Blake's day, excess is still the road to the palace of wisdom, even though some stylistic travelers have taken up permanent wayside residence.

The piece of junior writing illustrates one other transformative sequence for pedagogical use. Teachers can expect student ideas for sentences to be in developmental advance of their syntax. This follows an old pattern of language acquisition, where comprehension typically precedes execution. As children, we understood more than we could say and read at a higher level than we could write (we still do). But as I have said, although knowing this pattern may enlighten expectations and sharpen interpretation, it does not authorize a top-down approach to the sentence. Doubtless much of the employee sentence strategy feeds off a stock of intellectual, affective, and social frames larger than the student owns, but that does not argue that experimentation in sentence-work must wait until these frames are learned. Nor must sentence-work wait on procedures of invention, knowledge about format, or awareness of audience. Form and expression travel step in step, one aiding the other. Kerek, Daiker, and Morenberg's students at Miami University ended a semester of sentence-combining practice with improvement in "voice" as well as in "sentence structure."

So it is no paradox that the employees here enlarge and thicken their sentences while relaxing their grasp of sentences as definite or single forms. Their separate skills have become less so, less hard-wired. The maturing sentence grows because it is taking on more of the functions of the larger rhetorical operations, such as production, coherence, and—as we will see in the next chapter—essay organization. For composition teachers, the most important conclusion is that the way to graduate students from studio writing is to keep exercise in content and exercise in form on the move, hand in hand.

CHAPTER 10

Organization:
Closed and Progressive

AS WITH THE SENTENCE, IT IS NOT EASY TO interpret the traces teachers leave of their interpretive encounters with essay organization. How do we think the student goes about putting a whole essay together? Even with a put-together essay, whether and how it is organized becomes a topic about which a typical group of writing teachers are divided, unsure, and untypically inarticulate. In Sarah Warshaver Freedman's fascinating 1979 study of the way teachers read student essays, organization was a potent and cryptic influence on other writing measures, and only when teacher-evaluators felt organization to be strong did differences in mechanics and sentence structure begin to affect their overall quality ratings. Yet teachers achieved less concurrence on organization than on these two other traits. Sometimes it seems teachers simply do not want to think about the topic. When Thomas R. Newkirk, Thomas D. Cameron, and Cynthia L. Selfe asked freshman-composition teachers to rank weaknesses in student writing from the most to the least important, inability to organize essays fell sixteenth, after, for instance, failure to proofread and overuse of the passive.

The wording of this sixteenth weakness suggests that part of the problem may be perceptual: "Students are aware of only one organizational pattern—the five-paragraph theme." Five paragraphs, of course, make a stylistic uniform, not a pattern of organization. As we shall see, freshmen in the Sample generated a good variety of organizational patterns, even when writing impromptu on the second day of class. Composition teachers may not distinguish extended organization very well in student writing.

This is an ungenerous supposition (though I will offer more support for it later). But compare the uniform tale working writers tell about organization. Pearl G. Aldrich surveys top-level and mid-level managers on the weaknesses they find in *their* writing skills, and they rank "inability to organize content" among the top four. Time after time, surveys record the following list of qualities the working world expects in writing, beginning at the top: clarity, concision, organization. . . . Not surprisingly, the occupational tale often discovers its antagonist in the university teacher who misguides youths onto evil paths. The *Chronicle of Higher Education* reports this bearding of the lion in its 1985 NCTE annual meeting: "It may not be too outlandish to say that every effective writer on the continent announces the plan at the beginning, and every writer who saves the 'lead' until the end is in an English department" (Dec. 4: 29). That is truly ungenerous. It also conflicts with the evidence of the Sample, where, as we will see, it is not the employees who more often "announce their plan" at the beginning.

Still, the organizational technique of the employees—who, we should not forget, were selected as "effective writers" by their employers—differs enough from the technique of the students, and from the technique apparently taught and expected by their teachers, to support the feeling that college composition could improve its interpretation and teaching of essay organization. At the least, everyone—teachers, students, and employers—could benefit from some basic articulation of the various ways whole pieces of writing may be organized effectively and the ways students and professionals actually do so. That may reduce the confusion and improve the dialogue within and over the walls of the campus.

I announce my plan at the beginning. First I will classify the organizations of the Sample essays. Then I will use the classification to compare student and employee strategies and to trace some of the disagreement over organization to a developmental source. In the end I will argue that an interpretive problem lies buried at the root of the confusion. Students organize with better promise than teachers often see, and the working world organizes differently than it sometimes says.

A Classification of Essay Organization

Kenneth Burke said, "You can reduce any expression (even inconsequential or incomplete ones) to some underlying skeletal structure" (1950: 65). The rendered structure, however, will depend on the method of reduction. Researchers into discourse organization have sorted transitional expressions, identified relationships between sentences, plotted the sequence of superordination and subordination, constructed tree diagrams of logical embedding in paragraphs. With the Sample, my method has been to find and classify the top-level organization, that is, the one logically coherent arrangement of ideas embracing the largest number of words in the body or main thematic argument of an essay. The result looks teachable and easy: this essay basically organizes its thesis, say, by *causation*.

Such a method runs into major difficulties, though. I had to find a classification that passes a certain muster. It had to be ordered to show possible differences in the development of writers and generous enough to catch the sundry methods of top-level organization actually found in impromptu writing. It had to be fine enough to retain useful distinctions yet simple enough to make analysis by teachers and re-action by students practical. It had to respect the contemporary understanding of extended organization in writing as a hierarchical embedding of structures, where higher-level units embrace less inclusive units and so on down. Finally, the classification had to accept the fact that at any level the writers' use of a pattern need not follow the most effective rhetorical sequence. A part of a pattern conventionally occurring last may precede the first. The last part of one pattern may simultaneously express the first part of a second pattern (*overlap*), as where the solution to a problem functions also as the initial cause of an effect. Or two complete patterns may be expressed together (*overlay*), as where two stages of a chronology are also cause and effect or problem and solution. Such bidirectional or multilayered patterns embrace embedding that indented outlines or derivational trees cannot easily diagram (I resort to boxes that overlap and overlie).

I could not find such a classification ready-made, even for expressions as "inconsequential" as the fifty-minute impromptus.[1] The scheme I worked up is largely self-evident, and examples of analyzed writing in this and the next chapter should answer most questions about application. Two major distinctions in the classification are novel, however. One is the difference between *unchained* and *chained* patterns. By an unchained pattern, I mean a structure formed entirely of a single, enclosing logical unit—a causation or an inference, for instance—where all other logical patterns are subordinate to it, packaged inside it. By a chained pattern, I mean one formed by the overlapping or linking of two or more unchained patterns. At least

---

[1] Introductory reviews of previous classifications of logical organization are provided by Witte and Faigley 1981a and Haswell 1986b. Instructive efforts to classify discourse ideas by increasing complexity, with an implication for development and organization, are Moffett; Frederiksen; Klausmeier, Ghatala, and Frayer; Britton et al.; Wilkinson et al.; Freedman and Pringle 1980b; Hillocks; Kiniry and Strenski; Durst; and Newkirk 1987. My taxonomy owes its greatest debt to Frank D'Angelo's 1975 classification of paradigmatic structures, although his analysis does not handle an essay that combines more than one paradigm. A more thorough account of my classification can be found in the paper on which this chapter is based (1986b). For an application to student freewriting, see Haswell 1990a.

one section of the essay functions in a double role, as the terminal part of one pattern and the initial part of another. An unchained organization expands by embedding, by swallowing new subpatterns. A chained organization expands progressively, by overlapping or grafting another pattern onto its end to create a new and different organization.

The second distinction draws a logical division between *symmetrical* and *asymmetrical* patterns. Logical segments of a symmetrical pattern are categories of common class, as in a chronology where the parts are all units of time. The parts of an asymmetrical pattern need not be categories of the same class. For example, in a problem-solving pattern, the problem may be material (e.g., lack of money) but the solution psychological (change of expectations). Consequently, asymmetrical patterns are further distinguished by a mediating assertion, usually implied, that acts as a bridge between two different classes—the unstated premise in an induction, for instance, or the assumed agency of physical interaction between cause and effect in a causation. Given the progressive nature of chained patterns and the class-jumping and tacit nature of asymmetrical patterns, readers of previous chapters will not be surprised to discover that the major developmental finding of this analysis of organization is that older writers prefer the chained and asymmetrical patterns.

Table 1 shows the five basic subgroups of the fourteen basic patterns and identifies the internal logic of parts that differentiates one pattern from the others. It also provides a count of the results when this classification is applied to the freshman, junior, and employee essays, wherein will be readily seen a general shift of the older writers toward the higher-numbered patterns.

One feature of this classification has a direct relevance to the maturing of organizational skills. The fourteen major patterns, *collection* to *sequence*, are ranked by increasing complexity of the relationship between their constituent logical parts. Chained patterns are taken as more complex than

Table 1

Analysis of Top-Level Organizational Patterns

Pattern	Logical Parts of Pattern	Freshmen	Juniors	Employees
I. Unchained Patterns				
A. SYMMETRICAL				
Partition..................................		8	7	1
1. *Collection*	Overlapping categories			
2. *Classification*	Mutually exclusive categories			
Seriation		9	4	5
3. *Degree*	Categories that rank			
4. *Development*	Stages that evolve chronologically			
5. *Comparison*	Categories that compare and contrast			
B. ASYMMETRICAL				
Consequence............................		7	3	3
6. *Causation*	Cause and effect			
7. *Process*	Procedure and goal			
Argument................................		8	11	12
8. *Inference*	Premise and conclusion			
9. *Choice*	Options and final choice			
10. *Solution*	Problem and resolution			
11. *Dialectic*	Antithesis and synthesis			
II. Chained Patterns		0	7	11
12. *Causal Chain*	Chaining of cause and effect			
13. *Sorites*	Chaining of premise and conclusion			
14. *Sequence*	Chaining of parts of different patterns			
		32	32	32

unchained by reason of their overlapping section, which plays two logical roles at once. Logical asymmetry is assumed more complex than symmetry because it bridges two different classes: symmetrical pattern may be a mere dichotomy, but, as I note, the simplest asymmetrical pattern requires a third, mediating assertion. Within the five subgroups of the classification, increase in complexity is meant in its traditional developmental sense: a more complex pattern rises out of the ground of the patterns before it. *Classification* is a *collection* but differentiates categories so that they are mutually exclusive. *Development* adds to *degree* the notion of connected change. *Choice* involves at least one *inference* (one option is better than another for some reason) but adds a contrast between options. *Solution* implies not only a *choice* between possible options but a testing of the choice. And so on up. This concept of complexity is standard in both formative and transformative theories of development (e.g., Piaget's sequence of representation → classification → seriation → hypothesis formation). Complexity, of course, has no necessary connection with rhetorical worth.

Before we look at the developmental story this analysis tells of skill in essay organization, let's consider its value as a diagnostic tool. Using this scheme, teachers can analyze the top-level organization of many essays, in class and out, with one reading and a few pencil strokes. But intransigent pieces—and some are veritable Gordian knots—often prove more enlightening, both to teacher and to student. Here is a moderately difficult but typical junior essay from the Sample (figure 8).

The top-level pattern emerges as a *sequence*: a *causation* chained to a *solution*. *Causation*: the uniformity required by conduct codes (paragraph two) causes disillusionment when outgrown (paragraph three) and feelings of unfairness when applied to different groups (first three sentences of paragraph four). *Solution*: this double effect becomes the problem solved by a proper education (last two sentences of paragraph four). My guess is that many college teachers would miss this organization and assume one much simpler. Judged as a "five-paragraph

<table>
<tr>
<td>Intro-
duction</td>
<td>In the world today most men live in some type of civilization. Civilization itself is what dictates an individuals code of conduct. This can be easily seen by comparing an African society to an Indian society, or any other combination from an almost infinite variety of living groups.</td>
</tr>
</table>

| **Cause** | A uniform code of conduct is necessary to the survival of each particular society. Very often the laws are laid through some sort of message from God. In this way no one in the group is inclined to dispute the rules just for the sake of causing trouble. The idea is to get things functioning in a normal fashion and work out future problems as they comealong. |

| **Effect** | The problem with codes of conduct is the lack of an effective way to abandon them when they become unnecessary. The people become disillusioned with patterns that were set hundreds of years before, and which no longer deal effective with current issues. |
| | Most codes vary in meaning or importance depending on who they are applied to. Children will be dealt with differently from adults when punished for a crime. This it seems would be only fair as a child with limited experience can not be expected to know what an adult knows. | **Problem** |

| | However men (women & children) should not have trouble dealing with the society's laws because of their sex or age. Although all the laws for men may not be the same for women, they should have been raised with this expectation and adjust to it at an early age. | **Solution** |

| **Conclusion** | All men are born into a society that believes in certain ways. Each person deserves the opportunity to choose that particular way of life or leave to find another more suitable. |

Figure 8.

256

theme" by its stylistic uniform, the essay will not cohere. There is a very serious failure to signal logical progression. The fourth paragraph has all the indications of a new topic when logically it continues the third paragraph, and the crucial point of the entire essay, the solution to the problem set forth, is buried in the fourth paragraph, heralded with only a weak However and elaborated with only one sentence. The introduction does not forecast the main direction of the essay, and the summary seems to contradict it.

For students, herein lies the main virtue of the method of structural analysis. It forces a writer to see logical patterns self-made and followed, despite appearances and sometimes despite what can be articulated. Re-action can proceed from the student's own logical framework (consciously intended or not) rather than from a counterdevelopmental one urged by the teacher. For teachers, the method clears pedagogical trails as well as diagnostic eyes. The structural needs of this junior, now highlighted, can be meta-cognitively appraised, and revisions after more mature practice can be considered for appropriation: rewriting the introduction to show the tropical direction of the main logical sequence, providing salient transitions at major logical junctures, and elaborating short-shrifted yet major points near the end of the essay. (It is not surprising that students write through to their logically most complex idea and hastily throw it, as after a departing pickup, into the last paragraph.) Use of chaining to integrate the final idea here would create a small essay of quite respectable depth. Perhaps the idea that Each person deserves the opportunity to choose could stand as antithesis in a *dialectic,* suggesting some resolution of the clash between conformity to codes and freedom of choice.

Group Differences in Organization

What growth in organizational strategy does the Sample show? First, versatility seems to increase during college, with older writers slowly acquiring the more complex patterns. The entering freshmen display the most meager repertoire, failing to produce examples of *process, solution, causal chain, sorites,* and *sequence.* Second, contrary to the impression of the teachers surveyed by Thomas Newkirk, all student groups still use a respectable variety of patterns. Third, there are valuable trends in the kinds of patterns preferred. With students, the most popular patterns are, in descending order, *causation, collection, classification, development, choice,* and *comparison* —all symmetrical except for *causation* and *choice.* With employees, the most popular are *sequence, inference, causation,* and *solution* —all asymmetrical. Under half of the patterns selected by freshmen and sophomores were asymmetrical, about two-thirds by juniors, over four-fifths by employees. Chained essays also grow steadily, from none with freshmen to over a third with the employees. Conversely, nearly a fourth of all students used partition to organize their essays, but only one employee.

Fourth, with students there is a rough inverse correlation between structure and production. The more complex the pattern logically, the fewer words contained by it. But as the older writers select more complex patterns, they do not pay for the choice with loss of fluency. There is a general trend for older writers to fill patterns with more and more words. Freshmen manage top-level patterns only about 200 words long, sophomores about 260, adults about 330. This trend should not be taken lightly, for it indicates a capacity to embrace within one unitary top-level logical structure increasingly complex systems of embedded structures. Nor does this increase in the size of the top level reflect merely an increase in the space devoted to sublogical elements such as illustration, repetition, or restatement. Analysis of the longest logical segment of each essay shows a highly consistent increase from freshmen to employees in the number of levels of embedding.

Fifth, comparison of the top patterns with the patterns embedded in them finds a telling difference between collegiate and workplace strategies of organization. In their top-level pattern, employees tend to reverse student practice whereby patterns shrink in size as they grow more complex. For instance, with students, symmetrical patterns are about sixty words longer than asymmetrical ones, but with employees asymmetrical are thirty-five words longer than symmetrical. Students may need to use simple organization to express complex ideas, whereas adults have learned to make the main organization more complex as the number and complexity of their ideas rise. With embedded patterns, however, student and adult practice is the same: the simpler the pattern logically, the more the use. Students, then, organize logically on the top level little differently than they organize beneath, but competent adult writers apparently have distinct approaches to the two levels.

Last, there were no such differences between student and working-world practices in explicit signaling of the top-level pattern. Consider just the boundaries between main segments of the pattern and between them and introductory and summary material. The range of group performance is narrow. Junctures are marked by a new paragraph from 70 to 80 percent of the time and by an explicit transition from 40 to 55 percent of the time. And the percent of essays written in five paragraphs remained as constant—at about 30 percent. But the number of essays following the classic "five-paragraph theme" format—introduction, point one, point two, point three, summary—achieved a significant rise and decline: beginning-of-the-semester freshmen produced three, end-of-the-semester freshmen eight, sophomores nine, juniors three, employees one. Evidently it is college composition teachers themselves who help spread the five-paragraph theme, and it takes a year for older students to convalesce.

Appropriation by Student and Teacher

This is not to forget that one improvisation following this five-part format, a simple *collection,* is E. M. Forster's consummate essay "My Wood." It bears repeating that logically simple and logically complex are not prescriptive terms and that these patterns have equal rhetorical worth. Nor do these findings in any way argue that the "higher" patterns hold some sort of ultimate developmental sanction. To argue that would be to exalt or, as Bruner exactly puts it, to "vulgarize" one discursive skill over all the rest. It would say that Katherine Anne Porter's "Noon Wine" (a *development*) is more immature than the next political speech you may hear (quite likely a *sequence*).

And this is not to forget that the teacher's role is to prescribe—at least to the extent that prescription serves to help dislodge students from easy *Unmündigkeit*. As the above data implies, undergraduates have a good deal to learn from the employee organizational strategies, which must have aided higher production and holistic rating. As a group, students moving through college are still appropriating some of these schemes, and none too quickly. Fortunately, the chart of the acquisition of competent organizational skill—crude as my instrument has been—maps a general development clear enough to disperse some interpretive legends and to give teachers some solid purchase. Students demonstrate three existing strengths to lead from. They arrive at college with a command of a variety of organizational patterns. They show a creaturely growth in their ability to handle logical complexity both in breadth, the amount of ideas they can hold within one pattern, and in depth, the number of subordinate structures they can embed. And they possess an intuitive sense of formal logical coherence. This last may contradict the most unrealistic tale of all: that students arrive at college still thinking pre-formally in Piaget's sense. Although from sentence to sentence their writing may be so incohesive, repetitive, and unemphatic that from beginning to end it may seem illogical, rarely does it prove so. Only 2 of the 128 student essays were ordered by quasi-logical patterns such as fantasy, dream, free association, chance, or nonthematic narration. Fourteen more might be called incomplete, where the main body could not be entirely organized under one logical pattern. But these 14 suffered merely from a double thesis, again lacking cohesion more than logic. With a better introduction, each would have been a *collection*, like Forster's essay.

The above findings also chart some potential zones of proximal development. They suggest that teachers might expect more learning leeway in top-level than in lower-level patterns. When students organize their whole essays, they tend to adopt the simpler patterns, like *collection* and *comparison* and *causation*—the kinds of structures that are easy to produce and common all the way down to the level of sentence and even clause. The employees have found instead that it is the most complex patterns—structures rarely occurring within sentences or even paragraphs—that serve best for top-level organization. The implication is that good plans for long stretches of discourse are not always chosen out of ease. Teachers might therefore approach essay organization with unusual openness, placing unconscious and sometimes contradictory forestructures on the conference table. For some students, to detect and even map the patterns in their previous writing may help them see the virtue and limitations of some schemes, to see perhaps how a *collection* has thwarted an attempt to back a position or find a solution.

Most freshmen could benefit from schemes increasingly used by older students: *inference, choice, solution, dialectic,* and their chained combinations. This means teachers will need to become more aware of these complex patterns. Although we may be disheartened to see spreading the scheme we dislike the most, the rote five-paragraph *collection*, we might ask how much we are part of the reason for it. When we encourage long essays without teaching feasible organizational ways to achieve length, or when we insist on structured essays without identifying either a good variety of structures or a clear method of newly creating a structure shaped to the subject, we may force students to take recourse—or re-course—to a high-school tactic.

To teach more complex patterns, teachers must dwell on the tactic of chaining. Chaining is the organizational mechanism allowing what Mina P. Shaughnessy calls the "developing patterns" of accomplished writers (1977: 244). The mature advantage of chaining lies in the fact that it is open-ended. Just as we have seen with the sentence subject and with the paragraph topos, with an essay topic students have a tendency to box themselves in right from the beginning. They seize on unchained patterns, usually initiated with an enclosing statement of full scope (figure 9). With chained patterns and a tropic lead, writers can simply set a direction (figure 10). Ways to round off the inquiry will come naturally when the logical conclusion is arrived at (effect, solution, resolution, choice, concession, etc.).

The key to chaining lies in the asymmetrical patterns. Asymmetry moves. Just as in Victor Yngve's right-branching or "progressive" syntactic structures, in organizational patterns that function like Frank D'Angelo's "progressive" paradigms (syllogism, causation, process, narration), the writer can keep

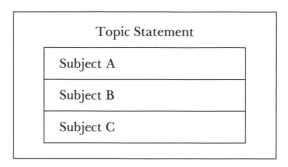

Figure 9.   Unchained pattern.

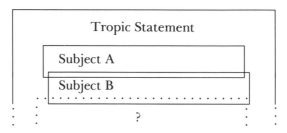

Figure 10.   Chained pattern.

adding parts without losing the logical thread. Since the parts jump from one classificatory unit to another, the asymmetrical patterns are the only ones that overlap or chain easily. Via *causation,* a writer can move from human standards of fashion to endangerment of fur-bearing species, and this effect can metamorphose into a dialectical thesis that moves from unrealistic ecological goals to modification of fashion standards. By contrast, symmetrical patterns limit themselves by their initial classificatory plan. A freshman begins with a thesis statement (taken right from the essay prompt): <u>The conceptions of 'right' and 'proper' are different for different age levels.</u> How can the symmetrical pattern preordained here, a *development* or *comparison,* be chained to another? Inclusive disjunction might find something in common between two categories of different seriations, moving perhaps from the drinking by adults (their "right") to alcohol as a more destructive addiction than marijuana, but if so, then already the writer has betrayed the stated plan and is writing a double-thesis essay.

Asymmetrical construction lends itself to the adventurous kind of writing that the competent employees tend to favor, "announcing a plan" or thesis only to the extent of emphasizing a particular idea to explore and a direction of inquiry to follow. That requires confidence, but confidence can be taught. Teachers might let students find out for themselves the generative power of asymmetrical patterns much as the employees probably found out, by using the patterns. Students might be given a progressive employee beginning to write from: <u>In considering the question of 'beauty' we have to remember</u> . . . A more forceful exercise, a kind of pattern generation on the same principle as Christensen's sentence generation, would have students add to a pattern they have already composed by using the last part as the beginning of a new pattern. Recursion of *sorites, dialectic,* and *solution* schemes produces natural and sometime elegant results. Most productive of all are *sequences.* They foster the genuine confidence and genuine pragmatism lying behind Jean-Paul Sartre's shocking comment: "There is nothing to be said about form in advance. . . . Everyone invents his own, and one judges it afterward" (20).

No doubt for the student, schemes of partition will still be doubly tempting, and not just for writing an impromptu piece. Quickly conceived and easily tracked, they allow for high output of words. Facile logical compartments can be plumped with examples and detail. And it is the long, fully supported, conspicuously sectioned essay that teachers often react to positively. If matriculating students do not know this, they soon find it out. For the freshmen essays in the Sample, the correlation between the pattern ranking by complexity and the holistic rating was −.35. The simpler the organization is logically, the higher the rate. Perhaps the simpler the organization, the better the students were able to compose in other ways during a timed writing situation. But the correlation figure also suggests the reverse effect: that teachers tend not to appreciate—probably not to recognize—complex logical schemes, what with the scanty cohesion, thin elaboration, and low fluency that often accompany them.

That common configuration is more properly the subject of the next chapter. However, the irony that teachers reward immature designs with high esteem bears directly on the question of why they are so divided and unsure about large-scale organization. The irony is rooted in one sure fact about language. At all levels, from the sentence on up, the great bulk of verbal organizing is implicit. Ninety-nine percent of the time, both writer and reader are unaware of the frames—ideational, emotional, cultural, discourse-communal—that give a sense of coherence to discourse. In part it is the implicitness of these frames, in fact, that gives them their great efficiency. Were writer or reader aware of all the interlocking and embedded schemes that uphold their sense of continuity, little would get written or read.

The problem is that running counter to this quotidian fact is a pedagogical one: that a basic sequence in the learning of verbal ability is from explicit to implicit. Linguists provide delightful illustrations of this sequence in the early acquisition of syntax, for instance where explicit oral expressions of causation ("I *made* that fall down") occur earlier than implicit ones, whether correct forms ("I pushed that down") or transitional errors ("I fell that down") (Bowerman: 127). But the overt → covert sequence keeps recurring at advanced phases of composition. It underpins the common tale of instructing and learning any new technique: a tactic is explicitly pointed out, defined, and consciously practiced—at first with awkwardness and other errors because it is conscious and at last with fluency because it has become automatic (indeed, Michael Carter finds this sequence in every discipline where novices develop into experts). The point is that the situation sometimes leads to a mismatch between the aims of reading teachers and the ambitions of writing students. Teachers intuitively interpret toward the explicit start of the learning sequence, students intuitively strive toward the mature and implicit end. Sarah Freedman's insight may touch on an unconscious and basic interpretive tale of teachers: that they need an overt organization before they will assess other facets of writing. The students who are organizing tacitly, or perhaps simply attending to the other facets of writing first, will pay.

The burden on the teachers is double. They need to discern logical patterns in student writing, no matter how cryptic, at the least to avoid requiring a revision more elemental than the original simply because the student can do it better (Heinz Werner notes that a decorticated frog catches flies better than a normal one). And they need to encourage adventurous writing, even though it means pushing some writers toward complex organization that seems to penalize them and pushing other writers away from simplistic patterns that probably have allowed classroom success. All this will be giving students double developmental allowance that other, more pragmatic teachers may disparage. The defense can be as pragmatic, however. Mina P. Shaughnessy points out, "Accomplished writers rarely proceed along set design of the sort teacher and texts often impose upon their students" (1977: 244). In the long run the "flexibility" we have seen required even for daily workplace writing (chapter 3) will not be learned by practicing simplistic, set formats alone. The occupational need to organize better is defined by the need to organize according to the demands of the job, which are much more than "announcing a plan at the beginning." As research has shown, those demands include adjusting plans in the middle, shaping plans to meet special audience needs, absorbing complexities of subject, improvising midstream ways to keep readers on track in "first-time-final" copy, and modifying formats, even those as supposedly set as the formal report.

In short, the teacher needs to find developmental ways beyond the studio essay as much as beyond the studio sentence. Here the student and employee impromptus provide a final insight: the ways the rhetorical dynamics of whole and part, essay and sentence, develop together ("embeddedness"). The maturing of the essay and that of the sentence follow the same road. In employee pieces, paragraphs as well as sentences could have been started at several points without loss of effect, so strong was the flow. Both employee essay and sentence prefer brief, more restricted openings that avoid an initial multiple focus or premature definition, both go on longer and demand longer memory spans, both find progressive ways to handle the attention load of complex relationships, both contain deeper restrictive embedding yet organize it with an open-ended and often simpler overframe, both prefer to leave connections tacit when possible, both take improvisational risks with the knowledge that writing competence will find ways out, and both tend to be incremental or accumulative, with new meaning building up toward the end. Student essay and sentence reflect their own shared dynamics: more timid than adventurous, more closed than open-ended—backward-looking and head-heavy—incohesive, short, and thin. For and from the prospects of instruction, this means that advance at one level will pull along the other and that self-contradiction between levels will serve as an ideal point to initiate that advance.

266

CHAPTER 11

Remediality:
Bottom and Top

"DEVELOPMENTAL" IS ONE OF THE MORE RECENT labels for students who write so badly that administrators and teachers do not want them in regular composition sections. Developmental? Ideally such a label should honor the interpretive frame used to determine what it means to write "badly." In this case, the frame pictures human development as progressing, for instance, from ego-centered feeling during childhood to other-centered abstracting during adulthood. Compared with other students, certain students entering college fall toward the childish side of this frame, since they don't write other-centered abstractions. So they are declared "developmental" and put in remedial sections where they can catch up—or climb out.

Many teachers have written in opposition to this method of determining remediality (e.g., Bizzell 1979; Berthoff; Kogen; Rose 1988; Martinez and Martinez). Part of the teacher fear of the developmental perspective in general stems from the suspicion that it will be used specifically and maybe exclusively in this way (see chapter 4). It hardly needs saying, but to the extent that the suspicion has been justified by actual practice in the profession to date, this book stands with the opposition. But that is because I have a different view of development. The way certain students are judged as "developmental" I take to be a travesty of current knowledge about human development. It simplifies multilateral human growth, it treats regression negatively, it applies an ideology rather than an "anticipatory regulative idea" in that it allows for no dialogue between subject and program, and it misunderstands normal postadolescent maturing, which in fact leads to something more than other-centeredness and abstracting.

How then would the transformative determine remediality? Or would it deny the concept altogether? This chapter will sketch an answer to these two questions. It will do so by returning to the contrast between a genuine developmental assessment of the Sample essays and the holistic procedure applied by the fourteen young composition teachers.

Bottom Writers: Lacking or Lean?

Something akin to the holistic procedure, of course, is the most common way of determining remediality. Entering students write impromptu, the impromptus are read by young but trained writing teachers following what I have called ungrounded criteria, certain students are culled out—or placed in. Let's see what happens when we treat the holistic rating of the Sample as a placement test. If we take as remedial an average score of 2 or below on the holistic scale of 1 to 8, we end up with nine essays from the freshman, sophomore, and junior groups—about the bottom 10 percent. Since the Sample tapped all composition classes at a land-grant university offering at the time no special writing courses for students with severe writing problems, and since enrollment in remedial sections across the nation averages between 10 and 15 percent of the entering class, our subsample of nine essays seems representative.

Before we confirm that with a look at the writing itself, there is one outcome of the holistic that the transformative immediately regards with suspicion: the way the teacher-raters tended to agree most on these bottom nine. Three essays received rates of only 1 and 2, five received rates of 1 to 3, and one received rates of 1 to 4 (the mean standard deviation of their rates is 0.75). By comparison, of the nine top essays, all with an average rate of 7 or higher, five received rates of 6 to 8, three of 5 to 8, and one of 3 to 8 (the mean standard deviation of their rates is 1.06). Not that this outcome is abnormal—just the reverse. Essays that settle to the bottom of holistic assessments almost always have the highest concordance of independent scores, higher even than the topmost essays. Teachers of writing apparently agree more on who are bad writers than on who are good. The transformative takes this customary outcome as a curiosity worth a closer look.

It takes no more than a glance at the bottom nine essays to see one possible explanation for this difference in assessment. They have all the classic signs of writing called "incompetent." They are halt with mechanical errors, quirky in paragraphing, and backward in production, averaging 196 words compared with 364 for the higher-rated student essays. They are scant of title and topic sentence and introduction and supportive elaboration and other reader amenities. Perhaps remedial writing is easy for evaluators to categorize because it bears, or bares, its earmarks flagrantly, on the surface.

Now the nine essays could be termed "developmental" because their performance on most of these surface traits stands at the end of the student distribution away from the maturing direction. But as with Sam in chapter 6, when we look under the surface, the picture changes, in some ways dramatically. The most dramatic is top-level logical organization. Measured by the classification of patterns outlined in the previous chapter, these basement essays perform more like the competent employee essays in comparison with the eighty-seven student essays higher up in the scale. Two of the nine were organized by *comparison,* two by *inference,* one by *choice,* one by *dialectic,* one by *sorites,* and two by *sequence.* Only around a third of the higher-rated student essays followed progressive or argumentative designs, strategies adopted by three-fourths of the lowest-rated and three-fourths of the employee essays. Considering the number of studies that have argued that "basic" writers lag in cognitive maturity (Bradford; Lees; Lunsford 1979; Stotsky), the transformative may be justified in looking askance at that uniform rating of "lowest" and in looking, beneath the surface of error and ineptitude, with more care at the way these nine bottom essays are organized. We will postpone other contradictory evidence for a moment.

Here is one of the nine (figure 11). I have blocked out what I take to be the main logical organization. The top-level pattern is *inference:* SINCE struggle forges talent, and SINCE unattractive people struggle more than attractive, THEN unattractive people

Intro- duction	Physical appearance or attractiveness needs to be down played in todays thinking. The obsession of people worrying about their physical appearance creates prejudices. Many people through out time have been caught in the appearance trap.
Logical Conclusion	Many jobs requir some physical attractiveness, such as: Stewards; stewardesses; and models. Some employers will not hire over weight people, short people, or tall people with out judging their ability to produce the work which is required of the job. Many of the people which are rejected for work because of their physical shape or uglyness might be just the people suited for that particular job.
Premises	Take for instance an over weight woman wants a job as a stewardess. Many over weight people have found that to over come their social block of their shape, they have to be more out going, more talkitive and have more general knowledge. A person who does not have this disability and on the other hand is pleaseing to the eye would not have this maturing strugle.
Conclusion	The poudgy stewardess might make a better personality than the thin attractive one.

Figure 11.

may be best for a job. The writer has made this logical construct remarkably difficult to see. The premises, mislabeled as an in-stance, follow the conclusion; the introduction misleads (are the people of the third sentence the employers, the applicants, or both?); and there is no paragraphing to graph logical bound-aries. Yet when the logical sense is finally made explicit, one peculiar behavior of this short piece becomes evident: how rapidly and how far the writer's thinking presses on. There is a social block against overweight people; THEREFORE employers worry about physical appearance; ALSO THEREFORE many jobs require attractive employees; ALSO THEREFORE overweight peo-ple must struggle harder; AS A RESULT they are often talented; CONVERSELY AND COMPARATIVELY attractive people are often less talented; AS A COMBINED RESULT some employers reject peo-ple without testing their worth; AS A RESULT the best person is not hired; THEREFORE GENERALLY people should downplay physical appearance.

So analysis by logical organization reveals a character dis-tinguishing this piece from much impromptu student writing: highly compressed sequential logical meditation. This is cer-tainly not a character one expects to find in "developmental" writing, yet others of the nine bottom essays divulge a like de-meanor. For the moment, let's avoid terms connoting deficiency or proficiency and call this a "lean" style. Obviously, when car-ried to an extreme, as in this case, lean writing will generate excesses in need of remediation. But given the employee per-formance on logical organization, this piece hardly deserves to be called "developmental."

Judged by the employee organizational "competence," what would be "developmental" writing? In the Sample it is the five-hundred-word essay based on a gimcrack partition of the subject, typically an unconsidered listing of parts (*collection*) or a division into simplistic stages (*development*)—with top-heavy introduction, truckling summary, restatements and examples of every common point, facile words and sentences, and boxy paragraphs of the same size. Equally a rhetorical exorbitance in need of remediation, it seems to have everything but ideas that spring one from the other in a thoughtful, fecund sequence. Let's call it "stout" writing.

At the other end of the holistic spectrum, among the nine top-rated student essays, is one I would call an extreme of stout writing. In five paragraphs and 521 words, it argues that physical appearance plays an important role in people's attitudes—not an argument that, it seems, the writer has many doubts about or expects the reader to have many doubts about. The essay sorts its subject into three main cabinets: youth and dating, males and females, and society. *Collection* is the right name for this method of arrangement. The categories seem erected independently of one another (they are taken verbatim from a list of suggested topics in the essay prompt), and the way they are muddled logically suggests that they serve essentially as preset catchalls, not as a sequence where one category logically evolved from another.

This essay shows its stoutness not only in its main logical pattern but also in its embedded patterns. Here is its fourth paragraph—the third cabinet (figure 12). The paragraph

And last, we must deal with physical beauty and it's effect on society. As you all know, outward appearance and charm is very important in the political scene. As was true in the Presidential election of 1960, the candidate with the most charm, best image, and best physical appearance often wins. People go on ridiculous diets and spend money hand over foot in order to lose weight and be "beautiful" again. And even more sadly, people with physical handicaps are often stared at or rejected as if they were some kind of monster carrying a communicable disease. It often seems as though Brittania Jeans, Pierre Cardin industries, Clairol, Faberge, and Vidal Sasson have complete control over the minds and bodies of the United States of America. Evidence of this can be found in all of us.

Part #1
Part #2
Part #3

Figure 12.

builds up another *collection,* again encasing three items taken from the prompt. Of its seven sentences, three serve as introduction and restatement. On even further embedded levels, by my count it generates six more logically confused *collections* (stared at or rejected), one feeble *degree* (even more sadly), and two *causations.* Rhetorically, the paragraph looks solid, like store bread, but part of that appearance owes to the simplicity and stasis of the logical relationships.

By contrast, here is a paragraph of about the same length from one of the bottom nine essays (figure 13). It serves as the

Problem	Girls in Highschool that are overweight never get asked to go to a dance. Although these girls may have the appearance of having a pretty face it is just because they are overweight. To the guy he may think of being laughed at by his friends. Even when these girls come to college thing will never change. When these girls go out with their friends to get picked up in a single bar, usually the girls that are not overweight will get picked up, whereas the girl that is overweight will not. You'll never find an overweight girl competing for the Miss America or Miss Universe. There is a lot of drawbacks for these girls. They may think it is some kind of handicap. Girls must have special	
Solu-tion	clothing to fit themselves. When they go out to eat or just standing in a lunch line, they asked for the calorie-cutter. Even for blind dates, girls overweight are turned down. There's no other	Options
Thesis	alternative but for these girls to stay home.	
Anti-thesis	But I understand that these girls try there best to compete with girls that aren't overweight and beautiful.	Choice

Figure 13.

273

entire body of the essay, accompanied only with a two-sentence introductory paragraph. This paragraph is anything but static, forging on from a problem with a failed *solution* through a *choice* of options to an unresolved *dialectic*. The logical restlessness spreads to embedded levels, where I count two *degrees*, six *comparisons*, four *causations*, and two *inferences*.

I am not going to hypothesize a motive for stout writing (although it is tempting to do so simply by citing the second sentence of the previous example: As you all know, outward appearance and charm is very important in the political scene). But I am going to hypothesize a motive and narrative for extreme lean, since this student style and its relative maturity have been little recognized. First and last, the writer wants to work out the logical ramifications of an idea set by a teacher. But tracking logical trails and inferring where they lead take time. Minutes pass between the writing of one proposition and the acceptance of its implications. Flow is lost, sometimes even grammatical and syntactic linkage, as with Ann Matsuhashi and Karen Quinn's student sentence cited in chapter 9. Most easily left unrecorded are logical steps because it is the logical end itself that is being most ardently pursued. The writer certainly does not want to be sidetracked with information tangential to the main logical path, such as background, definitions, restatements, summaries, illustrative examples, rhetorical color, or emphasis.

Holistically, the essay with the paragraph of stout writing above got nearly the top combined score from my seven teachers, with rates of 8, 8, 8, 8, 7, 6, and 5 (standard deviation = 1.21). The essay providing the example of lean writing got the very lowest, with rates of 1, 1, 1, 1, 1, 2, and 2 (standard deviation = 0.49). Why then should the raters have concurred less on their judgment of the one essay and more on the other? Judged by the transformative, both are *unmündig*, conveniently lazy, though in different ways. Judged by developmental measures, both essays combine virtues and deficiencies. Apparently one "disability" of the nine bottom writers is in getting a teacher to see such writing abilities they do have.

Incompetent or Noncompetitive?

Logical organizing is not the only area where the bottom-rated essays as a group more nearly matched the performance of the employees than did the higher-rated essays. Another area I can designate only by a term almost as outmoded today as "point," "theme," and "sentence": *verbal wit*. Here the bottom nine ally with the employee essays in a style of shrewd or worldly practicality. This again is perhaps a surprise. Not only impromptu essay tests but also quick-answer, SAT-like examinations tend to put bottom writers down. When juniors or seniors in high school, these particular nine writers earned an average score on the verbal parts of a statewide diagnostic that placed them in the bottom 15 percent of their class. But wit concerns more than the semicolons, spelling demons, and learned words of such high-pressure, verbal competition, and the stylistic output of shrewdness and practicality may take forms below the threshold of the English-teacher moral vision.

It does not take much rereading of these nine short essays to catch their peculiar verbal intelligence. They appreciate the power of streetwise, face-slapping words: Your just not good looking enough so bug off. Their sentences can be refreshingly brisk: Conduct codes are created to protect people from criminals. Their ideas are often more compressed than one is used to seeing in student writing, in class or out: The obsession of people worrying about their physical appearance creates prejudices. (Clauses in their essays average 10.3 words, equal to the achievement of the older writers and a full word higher than that of the other students.) They relish the thrust of syntactic parallelism: The age has little to do with the fact, but much to do with the morals of society. (Their parallelism rate is 20 percent higher than in the other underclass essays.) They often attempt a dry, sardonic humor: <u>Even for blind dates, girls overweight are</u> <u>turned down</u>, or <u>Quite often these people are overlooked be-</u> <u>cause they are fat</u>. Their metaphoric language stands close to life: <u>Young adults clinging to their family</u>, or <u>Some overweight</u> <u>people are like dark shadows, they are there, but are never really</u> <u>noticed</u>. And throughout they show an unusual honesty, not the fact-slinging of one power at another but the disinterested soothsaying of the outsider with little to lose: <u>Am I so ugly I</u> <u>can't get dates?</u> or <u>We are all criminals</u>. All in all, the idiographic signature of the individual flourishes more in these nine essays than in the other eighty-seven.

I am going to hypothesize a motive and narrative for this kind of verbal wit. First and last the writer feels noncompeti- tive. Thinking of oneself as out of competition prompts the freedom and the devil-may-care attitude and the unhurriedness from which issues writing characterized by introspection, hu- mor, laconism, and that pithy irony with which the rustic jives the city-goer. "The recklessness which makes for originality," writes Edward Hoagland, who not incidentally is a stammerer, "often grows out of despair." Or in reverse order, the idling anomie of the noncompetitor may produce good patches of writing and poor scores on verbal tests, both through a refusal to reck—to reck convention and consequence.

Both noncompetition and competition are deep motiva- tions for writers. The second, of course, is much more familiar to most of us. We assume our writing *vies*—it is not necessarily better than that of others, just in the same league. But bottom students know they do not compete with their peers, even if they have not been put out of the regular classrooms and into special cubicles. The coach can't fool the player at the far end of the bench, who probably regrets the effort of having suited up and adopts that distrait, cutoff, sitting-in-the-audience slump of those who are inside but not in. This is the vital and sometimes deadly meaning of "competence"—if you have it, you are al- lowed to compete. If you don't, you live beyond the pale, outside the normal grades of society, in a bottommost category so different that it forms a class of its own and cannot be judged by the same standards. Students in special classes for bottom-dwellers do not get grades, or the grades do not mean the same thing. The students are there because they did not make the grade in the first place. So what they write is slovenly, broken, and graceless—humorous, involuted, and honest.

The transformative returns to its initial curiosity. The teachers' conception of bottommost seems to place it in a tidy world apart, unendowed with the lively self-contradictions that accompany the natural growth of higher beings. One of the curiosities here, then, is why so unstratified a block of our population has attracted such a diversity of labels: "slow," "beginning," "disabled," "deficient," "remedial," "basic," "novice," "developmental." Our culture also cannot agree on one name for the sorts of people who show up at unemployment centers, and we are apparently as fuzzy about the essential condition that leads people to writing centers. Are they laggard and in need of prodding ("slow"), fledgling and in need of orientation ("beginning"), lame and in need of prosthesis ("disabled"), lacking and in need of supplies ("deficient"), sick and in need of cure ("remedial"), well-based but in need of cultural refinement ("basic"), green and in need of expertise ("novice"), poorly equipped and in need of gear ("unprepared"), or immature and in need of catching up ("developmental")?

The answer is that bottom writers may not be any of these, or may be any combination of them. What they won't be is any one of them. "Human cognition—even at its most stymied, bungled moments—is rich and varied," agrees Mike Rose, warning of the "cognitive reductionism" toward which each one of these epithets lures us (1988: 297). Each label stands as a gist of a motive or narrative for the kind of writer who ends up at the bottom of verbal tests or holistic ratings: they lack confidence, they fear writing, they are confused with an unfamiliar interpretive community, they trust everything to rules, they suffer from counterproductive cognitive styles, they suffer from a learning disability acquired at an early age, they operate from an inappropriate oral dialect, they are fixed in the security of an immature formative stage and can't cathect or decenter or generalize or abstract or think relativistically or imagine any way but narratively. And, as Rose points out, often the epithet and the single rationale behind it are sanctioned by a single method of evaluation—whether it be a count of clause length, a test of writing anxiety, a spoken protocol, a Perry scheme, a holistic apparatus, or a measure of logical organization. And epithet, rationale, and method feed the interpretive tale that generates a single, monolithic reading. Compounding this danger is the other fact that the error-ridden and unstylish surface of bottom writing *glares*, shielding the depths where the complexities are. Teachers agree on what constitutes the worst student writing not because they recognize it easily but because they simplify it.

The transformative argues that in most bottom students these negative capabilities are mixed, and are further mixed with positive capabilities, such as the two we have been looking at: a devotion to the pursuit of ideas, and a fondness for the play of verbal wit. And that has something to say about the academic fate of writers who have penned themselves into the bottom stall, through whatever excesses or regresses or fear or confusion or thoughtfulness or honesty.

Instruction for Bottom Writers, and Top

Montaigne, the least competitive of all the great outsiders, noted that the honest is more lovable than the useful. Still, my fondness for bottom prose must admit the writing's ineffectiveness under the set conditions. Noncompetitive may not mean incompetent, and lean may not mean lacking, but they both certainly mean a rotten grade. Selective quotes, and a deliberate setting aside of skills like punctuation and spelling, cannot hide the fact that, in the end, these writers have more to learn than the other students do about sharing thought. They mutter, stutter, mislead, skim, omit.

The transformative suggests a little-used pedagogy for remedial students. A teacher starts with those skills they already
possess and in which they actually surpass the students above—
their grasp of concrete language, their effective compression of
syntax, their truthfulness, their original wit and feeling for
metaphor, their finding out and tracking down trails of thought.
Students at the bottom think of themselves not only as shadows
but as dark shadows, as worse writers than they really are. If
they can be shown that they are better than other students in
some ways, they may regain that vital sense of competition.

But therein lurks a vitiating cajolery. With the competition
come the rules, with the rules the compromises, and with the
compromises the regressions—contradictions all. The leisurely
and time-consuming pursuit of logical ramifications will have a
difficult time fending off the academic demands for bulk, high
readability, and orderly pigeonholing. Even more bleak looks
the fate of the down-turned wit under the gaze of academic
solemnity, or the worldly slang against the Latin legions of poly-
syllables, or the patient and compressed syntax caught in the
rush for length. The fate of bottom writers during the first
years of college is often a retreat from familiar impediments
and an advance toward uncomfortable accommodations.[1]

I cannot think of any more difficult task of a teacher than
to find ways to block this retreat and still improve the writing of
these students. An initial step would be to accord lean or witty
writing the same respect as any other personal style. As chapter
6 recommends, bottom writers could be shown developmental

---

[1] The Sample offers a remarkable support for such a retreat. If we analyze
only the top and the bottom holistically rated essays, those one standard
deviation above and below the mean, and correlate rate with the degree of
complexity of the top-level organizational pattern, we get the following
trend from entering freshman to exiting freshman to sophomore to junior to
employee: -.66, -.23, -.02, .21, .38. In sum, on entering college, the best
writers find and the poorest writers discard the advantages of the asymmetrical and chained patterns.

goals in competent writing of companion styles. Some of the employees made use of conventions that assist readability and production and yet maintained complex organization, wit, honesty, even gritty vernacular—as in this piece from a 458-word essay:

> Mom always said you had to suffer if you wanted to look good. So we tortured ourselves with girdles, outrageous pointed-toed shoes, smelly padded bras, overbaked perms. We even went around for a few years looking like the brides of Daracula with our white lipstick and nail polish. And then came beehive hairdos, sprayed brittle. No wonder fashion rebelled and went natural in the 70's. What a relief!
>
> And yet I and my beauty values system can't go "natural." I have to force myself to find the "beauty" in the "beast," and when it happens, as it so often does, once again I walk the treadmill of being ashamed.

The bottom skills could be identified and praised along with titles, examples, and correct spelling.

Another step recommended by the transformative is to take bottom writers out of special cubicles, or never to put them in. If some college students do occupy a space one can legitimately define as a lag in development, then other students will provide the best zone of proximal development. According to the transformative belief in uneven, multilateral advance, mixing students will also give bottom students the opportunity to help the ones on top. Sophisticated sentences and logical patterns hidden in lean in-class writing could be plotted and suggested to all students as a plan for more fully elaborated out-of-class essays. For both bottom and top students, much can be gained by the nondiscriminatory therapy of leading from respective strengths.

Actually, before instruction, teachers ought to discriminate, in another sense of the word. They ought to further sort the unfortunates who have been sorted into the bottom, to distinguish lean from noncompetitive from second-languaged from dialect-languaged from culture-shocked from what Janice N. Hays calls "suburban basic" (1980: 145) and so on. Annette

N. Bradford suggests tests in thinking to screen the "cognitively immature," a procedure that at least might keep teachers from confusing "slow" minds with what is just slow writing. What the transformative suspects such a testing would show—assuming that it has some workable validity—is little or no correlation between "backward" writing and "immature" thinking. Against studies that argue the presence of cognitive lag, the developmental approach sets an axiom from two of its founders, Inhelder and Piaget: "Verbal productions can by no means fully account for the structures of intelligence" (246 n. 1). This suggests that for teachers the first test of cognition would be to scrutinize the verbal productions of writers deemed "basic" for structures of intelligence, as this chapter has tried to do. The paragraph of lean writing above may seem innocent of nearly every writing convention, but its final position of uncertain, unresolved dialectic is unusually mature for a college student, at least according to life-span studies we will be reviewing in the next chapter. Teachers should deeply question any inference about intellectual maturity based only on skill in following writing conventions. In comparing high-school senior and college junior writing for courses outside of English, Freedman and Pringle found that the complexity of abstract thinking did correlate with educational level but not with the grades of teachers. Some B and C essays abstracted at higher levels than any of the A essays (1980b).

And before any step is taken with students, the conventions themselves could stand the kind of questioning Habermas and Gadamer apply to all social presuppositions. Mina P. Shaughnessy (1977), David Bartholomae (1986), and others recommend teaching university conventions to "novice" students openly and systematically. There is a healthy pragmatism in this, but such pragmatism could use an equally healthy dollop of skepticism, or at least an awareness of the price paid. Should stoutness, for instance, be a necessary convention of in-class writing? In the confines of a one- or two-hour placement essay, good exploratory thinking may be disabled by many of our beloved crutches for the reader: examples, extended analogies, restatements, clever introductions, even perfect spelling and punctuation. In her observation of revision practices, Glynda Hull noted that "less skilled" writers, compared with "more skilled," focus more on mistakes of meaning and less on mistakes of surface form and that they more often "expressed a concern for making a text literally true or accurate." If, as she argues, writers with such a focus and concern show less skill because they have "not yet learned to distinguish between matters of necessity and matters of choice" (25), then maybe university writing teachers ought to start making surface form more of a choice and truth and accuracy more of a necessity. Andrea Lunsford found "basic" writers using the first person more often than "skilled" writers (1980); Sandra Stotsky found "poor" writers creating simpler subjects of sentences than did "good" writers; and David Bartholomae found "developmental" writers often attempting "syntax that is *more* complex than convention requires" (1980: 254). But a greater use of the first person and simpler subjects and more complex syntax all characterize the writing of competent workplace writers. Teachers should do their part in developing conventions to match and support the development of students.

They should do so even if one effect of such a spiral transformative process is to lower inter-rater reliability coefficients on holistic assessments. That ominous conformity among teacher ratings of bottom essays smacks too much of Habermas's "false ideology" or Gadamer's "hidden prejudice." One of the virtues of the developmental interpretive frame may be the way it exposes the holistic frame as subjecting remediality, under the guise of evaluative discrimination, to a discrimination of another kind.

Cobbett's Protest

As we have just seen, another epithet for bottom writers is "poor": they are poor writers. It may be one of the more subtle discriminatory labels. Compare the early-nineteenth-century British appropriation of the idea of "pauper." To be a "pauper" was to be placed beyond the point of no return in a time-honored, almost mythic journey to ruin: rich man, poor man, beggar man, thief. As "rats" and "parasites of the state," paupers were assigned to workhouses to pick oakum and to cobble roads, separated from spouses and children if married, jailed if in debt, and, if dying, sometimes carted by night to be discarded beyond the bourns of their home parish. Once during those years, the journalist William Cobbett (another great outsider) registered a telling protest: "What is a pauper? Only a very poor man." Today we would say that Cobbett's line deconstructs the interpretive frame of "pauper" toward the idiographic.

What is a student at the bottom? Only someone who needs to learn a lot. But not everything. "Poor" writers do not deserve to be stripped of the peculiar skills they already have, wrested midpassage from the personal history they have already created for themselves, and enrolled in some disconnected one-way intellectual trek. Developmental frames are as liable as any other to impoverish categorization of bottom writers, as Hays 1987a, Kurfiss 1982, and other developmentalists interested in composition curriculum themselves have noted. However, the transformative, with its theories of embeddedness, self-contradiction, beneficial regression, interaction, and dialogue, resists such categorization more than most other frames.

In the final analysis, the transformative takes a highly ambivalent stance toward the general interpretive frame of remediality, the expectation that there will always be some students who are somehow categorically behind. The transformative has a working concept of normal sequences in the acquisition of cultural skills, and that allows for a *placement* assessment that puts some students behind others, but its idiographic belief in creaturely growth and in the relativity of cultural standards disallows any *categorical* assessment of those students. For teachers and administrators involved in the admirable quest to help

283

low-rated writers, the transformative recommends one basic or beginning developmental step: to forget the expectation that there will be a remedial group, sui generis and unstratified, and to try to see the group placed in the nether cubicle individually, as eccentric and diverse as any other group.

PART V

Sequence and Development

It is a desideratum in works that treat *de re culinariâ*, that we have no rationale of sauces, or theory of mixed flavors; as to show why cabbage is reprehensible with roast beef, laudable with bacon; why the haunch of mutton seeks the alliance of currant jelly, the shoulder civilly declineth it; why loin of veal (a pretty problem), being itself unctuous, seeketh the adventitious lubricity of melted butter; and why the same part in pork, not more oleaginous, abhorreth it; why the French bean sympathizes with the flesh of deer; why salt fish points to parsnip, brawn makes a dead set at mustard. . . . We are as yet but in the empirical stage of cookery.

—Charles Lamb,
"Table Talk," *Athenaeum* (1834)

CHAPTER 12

Sequencing:
Two Interpretive Tales

OVER THE YEARS, A COMPOSITION DIRECTOR steps again and again into a river of questions from about-to-be teachers of freshman or advanced composition. It is a deep and tricky stream, never the same and always the same. Novice teachers, for instance, come bearing instructional motives that take a new tack several times a decade. Some years they expect their course to facilitate the act of composing, other years to improve the result in the eyes of others—this year to awaken students to the pleasures of language, next year to enhance their appreciation of famous writers. Paradoxically, about these fluid goals the new teachers rarely have questions. Yet they almost always ask the director where their instruction should begin. What should they start with? Minded to chart a course, they seem sure of its destination but not of its route. As Burke would put it, they have trouble converting motive from essence to temporality.

So have we all. That conversion, however, is forced on us when we teach, just as when we speak, we are forced to turn spherical feelings and thoughts into a linear syntax. We can no more avoid the sequential nature of instruction than the sequential nature of language. Teachers do not just teach writing. They teach a course in writing, divided into weeks and days.

The linear syntax of learning to write raises three major questions about sequence. At present, directors of composition can offer no sure answers. (1) In the four undergraduate years, what course should be taught first? This query assumes a "best" curricular sequence for an undergraduate composition program, or what I will call an *articulation*—a best order to beginning and advanced courses. (2) In any one writing course, what subject or activity should be broached first? Within an ideal articulation, there further must be a best *syllabus* or order to the parts of each course. (3) In the syllabus, what should any one student do first? Teachers ought to provide a best *diagnosis,* a most productive order to the task of improving each particular student's writing.

Articulation, syllabus, diagnosis. If teachers are ever in need of valid interpretive tales, it is when they set about constructing these three sequences. And sequence is what conventional English-department lore lacks. On the other hand, it is precisely sequence that the study of development has in abundance. There, before and after remains an explicit sine qua non. Even the most leveling of developmentalists cannot reduce theory beneath a certain baseline sequentiality. In a famous article on development and learning, Donald M. Baer attacks the notions of readiness and stages and concludes with the radical pronouncement: "Age has no relevance to development." But he instantly adds, and not as an afterthought: "Sequence or program has" (244).

Here, in the last turn of this book, we are almost ready to see how development's view of natural sequence or program may change our discipline's view of curricular sequence or program—of articulation and syllabus (chapter 13) and of individual diagnosis (chapter 14).

Almost ready—but not quite. First, in the present chapter, we need to uncover two basic and contradictory interpretive tales of instructional sequencing. Teachers may be unsure what to teach first, but ironically that is not because they lack fore-structures of sequence. Assumptions can befuddle as well as guide. It may be largely due to the one most common presupposition of the profession—I will call it the "instrumental" tale— that we so often face the issue of sequence and teaching with either a rudderless eclecticism or a kind of cloudy, underwater panic. The alternative perspective, which I will call the "life-course" tale and offer as preferable, rests on an understanding of postadolescent development in psychology, sociology, and thinking. This tale of sequence offers the hope that new curricular ways can be found to utilize the powerful current of certain common transformative changes continuing to flow through the college years.

The Instrumental Tale of Sequence

Consider the enigma that our trade lacks a standard beginning-advanced articulation in college, lacks even a conventional syllabus for the first course. In gymnastics, the coach knows to train a beginning class in the forward roll before the front-shoulder dive, in the dive before the front aerial. Writing coaches in college must yearn for such instructional sequences. Their colleagues know where to begin. A first course in literary criticism begins with the *Poetics,* a first course in linguistics with the phone and phoneme. Composition, famously, has neither history nor matter. How can it have a start?

What writing teachers think they have, of course, is something more functional than a history or a subject. They have an instrument: the rhetorical machine of discourse. That machine they may imagine lying outside the writer, as when they refer to paragraphs as "structures" or words as "tools" of the "trade." Or they may imagine it lying within, indulging in the convenient metaphor of the human mind as an instrument (Lakoff and Johnson: 47–48). Either way, they think of their task as training the student in the operation of this complex machine. Such training would seem to have one natural start. Students are made to write, the writing shows what they cannot do, and that inability tells the teacher where to begin.

In this way the instrumental course begins ex nihilo. Sandra Schor speaks for the great majority of the discipline when she says, "The student's life as a writer begins with her placement essay" (206). We have seen a similar blank start assumed by previous interpretive tales and have been at some pains to show how a developmental perspective rejects the assumption. Development cannot imagine any way a collegiate act of learning could begin in nescience. It sees a natural growth always in medias res. Its transformative version replaces the imitative tale of an unformed student taste with the tale of judgment at any age conditioned by prejudgments. It denies that students are too immature to have a style, arguing instead that style is an expression of an ongoing creative and self-actualizing encounter with the world.

The instrumental tale of sequence need not deny previous development. But it usually assumes that development relevant to college learning has been completed by the time students are in college—just as it assumes that students arrive at college with their rhetorical instrumentation complete. Only the operational skill is lacking. Without the luxury of a class of ten-year-old gymnastics students who have never attempted a front aerial before, but with a class of students seventeen to you-name-it years old who have been trying to write since grade one, the teacher cannot or does not systematize that previous life and so has to begin with what the student can't do, now.

Teachers then measure the rest of the course with the same instrumental frame. They think of instruction as prompting the betterment of some "skill" or "knowledge" through "training," by "assembling," "sharpening," "polishing," "refining," "testing," "prodding," and "stretching." They think of the course as getting students to "use," "exercise," "imitate," and "practice" until they are "made good writers," that is, until they have "mastered" a "level of achievement" that qualifies them for an advanced class.

Although these terms can be found everywhere (including in the pages of this book), they are all taken from an article we have seen before, by Eugene Hammond on the "co-ordination" of freshman and junior composition courses (1984). Hammond's study provides the Kitzhaberian map of decline in writing during college, reproduced in chapter 2. Indeed, the legend of deterioration and the instrumental tale merge easily, since instruments as well as operators deteriorate or depreciate without "use." I return to the article because it shows how an instrumental perspective generates a distinct understanding of pedagogical sequencing.

As for the beginning-advanced articulation, Hammond argues that freshman composition should not be "sub-ordinated" to junior composition. The first course will "cover" all major component skills and knowledge, and the second course will follow by "refining" them: "We need not, indeed we should not, leave the students at the end of 101 thinking that we have kept back certain 'material' which will be covered later; we should leave them thinking that they *need,* that they *want,* more practice" (218). So the sequence is defined not by the introduction of new and different tools but by the upkeep and improvement of the existing tools. The method of instruction is a variant of Kitzhaber's "steady pressure," namely "repeated practice" (217). All told, Hammond provides a rationale for probably the most common form of articulation nationwide between beginning and advanced composition: repetition with refinement of the same machinery (invention, argument, audience awareness, support, and so on). Discourse, that vehicle of thought, is brought around for its annual or biennial tune-up.

As for curriculum, the instrumental perspective will set it by default. Since the instrumental assumes a ready-made body of knowledge or repertoire of skills, and since it aims to give students what they currently lack, it will train skills in an order based on the nature of the machinery the students are operating. The apparatus of language provides teachers with one such order. Words make up sentences, sentences make up paragraphs, paragraphs make up essays. The ordering sets the sequence ("Students, we will begin the semester with vocabulary work"). The process of discourse production provides another order: invention precedes ideas, ideas precede first drafts, first drafts precede revisions, revisions precede final draft, final draft precedes proofreading, proofreading precedes essay, essay precedes audience reaction ("We will begin with Burke's pentad"). The internal structure of rhetorical mode provides another: narration underlies description, description underpins exposition, exposition underwrites argument ("We will begin with a personal narrative"). The engine of verbal logic provides another: definition is necessary for substantiation, substantiation for evaluation, evaluation for recommendation ("We will begin with a definition paper"). There seems no end to such sequences, so complex a tool is rhetoric.

In reality, this virtual plethora of orderings belies an actual poverty for instruction. It soon becomes clear that the instrumental tale lends equal authority to any number of teaching sequences. No wonder new teachers cannot decide where to begin. Since they assume an underlying writing mechanism that is essentially static and inviolate, they have no means to choose among ways to describe or approach it. In this, the closest literary analogue to the tale is the cookbook. For most recipes, ingredients can be thrown together in any order—only occasionally do whipped egg whites have to be added at the end. More important than the sequence are the quality and the quantity of the ingredients and the functioning of the tools.

Worse, instrumental orderings authorize sequences without much educational sustenance. As Gordon Allport points out about norm testing in clinical psychology, although the "cookbook method" may help clinicians assess and find "material," it does not diagnose individuals or lay out a plan for therapy (1968: 90–92). In composition, an instrumental bill of fare leads directly to the salmagundi concept of "service," which Richard A. Lanham argues causes a "failure of educational sequence" wherein "the humanities curriculum disintegrates into an intellectual A & P" (34). For most new writing teachers, of course, the default source of curricular sequence is that best-selling cookbook, the composition textbook ("Students, we will begin with chapter one").

There are worse implications yet. The way the instrumental frame, fully extended, reduces a potentially beneficial and social act of rhetoric to a self-serving "knack" no different from "cookery" is explained once and for all by Plato in the *Gorgias*. More to our immediate purpose, Alfred North Whitehead explains why the instrumental approach fails to lend a true perspective on the learning of writing. In *The Aims of Education* he asks why an educator, careless of sequence, would, for example, teach children quadratic equations when they as yet have no use for them.

> There is a traditional answer to this question. It runs thus: The mind is an instrument, you first sharpen it, and then use it; the acquisition of the power of solving a quadratic equation is part of the process of sharpening the mind. Now there is just enough truth in this answer to have made it live through the ages. . . . But whatever its weight of authority, whatever the high approval which it can quote, I have no hesitation in denouncing it as one of the most fatal, erroneous, and dangerous conceptions ever introduced into the theory of education. The mind is never passive; it is a perpetual activity, delicate, receptive, responsive to stimulus. You cannot postpone its life until you have sharpened it. (6)

If the mind may be compared to a machine, an instrument, or a tool, it is one unlike any fabricated by humans. It is alive, and its entire nature keeps changing even while one of its parts is being refined.

That makes a new and strange tale indeed. But in that tale lies the source for less ambivalent instructional sequences in writing, and perhaps more productive ones.

The Lifework Tale of Sequence

By now this book does not need to list the numerous ways the instrumental and the developmental frames oppose. Three differences, however, bear centrally on the question of sequence. First, development directs its gaze more at the worker than at the instrument. This shifts the definition of "curriculum" from its rather loose meaning as the matter of a course ("In our department, the 101 curriculum emphasizes the research paper") to the way that matter impinges on the student. Optimal instructional sequence is no longer the way to cover the "material" the most completely but rather the way to get students to develop their writing the furthest. With that shift, radical things happen to the "material." Joseph Katz and Nevitt Sanford, two leaders in the effort to revise college education from a developmental view, put it bluntly: "Once the question is raised, what is the impact, or lack of impact of the curriculum on the student, the notion of the inviolability of the 'body of knowledge' disappears" (419).

Second, the developmental assumes that both matter and student have been and will keep on changing. The field or craft of writing—standards and methods—changes under our very hand. Nor will the life of the student mysteriously and conveniently stabilize and mature the summer before entering college or docilely postpone its growth during college while it is being tested, refined, and sharpened for some future use. With the transformative view, the metaphor of instrument and operator breaks down. The student *is* the instrument—especially in the case of discourse, which acts less as a tool to express the changing life of the student and more as a product of that life. The operative term is not *machine* or *trainee* but *work*. If anything here is instrumental, it is all the evolving aspects of the human—material, emotional, intellectual, social, linguistic. Together they produce the lifework of the student, a creation that never stops developing.

Which means that another ingredient without stability is the teacher, who if still alive while teaching will still be changing as well. This leads to the third and most far-reaching difference between instrumental and what I can now call the lifework tale of sequencing. The instrumental tale creates a bifold picture of two active agents determining curriculum: domain and docent. The tale effectively eliminates the mentor's role, just as the cookbook eliminates the recipe maker. As Hammond sees it, teachers defer to the tool, merely detecting flaws and overseeing repairs: "We put the students to work the first day, writing. After that, we will teach them anything they need to know" (1984: 219). By contrast, the transformative brings the teacher back in, creating the trifold concept of education that chapter 5 analyzes and that the beginning of this book pictures (see figure 14). With the recognition of cultural and personal development, as David Henry Feldman says, "Curriculum formation becomes a joint function of child, field, and their continuing relationship under the guidance of teachers who understand development within domains" (1980: 168).

The lifework tale of sequence, then, begins in medias res with a vengeance, at a point where three rivers, all midcourse,

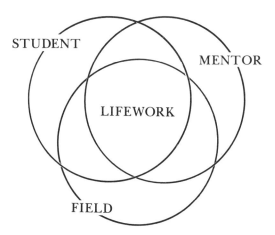

Figure 14.

meet in conflux. The instructional task will not be so much to introduce students to a machine important to their future, or to train them to run it, but more to join in some work. It will be the kind of work whose ends evolve with the work itself, as in the growth of a town or a home. If tools are needed, they will be the kind that are selected, modified, and devised as the work proceeds—an electric typewriter one year, a PC the next—a legal pad for one student, a tape recorder for another. And how will the work start and how proceed? From a point faithful to the current turn in the life courses of all three participants— field, teacher, and student—toward a point beneficial to the development of all three.

Such a sequence is not as chimeric, chaotic, or self-serving to the teacher as it may seem. The field of writing grows very slowly. And the growth of teachers will be much slower than that of their students, assuming that usually teachers are older and that the tempo of human development relaxes with age. In instructional sequencing, the development of the student will take precedence. But it will never have to compromise field or teacher, though it will often challenge and sometimes enrich them. "Recognizing and responding to life cycle concerns and helping students address developmental needs," affirms Arthur W. Chickering, "can be synergistic with achieving more immediate instrumental ends" (1981: 8–9).

In sum, lifework instruction will synchronize its own sequences to fit and further the continuing developmental sequence of the student. Coherent lifework programs will not produce instructional sequences like recipes. They will be more like dietary programs, if we think of diet in its full, household sense. What is the true historical nature of food in any family? Ages, tastes, and nutritional needs of the members change. Foodstuffs rotate with season, availability, price, industrial advance. Culinary instruments develop. Nutritional knowledge grows. Interest, time, and expertise of the cooks shift. Yet all of these changes can be and usually are absorbed into good dietary plans created by households. Again Whitehead puts it best:

> It must never be forgotten that education is not a process of packing articles in a trunk. Such a simile is entirely inapplicable. It is, of course, a process completely of its own peculiar genus. Its nearest analogue is the assimilation of food by a living organism: and we all know how necessary to health is palatable food under suitable conditions. When you have put your boots in a trunk, they will stay there till you take them out again; but this is not at all the case if you feed a child with the wrong food. (33)

The literary analogue to the lifework tale of sequence is not a cookbook. It is the narrative of youth and mentor, in adverse environs, devising a plan that changes all three for the better. Its type story is Joseph Conrad's "The Secret Sharer," and its diabolic inversion is Flannery O'Connor's "The Artificial Nigger." The composition textbook for it has not yet been written.

Developmental Sequences Spanning the College Years

Where will instructional sequences in composition be found under the developmental—or more precisely under that brand of the transformative that I call, following the usage of sociologists, "lifework"? Sequences will emerge from the three arenas pictured above, each as it interacts with the other two. One source will be the common histories of the influence that *mentors* (parents, peers, teachers) have had in assisting change in students through experience and critique. Chapter 5 outlines my analysis of one essential narrative, with its sequence of contradiction, dialogue, re-action, and appropriation. In my account of this narrative, I have left the part played by the development of the field largely tacit, and I have completely disregarded the part played by the development of the teacher.

A second source of sequencing will be the normative steps with which the craft in the *field* of writing is acquired, given the way mentors instruct and students appropriate today's discourse goals. Chapters 6 through 11 extract a number of those sequences, long and short. A brief catalogue here will be useful for the next two chapters. As writers continue applying the trade of writing in college, they gradually move toward more fluency, flow, and literary self-assurance. They shift toward a more technical vocabulary. They build on a growing meta-cognitive awareness of certain techniques, such as enhancing readability or shaping introductions and conclusions. Other tactics become more automatic: explicit coherence slowly gives way to tacit, concentration on form loosens with a greater attention to ideas, closed organizations yield to more adventurous and progressive ones. Certain concerns precede others: ideas move in advance of syntax, errors precede mistakes, the testing of new repertoire in organization and vocabulary attracts before the polishing of old repertoire. Everywhere writers progress toward a grasp of greater complexity; clauses, sentences, logical segments, and essays grow in breadth and depth. Writers move from a more piecemeal or hard-wired facility with discourse toward a fuller and more integrated one. And all along, regressive sequences take place: final free modification grows along with comma splicing; bound modification increases along with embedding and reference errors; students quicken their writing pace and raise their rate of production mistakes, attempt more midstream improvisation and write more awkwardly, focus more on ideas and less on specificity. To this catalogue may be added findings from a few other studies. College students grow in their abilities to take stock of their readers (Hays 1983b), to see both sides of an argument (Whitla 1981), to meet an opposing argument (Hays, Brandt and Chantry), to include more situational information in persuasive discourse (Beach and Anson), to make better rhetorical use of pauses while writing (Schumacher et al.), to access a wider range of rhetorical frames (Birnbaum), to express greater logical abstraction (Freedman and Pringle 1980b), and to use metaphoric language (Fox).

Clearly the evidence for normal development in the field of writing is scattered at present, although Michael Carter recently has offered an important synthesis. Despite what we know about the process and the product of writing, our understanding of the way students acquire the craft of writing has hardly reached Lamb's "empirical stage of cookery." What we have, however, can be used. These craftwise progressions—David Henry Feldman calls them "discipline-based" and Susan Carey "weaker restructurings"—operate largely at Sidney Strauss's "middle level" of learning. They involve reorganizations of knowledge that can occur within a semester, a week, even a few days (1987: 133). Therefore, they may be especially apt for syllabus sequencing, as Carter argues.

For articulation between courses, the best developmental frames come from the third arena above, the *student.* Here are transformations that may change not only specific recipes but whole styles of cooking—Feldman's "culture-based" development that all citizens may be expected to undergo, involving Carey's "strong restructurings" that "carve the world at different joints" (1985: 181). Direct evidence for such personal-cultural development will be found in even fewer studies of writing. But a rich volume is now available in lifework or "life-span" research, especially in psychology and sociology. I have referred to a number of studies throughout this book and now bring them and others together in a synopsis to complete our preparation for the next two chapters.

For instructional sequencing, the great utility of life-span theory is that it proposes developmental frames, fore-structures and end-goals, that extend before and after the college years. Only a few decades ago, of course, such framing was not much sought after or even surmised. It rests on the premise that "primary" or constructive changes in the personal occur beyond the age of fifteen or sixteen, beyond the end point that even the most ardent developmentalists such as Freud, Piaget, and Vygotsky had envisioned. The first half of our century saw only a few isolated voices arguing that formative growth does not cease when adulthood begins: G. Stanley Hall, Whitehead, Jung, Charlotte Bühler. Then three landmark books suddenly legitimized those voices: Erik H. Erikson's *Childhood and Society*

(1950), Robert J. Havighurst's *Developmental Tasks and Education* (1951), and Robert W. White's *Lives in Progress* (1952). Such an outpouring of studies and theories followed that today the life-span approach is as familiar in psychology and sociology as poststructuralism is in literary studies, constructivism in philosophy and history, or the ethnographic method in composition—with all of which it shares a number of affinities.

Lawrence Kohlberg and William Perry, Jr., however, are about the only life-span names with any currency in our field. Here I intend the following catalogue only as a rough classification and synopsis of some documented theories that I feel have the most to contribute to a revision of sequencing in undergraduate composition.[1] In four overlapping spheres—the cognitive, affective, psychological, and social—I list some of the better-supported developmental shifts from precollege to postcollege years. The charts, of course, do not intend to say that these shifts are completed during the college years, only that most college students will tend in these directions.

Cognitive (see a–f, pages 301–2). Generally with their ways of thinking and knowing, college students struggle beyond the static and abstract systems of formal logic. This development is of major importance and perhaps of some surprise to writing teachers. Advancing beyond Piaget's stage of formal operations, people of college age leave the security of tidy and

---

[1] Under the term *life-span,* I have collapsed theorists—more often psychologists and cognitive scientists such as Pascual-Leone or Perry—who want to extend a stage-like development past Piaget's formal operations, with theorists—more often sociopsychologists or social historians such as Robert White or Jerome Kagan—who reject or dilute the notion of stages. There is no full survey of postformal stage or life-course theory, although Jane Loevinger and Elizabeth Knoll and Deirdre Kramer attempt partial synopses of the former. The most convenient entries into this multidisciplined field are the essays and bibliographies in Brim and Kagan; Chickering et al.; Commons et al.; the journal *Human Development* (1958–); and the series *Life-span Development and Behavior* published by Academic Press (1979–). A college textbook on the subject of life-span development, with excellent bibliography, is Helen L. Bee. Chickering 1981 and Karen S. Kitchener 1982 summarize implications for college educators.

	(PRECOLLEGE)		(POSTCOLLEGE)	
(a)	Belief in *abstract, formal* systems of thought:	→	Belief in *concrete, relativistic* systems of thought:	(Sinnott; Chandler 1987)
	allegiance to stable and noncontradictory ideas	→	resignation to contradictory ideas always in dialectical flux	(Basseches)
	trust in absolute logical systems	→	trust in pragmatic systems where formal logic is qualified with action, affect, interpersonal relations, and other real-world frames	(Labouvie-Vief 1982)
	expectation of neat, schoolbook problems	→	expectation of messy, real-life problems with multiple causalities, interpretations, and solutions	(Cavanaugh et al.)
(b)	Trust in *objective, incontestable* systems of thought	→	Trust in *subjective, constructed* systems of thought	(Kramer; Koplowitz)
(c)	Assumption that principles have *universal application*	→	Assumption of a *contextual application,* appropriate in different ways under different circumstances	(Chinen; Gilligan 1981)
(d)	Tendency to remain *bound* within one framework:	→	Tendency to *displace* or judge one system by another:	(Schon)
	thinking in terms of self-consistency	→	thinking in terms of analogy	(Sternberg 1984a)
	thinking literally	→	thinking metaphorically	(Boswell)
	self-relational thinking	→	relativistic thinking	(Arlin)
	thinking dualistically (one authority is right and the others are wrong)	→	thinking multiplistically (any number of authorities may be right) or committedly (one system is best for me)	(Perry 1968)

301

(e) Leaning on *performative* → *thinking* (according to the system, how must I do this now?):	Attraction to *meta-thinking* (why does the system have me do this?):	
unreflective awareness →	reflective awareness	(King et al.)
cognitive handling of → problems (e.g., computing, memorizing)	meta-cognitive handling of problems (e.g., knowing when a list should be memorized), and epistemic handling (e.g., knowing whether a problem can be verified experimentally or not)	(Karen S. Kitchener 1983)
(f) Confinement to *implica-* → *tional* thinking (what does this mean?)	Desire to pursue *represen-tational* thinking (how well does this fit reality?)	(Labouvie-Vief 1984)

self-consistent systems of thought and engage the real world with more complex and ambiguous weapons: probability, analogy, dialectics, pragmatism, relativism, meta-cognitive reflection, existential commitment, subjective or constructive interpretation. The advance will have major repercussions on their learning and unlearning to write.

Affective (see g–k, page 303). Contrary to folklore, or parent-lore, people do not become less emotional as they grow out of their teens. They simply learn better to express affect, with less embarrassment, more openness, greater appropriateness, greater understanding. The implications debunk much teacher-lore directed toward the handling—usually the suppression—of emotion in college writing. As the discipline comes to understand more about the presence of affect in all kinds of writing (see Haswell 1990a), the developmental history of human emotions will grow in pedagogical use.

Psychological (see l–p, page 304). The psychological transformations taking place during the college years have been studied in some depth. Pervasive and powerful, they largely make up that obscure but precise feeling of being more grown-up.

	(PRECOLLEGE)		(POSTCOLLEGE)	
(g)	A closed *guarding* of emotions	→	A more *open* and *flexible* expression of emotions	(Chickering 1969)
(h)	*Distancing* from emotions:	→	Greater *closeness:*	(Erickson 1950)
	the emotional diffusion of anger, frustration, and love	→	the more directed emotion of intimacy	(Douvan)
	coldness toward others and toward ideas	→	fidelity to a group, policy, moral code, or ideology	(Damon)
(i)	Emotion under *less control:*	→	Emotion *better controlled:*	
	emotion and cognition more separate	→	emotion better integrated and mutually organized with cognitive structures	(Sigel)
	emotion largely expressed instinctually	→	emotion handled more linguistically	(Buck)
(j)	Emotions *private* and confused:	→	Emotions more in tune with accepted *public* norms:	(Santostefano)
	social rules of affect poorly understood	→	appropriate social rules better internalized	(Averill)
	affect badly expressed via emotional games people play	→	better organized through conventional scenarios	(Sarbin)
	emotion less reflected upon	→	more meta-emotional understanding	(Bearison and Zimiles; Boelen)
(k)	*undifferentiated* gender-role identification	→	*"cross-over"* where males adopt more female affective roles and females male ones	(Giele)

Generally, a sense of adulthood evolves through a self-appraisal both positive and negative. College students feel on the one hand that they are becoming more self-assured, autonomous, and responsible and on the other hand more complex, self-limited, and nonsignificant. Motivations to change one's writing emerge rather directly from these motives for personal growth.

	(PRECOLLEGE)	(POSTCOLLEGE)	
(l)	*Diffuse* self-identity:	→ More *unified* self-identity:	(Erikson 1968)
	anxious feelings of inner-outer split	→ positive feelings of integration	(Marcia; Astin)
	repressed and discontinuous sense of one's past	→ understanding of one's past as a narrative connected to present and future	(Cohler)
(m)	*Conforming* or unconscious need to act like others	→ *Conscientious* or self-critical need to act mutually and responsibly	(Loevinger 1976; Weathersby)
(n)	*Oriented toward belonging,* under the control of others:	→ *Oriented toward autonomy* or self-actualization, under one's own control:	(Chickering 1969; Maslow)
	coping with tasks at hand under the guidance of others	→ reciprocating and cooperating and relying on personal risk-taking	(Knefelkamp and Slepitza; Blocker)
	egoistic pride in self-consistency	→ feeling of "self-inconsistency" or awareness that one cannot have total control over oneself	(Blasi and Oresick)
(o)	*Sanguine* expectations:	→ *Realistic* appraisal:	
	trust that one's ideals will be achieved	→ hesitation and awareness of constraints and self-limits	(Viney)
	trust in personal competence furthered by formal education	→ hope for a critical interpersonal competence balancing incongruities among wishes, strategies, and actions	(Torbert)
(p)	*Egocentric* concerns:	→ *Allocentric* attention to others:	
	aloofness, coldness	→ empathy, feeling for others	(Benack)
	self-centeredness	→ interest in others	(Heath)
	egoism	→ relativism, seeing the world through someone else's eyes	(Kimmel)

Social (see q–w, pages 306–7). There is no need to argue the dominant influence of the social context on writing learners. In terms of development, the psychological shades into the social, especially since the late-teen self obeys a tropism toward the light of others. But social development does not at all proceed simply outward from the isolated and private ego to the larger and cohesive group, and the dichotomous term *decentering* poorly describes the realities of becoming a socially independent adult. Better is Michael J. Chandler's dialectical term *recentering* (1975). Generally, social concepts tend to evolve out of the teens via three positions, from (1) a narrow and personal sphere involving family or clique values, need to conform, striving toward solution of immediate social problems, and dependence on local authorities, through (2) a broad impersonal arena governed by institutional or universal values, need to compete, questioning of local norms, and independence within the hierarchy of a work organization or educational discipline, to (3) a manageable space involving interpersonal values, need to accomplish or build, finding of commitments within a pragmatic set of beliefs, and interdependence within local communities of family, friends, work, and culture.

To these sequences can be added a number of more diffuse maturing shifts spanning the college years. Supported by a wealth of studies from many different disciplines, and in most cases by common intuition, these reflect slow and general progressions, "a natural ripening of the mentality" (Werner: 24). Ideas increase in complexity, differentiation, hierarchic integration, implicitness, internalization, automaticity, and flexibility. Also growing are abilities to access and integrate information already acquired, to reflect meta-cognitively on one's own cognitive processes, to speculate hypothetically and probabilistically, to frame or chunk information, to deal with higher-order relations, to induce rules, and to pick and choose among the various ways to represent knowledge. Also expanding are general experience and store of knowledge structures, with accompanying growth in confidence and purposefulness.

	(PRECOLLEGE)	(POSTCOLLEGE)	
(q)	*Dependence* on a center of family or clique relationships	→ *Independence* on "institutional" relationships (university or work), evolving toward *interdependence* on relationships of love or friendship	(Kegan)
(r)	*Conformity* to beliefs of others:	→ *Construction* of one's own set of personally valid beliefs:	(Chickering 1969)
	conventional group values, with retributive punishment	→ social-contract values or values sanctioned by universal principles standing free of specific cultural norms, where punishment is legal or self-imposed	(Kohlberg)
	Unthinking acceptance of authorities	→ Questioning of authorities leading to conscious commitment to set of beliefs	(Perry 1968)
(s)	*Ineffectiveness,* or the sense of stagnation in useless or idle work:	→ *Generativity,* or the sense of working to benefit others and passing on one's achievements:	(Erickson 1985 [1950])
	attention to needs of oneself	→ attention to solidarity and partnership in the community	(Robert W. White)
	reciprocation or tit-for-tat cooperation for self-interests	→ collaboration with others for the sake of mutual interests	(Selman et al.)
(t)	*Achievement:*	→ *Responsibility:*	
	Goal-directed competition, using passive intelligence and the ability to generalize	→ Situation-directed competence, using active pragmatism and the ability to deal with specifics	(Schaie and Parr)
	Problem-solving	→ Problem-finding	(Arlin)
	Automaticity in following group rules	→ Conscious weighing of moral options with a "meta-ethic"	(Gibbs)

306

(u) *Decentering*, alienated by formal thinking to an abstract and impersonal world	→ *Recentering*, returning to the concrete and the personal of specific cultural traditions and affectively meaningful events	(Chandler 1975)
(v) *Merely learning:*	→ *Working*, in which college may serve as a good surrogate:	
status of novice, with a potential competence or repertoire of untried skills →	status of expert, with a proven capability to deploy skills in real-life situations	(Neimark)
social sycophancy →	work-world role, with an earned place and opportunities to bond, territorialize, and nurture	(Garfinkel; Vaillant)
(w) Limited *youth culture:*	→ Fuller *adult world:*	(Opler)
staying dependent on family and youth group →	Leaving and becoming independent: preparing for life-partnership with a mate, finding areas of competence, choosing a career, developing an ethical system	(Havighurst)
Adjusting to life; absorbing information →	Adjusting life to oneself, through college-age tasks; accommodating information	(Chickering and Havighurst; Haan)

Cautions

The next two chapters will sketch a method by which these life-span sequences, here stated so baldly, may be appropriated to devise curricular and diagnostic plans in time and in tune with the concrete and interactive way the maturing student, maturing teacher, and maturing field together develop.

Appropriation of regulative ideas, however, always warrants preliminary cautions.

If the static basis of the instrumental perspective makes decisions about sequencing ambivalent, the dynamic basis of the developmental makes them dangerously clear-cut. But to turn the lifework diet into a regimen is to counter the very foundation of the transformative itself. Forcing freshmen through a Perry series of assignments requiring first dualistic, then multiplistic, then committed-relativistic stands, for instance, would put review where re-action is needed (few students enter college as pure dualists) and would exceed any reasonable zone of proximal development (few students have achieved thoroughly committed relativism even as seniors). It would mock the transformative narrative as a "set of formulae" (Spear: 60), when in reality it describes a slow, complex, and deep-seated act of human change. Similarly, to use any of these developmental sequences as a carrot to hurry up change also offends their nature. Making students jump ahead to severely decentered writing denies the benefit of regression and the dialectical nature of the transformative ("Egotism appears to have its uses," as Lee Odell notes: 112). The proper application of these lifespan sequences will integrate them with all other facets of writing, in accord with the interactive nature of human growth. The resulting writing curriculum can take a variety of shapes: as a recursive series where general sequences are applied to new interest areas (Miller); as a single step forward under plus-one modeling, perhaps in collaboration with more advanced peers (Hays 1987a); as a mastery learning program where one step is appropriated before the next is taken (Hays 1987a) and where, I would hope, options of the next step are freely given students; and best of all, as "a series of dialogic encounters" with teachers, peers, and experts in the field (Dixon).[2]

---

[2] Lockstep sequences for college instruction have not been recommended by any composition developmentalist. In fact, even general curricular sequences are absent from the main discussions applying specific developmental theories to writing instruction: Lunsford 1979 (Piaget); Miller (Kohlberg); Sternglass

The mistake is to apply developmental sequences in isolation, hoping to promote development itself with writing or hoping to mature writing on the basis of rendered-out theories of human maturation. If the developmental transformation takes place at many levels in unison and fruitful contradiction with all aspects of the human, inner and outer, then psychological and social developmental sequences will be best combined with sequences from other aspects of the activity of writing. For example, today's professional need for collaborative writing at first suggests a series of exercises following a chronological process: assess writing circumstances → agree on goals → divvy up labor → write parts → find ways to meld parts (and so on). The developmental would not abandon these ingredients but would possibly alter the sequence. In a freshman class it might put the division-of-labor step first, as developmentally of active interest to younger students (see h, m, and q above). In an upper-division course it might place the whole task toward the beginning of the course to allow time later for older students to pursue autonomy and risk-taking and to experience themselves free of institutional constraints (n, q). For another example, the social-context approach to writing might suggest a private-to-public sequence segmented by basic human interests: writing for play → writing for personal power → writing for work → writing for public debate. Given the turn toward meta-cognitive and meta-emotional recentering that seems widespread with older students (e, j, u), the transformative might rewrite the sequence: debate → power → work → play.

Obviously, application of lifework sequences, especially those bridging the postadolescent years, will challenge many familiar instructional plans. The traditional word → sentence → paragraph → essay sequence may be backward developmentally, given the lower-division student's interest in large,

---

1981 (Wilkinson); Hays 1983 (Perry); Bradford (Piaget and Robert Gagné); D'Angelo 1983 (Werner); Neulib and Fontune 1985 (Piaget); Spear (Benjamin Bloom's cognitive taxonomy of educational objectives).

abstract orderings (a, d, t, v). The personal narrative paper, often assigned first because it is thought easiest, may be the hardest for entering freshmen to write because they have such a weak conception of a meaningful life history (l). In the chronology of a piece of writing, audience reaction may come last, but for older students analysis of it might be the place to begin, with their turn toward interpersonal relationships (h, o, q, r).

By the same token, transformative age-span sequences will also challenge instructional plans based on the old formative developmental theory, in particular on the schemes of Piaget, Moffett, and Britton. For one important instance, these schemes are based on school-age subjects and therefore end with formal abstractions. But college-age development shows clearly that apparent immaturity or "regression" in logical thinking often is actually a sign of mature advance toward postformal positions of relativism, pragmatism, existentiality, and emotional openness (a, c, g, t; cf. chapter 11). Taking formal operations (classification, deduction, control of variables, etc.) as the goal of instructional sequences, especially with upper-division students, may be asking them to appropriate what they already own and what they are already beginning to transform as contradictions. In the application of development to writing instruction, the original sin is to assume that prior is inferior. The dialectical or recursive nature of the transformative argues—and life-span studies experimentally confirm—that such an assumption rests on a dangerously simplistic and linear notion of human growth. Early traits recur, transformed. The undifferentiated emotions of the early teens become the reflective and directed emotions of adulthood, egoistic reluctance to decenter becomes a pragmatic need to recenter, trust in narrative becomes a distrust of the abstract, concrete-operational thought provides a dialectical path out of the excesses of formal thinking.

These are radical notions, no doubt, although some developmentalists in composition have expressed similar views (Bizzell 1979; Odell; Dixon; Onore). So there is one final caution for teachers who want to shape instructional sequences in sympathy with lifework sequences. Their new plans will offend some of the most established practices of academia. The teachers will have to transcend the detached, principled formalism of the institutional, as Kegan argues, when they urge their students to take a maturing turn toward inclusion and intimacy. They will have to revise the language promoted by the university with the more mature language heard by Labouvie-Vief in her postgraduate subjects (the same we have heard in our competent employees): "It was a language, I believe, in which individuals grapple with the fact that culture not only has sustained their cognitive productions but also has constrained them, stunted them, and provided only a partial vocabulary for the interpretation of their experience" (1984: 110). Teachers will have to question the academic insistence on order and the past success of academic disciplines, teachers who, as Perry puts it, wish to "teach dialectically—that is, to introduce our students, as our greatest teachers have introduced us, not only to the orderly certainties of our subject matter but to its unresolved dilemmas" (1981: 109). Someone once said that good teachers do not make disciples out of their students. Good lifework sequences will not adulate educational disciplines. As the next chapter will show, by their very nature, life-span sequences lead beyond college, the student soon viewing many of the endemic ways of "higher" education as contradictions to surpass.

CHAPTER 13

A Curriculum

PERIODICALLY, EACH ENGLISH DEPARTMENT'S composition curriculum should be renegotiated in a way none have ever been, in open forum of interested parties. Today such a curriculum would have to reconcile sequences advocated by many different perspectives: cultural literacy, social acculturation, technical preparation, academic service, and others. For this reason, my lifework perspective will not propose a curriculum in the form of a finished course plan, such as one might adopt for next fall and mail to teachers during the summer— nor even in the form of an exemplary course plan around which teachers might devise their own concrete variants. It can be only a model plan or "anticipatory idea," tendering the sort of curriculum that accords best with developmental lore.

In truth, at present it can aspire to be no more than an interim model. Given the paucity of knowledge about expected writing development during college, it only projects from such information as we have at hand and builds from such principles as we have in mind, awaiting new investigations at other colleges and universities, each with its unique field of student backgrounds, teacher personalities, departmental politics, administrative wish fulfillments. The interim sequence offered in this chapter expects to shadow forth less the ultimate model than the way that model might be created. That is why the chapter follows its anticipatory curriculum with some principles that might underlie the construction of a better one. A utopian enterprise, doubtless. But it is not a blind one, as we will see, and it leads in the end to reflection on what may be an irreconcilable contradiction with other four-year plans.

Inside the Traditional Curriculum:
From Freshman to Junior

My sample instructional sequence attends less to syllabus than to articulation. The advantages of a lifework curriculum over an ungrounded one accrue to a well-designed course plan, but obviously not as much as to the linking of two courses, which will span more of the student's own development. There are two prerequisite issues. First is the question of whether a second, "advanced" writing course is needed at all for undergraduates. I believe the record from four-year institutions argues that it is. If so, there is the second and more difficult question of timing. When during the four years should an advanced course be offered? I will argue for the benefits of waiting at least one year after the traditional first-year course. As with all curricular issues, the situation is problematic, and we will have to rely on piecemeal findings from the Sample and similar studies to probe two other issues, the two murky questions raised in chapter 2. What skills do students typically gain in a beginning writing course, and what of that gain do they maintain until a second course?

The need for a second course in composition depends on the particular success of the first course. This is not easy to know, however, given the variety of syllabi, students, teachers, testing procedures, and tester prejudgments that have met and mingled in the periodic attempts of the profession to see the forest. Perhaps the most objective source of information is formal research, where researchers often report precourse and postcourse performance of randomly selected students from "traditionally taught" sections serving as control groups. To that we can add a few unusually careful studies of the traditional course itself.

All told, freshman-composition students make only modest progress to the English-teacher vision. Final in-class essays register between a 6 and 20 percent improvement over beginning essays on holistic rating scales. Typically this kind of advance means that only between 60 and 70 percent of the students write an essay at the end of the course that is better than the one they wrote the first week. Chance alone would account for 50 percent.

Still, some improvement is consistently found. The major global change is in fluency, with students writing essays at the end 10 to 30 percent longer. These end-of-the-course pieces improve most in support and organization, least in ideas. Without specialized intervention such as sentence combining, syntax hardly changes at all, although a small gain in free modification is regularly reported and—not surprisingly, as we will see—a small drop in T-unit length and often in clause length as well. Gain in vocabulary looks ambiguous. The most thorough study, by Michael Holzman, reports that students at the University of California, San Diego moved both toward the distribution in adult published writing and toward each other's distribution. This second effect, a decrease in group variance during the course, occurs very consistently, especially with syntactic measures. Part of the decrease can be attributed to an outcome that rightly disturbs teachers when they become aware of it. Improvement during the course often occurs unequally, with lower-ability students advancing more and higher-ability students less.

In the Sample, the group of students writing at the end of the freshman course registers all these typical outcomes.[1] Their

---

[1] Compared with the other three undergraduate groups in the Sample, this selection of exiting freshmen may represent somewhat better writers. A number of students had dropped the course before the essay was given, and the subjects were selected from only nine sections, increasing the chances of

essays surpass the holistic rate of the entering freshmen's by a fourth, and their length by a third. There is a greater amount of exemplification and more material stored in the logical compartments of the top-level organization, both measures indicating an expansion of ideas. Associated with the faster writing pace are other changes, some positive, some not. Three head toward the employee competence: more appositives, fewer sentence fragments, and more coordination of nominals rightward of the subject. But comma splicing, rote five-paragraph themes, simple *collection* organizations, and—unexpectedly—the rate of stative as opposed to process verbs, all increase. This last may reflect course pressure to provide support with static examples and descriptive detail and to write faster, since stative verbs often come to mind more easily than nonstative. The essays also improve in audience awareness, with much better introductions and more transitions between paragraphs. Finally, they double the rate of long words (nine or more letters long), though it is important to note that their rate of "unusual" words remains unchanged.

This picture of improvement during the freshman composition course emerges as highly ambivalent. Quid-pro-quo trade-offs are operating at top-market rate. Higher production is achieved along with some simplification of organization, fuzziness of word choice, and increase in error. There is also

------

an influence from one or two unusually fine teachers. The fact that these students were writing for grade rather than for diagnosis may also have influenced the improvement in quality of the essays. On the other hand, this group had the same range of pretest writing-ability scores and earned the same range of final grades for freshman composition as did the other three groups. At the time, their freshman course was quite traditional, with a middle-of-the-road rhetoric and an anthology of essays by very talented writers such as Joan Didion and James Baldwin, with a required writing assignment of around four hundred words a week including three in-class essays and an optional research paper, and with an eager corps of young teaching assistants who spent a prodigious amount of time marking papers, holding conferences, and inciting class discussion. There were no systematic coursewide exercises in syntax, error avoidance, heuristics, or anything else.

perhaps some regression in syntactic play. Sentence, clause, and T-unit lengths decline slightly in size, and T-unit variance decreases—all statistically nonsignificant but symptomatic of the conservatism that exiting freshmen show everywhere. Out of 105 measures covering the whole range of analysis, the exiting group shows less variance than the entering in 91. In syntax alone, something is holding the freshmen back from participation in the subclausal advances recorded by the sophomores and juniors, for instance in final free modification and nominal modification. The main concerns of the freshmen at the end of the course seem to be length, support, and explicitness. Since these concerns were the writing tactics the course probably emphasized, many teachers would see, even in this imperfect expression of impromptu writing, a sign of course success. The same teachers would likely also see many tactics taught but unlearned.

A different kind of unlearning, of course, seems to occur after—and probably just after—the exiting students close the door on the course. "What would happen at Harvard or Yale if a prof gave a surprise test in March on work covered in October? Everyone knows what would happen," says John Holt. "That's why they don't do it" (135). But teachers of advanced writing do it, the first week of class. In the Sample, here is what happens to the January students the next September. Compared with the exiting freshman holistic, entering sophomores fall back by a sixth. Their essay length is cut by a fifth. Specificity plummets: exemplification drops by one-third and logical restriction of sentence subjects by nearly half. Transitions between paragraphs decline by 20 percent, the quality of introductions by 15. The rate of long words falls by a third. And the rate of six of the eight formal solecisms studied in chapter 7 increases even from beginning freshman levels. It is enough to dismay any teacher. Teachers may attribute this Kitzhaberian "backsliding" to a lack of reinforcement for writing in noncomposition classes and to the reduction of pressure in a first-week diagnostic essay. Since, as chapter 2 shows, teachers are not very attentive to the ways the sophomore group is advancing otherwise, they will see many of the very objectives they worked hardest to achieve and did achieve in freshman composition lost once the course is over. Even should the objectives be regained with some heavy-handed review in advanced composition, the teachers can still imagine how sophomores must be writing, if they are at all, in courses outside the department.

The understandable impulse is to require more composition coursework as soon as the student's schedule allows, and indeed many academic departments insert an advanced writing course into their program for majors at the sophomore year. But there is some evidence that juniors are more open than sophomores to a substantial advance in the milieu of a second composition course. In the Sample, sophomores show an unease or insecurity or milling around, call it a temporizing, a writing plateau, a period of gestation, a beneficial regression, or a sophomore slump (for further confirmation, see Rubin, Graham, and Mignerey). Not only do they make more errors, they rely more on modals of qualification such as "could" and "might," avoid first-person subjects, and write shorter sentences. They do move with the major tidal undergraduate advances—in vocabulary, in nominal modification, in final free modification, in syntactic postpositioning, in logical organization. But in each case juniors have advanced more, and besides they have recouped some of the sophomore loss in the tactics preferred by the freshman-composition teachers—in introductions, transitions, specificity, and essay length. A sophomore slump makes sense in terms of motivation. Most of the sophomores in the Sample had been writing comp-teacher essays for five years straight, since they were freshmen in high school, and they may have looked with weariness and ennui toward taking another writing course (the same one?). The juniors had a one-year break from comp and may have been energized by the proximity of upper-level courses in their major with known assignments in research papers, case studies, laboratory reports, and other kinds of technical writing.

318

The scanty evidence makes any conclusion tentative, but by and large it supports the recommendation of a long-surviving remnant of teachers: students profit most from a hard-hitting advanced-writing course in their junior year when, as John L. Kimmey observes, their vocabulary is larger, their sentence structure more varied, and their control over the material tighter (cf. Miller and Selzer; Calabro; Acton; Fahnestock). The recommendation has not been much heard in the land, though. More than thirty years ago, Hubert Smith's CCC panel thought a second, upper-division course was "gaining ground" in the United States (167). The prediction has proved only mildly accurate. Although a 1988 survey finds one out of three colleges and universities requiring an upper-level course with a designated writing component (probably connected with some form of writing across the curriculum), only one in ten requires an upper-level composition course outright (Daniel with Ludgewalt).

An Anticipatory Articulation:
Freshman Writing, Junior Writing

The problem may lie partly in the way the advanced course, required or not, is currently designed. As we saw in chapter 2, a common reaction to the legend of deterioration is to make students take again the course that apparently did not take. Michael P. Hogan's 1980 survey found advanced-composition teachers adhering to Eugene Hammond's plan of repeated practice. Typically they imagine a second course as "covering the range of the freshman course but in greater depth" (22). Clinton S. Burhans, Jr.'s 1983 survey of beginning and advanced course descriptions also found "a high degree of repetition across levels" (646). Bernice W. Dicks's 1982 review of articles on advanced composition found most of them promoting the same format as the freshman course only with "harder" textbooks. She cites a teacher who says, "The course has not proved to be very advanced, because most of the students are not."

Dicks guesses, "Perhaps what the students really want is to back up, in effect, and start over with smaller units." She ends with the sad advice to new teachers that they read articles on individualized approaches to composition in the hope that they might be inspired "to try something that has worked in a freshman or other writing course" (185–87).

I offer here just the opposite: a generalized and untested curricular sequence based on the developmental assumption that what works best in freshman composition will not work best in advanced composition. The articulation aims for two courses, provocatively distinct, whose differences in coverage mesh with lifework changes reported during college and link together in transformative sequence. I will describe the sequence first, defend it afterward.

Freshman composition. There would be a double concentration on organizing and generating college-level ideas. Logical schemes would be analyzed and practiced in the following sequence: complex causation, process, inference, choice of options, multiple solutions to problems. Progressive chaining of these and other asymmetrical patterns would be encouraged all along. Rhetorical ways to handle such energetic thoughts would be worked on, first with conclusions that expand implications, then with tactics of internal coherence such as signaling of major logical shifts and providing transitions between paragraphs, finally with introductions that utilize simple heuristic direction-setting. The work on generation of ideas—using freewriting and other familiar heuristic exercise—would usually follow organization within course units. Rhetorical ways to produce ideas would include some of the tactics listed in chapter 8, beginning with the use of logical chaining, then with forward revising and tropic sentences, and then with appositives and other open-ended, midstructure syntactic devices. Otherwise there would be no specific study or exercise in syntax, nor in cohesion, nor in support, description, or specificity except perhaps to practice the recording of particulars as a useful mid-writing heuristic.

Composing dynamics would stress the individual writer working in an intellectual world of ideas. It would begin with exploration and appropriation of readings (with writing tactics such as questioning of authorities, entertainment of divergent views, application to related situations), then move to the sharing of such ideas and the arguing about them with teachers and especially fellow students (tactics such as selecting and paring quotations, defining new terms, identifying sources, allowing alternate explanations and arguments, producing clean copy). Writing topics would deal with intellectual issues of student interest and with arguments emerging from them.

Junior composition. The major work would be in flow, syntax, and diction (in that order) and in meta-linguistic analysis of the relationship of language to reality and to audience (in that order). For flow, students would analyze and exercise distinctions such as new and old information, agent and goal, state and process, active and passive, in order to improve intersentence dynamics. Local frames creating coherence could be studied and practiced, such as refutation, concession, discarding of possibilities, definition through negation, explanation through analogy, logical analysis, exemplification, dialectics. For syntax, students would practice and critique ways to lengthen sentences (through parallelism, expansion of sentence objects, final free modification, and nominal restriction through postpositioning and logical progression of modifiers), then ways to increase sentence variance, then ways to improve cohesion between sentences. Vocabulary work would deal with problems of pretentious diction, technical jargon, underspecificity of nouns, noun-adjunct clustering, and so on. In connection with all of the above, some types of solecisms could be treated in class: sentence fragments with the work in free modification and sentence-length variance, comma splicing and faulty parallelism with the work on sentence lengthening and parallelism, predication error and perhaps some common types of misspelling with the vocabulary work. But the majority of the time would be spent with other kinds of meta-analysis, in discussing the representational, symbolic, cultural, interactive, and potentially oppressive nature of language.

Composing dynamics would stress the collaborative writer in a pragmatic world of shared work and shared ideas. It would begin with group writing projects (applying techniques of audience analysis, format adaptation, labor division, multiple-author drafting, etc.) and would end with more intimate, oppositional pieces directed to a select readership (applying techniques utilizing features of an individual style). Writing topics would deal with nonacademic interests and with the utilitarian projects, language criticism, and personal positions that emerge from them.

This articulation, and to a certain extent the two syllabi within it, look for transformative learning where supported by the life-span sequences mentioned in the last chapter. The first course, then, will stand contradictory to the second in many ways. The first announces a position beyond high school with its basic motive of exploring university ways of knowing. It agrees with Joseph Katz and Nevitt Sanford that "the major aim of the freshman year should be to win the student to the intellectual enterprise" (433) and offers a Whiteheadian stage of romance with ideas. The second course transcends the first by critiquing academic ideas, offering a Whiteheadian stage of precision with the basic motive of looking ahead to the pragmatic world beyond college. The first encourages an idealistic pursuit of formal ideas associated with institutional methods and a multiplistic approach to beliefs and values. The second encourages a worldly pursuit of facts, associated with personal methods and a recentering, contextual acceptance of life. The first course asks the student to re-act an immature conformity to rules of family or convention and then to transform them into institutional or public principles. The second asks the student to re-act public, postconventional principles and transform them into something more private. Beginning with a performative focus on invention, the first course hopes to instill in the student a confidence in his or her writing by dwelling on the production of ideas in partial connection with university writing. Continuing with a meta-cognitive focus on linguistic critique, the second course hopes to promote a student's self-critical view of his or her writing by analyzing the representational nature of language in partial connection with technical and collaborative writing. The beginning course helps the student switch allegiance from school cliques to a more universal group of respected thinkers. The advanced course helps the student switch again to a more autonomous and intimate group. The first offers a socialization into college, the second an individuation out of it.

Below I will explain how a few developmental principles of curriculum building support other features of this two-course sequence. Enough of it has been presented, perhaps, to clarify the advantages of a truly articulated sequence over the customary beginning-advanced program. More will be gained than just distinguishing the advanced course from what one instructor calls the "amorphous quality of its ilk across the nation" (cited by Shumaker, Dennis, and Green). Two distinct but sequential courses will give students a sense of change and will feed curiosity for something new ahead. They will provide a sense of connected learning, the feeling that one is enjoying transformative growth by building new skills on and beyond previous skills. An articulated sequence will generate a sense of appropriateness, the intuition that skills being learned are designed to meet current needs. And it will cultivate a sense of satisfaction when exercise also fits the internal ripeness that, in learning, as Lear discovered, may be all. At a minimum, it will help keep alive throughout the first three years of higher education that vital drive of creaturely growth described in chapter 2, with its restlessness, curiosity, venture, and acquisitiveness.

A Developmental Building Code for Curriculum

As I warned at the beginning of the chapter, this proposed curriculum is only an interim model. A number of comparable articulations could be built from developmental information so far available. Future curricula will be tailored to the individual

323

talents of teachers and the unique shapes of institutions, in accordance with the transformative tenets of plasticity, interaction, and self-actualization. For the future, here is a start on some principles underlying any construction of curriculum sensitive to lifework sequences.

1. Skills will be scheduled for instruction on the evidence that students will permanently appropriate them. The principle is based on Habermas's test for genuine change: that it appear later as part of the subject's uncoerced life history. Since beginning sophomores retain much of the improvement in introductions achieved by freshmen, and since as juniors the experimental students of Kerek, Daiker, and Morenberg retained the gains in appositives they had achieved via sentence combining as freshmen (whereas junior control students had still not caught up), then introductions and appositives appear suitable for instruction in the freshman course. Often this will be a hard principle to swallow. Like most writing teachers, I love graphic, concrete detail and would like to find student essays as populated with it as Emerson found England "paved with quails." At the expense of considerable instructional time, first-course teachers manage to increase the student use of exemplification. But it appears a counterdevelopmental gain, bucking some lifework tidal swing, and beginning sophomores have cast it away.

2. Conversely, direct instruction will be avoided where students seem to progress on their own. Both vocabulary sophistication and nominal restriction, for instance, grow steadily toward matured practice apparently whether attended to in writing classes or not. The control students of Kerek, Daiker, and Morenberg caught up to the experimental students in virtually all the syntactic gains the latter had acquired through a semester of sentence combining. Hence specific work in syntax and vocabulary is relegated to the junior course above.

3. The best time for students to transform a skill will be after it has grown to excess. In the beginning course, freshmen practice progressive logical schemes because they have already

come to rely too much on partitional schemes. Meanwhile, the course lets them try to mature their vocabulary with long words on their own before having them study, as juniors, the virtues and dangers of "unusual" words. It lets them stack up nominal modification until the junior year, when that symptom of academic study has grown lopsided with undue front-loading. The sequence lets them enjoy the concoction of long sentences, along with attendant comma splicing and embedding errors and faulty cohesion, before analyzing the problems. It fosters the enthusiasm for abstract ideas in the first course before broaching their dangers in the second. Prevention is always poor pedagogy. Put in transformative terms, frames have to be appropriated before they can be broken and transformed into more mature frames.

4. Sequencing will focus on key points, not attempt full coverage. The principle obviously heightens the sense of advance in moving from one course to another or in moving within a course from one section to the next. Developmentally, the principle follows from Heinz Werner's fruitful notion of embeddedness: that different interactive aspects of the human develop at different rates and that advance in one aspect may have "a pulling influence" on other aspects (Feldman 1980: 81). In the beginning course it may seem an inexcusable omission to disregard skills in sentence coherence, but they will not lie entirely dormant. The focus on progressive organizations (with some work in paragraph transitions) will eventually transform the student's sense of flow for the better.

5. Tactics and strategies will be taught together when they tend to cluster and interact generatively. The combination of chained logical schemes, idea production, and paragraph transitions in the first course is a case in point. Chaining stimulates new ideas and discovers boundary transitions; ideas discovered midprocess generate progressive schemes and require transitions as mnemonic signposts for writer and reader; paragraph transitions quicken writing pace and lead to a flow of progressive ideas. Teaching such clusters and their circular

quid-pro-quo interrelationships is important. Internal clashes can be made explicit, as the inevitable give-and-take of the writing task and as a challenge to overcome. In the junior course, a more conscious awareness of vocabulary will slow down writing pace, which in turn will interrupt good flow—an important point for students facing more cautious writing outside the course and a problem dealt with by techniques of multi-author and multidraft composing.

6. Instruction in a skill will work best when other skills on which it depends are developmentally active. Consider specificity again, reserved for junior-level work in the sequence. In the Sample, the employees achieve specificity not through exemplification, as is often taught, but through nominal restriction, technical exactness of vocabulary, and exploitation of the first person. Freshmen show no increase, natural or forced, in any of these tactics during their course, whereas sophomores show a steady growth in the first two and juniors a sudden surge to matured levels in the third (cf. the similar finding of Marcia B. Baxter Magolda). Furthermore, the employees avoid the stagnancy and obscurity that specificity risks in ways that sophomore and junior writers have been developing but that freshmen show little progress in: top-level progressive organization, confining of static classifications to the sentence or paragraph level, simplification of sentence subjects, breaking apart of nominal clumps with free modifiers, syntactic postpositioning. As Susan MacDonald has well argued, specificity cannot be taught free of its complicated rhetorical context—or its developmental context, I would add.

7. The skills taught will coincide with change in student impulses and needs. Specificity could be stressed in the first course and allowed its excesses, but we have seen that the techniques for it are little retained. The students may not yet see much need for it. (With their descriptive sentences in personal narratives, Richard Beach's college freshmen stood below the rate of seventh-graders by a third and below the rate of English teachers by more than half.) In contrast, as life-span studies

indicate, freshmen show a deep engagement in the construction of abstract and formal ideas. Certainly on entering college, they face at once a novel academic demand for the rapid understanding, recording, and invention of logical and complex ideas. They will receive with more enthusiasm a course that explicitly practices these skills, and practices them thoroughly, than one teaching them colorful and interesting detail. Two years later, juniors may better engage in a scrutiny of specificity as part of their forward gaze toward the world of technical work.

8. A more inclusive skill will be scheduled first. This derives from a self-evident rule of learning efficiency of which many composition course-plans seem unaware. It is expressed everywhere, from the hermeneutic prerequisite of general fore-structures for special interpretations to Werner's basic developmental rule of differentiation, that organisms progress from global to more specialized behavior. There is developmental sense in the way people experience a love of ideas before a desire to substantiate them (Whitehead), or in the way they morally wrestle first with universal principles and then with particular circumstances (Kohlberg), or in the way they "develop sooner, more irreversibly, and more comprehensively with respect to reasoning about matters in the non-social world" (Bruner 1986b: 26–27). It is more efficient to adjust an abstract law to actual events than to create a general law from local contingencies. The above curriculum applies the rule not only at this cultural level but also at the level of domain. The junior syllabus treats flow first, syntax second, and diction third, under the assumption that some of the more inclusive principles of flow (e.g., the dynamics of given-new information) will automatically prompt beneficial changes in syntax and that some of the principles of syntax (e.g., parallelism) will intuitively foster improved choice of words. Elsewhere the curriculum puts work with logical framing before idea production, conclusions before introductions, generation of ideas before syntax, fluency before cohesion. The basic development premise is that changes in frame, concept, or affect precede changes in style (cf. Durst).

In the teaching of writing, beginning small with sentence work or lists of logical transitions or vocabulary drill seems natural and easy, but at best it will produce assimilative learning, at worst entrench larger difficulties. Solving larger problems, such as maintaining reader suspense, will solve along with them many smaller problems.

9. Sequencing will begin proleptically. "Proleptic learning" describes traditional apprenticeship systems, such as tailoring or journalism where apprentices are allowed to take on tasks a little ahead of their competence (Brown and Reeves: 179–84). It follows Vygotsky's formula "that the only 'good learning' is that which is in advance of development" (1978: 89) and the transformative principle that generative change starts with reaction, not review. So the freshman course above begins not with the simpler logical patterns, classification or chronology, but midstream with complex causation on the expectation that entering freshmen already have simple linear causal frames and that they will find analysis and practice of multiple causes, multiple effects, and causal circularity alien enough to stimulate growth. There is a danger in making students walk through developmental sequences from the beginning (as recommended by Kiniry and Strenski; Tremblay). That will help make automatic Kant's "convenient" immature strategies when these are the very ones students need to deautomaticize, to reflect on meta-cognitively as contradictions to be transformed. Although freshmen may seem to have trouble handling simple "formal" writing tasks (decentering, classifying, comparing, etc.), they don't need to start by mastering these tasks but by unlearning them in order to reintegrate them under more complex inclusive frames, as freshmen probably are already attempting to do, thus giving the appearance of immaturity.

10. Sequencing will end proleptically. Eugene Hammond says that as teachers, "we need not, indeed we should not, leave the students at the end of 101 thinking that we have kept back certain 'material' which will be covered later" (1984: 218). Yet that is exactly where a developmental curriculum wants to leave

them. It is not culpable but simply reasonable and human to let students know that what they have learned will be augmented, contradicted, and transformed in the next course. In fact, the same should be said to students leaving the most advanced course the university has to offer. Just as the freshman course transcends high-school ways with a focus on university-level academic writing, the advanced course transcends academic discourse with a focus on pragmatic writing. In a life-course curriculum, life always projects a more advanced course over the horizon.

Beyond the Curriculum

This last principle looks directly at what may well be to-day's most salient feature of a lifework writing sequence: its iconoclasm. As we have seen over and again in this book, the developmental approach challenges composition orthodoxy on many fronts. Of all the means of writing instruction, however, curricular sequence (both matter and timing) attaches the most thoroughly to motives that may have the least to do with generative learning. Conservative and highly visible, sequence is bound with ties to department entitlement, faculty salaries, faculty prestige and hierarchy, institutional service, convenience of scheduling of students in other departments, enrollment constraints, competency testing, and legislative funding. The particular educational experience that curriculum shapes for students typically has only a partial regard for the maturing that stands as the core of a developmental pedagogy. Ensconced curriculum and a possible transformative curriculum are bound to clash.

No doubt curriculum will be one of the last bastions of the current-traditional pedagogy to fall. But fall it will, and as the discipline looks toward new sequences, negotiating among the priorities of different perspectives, I would like to put in a clear word for life-course needs. Loosely, curriculum can influence human development in five ways (I am adapting and expanding Gollin: 237–39). It can *primitivize* development, forcing students to discard more mature skills in order to adapt to its conditions, just as some beetles lost their eyesight when they evolved into parasites on mammals, or just as students may lose their sense of complex logical design if forced to use nothing but preset formats. It can *misdirect,* fostering a development harmful in the future, as park wildlife can be conditioned to rely on summer tourists' garbage, or as students can be trained to rely on teachers' corrections. It can *maintain,* preserving the conditions for further natural growth, as hen body temperature allows eggs to hatch, or as a course climate for experimentation allows students to acquire rhetorical flexibility. It can *facilitate,* easing and accelerating maturity, as exposure to sunlight allows eggs to hatch sooner, or as proleptic teaching allows students to write functional conclusions sooner. And it can *direct,* fostering beneficial skills that otherwise would not be learned from the environs, as higher primates can be taught to find new foods in their natural surroundings, or as students can be taught to question academic abstractions. Obviously, life-course priorities ask for a curriculum that does no worse than maintain development while providing teachers with opportunities to facilitate and with leeway to direct.

Perhaps not so obviously, it is especially this last function—directing development—future university curriculum builders will be the most reluctant to allow. The current instrumental sequence is certainly antipathetic to directing, since its machinery sets its own parameters or environmental conditions, pushing students no further than ungrounded "practice" in writing or, at best, than "service" for other departments. In contrast, as we have seen in chapter 5, it is a law of transformative development to continually alter and escape itself. Any university curriculum based on lifework sequence will end by reflecting on the university, meta-cognitively. One reason higher education has so little welcomed the developmental perspective may be the implied self-attack in doing so.

The point, made in the last chapter, bears repeating. All serious life-span sequences lead beyond the traditional academic ends of abstract, universal, dispassionate knowledge: Erickson's intimacy, Riegel's historical relativism, Loevinger's individual autonomy, Perry's personal commitment, Gilligan's nonformal ethic of caring, Labouvie-Vief's interpersonal pragmatics. The same will be true of any serious philosophy of mature, human change. Imagine a person who has genuinely achieved *Erlebnis* in Gadamer's sense: open to negative experience, "skeptical in action" (1975: 317), constantly ready to question presuppositions, unceasingly aware of human "finitude" and self-limitations due to history, knowledge, and culture. Now imagine that person studying for a typical comprehensive exam. Could such a student tolerate the role expected of students? Imagine an undergraduate who has achieved the true *Mündigkeit* of Habermas's final, post-Kohlberg stage of moral development: aware of the symbolic structure of all human motives and the fictive base of all value systems, committed to the ultimate privilege of individual beliefs, engaged in the revision of communal norms through open dialogue in which speakers are absolutely equal (1979: 69–94). Could that person stand the ordinary multisection lecture course? Clearly, undergraduates cannot be brought to such mature positions by even a lifework curriculum. But perhaps only a lifework philosophy will be willing to create a curriculum honestly moving students—and teachers—in that direction.

CHAPTER 14

Diagnosis

A CURRICULAR DECISION SERVES MANY TIMES over, once for each student enrolled in a course or a run of courses. Whenever curriculum works for everyone—such is its nomothetic power—we can turn the size of our clientele from adversity to advantage. Yet how often does it work for all students in a course? The eccentric student introduced at the start of chapter 1, the twenty-two-year-old Greek in freshman composition, returns here at the end to remind us once again of the diversity that faces teachers across the classroom arena. Nearly a third of the students in the beginning composition course tapped for the Sample freshman group were not eighteen years old. And that course is the most homogeneous that English departments can hope for.

It is the idiographic power of individual diagnosis that corrects curricular mismatches. When a syllabus or articulation schedules redundant or indigestible work for a student, then the teacher assesses (*ad + sedere:* sits down with) the student's writing and from it deduces a personalized schedule. There are, of course, many other kinds of assessment, and it needs to be made clear that when teachers diagnose, they engage in an interpretive procedure quite different, for instance, from grading, rating, norming, or correcting. In the exact sense of the word, *diagnosis* is that act of finding out what a student should do next to improve her or his writing. It is simply the individualized form of curriculum. Both aim to discover the best learning sequence. Just like curriculum, true diagnosis is an activity little discussed in the profession (neither word appears in the index to Gary Tate's *Teaching Composition: Twelve Bibliographical Essays*). It will be the main argument of this chapter that like curriculum, diagnosis can be especially well informed by a developmental perspective. In the end, in fact, diagnosis may turn out to be the most characteristic interpretive act of that perspective.

Diagnosis, Pseudodiagnosis, and the Uneven Essay

The assessment activity opposite to diagnosis is placement. Essentially, placement is passing muster—assigning place before the course begins, conferring grade during the course, keeping gate at the end. The difference between placement and diagnosis is radical. Teachers place or pass pieces of writing: they judge what the students have accomplished on the spot or in the past (on evidence of high-school English grades or standardized tests). Teachers diagnose students: they look through pieces of writing—I mean *through* them—toward probable future accomplishments of the authors. The two interpretive procedures should never be confused—although they frequently are, as when teachers are asked, to their distress, to both place and diagnose students on the basis of a first-week essay.

Here is a true tale of the way the discipline has trouble keeping placement and diagnosis apart. A quarter of a century ago, a new teaching assistant appeared at the office of his director and said that there was a student in his Comp 101 he did not know what to do with. He showed the director an essay that was half brilliant and half logical. The director, who cultivated a cigar and an office like H. L. Mencken's, studied the piece for

334

a while. Then he said, "Give it a B–." The TA said no, he could figure out a grade—he needed some advice on what to have the student do. The director studied the piece some more and said, "Tell her to drop and take 201." And then he added, handing me back the essay with the hand that also held his cigar, "Or give her an F." I had asked the diagnostic query of where to begin with the student, and had been given the placement answer of where to end with her.

It is a rare teacher today who so narrowly assesses writing. But often when teachers think they are truly diagnosing student writing, they are still placing or passing muster on it. I will call this *pseudodiagnosis*, without anything negative necessarily implied by the term. The interpretive process derives directly from the instrumental perspective and ultimately from the ungrounded English-teacher vision and therefore needs little explication here. Early in the course, the teacher finds a student piece that does not fit the set curricular sequence of the course. Perhaps the teacher has scheduled work on introductions next, yet the piece carries off its introduction at or beyond the projected level of mastery. Or the piece betrays a grasp of introductory technique more rudimentary than the level at which the teacher plans to begin. In either case, the teacher assigns the student special work, literally "extracurricular," perhaps to skip ahead in reading assignments or to take on remedial work at the writing center.

This has the guise of diagnosis. The teacher is predicting future accomplishment, guessing that in the upcoming session on introductions the student will learn nothing. But notice that the prediction actually imagines what the student will not do, and that it is based on what the student has already done. The interpretive act is no different than an act of placement in which someone deems from a sample of writing that a student will learn nothing from course N (or has learned nothing) and ought to take course M or O (or take N over again). This all bears the unmistakable signs of the instrumental perspective. A writing class is viewed as a training course in the running of a machine that has only so many parts to master, one of them being the construction of passable introductions. Instruction is geared to what the trainee lacks or cannot do to handle those parts. Levels of mastery arc sct to initiate and cease instruction. Decisions do not really depend on the student or on how the student might change, nor on the teacher, who ideally is eliminated in the interests of objectivity, but on the machinery of writing, which is absolute.

What is true diagnosis? As with lifework sequencing, it focuses not on an ungrounded instrument or "subject area" but on an individual student. And it does not restrict its gaze to the student of past accomplishments but looks through that to the learner the present student will become when engaged with new writing tasks. Diagnosis sets extracurricular work on the basis of the student's capabilities and desires, not on the abstract value of the student's present work. So the student's *introductions* may need work but the *student* may need first to acquire a better sense of conclusions or of logical sequence before work on introductions will much progress. Or the introductions may appear perfectly mastered, when the student could benefit by re-acting that mastery because it is contradictory and in need of transforming to allow advance in other techniques, perhaps in setting epistemic goals or in maintaining reader interest. Or what appear to be remedial problems in introductions may turn out to be the residual from a trade-off with attention given elsewhere, quickly resolved as the student's engagement with writing evolves in a new direction. Diagnosis is well named. It is knowledge (*gnosis*) that looks through (*dia*)—through present performance to the underlying developmental forces that will bring about a different future performance.

There is a strong pedagogical voice discrediting diagnostic knowledge, and some of it naturally unites with those voices discrediting the use of developmental knowledge in teaching. John B. Biggs, for instance, argues that Piaget has little to say about teaching method because he is interested in development whereas educators are interested in "attainment." Since development is internal, it is hypothetical, unobservable, and unmeasurable. "The teacher is concerned with the immediate outcomes of learning, vis-à-vis the particular learning task. He or she is not a psychologist whose job it is to 'diagnose' from a particular task performance the student's 'level of cognitive development'" (108). For Biggs, then, the kind of interpretive knowledge needed by teachers to assess essays should do no more than fulfill the placement requirements of the familiar Standard Learning Objective or, as he names it, "SOLO: Structure of Observed Learning Outcome." The "level of learning" is determined, "norms for the task" are established, "outcome objectives" are set, and the teacher interprets the piece of student writing by placing it against the SLO or SOLO rubric (114).

The exact point of departure from this behaviorist program is identified by a developmentalist educator we have met in chapter 7, S. Pit Corder. He argues that once the teacher knows that a learner does not match the task, then the teacher needs to exercise a different kind of knowledge to determine remedial, or in our terms, extracurricular action:

> The problem of the nature of such action has to be solved. In other words, we have to decide what aspect of knowledge, skills, or ability the learner lacks in order to cope with the situation. Whereas a degree of mismatch is a quantitative assessment, the nature of mismatch is a *qualitative* assessment. We can call this a problem of diagnosis. This is essentially an applied linguistic problem, since it involves a study of the *nature* of the learner's knowledge of the language (not a measurement of the knowledge). (47)

The kind of knowledge required for genuine diagnosis, then, will be subjective and qualitative, interested not in the behaviorist's "immediate outcomes" but in future betterment, aiming not to measure or rank a student but to help the student find the best way "to cope with the situation."

The interpretive acts of pseudodiagnosis and diagnosis tend to line up with distinctions advanced by other authorities we have met before. Pseudodiagnosis uses Schleiermacher's "grammatical" method of dealing with unfamiliar discourse by setting it negatively against the bounds of conventional usage; diagnosis uses the "psychological" method by reading positively through the new language to the unique intentions of the writer. Pseudodiagnosis operates on the level of Habermas's "instrumental understanding" by *recognizing* via dogma agreed upon in the past; diagnosis operates on the level of "critique" by *proposing* via future-directed theory or hypothesis. Pseudodiagnosis engages in Gadamer's "method" or technical explanation, which questions texts; diagnosis engages in "dialectical experience," which is open to being questioned by texts.

There is little surprising in any of this. But there may be in the way the two follow a distinction discussed in chapter 3. Pseudodiagnosis aligns with the holistic method of assessment, diagnosis with the analytic. The holistic, of course, admits openly that it is a method of placement and not of diagnosis (Edward M. White 1985: 28). It is an evaluative instrument fitting an instrumental view of writing hand in glove: preset criteria, rubric covering all components of the writing machine, scales arranging levels of mastery, isolation of product, erasure of influence of temperament of rater and of writer (reliability training, masking of gender and handwriting, etc.). What is surprising, and worth some reflection, is the way the final goal of the procedure, an intuition of holism or a synthesis of parts, clashes with the end of diagnosis based on developmental principles. Chapters 3 and 11 point out that the range of criteria traditionally set for holistic ratings does not do much justice to the range describing college-age writing development. Holistic values may also reflect an interpretive community that excludes evolving student interests (Scharton), and its scaling may be too crude to measure slow development (Knoblauch and Brannon). Here the point is that developmental knowledge, and diagnosis based on it, has a certain antipathy toward the holistic vision of a balanced whole.

By now in this book we are able to see why this is so. The basic impetus for human development is imbalance, and the route of human development spirals through internal contradictions, regressions, and re-actions. The multiplex writing competency of an undergraduate writer has not progressed in the past nor will it progress in the future uniformly, all of a block in military parade formation. In effect, the odds are low that one will find a student essay of equal knack throughout. The embedded or interactive nature of human beings counters it: one faculty preempts another—verbal memory dims as sight-reading improves, handwriting elegance flags as velocity increases. The history of students counters it: contradictory precollegiate writing advice, the faulty current of competition, late-teen fluctuations in other primary motivations, the plastic stop-and-go of temperament and style. Above all, the circular quid-pro-quo negotiations of learning a complex skill counter it: fluency battles thought, syntax battles flow, vocabulary battles fluency. To enrich a conclusion may be to impoverish an introduction, to sharpen an introduction may be to dull the logical organization, to enliven the organization may be to weaken the support, to shore up convincing particulars may be to undermine a pointed conclusion.

In terms of lifework diagnosis, this muddled situation can be seen with rather startling clarity: it is the uneven essay that is easiest to diagnose. Unevenness helps identify which skills tend to concur negatively and which positively with another. It helps spot performance that, however conventional or correct, lags behind age-related sequences, and it helps measure tolerances of style. It highlights skills with good potential for trial. And not least, it gives the teacher ways to react positively, making it easy to praise tactics that are more advanced than those of peers, departures from the norm that are eccentric yet workable, even infelicitous attempts that move in the direction of mature writing. As we have seen throughout this book, when only ungrounded criteria are applied, negative reactions sprout only too easily. According to Winifred Hall Harris's count, high-school students found their essays returned with 60 percent of the end comments and 99 percent of the running comments negative—and surely college students receive fare no less bitter. The teachers are not vindictive. They just tend to notice what a piece has not done right, since they lack clear ideas of what the author should do new.

Now what is a boon for developmentalists is the bane of holistic assessment. It is the uneven essay that generates poor concordance among raters and low reliability coefficients. And just as the way to notice unevenness in writing is through analytical breakdown, the way to obscure it is through an interpretive push toward holism. Evaluators train their raters intensely in norming flat uneven writing to achieve high concordance, and afterward, interrater reliabilities are displayed with pride if they are high enough. A winning coefficient of, say, .8 means that if the encounter was to be staged again under comparable circumstances—similar raters using the same systematic weaponry versus the same wily essays—the new rates would correlate with the old ones at about .8. Such a figure expresses the victory of an orderly system of placement waged successfully against a mob of anomalies. The question, of course, is whether it is not a Pyrrhic victory.

The anomalies may have been momentarily vanquished, but they have not vanished. The writers could display a reliability figure of their own, though to my knowledge researchers in writing assessment have not yet thought fit to give it birth. That figure would be a correlation not of summed rates but of the *variances* of the individual rates making up each score. This correlation would not show how reliable raters are but how reliable certain essays are in eliciting a concordant or discordant reaction. From an actual rescoring of the Sample essays, I predict that the figure would fall around .5—not in the same league as that holistic rating's .9 interrater reliability but an honorable enough testimony to the tenacity of some student writing to remain irreducibly uneven even under intense, well-trained holistic pressure.

No doubt the quality of unevenness will itself be spread unevenly among any sample of writers of the same age and experience. The point is that the profession has trained English teachers to interpret that fact very nearly the reverse of the way developmental educators would interpret it. Traditionally, whole essays with balanced parts are the goal of writing classes and the basic criterion on which placement decisions are made. For developmentalists, such essays may very well be taken as a sign of stalled growth. And for diagnosticians, such essays resist projections about future progress just as round, highly polished agates resist the grasp. In their brilliant self-study of diagnostic interpretation, Loren Barritt, Patricia L. Stock, and Francelia Clark delve right to the heart of the issue. They argue that even for placement of entering students into a curriculum, it is essential that an assessor envision what they call the "imagined" or "prospective" student. But that happens only when the assessment method of "pre-established criteria" breaks down and produces discrepant readings, forcing assessors to think of the writer behind the writing. Concordant readings mean the interpretive process has stopped with the writing: "When an essay matches our expectations, the student as author goes otherwise unnoticed" (321).

Unfortunately, no one has written a procedure to train assessors in breaking down student writing to produce discrepant and diagnostic readings. As Gadamer says, "There is no such thing as a method of learning to ask questions" (1975: 329). Or as I would say, the method of placement or pseudodiagnosis is easily taught but tends to the loss of the student, the method of true diagnosis is little understood but leads to the regaining of the student through dialogue.[1]

---

[1] Feldman provides a classic description of the way development of a complex skill proceeds multilaterally, and of the need of an analytic procedure to study or even envision that process (1980: 41–85). He documents the development of map drawing in children, but I have no doubt a similarly fine-grained analysis of essay writing by college students would find the same irregular, recursive, interactive movement of different subskills. For skepticism regarding the ability of holistic methods to detect growth in writing,

A Last, and the First, Diagnostic Essay

To illustrate the way teachers can lose and gain students, this book began with a partial glimpse of a junior "diagnostic" essay seen through the teacher's window of interpretation. Let's circle back to the piece and look at it whole. It will be this book's final trial of the developmental perspective as a guide for pedagogical interpretation and practice. It is also an example of unevenness. Of all the essays in the Sample, it aroused the most interrater variance, the only essay to receive both the highest and the lowest rates on the eight-point scale. The seven rates were 1, 4, 5, 5, 6, 7, and 8. If nothing else, one wants to see what amphisbaena of an essay could earn such a divergence of reactions from college teachers trained in holistic norming.

> I believe that conceptions of human "beauty" and "handsomeness" differ greatly between age groups. There are, however, certain basics which are common to all. Children as well as adults seem more attracted to people who are well-groomed, well-dressed, and confident of manner. Children seem more apt to base all of their judgements on these three criterion, while adults are more likely to recognize physical beauty, or potential, under a shy or poorly dressed person.
>
> On the other hand, children are quick to ostracize an extremely homely or handicapped individual in spite of that person's efforts at being well-groomed and outgoing. I find that as I grow older I am more likely to incorporate someone's personality into my conception of their looks. When I was a child, though, I didn't wait to get to know a person. I formed a permanent judgement based on personal appearance and projected attitude only.
>
> That is why I feel it's especially important for young children to start out with a positive self-image. With confidence, a plain child can fool other kids into thinking he or she is physically flawless. The other children's attitudes will keep reinforcing this self-image, and as an adult, that person will carry a confident manner

see Nold; Applebee, Durst, and Newell; Knoblauch and Brannon: 151–71; Lucas; Scharton; and especially Warantz and Keech: "Beyond Holistic Scoring: Rhetorical Flaws That Signal Advance in Developing Writers."

that overrides physical appearance. Since our society places such emphasis on beauty, a child without that gift must learn early how to "be beautiful."

Once it is known that a particular essay produces wildly discrepant ratings, the reasons usually can be detected at a glance. Even for a junior writer, this piece displays an unusual sophistication of vocabulary and facility with mechanics. The penultimate sentence alone shows a correct apostrophe for a tricky possessive (children's), a nonobligatory but helpful hyphen (self-image), an unusual but apt verb (overrides), and a faulty predicate—the only one in the essay—that borders on justifiable poetic license (carry a confident manner). The two unarguable solecisms (judgements and three criterion) bear the unmistakable signs of developmental error rather than mistake. These virtues and others, such as an unusually complex logical design, entwine with major problems. The output is low for an hour's work. Introduction and conclusion are perfunctory. Concrete detail, color, and support are nearly absent. So is variety of syntax. Although T-units are longer than those of most juniors, they are monotonous in length and construction, with little but multiclause sentences, no passives or inversions, and a rate of stative verbs higher than in any of the employee essays. Worst, the reasoning, although complex, wends its way to serious logical contradictions. The second paragraph argues that a homely child cannot keep from being ostracized by being outgoing, and the next that a child can hide homeliness by being confident. In the last sentence the author says society emphasizes physical beauty, yet she earlier argued that adults judge by personality.

Clearly, placing the piece—say, giving it a grade or assigning it a pass or fail on a "rising junior" qualifying test—will be a vexed decision. If we judge the language ability of this author, the effort probably deserves the 8, but if we ask whether she got a point across and convinced us of it in the fifty minutes, the effort probably deserves the 1. On the other hand, pseudodiagnosis may come too readily. A teacher would have no trouble listing at the end of the essay the rhetorical subskills that the student has not passed muster on: support, introductions and conclusions, transitions, variety, logic. Some teachers have rubberstamp checklists just for the purpose. Unfortunately, since such a rubric does not consider which of these recommendations are going to undermine and which further the energy-rich accomplishments of the author, and since it gives no indication of an order of attack on the deficiencies, the student would have little idea of where to begin.

For true diagnosis, the teacher can rely on personal experience in learning the craft of writing, on knowledge of normal age-span developmental, and on the principles proposed for curricular sequencing in the last chapter. Let's assume we have seen enough writing from this student to be sure the above sample fairly demonstrates the present turn her writing has taken. Let's also assume that she is starting a junior-level course that is about to take up, as suggested in the previous chapter, semantic analysis of language and local problems of flow. Here is my diagnosis. I would suggest to this student that for her next writings she concentrate on finding and using organizations that (as Hegel put it so radically) rise from the abstract to the concrete. To explain, I would offer some illustrative tropic statements: Let's look at misconception X and see where it goes wrong. What are the beliefs or assumptions of group X and which of them am I able to accept? What are the different effects of X and how can they be reconciled? What is the ideal goal of X, how far have we progressed toward it, and what is our next step? What of X remains viable when we view X from the viewpoint of Y, and then from the viewpoint of Z?

Here are my reasons for choosing this particular coaching advice. (1) The focus on logical organization leads from a strength shown by the chained structuring of her essay, which analyzes a problematic situation in the first two paragraphs, suggests a solution in the first sentence of the last paragraph, and follows that with an analysis of the results of the solution. (2) The particular logical pattern recommended begins at a point of strong contradiction in her essay. This is where the writer's yearning to categorize, grown excessive, has produced various classifications that overlap, clash, and begin logically to break down. For instance, her categorization of adults as being able to see through shyness in paragraph one vibrates against her categorization of them as being fooled by a confident manner in paragraph three. (These contradictions would be the spot to start discussing the essay with the student.) Such problems with categorical thinking are resolved by the recommended modes of relativistic, dialectical, and pragmatic thought. (3) The new writing task would force the writer to re-act meta-cognitively her problems with formal thought. (4) As we have seen, progression from abstract to concrete thinking follows a pervasive, early adult sequence and is especially appealing to women (e.g., Marcia B. Baxter Magolda). (5) This work on top-level, concrete logical organization would reinforce the concurrent coursework in sentence flow and in the analysis of language and reality—in part because it is more inclusive. (6) Intuitively, it strikes me as a key point whose pulling influence will likely help this writer with other problems. Setting up a tropic and progressive purpose may lend substance to introduction and conclusion, and the step structure of a logical plot may quicken the pace of writing, resulting in fewer but more efficient transitions and a better variety of syntax. (7) I respect such logical maneuvers and am interested in seeing how advanced students take to them. (8) I am eager to see if she will accept the diagnosis.

This last reason needs an explanation. Just as Habermas's models for critique are "anticipatory" and theories of development are "probabilistic," every true diagnosis is speculative. It has to be, since like the other interpretations, it deals with the future. The only way to *know through* the present is by intuition and imagination. Although this particular tactic may seem as simple as learning to throw your tools over the fence before you climb over it yourself, it is advice submitted to one particular student at one particular time of her life. So the narrative of true diagnosis requires one turn beyond that usually taken with the acts of placement or pseudodiagnosis, and that is truly to assess, to *sit down with,* the student and together decide what will be the next best step. This will be a dialogue in the deepest sense of both Habermas and Gadamer, in which the teacher will propose a critique based on a probable lifework scenario and the student will freely accept it or not, in which the teacher will let the temperament of the student openly question the diagnosis and the student will openly let the diagnosis contradict and re-act her prejudgments. Together they will try to find the catch that both teacher and student are always in search of, that switch releasing an energy surge in rhetorical effect or efficiency.

Development and the Act of Diagnosis: The Teacher As Good Mechanic

There is no hiding the fact that true diagnosis is time-consuming. A syllabus and articulation based on normative lifework sequences may act diagnostically in a collective and tacit way. But a certain amount of individual diagnostic attention will be required due to the very nature of plasticity that shapes our ends. The uneven essay is not anomalous, just pedagogically easy because it does not hide the contradictions that vitalize all acts of learning. Indeed, there is no reason to hide the fact that developmental theory would lead, if it could, to diagnosis in a master-apprentice situation as part of an on-the-job, proleptic tradition of curriculum much older than the current one.

Educators must make do with what they have. The loss of time entailed by diagnosis, nevertheless, is bought back for the teacher by the gain of the student—and by a certain peace of mind as well. Barritt, Stock, and Clark describe the release when a teaching corps openly admits and discusses discrepancies in assessments of student writing, and they note that concordance on preestablished criteria does not guarantee the satisfaction of validity, only a kind of free-floating reliability. I would go further. Hidden in the act of placement is a kind of root dishonesty that partly explains the uneasiness many people feel when required to direct or apply it. The kind of high variance displayed by the seven teachers' ratings of the junior essay above has been seen as a shame for our profession (can't we agree on standards?), as a fear of directors of composition (what if the student took the essay to another teacher for a grade?), and as the despair of holistic evaluators (there goes the reliability coefficient). Yet when I watch holistic raters or teaching-assistant graders struggling with their scales, trying to decide what to do when an essay fits a "7" or a "B" in one category and a "3" or a "D" in another, I am reminded of the despair of William Blake's nomothetic Urizen on seeing "That no flesh nor spirit could keep / His iron laws one moment." To my mind, the seven rates of 1, 4, 5, 5, 6, 7, and 8 describe the essay more accurately than any less varied set. They are more truthful, and therefore more useful for any pedagogical effort to help the student.[2] "Assessing growth in writing," says Janet Emig, "is a far larger, more complex, more individual and more interesting matter than testing" (143).

This is not to assign placement any less rightful place than diagnosis in the teaching of writing. Placement and diagnosis, in fact, form another hermeneutic circle, along with grammatical and psychological reading, rule and example, presupposition and experience, understanding and explaining, knowledge and hypothesis. Set cultural values guide diagnostic conjectures, and the developmental realities that underlie diagnosis validate placement standards. There is a persuasive defense for

---

[2] Currently, in the profession's evaluation of the writing competence of individuals, we are beginning to turn away from the holistic (e.g., Catharine Keech Lucas), a shift I hope this book will further. But we should not forget that this advance is also a historical regression. So in 1949, before the popularity of holistic assessment, Stephen Wiseman argued that "lack of high inter-correlation is desirable, since it points to a diversity of viewpoint in the judgment of complex material, i.e., each composition is illuminated by beams from different angles" (206).

the spirit of holism that inspires accurate placement of writing: "Even the meanest bit of halting prose, even the most down-trodden of our fellow creatures, deserves to be taken as a living and vital unit of meaning, an artistic whole, not merely as a collection of scraps and parts" (Edward M. White 1984: 409). And there is an equally persuasive defense for human "scraps" and the spirit of analysis, which this study has embraced and which any study of development must embrace: "Each individual has a share in numerous group minds—those of his race, of his class, of his creed, of his nationality, etc.—and he can also raise himself above them to the extent of having a scrap of independence and originality" (Freud 1955: 129). Without the "units of meaning" that are interpretive frames, nothing will be understood, but without that "scrap of originality," the authority-bound stereotyping of the circle will never be broken and turned into Ricoeur's "living circle," into an interpretive spiral that moves.

Freud's appeal to the element of independence and originality in every human being reminds us of Mark Freeman's point that it is more toward the idiographic than the nomothetic that the narrative force of developmental thinking leads. So it is proper that with individual diagnosis, this book ends with one last turn through the idiographic. If there is one act most characteristic of developmental thinking, most central to the interpretive frame this book encourages teachers to assume, it is diagnosis. Diagnosis is that point in the full transformative tale when mentor—seneschal and trickster—submits a plan based on knowledge of past development to help a learner progress. It is the moment in "The Secret Sharer" when Leggatt conveys to the novice captain that he needs to take a risk to gain his crew's respect, or the moment in "Undr" when Bjarni sends Ulf away to discover on his own that he has his own style, or the moment in "Resolution and Independence" when the leech-gatherer shows the young poet-narrator that he can trust life. In the philosophy of change, diagnosis marks that turn when virtual change takes on the possibility of actual change—when experience converts to application in Gadamer, when knowledge converts to self-knowledge in Habermas, when understanding reaches toward that "terminal act" of appropriation in Ricoeur. In the teaching of writing, diagnosis reminds us that the truly victorious teacher concordance—achieved holistically and analytically—will be when we all agree on what a writer should do next.

This last sentence makes me reflect once again on a chronic metaphor running throughout this book: the image of the teaching of writing as a military act. Just as pervasive are two other metaphors, one medical and the other culinary. The images are worth pondering on, since they suggest a view of the student as adversarial, ill, or malnourished—any of which I utterly reject. But the view of the teacher of writing as tactician, dietician, or physician implies a status that I have come to see as more and more noble for our profession, that of diagnostician. The writing teacher can hardly aspire to a more respected image than that of the good mechanic: the coach, the decorator, the plumber, the tuner—those craft-wise fixers who can not only tell you what's wrong or what's going to go wrong but also suggest what to do about it. Isn't this really what students bring their writing to us for?

One last story. I will call it the tale of the good mechanic. I had read it so long ago it had assumed the disembodied power of one of Frederic Jameson's protonarratives, and I was able to trace its source only with luck. The good clinician Max Wertheimer often told it as an illustration of the way the mind can discover solutions by reorientation or restructuring, but for me it figures forth the essential act of diagnosis. Wertheimer once observed two boys, aged ten and twelve, playing badminton outside his window. The game was no fun for either. The younger boy was just learning and could not even return the serves of the older. After losing several games in a row, the younger one threw his racket down, said, "I won't play any more," and refused to answer the older boy's pleas to continue.

At this point in the story, Wertheimer often asked people what they would do were they the older boy. The answers that he received sound like the pseudodiagnosis I once got from my director of composition: promise him candy, find a different game, scold him for being a sissy, offer to treat him easy, forget him, give him a handicap. But instead the older boy, after studying the situation, suggested they just see how long they could keep the bird going between them. He would start with easy serves but make them gradually harder (172–76). Was it a stroke of genius or a solution any kid would have found? No matter. Either way it was an act of true diagnosis. A few days later Wertheimer saw the boys playing happily, the game of the younger much developed.

Re-Action:
A Consolatory Tale

Islands in the unnavigable depth
Of our departed time.
     —William Wordsworth, manuscript fragment

WELL, ONE MORE STORY. IN THE LAST OF HER
Winter's Tales, Isak Dinesen tells a brief story of infinite regress,
the kind that has so attracted the readers of this century.
Nasrud-Din, the prince of Persia, takes to wandering the
squalid streets of Teheran disguised as a wretched beggar. He
wants to know the people whom he will one day rule. The poor
are not fooled, of course, and give alms to their beggar-prince
liberally. Meanwhile Fath, a beggar by profession, capitalizes,
so to speak, on the situation, and disguises himself as Prince
Nasrud-Din disguised as a beggar. One night the two meet and
talk. When Nasrud-Din learns the truth, he laments that he has
become servant to a beggar. Whatever fame he achieves as a
prince will "serve to the greater glory of Fath." Fath replies that
he himself is equally enslaved, since he can rise no farther than
to the beggar whom Nasrud-Din feigns: "I am but the beggar's
mask of Prince Nasrud-Din." How can the two release themselves from their mutual enslavement?

I will let Dinesen tell that part of her story. For my purpose, the tale is complete when Fath explains the principle that
will lead to the solution: "My master, you and I, the rich and the

poor of this world, are two locked caskets, of which each contains the key to the other."

The teachers and the learners of the world, this book has argued, are two locked caskets, of which each contains the key to the other. Both are locked into interpretive boxes fashioned by time and development and the chance condition that one was born not richer than but years before the other. The key is perspective, or the ability to see through the natural disguises that time confers. "The only true voyage of discovery," Proust says, "the only fountain of Eternal Youth, would be not to visit strange lands but to possess other eyes, to behold the universe through the eyes of another." And the method of opening the boxes is through open dialogue, in which the separate developments of teacher and learner somewhat merge, somewhat change, and (since the change has been achieved by at least two people) somewhat add to the development of the culture.

All this was foreseen in the first pages of this book, with their project of regaining the student and the teacher through an enlargement of interpretive and developmental ground. But what I did not foresee and what the book has not really faced is the difficulty of such an open dialogue for both student and teacher. I have failed to treat a contradiction of major import in the study of development and teaching, and that is the problem of communication between people at different points in a life course. Wordsworth was right in fearing the "vacancy" that lies between the "two consciousnesses" of less experienced and more experienced. In a famous letter picturing development as a mansion of many apartments, Keats saw the developmental way Wordsworth was exploring as full of dark doors leading to dark passages. To me, such appears the way ahead for the application of development to teaching.

What will students make of a teacher who, as Mina Shaughnessy imagined, reaches the fourth stage of his own development, "remediates himself," and makes students his study (1976)? How will students respect the teacher who uses dialogue in a genuine Gadamerian sense, not to prove herself right but to gain insight? In their own developmental phase, ardent in the pursuit of formal or factual truths, how can students be kept from seeing as threatening or insignificant any genuine Habermasian dialogue, which aims to create operational "truths" by consensus? And from the angle of the teachers, how will we be able to revisit that strange land of the student when our memories of that time are only "Islands in the unnavigable depth / Of our departed time"? How can we know again those old transformations of knowing when, as developmentalists have often pointed out, it is the major frame-shifts that are most forgotten because they break the earlier frame by which we can know them? How eager will we be to take up positions we once abandoned precisely because we intuited them as constraints? Will we need special exercises to talk to students at their own level, as William Perry ponders (1981: 87), to train us for a professional form of dialogue in which we must re-act and reflect on old turns of development that most people our age have wisely left behind?

These are dark passages this book has left to others to illuminate. There are already a few pioneers, some of them exploring the promising Marxist synthesis of development and social dialogue in Lev Vygotsky, Mikhail Baktin, and Paulo Freire. I can only encourage reading Janet Emig and Robert P. Parker on changes in the way teachers interpret student writing when they reach middle age, Chris M. Anson on the largely undescribed "symbiotic relationships" between students and teachers at different Perry stages, Joy S. Ritchie on the ease with which development other than one's own can be squelched without real dialogue, Marx W. Wartofsky on the way theoretical views of development alter the actual development of students, Jerome Bruner on the classroom as a forum for negotiating and renegotiating meaning (1986a: 121–33), Joseph Williams on a teaching model of growth in which "we are in the figure along with the student" (1989: 250), Kathleen Dixon on the danger to teaching when growing students are visualized as "negatives of adults."

The teacher's consolation is not in knowing that one can pass on what one has learned. Nor is it in knowing that students will carry on. It is in knowing that students and teachers carry each other on.

In Dinesen's story, the encounter of Nasrud-Din and Fath is framed by another, more contemporary story, for which the parable serves as "a consolatory tale." A Parisian author has just finished writing a new book and is awaiting, in a state of depression, the reaction from the public (*"Omne animal post coitum triste,"* comments Dinesen). Artists are at the mercy of the public, he laments to a friend. A book is nothing until it becomes what readers make it, for good or bad. His friend consoles him with the tale of Nasrud-Din and Fath, which in effect points out that readers do not exist without books and can become no more than what books make them out to be. I refrain from applying the tale to the present author and his readers, now creating the last lines of this book together. Instead I extend the tale to teachers and their students. Doesn't the sadness that teachers feel after the final class period mean that they have not remained and will not remain what they were?

Works Cited

Acton, Gary. 1987. "Second Writing Experience at Eastern Montana College." *Teaching Writing* 9 (Fall): 52–57.

Adams, M. Ray. 1956. "A Cooperative Academic Enterprise in Defense of the English Language." *College Composition and Communication* 7: 86–90.

Aldrich, Pearl G. 1982. "Adult Writers: Some Factors That Interfere with Effective Writing." *Research in the Teaching of English* 16: 298–300.

Allport, Gordon W. 1961. *Pattern and Growth in Personality.* New York: Holt, Rinehart and Winston.

———. 1968. *The Person in Psychology.* Boston: Beacon Press.

Anderson, Richard C. 1980. "Schema-Directed Processes in Language Comprehension." In *The Psychology of Written Composition,* ed. James Hartley, 26–39. London: Kogan Page.

Anson, Chris M. 1989. "Response Styles and Ways of Knowing." In *Writing and Response: Theory, Practice, and Research,* ed. Chris M. Anson, 332–66. Urbana, Ill.: National Council of Teachers of English.

Applebee, Arthur N., Russel K. Durst, and George E. Newell. 1984. "The Demands of School Writing." In *Contexts for Learning to Write,* ed. Arthur Applebee, 55–77. Norwood, N.J.: Ablex.

Arlin, Patricia K. 1984. "Adolescent and Adult Thought: A Structural Interpretation." In *Beyond Formal Operations: Late Adolescent and Adult Cognitive Development,* ed. Michael L. Commons et al., 258–71. New York: Praeger.

Astin, Alexander. 1977. *Four Critical Years.* San Francisco: Jossey-Bass.

Averill, James R. 1984. "The Acquisition of Emotions during Adulthood." In *Emotion in Adult Development,* ed. Carol Z. Malatesta and Carroll E. Izard, 23–43. Beverly Hills, Calif.: Sage Publications.

Baer, Donald M. 1970. "An Age-Irrelevant Concept of Development." *Merrill-Palmer Quarterly* 16: 238–45.

Baltes, Paul B. 1979. "Life-Span Developmental Psychology: Some Converging Observations on History and Theory." In *Life-Span Development and Behavior,* ed. Paul B. Baltes and Orville G. Brim, Jr., vol. 2, 255–79. New York: Academic Press.

———. 1984. Foreword to *On the Nature of Human Plasticity,* by Richard M. Lerner, ix–x. Cambridge: Cambridge University Press.

Bamberg, Betty J. 1983. "What Makes a Text Coherent?" *College Composition and Communication* 34: 417–29.

Bandura, Albert. 1981. "Self-Referent Thought: A Developmental Analysis of Self-Efficacy." In *Social Cognitive Development: Frontiers and Possible Futures,* ed. John H. Flavell and Lee Ross, 200–239. Cambridge: Cambridge University Press.

Barritt, Loren, Patricia L. Stock, and Francelia Clark. 1986. "Researching Practice: Evaluating Assessment Essays." *College Composition and Communication* 37: 315–27.

Barron, N. 1971. "Sex-Typed Language: The Production of Grammatical Cases." *Acta Sociologica* 14: 24–42.

Bartholomae, David. 1980. "The Study of Error." *College Composition and Communication* 31: 253–69.

———. 1986. "Released into Language: Errors, Expectations, and the Legacy of Mina Shaughnessy." In *The Territory of Language: Linguistics, Stylistics, and the Teaching of Composition,* 2d ed., ed. Donald A. McQuade, 64–88. Carbondale: Southern Illinois University Press.

Basseches, Michael A. 1984. *Dialectical Thinking and Adult Development.* Norwood, N.J.: Ablex.

———. 1989. "Intellectual Development: The Development of Dialectical Thinking." In *Thinking, Reasoning, and Writing,* ed. Elaine Maimon, Barbara Nodine, and Finbarr W. O'Connor, 23–45. New York: Longman.

Beach, Richard. 1987. "Differences in Autobiographical Narratives of English Teachers, College Freshmen, and Seventh Graders." *College Composition and Communication* 38: 56–69.

356

Beach, Richard, and Chris M. Anson. 1988. "The Pragmatics of Memo Writing: Developmental Differences in the Use of Rhetorical Strategies." *Written Communication* 5: 157–83.

Bearison, David J., and Herbert Zimiles. 1986. "Developmental Perspectives on Thought and Emotion: An Introduction." In *Thought and Emotion: Developmental Perspectives,* ed. David J. Bearison and Herbert Zimiles, 1–10. Hillsdale, N.J.: Erlbaum.

Bee, Helen L. 1987. *The Journey of Adulthood.* New York: Macmillan.

Belenky, Mary Field, et al. 1986. *Women's Ways of Knowing: The Development of Self, Voice, and Mind.* New York: Basic Books.

Benack, Suzanne. 1984. "Postformal Epistemologies and the Growth of Empathy." In *Beyond Formal Operations: Late Adolescent and Adult Cognitive Development,* ed. Michael L. Commons et al., 340–56. New York: Praeger.

Bereiter, Carl. 1980. "Development in Writing." In *Cognitive Processes in Writing,* ed. Lee W. Gregg and Erwin Steinberg, 73–93. Hillsdale, N.J.: Erlbaum.

Bereiter, Carl, and Marlene Scardamalia. 1987. *The Psychology of Written Composition.* Hillsdale, N.J.: Erlbaum.

Bernstein, Richard J. 1983. *Beyond Objectivism and Relativism: Science, Hermeneutics, and Praxis.* Philadelphia: University of Pennsylvania Press.

———. 1986. "The Question of Moral and Social Development." In *Value Presuppositions in Theories of Human Development,* ed. Leonard Cirillo and Seymour Wapner, 1–18. Hillsdale, N.J.: Erlbaum.

Berthoff, Ann E. 1984. "Is Teaching Still Possible? Writing, Meaning, and Higher Order Reasoning." *College English* 46:743–55.

Bever, Thomas G. 1970. "The Cognitive Basis for Linguistic Structures." In *Cognition and the Development of Language,* ed. John R. Hayes, 279–362. New York: Wiley.

———. 1982. "Regression in the Service of Development." In *Regressions in Mental Development: Basic Phenomena and Theories,* ed. Thomas G. Bever, 153–88. Hillsdale, N.J.: Erlbaum.

Biggs, John B. 1980. "Developmental Processes and Learning Outcomes." In *Cognition, Development, and Instruction,* ed. John R. Kirby and John B. Biggs, 91–118. New York: Academic Press.

Birnbaum, June Cannell. 1986. "Reflective Thought: The Connection between Reading and Writing." In *Convergences: Transactions in Reading and Writing,* ed. Bruce T. Petersen, 30–45. Urbana, Ill.: National Council of Teachers of English.

Bizzell, Patricia. 1982. "Cognition, Convention, and Certainty: What We Need to Know about Writing." *Pre/Text* 3: 213–43.

———. 1984. "William Perry and Liberal Education." *College English* 46: 447–54.

Blasi, Augusto, and Robert J. Oresick. 1986. "Emotions and Cognitions in Self-Inconsistency." In *Thought and Emotion: Developmental Perspectives,* ed. David J. Bearison and Herbert Zimiles, 147–65. Hillsdale, N.J.: Erlbaum.

Blocker, Donald H. 1974. *Developmental Counseling.* 2d ed. New York: Ronald Press.

Boelen, Bernard J. 1978. *Personal Maturity: The Existential Dimension.* New York: Seabury Press.

Boice, Robert. 1985. "Cognitive Components of Blocking." *Written Communication* 2: 91–104.

Bok, Derek C. N.d. *The President's Report: 1976–1977.* Cambridge: Harvard University.

Borge, Jorge Luis. 1975. *El Libro de Arena.* Buenos Aires: Emecé. Trans. Norman Thomas Di Giovanni, under the title *The Book of Sand.* New York: E. P. Dutton, 1977.

Boswell, D. A. 1979. "Metaphoric Processing in the Mature Years." *Human Development* 22: 373–84.

Bowerman, Melissa. 1982. "Starting to Talk Worse: Clues to Language Acquisition from Children's Late Speech Errors." In *U-Shaped Behavior Growth,* ed. Sidney Strauss, 101–45. New York: Academic Press.

Braddock, Richard. 1974. "The Frequency and Placement of Topic Sentences in Expository Prose." *Research in the Teaching of English* 8: 287–302.

Bradford, Annette N. 1983. "Cognitive Immaturity and Remedial College Writers." In *The Writer's Mind: Writing as a Mode of Thinking,* ed. Janice N. Hays et al., 15–24. Urbana, Ill.: National Council of Teachers of English.

Brainerd, C. J. 1978. "The Stage Question in Cognitive-Developmental Theory." *Behavioral and Brain Sciences* 1: 173–82.

Brim, Orville G., Jr., and Jerome Kagan. 1980. "Constancy and Change: A View of the Issues." In *Constancy and Change in Human Development,* ed. Orville G. Brim, Jr., and Jerome Kagan, 1–25. Cambridge: Harvard University Press.

Britton, James, et al. 1975. *The Development of Writing Abilities (11–18),* Schools Council Research Studies. London: Macmillan.

Broadhead, Glenn J., James A. Berlin, and Marlis Manley Broadhead. 1982. "Sentence Structure in Academic Prose and Its Implication for College Writing Teachers." *Research in the Teaching of English* 16: 225–40.

Brodkey, Linda. 1987. *Academic Writing as Social Practice*. Philadelphia: Temple University Press.

Brooke, Robert. 1987. "Underlife and Writing Instruction." *College Composition and Communication* 38: 141–53.

Brown, Ann L. 1982. "Learning and Development: The Problem of Compatibility, Access, and Induction." *Human Development* 25: 89–115.

Brown, Ann L., and Robert A. Reeves. 1987. "Bandwidths of Competence: The Role of Supportive Contexts in Learning and Development." In *Development and Learning: Conflict or Congruence?* ed. Lynn S. Liben, 173–223. Hillsdale, N.J.: Erlbaum.

Bruner, Jerome. 1963. *The Process of Education*. New York: Vintage Books.

———. 1968. *Toward a Theory of Instruction*. New York: W. W. Norton.

———. 1972. "The Nature and Uses of Immaturity." *American Psychologist* 27: 687–708.

———. 1986a. *Actual Minds, Possible Worlds*. Cambridge: Harvard University Press.

———. 1986b. "Value Presuppositions of Developmental Theory." In *Value Presuppositions in Theories of Human Development*, ed. Leonard Cirillo and Seymour Wapner, 19–28. Hillsdale, N.J.: Erlbaum.

Buck, Ross. 1984. *The Communication of Emotion*. New York: Guilford Press.

Bühler, Charlotte. 1962. "Genetic Aspects of the Self." *Annals of the New York Academy of Sciences* 96: 730–64.

Burhans, S. Clinton, Jr. 1983. "The Teaching of Writing and the Knowledge Gap." *College English* 45: 639–56.

Burke, Kenneth. 1945. *A Grammar of Motives*. New York: Prentice-Hall.

———. 1950. *A Rhetoric of Motives*. New York: Prentice-Hall.

Calabro, John. 1987. "Advanced Composition at West Point." *Teaching Writing* 9 (Fall): 82–86.

Carey, Susan. 1982. "Face Perception: Anomalies of Development. In *U-Shaped Behavioral Growth*, ed. Sidney Strauss, 168–90. New York: Academic Press.

———. 1985. *Conceptual Change in Childhood*. Cambridge: Massachusetts Institute of Technology Press.

Carter, Michael. 1990. "The Idea of Expertise: An Exploration of Cognitive and Social Dimensions of Writing." *College Composition and Communication* 41: 265–86.

Case, Robbie. 1985. *Intellectual Development: Birth to Adulthood.* Orlando: Academic Press.

Cavanaugh, John C., et al. 1985. "On Missing Links and Such: Interface between Cognitive Research and Everyday Problem-Solving." *Human Development* 28: 146–68.

Chandler, Michael J. 1975. "Relativism and the Problem of Epistemological Loneliness." *Human Development* 18: 171–80.

———. 1987. "The Othello Effect: Essay on the Emergence and Eclipse of Skeptical Doubt." *Human Development* 30: 137–59.

Chickering, Arthur W. 1969. *Education and Identity.* San Francisco: Jossey-Bass.

———. 1981. Introduction to *The Modern American College,* ed. Arthur W. Chickering et al., 1–10. San Francisco: Jossey-Bass.

Chickering, Arthur W., and Robert J. Havighurst. 1981. "The Life Cycle." In *The Modern American College,* ed. Arthur W. Chickering et al., 16–50. San Francisco: Jossey-Bass.

Chickering, Arthur W., et al., eds. 1981. *The Modern American College.* San Francisco: Jossey-Bass.

Chinen, Allan B. 1984. "Modal Logic: A New Paradigm of Development and Late-Life Potential." *Human Development* 27: 42–56.

Christensen, Francis. 1968. "The Problem of Defining a Mature Style." *English Journal* 57: 572–79.

Christensen, Francis, and Bonniejean Christensen. 1978. *Notes Toward a New Rhetoric: Nine Essays for Teachers.* 2d ed. New York: Harper and Row.

Coates, Jennifer. 1986. *Women, Men, and Language: A Sociolinguistic Account of Sex Differences in Language.* New York: Longman.

Cohler, Bertram J. 1982. "Personal Narrative and Life Course." In *Life-Span Development and Behavior,* ed. Paul B. Baltes and Orville G. Brim, Jr., vol. 4, 205–41. New York: Academic Press.

Commons, Michael L., et al., eds. 1984. *Beyond Formal Operations: Late Adolescent and Adult Cognitive Development.* New York: Praeger.

Connors, Robert J., and Andrea A. Lunsford. 1988. "Frequency of Formal Errors in Current College Writing, or Ma and Pa Kettle Do Research." *College Composition and Communication* 39: 395–409.

Cooper, Charles R., and Lee Odell. 1976. "Consideration of Sound in the Composing Process of Published Writers." *Research in the Teaching of Writing* 10: 103–14.

Corder, S. Pit. 1981. *Error Analysis and Interlanguage.* Oxford: Oxford University Press.

Costa, Paul T., Jr., and Robert R. McCrae. 1980. "Still Stable after All These Years: Personality as a Key to Some Issues in Adulthood and Old Age." In *Life-Span Development and Behavior,* ed. Paul B. Baltes and Orville G. Brim, Jr., vol. 3, 65–102. New York: Academic Press.

Crain, William C. 1980. *Theories of Development: Concepts and Application.* Englewood Cliffs, N.J.: Prentice-Hall.

Crews, Frederick. 1983. "Composing Our Differences: The Case for Literary Readings." In *Composition and Literature: Bridging the Gap,* ed. Winifred B. Horner, 159–67. Chicago: University of Chicago Press.

Daiute, Collette A. 1981. "Psycholinguistic Foundations for the Writing Process." *Research in the Teaching of Writing* 15: 5–22.

Damon, William. 1986. "Affect, Cognition, and Self in Developmental Psychology." In *Thought and Emotion: Developmental Perspectives,* ed. David J. Bearison and Herbert Zimiles, 167–73. Hillsdale, N.J.: Erlbaum.

D'Angelo, Frank J. 1975. *A Conceptual Theory of Rhetoric.* Cambridge, Mass.: Winthrop.

———. 1983. "Literacy and Cognition: A Developmental Perspective." In *Literacy for Life,* ed. Richard W. Bailey and Robin M. Fosheim, 97–114. New York: Modern Language Association of America.

Daniel, Neil, with Wendy Ludgewalt. 1988. "Report of English-Department Survey of Spring 1988." Fort Worth: Texas Christian University English Department.

Daniels, Harvey A. 1983. *Famous Last Words: The American Language Crisis Reconsidered.* Carbondale: Southern Illinois University Press.

Dicks, Bernice W. 1982. "State of the Art in Advanced Expository Writing: One Genus, Many Species." *Journal of Advanced Composition* 3: 172–91.

Dillon, George L. 1981. *Constructing Texts: Elements of a Theory of Composition and Style.* Bloomington: Indiana University Press.

Dixon, Kathleen G. 1989. "Intellectual Development and the Place of Narrative in 'Basic' and Freshman Composition." *Journal of Basic Writing* 8: 3–20.

Douvan, Elizabeth. 1981. "Capacity for Intimacy." In *The Modern American College,* ed. Arthur W. Chickering et al., 191–211. San Francisco: Jossey-Bass.

Durst, Russel K. 1987. "Cognitive and Linguistic Demands of Analytic Writing." *Research in the Teaching of Writing* 21: 347–76.

Dyson, Anne H. 1987. "Individual Differences in Beginning Composing: An Orchestral Vision of Learning to Write." Center for the Study of Writing Technical Report No. 9. ERIC Document Reproduction Service. ED 287 170.

Eblen, Charlene. 1981. "Growth in Writing during College Years: A Preliminary Look." ERIC Document Reproduction Service. ED 217 423.

Emig, Janet. 1983. *The Web of Meaning: Essays on Writing, Teaching, Learning, and Thinking.* Ed. Dixie Goswami and Maureen Butler. Upper Montclair, N.J.: Boynton/Cook.

Emig, Janet, and Robert P. Parker. 1976. "Responding to Student Writing: Building a Theory of the Evaluating Process." ERIC Document Reproduction Service. ED 136 257.

Erikson, Erik H. 1985 [1950]. *Childhood and Society.* New York: Norton.

———. 1968. *Identity: Youth and Crisis.* New York: Norton.

Fahnestock, Jeanne. 1987. "University of Maryland's Junior Writing Program." *Teaching Writing* 9 (Fall): 6–11.

Faigley, Lester. 1979. "The Influence of Generative Rhetoric on the Syntactic Maturity and Writing Effectiveness of College Freshmen." *Research in the Teaching of English* 13: 197–206.

———. 1980. "Names in Search of a Concept: Maturity, Fluency, Complexity, and Growth in Written Syntax." *College Composition and Communication* 31: 291–300.

Faigley, Lester, and Stephen Witte. 1981. "Analyzing Revision." *College Composition and Communication* 32: 400–414.

Feldman, David Henry. 1980. *Beyond Universals in Cognitive Development.* Norwood, N.J.: Ablex.

———. 1987. "Going for the Middle Ground: A Promising Place for Educational Psychology." In *Development and Learning: Conflict or Congruence?* ed. Lynn S. Liben, 159–72. Hillsdale, N.J.: Erlbaum.

Fischer, Kurt W., Helen H. Hand, and Sheryl Russell. 1984. "The Development of Abstractions in Adolescence and Adulthood." In *Beyond Formal Operations: Late Adolescent and Adult Cognitive Development,* ed. Michael L. Commons et al., 43–73. New York: Praeger.

Fischer, Walter R. 1984. "Narration as a Human Communication Paradigm: The Case of Public Moral Argument." *Communication Monographs* 51: 1–22.

Flavell, John H. 1977. *Cognitive Development*. Englewood Cliffs, N.J.: Prentice-Hall.

———. 1984. "Discussion." In *Mechanisms of Cognitive Development*, ed. Robert J. Sternberg, 187–209. New York: W. H. Freedman.

Flavell, John H., and J. F. Wohlwill. 1969. "Formal and Functional Aspects of Cognitive Development." In *Studies in Cognitive Development: Studies in Honor of Jean Piaget,* ed. David Elkind and John H. Flavell, 567–720. New York: Oxford University Press.

Flower, Linda S., and John R. Hayes. 1980. "The Cognition of Discovery: Defining a Rhetorical Problem." *College Composition and Communication* 31: 21–32.

———. 1981. "Plans That Guide the Composing Process." In *Writing: Process, Development and Communication,* ed. Carl H. Frederiksen and Joseph F. Dominic, 39–58. Hillsdale, N.J.: Erlbaum.

———. 1984. "Images, Plans, and Prose." *Written Communication* 1: 120–60.

Flower, Linda, et al. 1986. "Detection, Diagnosis, and the Strategies of Revision." *College Composition and Communication* 37: 16–55.

Fox, Rhonda. 1984. "A Study of Metaphor in the Writing of Nine and Thirteen Year Olds, College Freshmen, and Graduate Students in the Humanities and the Sciences." Ph.D. diss., University of California, San Diego.

Frederiksen, Carl H. 1972. "Effects of Task-Induced Cognitive Operations on Comprehension and Memory Processes." In *Language Comprehension and the Acquisition of Knowledge,* ed. John B. Carroll and Roy O. Freedle, 211–45. New York: Wiley.

Freedman, Aviva, and Ian Pringle. 1980a. "The Writing Abilities of a Representative Sample of Grade 5, 8, and 12 Students." ERIC Document Reproduction Service. ED 217 413.

———. 1980b. "Writing in the College Years: Some Indices of Growth." *College Composition and Communication* 31: 311–24.

Freedman, Sarah Warshauer. 1979. "Why Do Teachers Give the Grades They Do?" *College Composition and Communication* 30: 161–64.

———. 1984. "The Registers of Student and Professional Expository Writing: Influences on Teachers' Responses." In *New Directions in Composition Research,* ed. Richard Beach and L. S. Bridwell, 334–47. New York: Guilford Press.

Freeman, Mark. 1984. "History, Narrative, and Life-Span Developmental Knowledge." *Human Development* 27: 1–19.

Freud, Sigmund. 1928. *The Future of an Illusion*. New York: Liveright Publishing Corp.

———. 1955. *Beyond the Pleasure Principle, Group Psychology, and Other Works.* The Complete Psychological Works, vol. 18. Trans. James Strachey. London: Hogarth Press.

Fulwiler, Toby. 1990. "Looking and Listening for My Voice." *College Composition and Communication* 41: 214–20.

Gadamer, Hans-Georg. 1975. *Truth and Method.* Trans. Garrett Barden and John Cumming. New York: Seabury Press.

———. 1976. *Philosophical Hermeneutics.* Ed. and trans. David E. Linge. Berkeley: University of California Press.

Garfinkel, Renée. 1982. "By the Sweat of Your Brow." In *Review of Human Development,* ed. Tiffany M. Field et al., 500–507.

Gebhard, Ann O. 1978. "Writing Quality and Syntax: A Transformational Analysis of Three Prose Samples." *Research in the Teaching of English* 12: 211–32.

Geertz, Clifford. 1983. *Local Knowledge: Further Essays in Interpretive Anthropology.* New York: Basic Books.

Gergen, Kenneth J. 1982. *Toward Transformation in Social Knowledge.* New York: Springer-Verlag.

Gibbs, John C. 1979. "Kohlberg's Moral Stage Theory: A Piagetian Revision." *Human Development* 22: 89–112.

Giele, Janet Zollinger. 1980. "Adulthood as Transcendence of Age and Sex." In *Themes of Work and Love in Adulthood,* ed. Neil J. Smelser and Erik H. Erikson, 151–73. Cambridge: Harvard University Press.

Gilligan, Carol. 1981. "Moral Development." In *The Modern American College,* ed. Arthur W. Chickering et al., 139–58. San Francisco: Jossey-Bass.

———. 1982. *In a Different Voice: Psychological Theory and Women's Development.* Cambridge: Harvard University Press.

Gleser, Goldine C., Louis A. Gottschalk, and John Watkins. 1959. "The Relationship of Sex and Intelligence to Choice of Words: A Normative Study of Verbal Behavior." *Journal of Clinical Psychology* 15: 182–91.

Goffman, Erving. 1974. *Frame Analysis: An Essay on the Organization of Experience.* Cambridge: Harvard University Press.

———. 1981. *Forms of Talk.* Philadelphia: University of Pennsylvania Press.

Gollin, Eugene S. 1981. "Development and Plasticity." In *Developmental Plasticity: Behavioral and Biological Aspects of Variations in Development,* ed. Eugene S. Gollin, 231–51. New York: Academic Press.

Gorrell, Donna. 1983. "Toward Determining a Minimal Competency Entrance Examination for Freshman Composition." *Research in the Teaching of English* 17: 263–74.

Gould, Roger L. 1978. *Transformations: Growth and Change in Adult Life.* New York: Simon and Schuster.

Graham, Janet Gorman. 1987. "A Comparison of the Writing of College Freshmen and College Seniors with a Focus on Indications of Cognitive Development." Ph.D. diss., University of Maryland.

Gubrium, Jaber F., and David R. Buckholdt. 1977. *Toward Maturity.* San Francisco: Jossey-Bass.

Haan, Norma. 1981. "Adolescents and Young Adults as Producers of Their Development." In *Individuals as Producers of Their Development: A Life-Span Perspective,* ed. Richard M. Lerner and Nancy A. Busch-Rossnagel, 155–82. New York: Academic Press.

Habermas, Jürgen. 1971. *Knowledge and Human Interests.* Boston: Beacon Press.

———. 1979. *Communication and the Evolution of Society.* Boston: Beacon Press.

———. 1980. "The Hermeneutic Claim to Universality." In *Contemporary Hermeneutics: Hermeneutics as Method, Philosophy, and Critique,* ed. Josef Bleicher, 181–211. London: Routledge and Kegan Paul.

[Hackett, Herbert.] 1954. "The Composition Career (of All Students) after the Freshman Year." *College Composition and Communication* 5: 114–16.

Halpern, Jeanne W. 1985. "An Electronic Odyssey." In *Writing in Nonacademic Settings,* ed. Lee Odell and Dixie Goswami, 157–201. New York: Guilford Press.

Hammond, Eugene. 1979. "Professional Writing Programs: Lessons for Freshman Composition." ERIC Document Reproduction Service. ED 176 325.

———. 1984. "Freshman Composition—Junior Composition: Does Co-Ordination Mean Sub-Ordination?" *College Composition and Communication* 35: 217–21.

Harris, Muriel. 1981. "Mending the Fragmented Free Modifier." *College Composition and Communication* 32: 175–81.

Harris, Winifred Hall. 1977. "Teacher Response to Student Writing." *Research in the Teaching of English* 11: 175–85.

Haswell, Richard H. 1986a. "Change in Undergraduate and Post-Graduate Writing Performance (Part I): Quantified Findings." ERIC Document Reproduction Service. ED 269 780.

———. 1986b. "The Organization of Impromptu Essays." *College Composition and Communication* 37: 402–15.

———. 1989. "Textual Research and Coherence: Findings, Intuition, Application." *College English* 51: 305–19.

———. 1990a. "Bound Forms in Freewriting: The Issue of Organization." In *Nothing Begins with N: New Investigations of Freewriting*, Pat Belanoff, Peter Elbow, and Sheryl I. Fontaine, 32–68. Carbondale: Southern Illinois University Press.

———. 1990b. "No Title: A Response to Sam Meyer." *Journal of Advanced Composition* 10: 396–99.

———. 1991. "Change in Undergraduate and Post-Graduate Writing Performance (Part II): Problems in Interpretation." ERIC Document Reproduction Service. CS 212 491.

Havighurst, Robert J. 1973. *Developmental Tasks and Education*. 3d ed. New York: David McKay.

Hays, Janice N. 1980. "Teaching the Grammar of Discourse." In *Reinventing the Rhetorical Tradition*, ed. Aviva Freedman and Ian Pringle, 145–55. Conway, Ark.: L & S Books.

———. 1983a. "The Development of Discursive Maturity in College Writers." In *The Writer's Mind: Writing as a Mode of Thinking*, ed. Janice N. Hays et al., 127–44. Urbana, Ill.: National Council of Teachers of English.

———. 1983b. "An Empirically-Derived Stage Model of Analytic Writing Abilities during the College Years: Some Illustrative Cases." ERIC Document Reproduction Service. ED 247 553.

———. 1987a. "Models of Intellectual Development and Writing: A Response to Myra Kogen *et al*." *Journal of Basic Writing* 6: 11–27.

———. 1987b. "Postscript." In *A Sourcebook for Basic Writing Teachers*, ed. Theresa Enos, 495–96. New York: Random House.

Hays, Janice N., and Kathleen Brandt. 1988 (forthcoming). "Socio-Cognitive Implications of Dialectical and Counterproductive Audience Activity at Four Levels of Argumentative Writing Performance."

Hays, Janice N., Kathleen M. Brandt, and Kathryn H. Chantry. 1988. "The Impact of Friendly and Hostile Audiences on the Argumentative Writing of High School and College Students." *Research in the Teaching of English* 22: 391–416.

Hays, Janice N., et al. 1988 (forthcoming). "Adaptations to Friendly and Hostile Readers in the Argumentative Writing of Students at Three Levels of Adult Socio-Cognitive Development."

Heath, Douglas H. 1968. *Growing Up in College: Liberal Education and Maturity*. San Francisco: Jossey-Bass.

Hillocks, George, Jr. 1982. "Inquiry and the Composing Process: Theory and Research." *College English* 44: 659–73.

Hogan, Michael P. 1980. "Advanced Composition: A Survey." *Journal of Advanced Composition* 1: 21–29.

Holt, John. 1964. *How Children Fail.* New York: Dell.

Holzman, Michael. 1980. "Theory, Research, and Pedagogy." *College English* 42: 343–49.

Hull, Glynda. 1987. "The Editing Process in Writing: A Performance Study of More Skilled and Less Skilled College Writers." *Research in the Teaching of English* 21: 8–29.

Hunt, Kellogg W. 1965. *Grammatical Structures Written at Three Grade Levels.* NCTE Research Report No. 3. Champaign, Ill.: National Council of Teachers of English.

————. 1970. *Syntactic Maturity in Schoolchildren and Adults.* Monographs of the Society for Research in Child Development 35, no. 1.

Inhelder, Barbel, and Jean Piaget. 1958. *The Growth of Logical Thinking from Childhood to Adolescence: An Essay on the Construction of Formal Operational Structures.* Trans. Anne Parsons and Stanley Milgram. New York: Basic Books.

James, William. 1961. *The Varieties of Religious Experience: A Study in Human Nature.* New York: Crowell-Collier.

Jameson, Frederic. 1981. *The Political Unconscious: Narrative as a Socially Symbolic Act.* Ithaca: Cornell University Press.

Jespersen, Otto. 1922. *Language: Its Nature, Development, and Origin.* London: Allen and Unwin.

Jewell, Ross M., et al. 1969. *The Effectiveness of College-Level Instruction in Freshman Composition.* Final Report, U.S. Office of Education Project No. 2188, Amended. Cedar Falls: University of Northern Iowa.

Kagan, Donna M. 1980. "Run-on and Fragment Sentences: An Error Analysis." *Research in the Teaching of English* 14: 127–38.

Kagan, Jerome. 1980. "Perspectives on Continuity." *Constancy and Change in Human Development,* ed. Orville G. Brim, Jr., and Jerome Kagan, 26–74. Cambridge: Harvard University Press.

Kagan, Jerome, and Howard A. Moss. 1962. *Birth to Maturity.* New York: Wiley.

Kaplan, Bernard. 1983. "Genetic-Dramatism: Old Wine in New Bottles." In *Toward A Holistic Developmental Psychology,* ed.

Seymour Wapner and Bernard Kaplan, 53–74. Hillsdale, N.J.: Erlbaum.

Katz, Joseph, and Nevitt Sanford. 1962. "The Curriculum in the Perspective of the Theory of Personality Development." In *The American College: A Psychological and Social Interpretation of the Higher Learning,* ed. Nevitt Sanford, 418–44. New York: Wiley.

Kaufer, David S., John R. Hayes, and Linda Flower. 1986. "Composing Written Sentences." *Research in the Teaching of English* 20: 121–41.

Kegan, Robert. 1982. *The Evolving Self: Problem and Process in Human Development.* Cambridge: Harvard University Press.

Keil, Frank C. 1981. "Constraints on Knowledge and Cognitive Development." *Psychological Review* 88: 197–227.

———. 1984. "Mechanisms of Cognitive Development and the Structure of Knowledge." In *Mechanisms of Cognitive Development,* ed. Robert J. Sternberg, 81–99. New York: W. H. Freedman.

Kerek, Andrew, Donald A. Daiker, and Max Morenberg. 1980. "Sentence Combining and College Composition." *Perceptual and Motor Skills* 51: 1059–1157. Monograph Supplement 1-V51.

Kessen, William. 1984. "The End of the Age of Development." In *Mechanisms of Cognitive Development,* ed. Robert J. Sternberg, 1–17. New York: W. H. Freedman.

Kimball, J. P. 1973. "Seven Principles of Surface Structure Parsing in Natural Language." *Cognition* 2: 15–47.

Kimmel, Douglas C. 1980. *Adulthood and Aging: An Interdisciplinary Developmental View.* New York: Wiley.

Kimmey, John L. 1975. "Freshman Composition in the Junior Year." *College Composition and Communication* 26: 347–49.

King, P. M., et al. 1983. "The Justification of Beliefs in Young Adults: A Longitudinal Study." *Human Development* 26: 106–16.

Kiniry, Malcolm, and Ellen Strenski. 1985. "Sequencing Expository Writing: A Recursive Approach." *College Composition and Communication* 36: 191–202.

Kinneavy, James L. 1983. "Writing Across the Curriculum." *Profession 83* (Modern Language Association): 13–20.

Kitchener, Karen S. 1982. "Human Development and the College Campus: Sequences and Tasks." In *Measuring Student Development,* ed. G. R. Hanson, 17–45. San Francisco: Jossey-Bass.

———. 1983. "Cognition, Metacognition, and Epistemic Cognition: A Three-Level Model of Cognitive Processing." *Human Development* 26: 222–32.

Kitchener, Richard F. 1978. "Epigenesis: The Role of Biological Models in Developmental Psychology." *Human Development* 21: 141–60.

Kitzhaber, Albert R. 1963. *Themes, Theories, and Therapy: The Teaching of Writing in College.* New York: McGraw-Hill.

Klahr, David, and J. G. Wallace. 1976. *Cognitive Development: An Information-Processing View.* Hillsdale, N.J.: Erlbaum.

Klausmeier, Herbert J., Elizabeth S. Ghatala, and Dorothy A. Frayer. 1974. *Conceptual Learning and Development: A Cognitive View.* New York: Academic Press.

Knefelkamp, L. Lee, and Ron Slepitza. 1978. "A Cognitive-Developmental Model of Career Development: An Adaptation of the Perry Scheme." In *Encouraging Development in College Students,* ed. Clyde A. Parker, 135–50. Minneapolis: University of Minnesota Press.

Knoblauch, C. H. 1980. "Intentionality in the Writing Process: A Case Study." *College Composition and Communication* 31: 153–59.

Knoblauch, C. H., and Lil Brannon. 1984. *Rhetorical Traditions and the Teaching of Writing.* Upper Montclair, N.J.: Boynton/Cook.

Kogen, Myra. 1986. "The Conventions of Expository Writing." *Journal of Basic Writing* 5: 24–37.

Kohlberg, Lawrence. 1981. *The Philosophy of Moral Development: Moral Stages and the Idea of Justice.* San Francisco: Harper and Row.

Kolb, David A. 1981. "Learning Styles and Disciplinary Differences." In *The Modern American College,* ed. Arthur W. Chickering et al., 232–55. San Francisco: Jossey-Bass.

Koplowitz, Herb. 1984. "A Projection beyond Piaget's Formal-Operations Stage: A General System Stage and a Unitary Stage." In *Beyond Formal Operations: Late Adolescent and Adult Cognitive Development,* ed. Michael L. Commons et al., 258–71. New York: Praeger.

Kramer, Deirdre. 1983. "Post-formal Operations? A Need for Further Conceptualization." *Human Development* 26: 91–105.

Krashen, Stephen. 1981. *Second Language Acquisition and Second Language Learning.* Oxford, England: Pergamon Press.

Kroll, Barry. 1980. "Developmental Perspectives and the Teaching of Composition." *College English* 41: 741–52.

Kuhn, Thomas S. 1977. *The Essential Tension: Selected Studies in Scientific Tradition and Change.* Chicago: University of Chicago Press.

Kurfiss, Joanne. 1977. "Sequentiality and Structure in a Cognitive Model of College Student Development." *Developmental Psychology* 13: 565–71.

———. 1982. "Developmental Perspectives on Writing and Intellectual Growth in College." In *To Improve the Academy,* vol. 3, ed. L. C. Buhl and L. A. Wilson, 136–47. Pittsburgh: Professional and Organizational Development Network in Higher Education.

Kutz, Eleanor. 1986. "Between Students' Language and Academic Discourse: Interlanguage as Middle Ground." *College English* 48: 385–96.

Labouvie-Vief, Gisela. 1981. "Proactive and Reactive Aspects of Constructivism: Growth and Aging in Life-Span Perspective." In *Individuals as Producers of Their Development: A Life-Span Perspective,* ed. Richard M. Lerner and Nancy A. Busch-Rossnagel, 197–230. New York: Academic Press.

———. 1982. "Discontinuities in Development from Childhood to Adulthood: A Cognitive-Developmental View." In *Review of Human Development,* ed. Tiffany M. Field et al., 447–55. New York: Wiley.

———. 1984. "Culture, Language, and Mature Rationality." In *Life-Span Developmental Psychology: Historical and Generational Effects,* ed. Kathleen A. McCluskey and Helen W. Reese, 109–28. Orlando, Fla.: Academic Press.

Lakoff, George, and Mark Johnson. 1980. *Metaphors We Live By.* Chicago: University of Chicago Press.

Lange, Phil C. 1948. "A Sampling of Composition Errors of College Freshmen in a Course Other Than English." *Journal of Educational Research* 42: 191–200.

Langer, Jonas. 1969. *Theories of Development.* New York: Holt, Rinehart and Winston.

Langley, Pat, and Herbert A. Simon. 1981. "The Central Role of Learning in Cognition." In *Cognitive Skills and Their Acquisition,* ed. John R. Anderson, 361–79. Hillsdale, N.J.: Erlbaum.

Lanham, Richard A. 1983. *Literacy and the Survival of Humanism.* New Haven: Yale University Press.

Lavers, Norman. 1981. "Strephosymbolia: A Possible Strategy for Dealing with It." *College English* 43: 711–15.

Lee, Laura L. 1974. *Developmental Sentence Analysis: A Grammatical Assessment Procedure of Speech and Language Clinicians.* Evanston, Ill.: Northwestern University Press.

Lees, Elaine O. 1983. "Building Thought on Paper with Adult Basic Writers." In *The Writer's Mind: Writing as a Mode of Thinking,* ed. Janice N. Hays et al., 145–51. Urbana, Ill.: National Council of Teachers of English.

Lerner, Richard M. 1978. "Nature, Nurture, and Dynamic Interaction." *Human Development* 21: 1–20.

———. 1984. *On the Nature of Human Plasticity.* Cambridge: Cambridge University Press.

Lerner, Richard M., and Nancy A. Busch-Rossnagel. 1981. "Individuals as Producers of Their Development: Conceptual and Empirical Bases." In *Individuals as Producers of Their Development,* ed. Richard M. Lerner and Nancy A. Busch-Rossnagel, 1–36. New York: Academic Press.

Liben, Lynn S. 1987a. "Epilogue: Approaches to Development and Learning: Conflict *and* Congruence." In *Development and Learning: Conflict or Congruence?* ed. Lynn S. Liben, 237–52. Hillsdale, N.J.: Erlbaum.

———. 1987b. "Information Processing and Piagetian Theory: Conflict or Congruence?" In *Development and Learning: Conflict or Congruence?* ed. Lynn S. Liben, 109–32. Hillsdale, N.J.: Erlbaum.

Linville, Jewell I. Holderby. 1982. "A Comparative Analysis of Textbook Theory and Business Practice in Report Writing." Ph.D. diss., University of Arkansas.

Loban, Walter. 1976. *Language Development: Kindergarten through Grade Twelve.* Urbana, Ill.: National Council of Teachers of English.

Loevinger, Jane. 1986. "On the Structure of Personality." In *Thought and Emotion: Developmental Perspectives,* ed. David J. Bearison and Herbert Zimiles, 65–74. Hillsdale, N.J.: Erlbaum.

Loevinger, Jane, with A. Blasi. 1976. *Ego Development: Conceptions and Theories.* San Francisco: Jossey-Bass.

Loevinger, Jane, and Elizabeth Knoll. 1983. "Personality: Stages, Traits, and the Self." *Annual Review of Psychology* 34: 195–222.

Lucas, Catharine Keech. 1988. "Toward Ecological Evaluation." *The Quarterly* 10: 1–3, 12–17 (no. 1), 4–10 (no. 2).

Lunsford, Andrea. 1979. "Cognitive Development and the Basic Writer." *College English* 41: 38–46.

———. 1980. "The Content of Basic Writers' Essays." *College Composition and Communication* 31: 278–90.

McCarthy, Lucille Parkinson. 1987. "A Stranger in Strange Lands: A College Student Writing across the Curriculum." *Research in the Teaching of English* 21: 233–65.

McCulley, George A. 1985. "Writing Quality, Coherence, and Cohesion." *Research in the Teaching of English* 19: 269–82.

MacDonald, Susan P. 1986. "Specificity in Context: Some Difficulties for the Inexperienced Writer." *College Composition and Communication* 37: 195–203.

Macrorie, Ken. 1963. Review of *Themes, Theories, and Therapy,* by Albert Kitzhaber. *College Composition and Communication* 14: 267–70.

Magnusson, David. 1988. *Individual Development from an Interactional Perspective.* Hillsdale, N.J.: Erlbaum.

Magolda, Marcia B. Baxter. 1989. "Gender Differences in Cognitive Development: An Analysis of Cognitive Complexity and Learning Styles." *Journal of College Student Development* 30: 213–20.

Maimon, Elaine P., and Barbara F. Nodine. 1979. "Words Enough and Time: Syntax and Error One Year After." In *Sentence Combining and the Teaching of Writing: Selected Papers from the Miami University Conference,* ed. Donald A. Daiker et al., 101–8. Akron: University of Akron Press.

Mair, David D., and Nancy N. Roundy. 1981. "The Composing Process of Technical Writers: A Preliminary Study." ERIC Document Reproduction Service. ED 200 994.

Marcia, J. E. 1976. "Identity Six Years After: A Follow-up Study." *Journal of Youth and Adolescence* 5: 145–60.

Martinez, Joseph G. R., and Nancy C. Martinez. 1987. "Reconsidering Cognition and the Basic Writer: A Response to Myra Kogen." *Journal of Basic Writing* 6: 79–83.

Maslow, Abraham H. 1970. *Motivation and Personality.* 2d ed. New York: Harper and Row.

Matsuhashi, Ann. 1981. "Pausing and Planning: The Tempo of Written Discourse Production." *Research in the Teaching of English* 15: 113–34.

Matsuhashi, Ann, and Karen Quinn. 1984. "Cognitive Questions from Discourse Analysis." *Written Communication* 1: 307–39.

Meacham, John A. 1981. "Political Values, Conceptual Models, and Research." In *Individuals as Producers of Their Development: A Life-Span Perspective,* ed. Richard M. Lerner and Nancy A. Busch-Rossnagel, 447–74. New York: Academic Press.

Means, Barbara, Susan Sonnenschein, and Linda Baker. N.d. "Organization and Content in Writing and in Speech." ERIC Document Reproduction Service. ED 208 403.

Mellon, John C. 1979. "Issues in the Theory and Practice of Sentence Combining: A Twenty-year Perspective." In *Sentence Combining and the Teaching of Writing: Selected Papers from the*

Miami University Conference, ed. Donald A. Daiker et al., 1–38. Akron: University of Akron Press.

Messick, Samuel. 1976. "Personality Consistencies in Cognition and Creativity." In *Individuality in Learning,* ed. Samuel Messick, 4–22. San Francisco: Jossey-Bass.

Milic, Louis T. 1965. "Theories of Style and Their Implications for the Teaching of Composition." *College Composition and Communication* 16: 66–69, 126.

———. 1971. "Rhetorical Choice and Stylistic Option: The Conscious and Unconscious Poles." In *Literary Style: A Symposium,* ed. Seymour Chatman, 77–88. London: Oxford University Press.

Miller, Carolyn R., and Jack Selzer. 1985. "Special Topics of Argument in Engineering Reports." In *Writing in Nonacademic Settings,* ed. Lee Odell and Dixie Goswami, 309–41. New York: Guildford.

Miller, Susan. 1980. "Rhetorical Maturity: Definition and Development." In *Reinventing the Rhetorical Tradition,* ed. Aviva Freedman and Ian Pringle, 119–27. Conway, Ark.: L & S Books.

Moffett, James. 1968. *Teaching the Universe of Discourse.* Boston: Houghton Mifflin.

Morrow, Lesley M. 1978. "Analysis of Syntax of Six-, Seven-, and Eight-Year-Old Children." *Research in the Teaching of English* 12: 143–48.

Mortimer, Jeylan T., et al. 1982. "Persistence and Change in Development: The Multidimensional Self-Concept." In *Life-Span Development and Behavior,* vol. 2, ed. Paul B. Baltes and Orville G. Brim, Jr., 263–313. New York: Academic Press.

Moshman, David, and Bridget A. Franks. 1989. "Intellectual Development: Formal Operations and Reflective Judgment." In *Thinking, Reasoning, and Writing,* ed. Elaine P. Maimon et al., 9–22. New York: Longman.

Moss, Howard A., and Elizabeth J. Susman. 1980. "Longitudinal Study of Personality Development." In *Constancy and Change in Human Development,* ed. Orville G. Brim, Jr., and Jerome Kagan, 530–95. Cambridge: Harvard University Press.

Neilsen, Lorraine, and Gene L. Piché. 1981. "The Influence of Headed Nominal Complexity and Lexical Choice on Teachers' Evaluation of Writing." *Research in the Teaching of English* 15: 65–73.

Neimark, Edith D. 1982. "Cognitive Development in Adulthood: Using What You've Got." In *Review of Human Development,* ed. Tiffany M. Field et al., 435–46. New York: Wiley.

Neulib, Janice, and Ron Fontune. 1985. "The Use of Sentence Combining in an Articulated Writing Curriculum: A Report on Illinois State University's NEH Project in Progress." In *Sentence Combining: A Rhetorical Perspective,* ed. Donald A. Daiker, Andrew Kerek, and Max Morenberg, 127–37. Carbondale: Southern Illinois Press.

Newkirk, Thomas. 1984. "How Students Read Student Papers: An Exploratory Study." *Written Communication* 1: 283–305.

———. 1987. "The Non-narrative Writing of Young Children." *Research in the Teaching of English* 21: 121–44.

Newkirk, Thomas R., Thomas D. Cameron, and Cynthia L. Selfe. 1977. "What Johnny Can't Write: A University View of Freshman Writing." *English Journal* 66: 65–69.

Nold, Ellen W. 1978. "The Basics of Research: Evaluation of Writing." ERIC Document Reproduction Service. ED 166 713.

North, Stephen M. 1986. "Writing in a Philosophy Class: Three Case Studies." *Research in the Teaching of English* 20: 225–62.

Odell, Lee. 1983. "Redefining Maturity in Writing." In *Learning to Write: First Language / Second Language,* ed. Aviva Freedman, Ian Pringle, and Janice Yalden, 96–113. London: Longman.

Ohmann, Richard. 1976. "The Decline in Literacy Is a Fiction, If Not a Hoax." *Chronicle of Higher Education* 13 (Oct. 25): 32.

———. 1979. "Use Definite, Specific, Concrete Language." *College English* 41: 390–97.

Olson, Gary A. 1982. "Clichés: Error Recognition or Subjective Reality." *College English* 44: 190–94.

Onore, Cynthia. 1989. "The Student, the Teacher, and the Text: Negotiating Meanings through Response and Revision." In *Writing and Response: Theory, Practice, and Research,* ed. Chris M. Anson, 231–60. Urbana, Ill.: National Council of Teachers of English.

Opler, Marvin K. 1971. "Adolescence in Cross-Cultural Perspective." In *Modern Perspectives in Adolescent Psychiatry,* ed. J. G. Howells, 152–79. New York: Brunner/Mazel.

Pace, Robert C. 1984. "Measuring the Quality of College Student Experience: An Account of the Development and the Use of the College Student Experiences Questionnaire." ERIC Document Reproduction Service. ED 255 099.

Palmer, Richard E. 1969. *Hermeneutics: Interpretation Theory in Schleiermacher, Dilthey, Heidegger, and Gadamer.* Evanston, Ill.: Northwestern University Press.

Perry, William, Jr. 1968. *Forms of Intellectual and Ethical Development in the College Years: A Scheme.* New York: Holt, Rinehart and Winston.

———. 1981. "Cognitive and Ethical Growth: The Making of Meaning." In *The Modern American College,* ed. Arthur W. Chickering et al., 76–116. San Francisco: Jossey-Bass.

Phelps, Louise Wetherbee. 1988. *Composition as a Human Science: Contributions to the Self-Understanding of a Discipline.* New York: Oxford University Press.

Piaget, Jean. 1970. *Science of Education and the Psychology of the Child.* Trans. Derek Coltman. New York: Orion Press.

———. 1973. "Genetic Epistemology." In *Jean Piaget: The Man and His Ideas,* ed. Richard I. Evans and trans. Eleanor Duckworth, xlii–lxi. New York: Dutton.

Popper, Karl R. 1965. *Conjectures and Refutations: The Growth of Scientific Knowledge.* 2d ed. New York: Basic Books.

Pulkkinen, Lea. 1982. "Self-Control and Continuity from Childhood to Late Adolescence." In *Life-Span Development and Behavior,* vol. 4, ed. Paul B. Baltes and Orville G. Brim, Jr., 63–105. New York: Academic Press.

Raforth, Bennett A., and Donald L. Rubin. 1984. "The Impact of Content and Mechanics on Judgments of Writing Quality." *Written Communication* 1: 446–58.

Raforth, Bennett A., and Warren Combs. 1983. "Syntactic Complexity and Readers' Perception of an Author's Credibility." *Research in the Teaching of English* 17: 165–69.

Rest, James R. 1979. *Development in Judging Moral Issues.* Minneapolis: University of Minnesota Press.

Ricoeur, Paul. 1973. "Ethics and Culture: Habermas and Gadamer in Dialogue." *Philosophy Today* 17: 153–65.

———. 1981. *Hermeneutics and the Human Sciences.* Ed. and trans. John B. Thompson. Cambridge: Cambridge University Press.

Riegel, Klaus F. 1972. "Time and Change in the Development of the Individual and Society." In *Advances in Child Development and Behavior,* vol. 7, ed. Helen W. Reese, 81–113. New York: Academic Press.

———. 1973. "Dialectical Operations: The Final Period of Cognitive Development." *Human Development* 16: 345–76.

———. 1979. *Foundations of Dialectical Psychology*. New York: Academic Press.

Riley, William K. 1964. "Sentence Openers in Freshman Writing." *College English* 26: 228–30.

Ritchie, Joy S. 1989. "Beginning Writers: Diverse Voices and Individual Identity." *College Composition and Communication* 40: 152–74.

Robbins, Edwin W. 1964. Review of *Themes, Theories, and Therapy*, by Albert Kitzhaber. *College Composition and Communication* 15: 60–62.

Roberts, Paul. 1952. "Pronominal 'This': A Quantitative Analysis." *American Speech* 27: 171–78.

Rose, Mike. 1984. *Writer's Block: The Cognitive Dimension*. Carbondale: Southern Illinois University Press.

———. 1988. "Narrowing the Mind and Page: Remedial Writers and Cognitive Reductionism." *College Composition and Communication* 39: 267–302.

Rosenzweig, Saul. 1958. "The Place of the Individual and of Idiodynamics in Psychology: A Dialogue." *Journal of Individual Psychology* 14: 3–21.

Rubin, Rebecca B., Elizabeth E. Graham, and James T. Mignerey. 1990. "A Longitudinal Study of College Students' Communication Competence." *Communication Education* 39: 1–14.

Ruth, Leo, and Sandra Murphy. 1988. *Designing Writing Tasks for the Assessment of Writing*. Norwood, N.J.: Ablex.

Salkind, Neil J. 1981. *Theories of Human Development*. New York: D. Van Nostrand.

Santostefano, Sebastiano. 1986. "Cognitive Controls, Metaphors, and Contexts: An Approach to Cognition and Emotion." In *Thought and Emotion: Developmental Perspectives*, ed. David J. Bearison and Herbert Zimiles, 175–210. Hillsdale, N.J.: Erlbaum.

Sarbin, Theodore R. 1986. "Emotion and Act: Roles and Rhetoric." In *The Social Construction of Emotions*, ed. Rom Harré, 83–97. Oxford: Basil Blackwell.

Sartre, Jean-Paul. 1965. *What Is Literature?* Trans. Bernard Frechtman. New York: Harper and Row.

Schaie, K. Warner, and Joyce Parr. 1981. "Intelligence." In *The Modern American College*, ed. Arthur W. Chickering et al., 117–38. San Francisco: Jossey-Bass.

Schank, R. C., and R. P. Abelson. 1973. *Scripts, Plans, Goals, and Understanding*. Hillsdale, N.J.: Erlbaum.

Scharton, Maurice. 1989. "Models of Competence: Responses to a Scenario Writing Assignment." *Research in the Teaching of English* 23: 163–80.

Scholes, Robert. 1985. *Textual Power: Literary Theory and the Teaching of English.* New Haven: Yale University Press.

Schon, Donald A. 1963. *The Displacement of Concepts.* Cambridge, England: Tavistock Press.

Schor, Sandra. 1986. "Style through Control: The Pleasures of the Beginning Writer." In *The Territory of Language: Linguistics, Stylistics, and the Teaching of Composition,* 2d ed., ed. Donald A. McQuade, 204–12. Carbondale: Southern Illinois University Press.

Schumacher, Gary M., et al. 1984. "Cognitive Activities of Beginning and Advanced College Writers: A Pausal Analysis." *Research in the Teaching of English* 18: 169–87.

Sears, R. R. 1977. "Sources of Life Satisfactions of the Terman Gifted Men." *American Psychologist* 32: 119–28.

Selman, Robert L., et al. 1986. "Assessing Adolescent Interpersonal Negotiation Strategies: Toward the Integration of Structural and Functional Models." *Developmental Psychology* 22: 450–59.

Shaughnessy, Mina P. 1976. "Diving In: An Introduction to Basic Writing." *College Composition and Communication* 27: 234–39.

———. 1977. *Errors and Expectations: A Guide for the Teacher of Basic Writing.* New York: Oxford University Press.

Shor, Ira. 1986. *Culture Wars: School and Society in the Conservative Restoration, 1969–1984.* Boston: Routledge and Kegan Paul.

Shumaker, Ronald C., Larry Dennis, and Lois Green. 1990. "Advanced Exposition: A Survey of Patterns and Problems." *Journal of Advanced Composition* 10: 136–44.

Sigel, Irving E. 1986. "Cognition-Affect: A Psychological Riddle." In *Thought and Emotion: Developmental Perspectives,* ed. David J. Bearison and Herbert Zimiles, 211–29. Hillsdale, N.J.: Erlbaum.

Sinnott, Jan Dynda. 1984. "Postformal Reasoning: The Relativistic Stage." In *Beyond Formal Operations: Late Adolescent and Adult Cognitive Development,* ed. Michael L. Commons et al., 298–325. New York: Praeger.

Sloan, Gary. 1984. "The Frequency of Transitional Markers in Discursive Prose." *College English* 46: 158–79.

Smith, Hubert. 1958. "The Advanced Course in Expository Writing: Aims, Texts, Methods." *College Composition and Communication* 9: 165–67.

Sommers, Nancy. 1980. "Revision Strategies of Student Writers and Experienced Adult Writers." *College Composition and Communication* 31: 378–87.

Spear, Karen I. 1983. "Thinking and Writing: A Sequential Curriculum for Composition." *Journal of Advanced Composition* 4: 47–63.

Spender, Dale. 1980. *Man Made Language.* London: Routledge and Kegan Paul.

Spivey, Nancy N. 1987. "Construing Constructivism: Reading Research in the United States." *Poetics* 16: 169–93.

Squire, James R. 1964. "Department Memo: Reassessing the Crisis in English Teaching." *College English* 25: 449–57.

Steinberg, Leo. 1966. "Contemporary Art and the Plight of Its Public." In *The New Art,* ed. Gregory Battcock, 27–47. New York: Dutton.

Sternberg, Robert J. 1984a. "Higher-Order Reasoning in Postformal Operational Thought." In *Beyond Formal Operations: Late Adolescent and Adult Cognitive Development,* ed. Michael L. Commons et al., 74–91. New York: Praeger.

———. 1984b. "Mechanisms of Cognitive Development: A Componential Approach." In *Mechanisms of Cognitive Development,* ed. Robert J. Sternberg, 163–86. New York: W. H. Freedman.

Sternglass, Marilyn S. 1981. "Assessing Reading, Writing, and Reasoning." *College English* 43: 269–75.

Stewart, Murray F., and Cary H. Grobe. 1979. "Syntactic Maturity, Mechanics of Writing, and Teachers' Quality Ratings." *Research in the Teaching of English* 13: 207–15.

Stiff, Robert. 1967. "The Effect upon Student Composition of Particular Correction Techniques." *Research in the Teaching of English* 1: 54–75.

Stotsky, Sandra. 1986. "On Learning to Write about Ideas." *College Composition and Communication* 37: 276–93.

Strauss, Sidney. 1972. "Inducing Cognitive Development and Learning: A Review of Short-Term Training Experiments, I: The Organismic Developmental Approach." *Cognition* 1: 329–57.

———. 1987. "Educational-Developmental Psychology and School Learning." In *Development and Learning: Conflict or Congruence?* ed. Lynn S. Liben, 133–57. Hillsdale, N.J.: Erlbaum.

Strauss, Sidney, ed., with Ruth Stavy. 1982. *U-Shaped Behavioral Growth.* New York: Academic Press.

Taylor, Karl K., and Ede B. Kidder. 1988. "The Development of Spelling Skills: From First Grade through Eighth Grade." *Written Communication* 5: 222–44.

Thomas, Alexander, and Stella Chess. 1977. *Temperament and Development.* New York: Brunner/Mazel.

Thorndike, Edward L., and Irving Lorge. 1944. *The Teacher's Word Book of 30,000 Words.* New York: Teacher's College Press.

Torbert, William R. 1981. "Interpersonal Competence." In *The Modern American College,* ed. Arthur W. Chickering et al., 172–90. San Francisco: Jossey-Bass.

Toulmin, Stephen. 1981. "Epistemology and Developmental Psychology." In *Developmental Plasticity and Biological Aspects of Variations in Development,* ed. Eugene S. Gollin, 253–67. New York: Academic Press.

Tremblay, Paula Y. 1986. "Writing Assignments for Cognitive Development." *College Composition and Communication* 37: 342–43.

Tyler, Leona E. 1978. *Individuality: Human Possibilities and Personal Choice in the Psychological Development of Men and Women.* San Francisco: Jossey-Bass.

Vaillant, G. E. 1977. *Adaptation to Life.* Boston: Little, Brown.

Van Bruggen, John A. 1946. "Factors Affecting the Regularity of the Flow of Words during Written Composition." *Journal of Experimental Education* 15: 133–54.

Van Dyck, Barrie. 1980. "On-the-job Writing of High-level Business Executives: Implications for College Teaching." ERIC Document Reproduction Service. ED 185 584.

Viney, Linda L. 1987. "A Sociophenomenological Approach to Life-Span Development Complementing Erikson's Sociodynamic Approach." *Human Development* 30: 125–36.

Vygotsky, Lev S. 1962. *Thought and Language.* Ed. and trans. Eugenia Hanfmann and Gertrude Vakar. Cambridge: Massachusetts Institute of Technology Press.

———. 1978. *Mind in Society: The Development of Higher Psychological Processes.* Ed. Michael Cole et al. Cambridge: Harvard University Press.

Warfel, Harry R. 1953. "Frequency of the Passive Voice." *College English* 15: 129.

Warantz, Elissa, and Catharine Keech. 1982. "Beyond Holistic Scoring: Rhetorical Flows That Signal Advance in Developing Writers." In "Properties of Writing Tasks: A Study of Alternative Procedures for Holistic Writing Assessment," by Leo Ruth et al., 509–42. ERIC Document Reproduction Service. ED 230 576.

Wartofsky, Marx W. 1986. "On the Creation and Transformation of Norms of Human Development." In *Value Presuppositions in Theories of Human Development,* ed. Leonard Cirillo and Seymour Wapner, 113–25. Hillsdale, N.J.: Erlbaum.

Watson, Cynthia. 1983. "Syntactic Change: Writing Development and the Rhetorical Context." In *The Psychology of Written Language,* ed. Margaret Martlew, 127–39. London: John Wiley and Sons.

Weathersby, Rita P. 1981. "Ego Development." In *The Modern American College,* ed. Arthur W. Chickering et al., 51–75. San Francisco: Jossey-Bass.

Werner, Heinz. 1978. *General Theory and Perceptual Experience: Developmental Processes.* Heinz Werner's Selected Writings, vol. 1. Ed. Sybil S. Barten and Margery B. Franklin. New York: International Universities Press.

Wertheimer, Max. 1959. *Productive Thinking.* Enlarged Edition. New York: Harper and Row.

White, Edward M. 1984. "Holisticism." *College Composition and Communication* 35: 400–409.

———. 1985. *Teaching and Assessing Writing.* San Francisco: Jossey-Bass.

White, Hayden. 1973. *Metahistory: The Historical Imagination in Nineteenth-Century Europe.* Baltimore: Johns Hopkins University Press.

White, Robert W. 1966. *Lives in Progress: A Study of the Natural Growth of Personality.* 2d ed. New York: Holt, Rinehart and Winston.

Whitehead, Alfred North. 1967 [1929]. *The Aims of Education and Other Essays.* Reprint. New York: Free Press.

Whitla, Dean K. 1981. "Value Added and Other Related Matters." ERIC Document Reproduction Service. ED 228 245.

———. N.d. *Value Added: Measuring the Impact of Undergraduate Education.* Cambridge: Office of Instructional Research and Evaluation, Harvard University.

Wilkinson, Andrew G., et al. 1980. *Assessing Language Development.* Oxford: Oxford University Press.

Williams, James D. 1985. "Coherence and Cognitive Style." *Written Communication* 2: 473–91.

Williams, James D., and Scott D. Alden. 1983. "Motivation in the Composition Class." *Research in the Teaching of English* 17: 101–25.

Williams, Joseph M. 1979. "Defining Complexity." *College English* 40: 595–609.

———. 1989. "Afterword: Two Ways of Thinking about Growth: The Problem of Finding the Right Metaphor." In *Thinking, Reasoning, and Writing,* ed. Elaine Maimon, Barbara Nodine, and Finbarr W. O'Connor, 245–55. New York: Longman.

Wiseman, Stephen. 1949. "The Marking of English Composition in Grammar School Selection." *British Journal of Educational Psychology* 19: 200–209.

Witkin, Herman A. 1976. "Cognitive Styles in Learning and Teaching." In *Individuality in Learning,* ed. Samuel Messick, 38–72. San Francisco: Jossey-Bass.

Witkin, Herman A., and D. R. Goodenough. 1967. "Stability of Cognitive Style from Childhood to Young Adulthood." *Journal of Personality and Social Psychology* 7: 219–300.

Witte, Stephen. 1983. "Topical Structure and Revision: An Exploratory Study." *College Composition and Communication* 34: 313–41.

———. 1987. "Pre-text and Composing." *College Composition and Communication* 38: 397–425.

Witte, Stephen, and Lester Faigley. 1981a. "Coherence, Cohesion, and Writing Quality." *College Composition and Communication* 32: 189–204.

———. 1981b. "A Comparison of Analytic and Synthetic Approaches to the Teaching of College Writing." ERIC Document Reproduction Service. ED 209 677.

Wolk, Anthony. 1970. "The Relative Importance of the Final Free Modifier: A Quantitative Study." *Research in the Teaching of English* 4: 59–68.

Woolf, Virginia. 1980. *Virginia Woolf: Women and Writing.* Ed. Michèle Barrett. New York: Harcourt Brace Jovanovich.

Wozniak, Robert H. 1987. "Developmental Method, Zones of Development, and Theories of the Environment." In *Development and Learning: Conflict or Congruence?* ed. Lynn S. Liben, 225–35. Hillsdale, N.J.: Erlbaum.

Yngve, Victor H. 1960. "A Model and an Hypothesis for Language Structure." *Proceedings of the American Philosophical Society* 104: 444–66.

Index

"incompetence" in, as sign of remediality, 269–75, 278; instrumental purpose of, 290; interpretation of, in advanced-writing course, 35; organizational patterns of, 250, 251, 253, 254 (table), 255–57, 260–61; progress with age in organization of, 257–58, 259; recording of postfreshman decline by, 317–18; sentence construction in, 230, 232, 233, 234, 237, 240–41, 243, 244; statistical difference between business writing and, 74; stylistic conventions of, 281–82; teacher's expectations about, in advanced-writing course, 36–38, 56, 57–58, 59, 60, 70–71; top-rated, 272–73, 274; verbal wit in low-rated, 275–76, 278. *See also* student essays

diagnostic tests, 275, 276

dialectic (essay organizational pattern), 254 (table), 257, 261, 263, 269, 274, 345

dialectical thinking, teaching of, 151

dialogue: composition course as, 148, 352–54; in diagnosis, 341, 346; in reactive process, 133, 135, 283, 297; restriction by curriculum, 331; of self-reflection, 127; therapeutic, 122. *See also* conversation

Dick, Bernice W., 319–20

diction: advancement of upper-division writers in, 87, 153; changes in (freshman to junior), 24, 28–29; comparison between business and student writing, 79;

developmental curve for, 199, 201; diagnosis of, 343; in holistic rating system, 38, 39, 40; imitation of, 96, 100; improvement of, 222; in lifework sequencing of instruction, 298, 321, 324, 325, 326, 327, 328; readiness for advanced course, 319; registering of improvement in freshman course, 315, 316; relationship of sentence construction to, 230; of slow writers, 215, 216, 222; student preferences in, 97; teacher's expectations about, for advanced students, 36–37, 40, 41, 59; uneven competence in, 339

Dillon, George L., 244

Dilthey, Wilhelm, 126

Dinesen, Isak, 187, 351–52, 354

diplomatic writing, 230

discourse analysis: on comprehension of sentences, 235; on construction of sentences, 237n; discounting of grammatical status of sentence, 229

disequilibrium, as impetus to developmental progress, 138

dispositio, 94

disposition, influence over choices of writers, 94, 99

Dixon, Kathleen G., 137, 308, 310, 353

Douvan, Elizabeth, 303

Durst, Russell K., 252n, 327, 342n

Dyson, Anne H., 186

Eblen, Charlene, 41, 224n

ego, subjugation of id by, 103–4

Eiseley, Loren, 186

Elbow, Peter, 208

About the Author

RICHARD H. HASWELL is professor of English at Washington State University, where he directed the writing program for nine years. He graduated Phi Beta Kappa from the University of Missouri in 1961 and was awarded a Woodrow Wilson Fellowship. He received his M.A. from the University of Washington in 1962 and his Ph.D. from the University of Missouri in 1967.